British Economic Fluctuations, 1790–1939

British Economic Fluctuations 1790–1939

Edited and introduced by

DEREK H. ALDCROFT

PETER FEARON

MACMILLAN
ST. MARTIN'S PRESS

First published 1972 by
THE MACMILLAN PRESS LTD
London and Basingstoke
Associated companies in New York Toronto
Dublin Melbourne Johannesburg and Madras

Library of Congress catalog card no, 77–178900

SBN 333 11642 9 (hard cover)
SBN 333 11643 7 (paper cover)

Printed in Great Britain by
RICHARD CLAY (THE CHAUCER PRESS) LTD
Bungay, Suffolk

Contents

List of Diagrams   vii

List of Tables   ix

Preface   xi

Acknowledgements   xii

Introduction   1
    Problems of definition and measurement. Duration
    and amplitude of cycles. International comparisons
    and international synchronisation. Characteristics
    of the cycle. Business cycle theory. The role of exports
    and investment. Schumpeter's innovations. Harvest
    fluctuations. Monetary factors. Random shocks.
    Long cycles in economic activity. The long cycle
    in Britain. The generation of the long swing.

1   Cycles in the British Economy: 1790–1914   *W. W. Rostow*   74
2   The Trade Cycle in Britain, 1790–1850   *R. C. O. Matthews*   97
3   British Economic Fluctuations, 1870–1914   *A. G. Ford*   131
4   The Role of Consumption in Interwar Fluctuations   161
    H. W. Richardson
5   The Causes of Business Fluctuations   *D. J. Coppock*   188
6   Long Waves in Building in the British Economy of the   220
    Nineteenth Century   *E. W. Cooney*
7   Fluctuations in House-Building in Britain and the United   236
    States in the Nineteenth Century   *H. J. Habakkuk*
8   The Long Swing: Comparisons and Interactions Between   268
    British and American Balance of Payments, 1820–1913
    Jeffrey G. Williamson

Select Bibliography   291

Bibliographical Name Index   295

Subject Index   298

List of Diagrams

Chapter 3

3.1 The cycles in outline   132
3.2 Trends   133
3.3 The cycles in detail   134
3.4 Short-term interest rates   141
3.5 Banking behaviour   144
3.6 British overseas issues and exports by areas   153
3.7 Home investment behaviour   156

Chapter 5

5.1 U.S.A. manufacturing production (Frickey): deviations   190
from trend
U.K. industrial production excluding building (Hoffmann): deviations from trend
5.2 U.K. industrial production excluding building (Hoffmann): deviations from trend   191
5.3 G.B. index of residential construction (Weber), 1900–9   196
= 100
5.4 U.K. volume of exports of home products (Schlote):   210
deviations from trend

Chapter 6

6.1 Building activity, timber imports and brick production,   226
1830–70
6.2 Building activity in U.K. and U.S.A.   228

Chapter 8

8.1 British imports deflated and in current prices, and home   277
investment: original data as percentage of trend, 1820–
1915
8.2 British exports and imports in percentage rates of   278
change, 1820–1915

8.3 British exports deflated and in current prices, as percent-   280
    age deviations about trend, 1820–1915

8.4 British exports to America and total British exports, first   283
    differences, 1850–1915

8.5 British trade balance and net capital exports, and   285
    American net capital imports, 1820–1915

List of Tables

Introduction

1   Duration and amplitude of cycles in Gross National   9
Product, U.K., 1836–1937

2   Duration and amplitude of cycles in industrial produc-   12
tion, U.K., 1785–1913

3   Cyclical amplitude of components of national income,   28
1836–1937

4   Aggregate amplitude of cycles in components of national   28
income

5   Signs of the first differences of the detrended ratio series   30
for selected pairs of variables, 1836–1909

Chapter 1

1.1   Annual turning-points, British trade cycles, 1788–1914   77

Chapter 3

3.1   Signs of first differences of deviations in national income,   135
exports and home investment, 1870–1909

3.2   Signs of first differences of deviations in national income,   138
exports, current account balance of payments and home
investment, U.K., 1870–1909

3.3   Signs of first differences of deviations in national income,   145
bank deposits and advances

3.4   Signs of first differences of U.K. export deviations,   147
1870–1909

3.5   Signs of first differences of deviations in overseas issues,   149
exports and national income

3.6   Signs of first differences of deviations in overseas issues   151
and home investment

3.7   Mean deviations in British exports and overseas issues to   152
selected areas, 1870–1909

3.8   Signs of first differences of deviations in gross investment   155
and its component series, national income and industrial
profits, U.K., 1870–1910

Chapter 4

4.1 Aggregate consumption, 1929–38   168
4.2 Indices of real consumption spending, 1929–38 (1929 =   170
     100)
4.3 Estimated indices of average annual real earnings,   174
     1929–38 (1930 = 100)

Chapter 5

5.1 Residential construction, U.S.A.   193
5.2 Construction workers in U.S.A.   194
5.3 Gross capital formation in U.S. railroads   194
5.4 Net immigration to U.S.A. as percentage of population   201
     growth
5.5 Changes in U.K. exports by geographical regions   208

Chapter 6

6.1 Imports of lathwood into the U.K., 1831–70   224
6.2 Imports of mahogany into the U.K., 1831–80   227

Chapter 8

8.1 U.S. balance of payments dating for long swings, 1817–   272
     1915 (smoothed data)
8.2 Long swings in exports and imports (deflated series),   282
     U.S. and U.K., 1821–1913
8.3 British exports to U.S.A., 1850–1913   284
8.4 Long swings in trade components and home investment,   286
     U.K., 1847–1913

Preface

As yet there is no comprehensive analysis of economic fluctuations in Britain since the beginning of modern industrial growth. In the interim this volume draws together a selection of writings on fluctuations in the nineteenth and twentieth centuries, while the Introduction attempts to provide a realistic overview of the main aspects and problems encountered in cyclical activity in Britain during this period. With one exception the eight essays reprinted below appear as published in the original apart from a few minor revisions and corrections. We should like to thank the authors for their co-operation and permission to reproduce their writings. We are also indebted to Mrs Joan Morrison for the speed and efficiency with which she completed many statistical exercises and to Miss Judith Watts once again for typing services rendered.

D.H.A.
P.F.

University of Leicester

Acknowledgements

THE editors and publishers wish to thank the following for permission to reproduce the essays contained in this volume. They are listed in the order in which they appear:

W. W. Rostow, 'Cycles in the British Economy: 1790–1914', chap. ii in *British Economy of the Nineteenth Century* (Oxford University Press, 1948).

R. C. O. Matthews, 'The Trade Cycle in Britain, 1790–1850', *Oxford Economic Papers*, VI (1954).

A. G. Ford, 'British Economic Fluctuations, 1870–1914', *Manchester School*, XXXVII (1969).

H. W. Richardson, 'The Role of Consumption in Interwar Fluctuations', adapted from chap. 5 of *Economic Recovery in Britain, 1932–9* (Weidenfeld & Nicolson, 1967).

D. J. Coppock, 'The Causes of Business Fluctuations', *Transactions of the Manchester Statistical Society* (1959).

E. W. Cooney, 'Long Waves in Building in the British Economy of the Nineteenth Century', *Economic History Review*, XIII (1960–1).

H. J. Habakkuk, 'Fluctuations in House-Building in Britain and the United States in the Nineteenth Century', *Journal of Economic History*, XXII (1962).

Jeffrey G. Williamson, 'The Long Swing: Comparisons and Interactions Between British and American Balance of Payments, 1820–1913', *Journal of Economic History*, XXII (1962).

Introduction

MOST economic history texts tend either to neglect cyclical fluctuations altogether or else they skip rather lightly over the subject.[1] This is regrettable given the fact that fluctuations in economic activity constitute one of the two main facets of macro-economic behaviour, the second being the study of long-term growth. Indeed, the cycle and the trend are often regarded as inseparable entities, though opinion is still far from unanimous on this issue.[2] However, the comparative neglect of the subject does mean that students of Britain's past development have tended to concentrate their attention on issues of long-run growth and on institutional changes and have paid lip-service to the question of instability.

This neglect can be explained quite readily. In the post-war years business cycle research became somewhat *démodé*; as fluctuations became shorter and more heavily damped, interest in the subject waned and the focus of attention ran towards what seemed to be the more pressing problems of growth, inflation and the balance of payments, though more recently there has been a renewed interest in questions of instability. Business cycle research, however, has never been as popular as in the United States where, for the past half-century or more, there has been a vast outpouring of literature on almost every conceivable aspect of the cycle. Data limitations too have set limits to the study of the cycle in Britain. It is only in the last decade or so that a number of long-run statistical series have been compiled which permit serious study of the subject. Thus most of the earlier literature, especially that written before 1939, was based on rather fragmentary data and a high degree of conjecture. Since the

[1] Though there is an increasing tendency for economic history textbooks to contain chapters on fluctuations. For a recent selection see R. S. Sayers, *A History of Economic Change in England, 1880–1939* (1967); P. Deane, *The First Industrial Revolution* (1965) and P. Mathias, *The First Industrial Nation: An Economic History of Britain, 1700–1914* (1969).

[2] We return to this thorny issue later, though reasons of space preclude an exhaustive analysis of the subject. For a short and useful introduction to the problem see R. M. Goodwin, 'The Problem of Trend and Cycle', *Yorkshire Bulletin of Economic and Social Research*, v (1953).

war a number of scholars have produced distinguished pieces of work on fluctuations, but for the most part these have been of a fairly specialised nature and there is as yet no comprehensive survey of business cycles in a historical setting. And indeed there have been very few texts published in this country on the theory of cycles.[1] No doubt it will be some time before these serious gaps in the literature are made good and the present volume cannot lay claim to providing a definitive account. But it seemed sensible, at least for a start, to provide students with a sample of the contributions that have been made on business cycle history in recent years, together with a discussion of some of the main issues at stake.

A brief comment is perhaps called for on the time-period chosen for the present volume. Readers may well ask why the particular dates, 1790 and 1939, have been chosen as the starting and terminal years of the survey. A number of reasons governed the choice. First, to have extended the time-span, either backwards or forwards, would have meant producing an unacceptably large volume and a more complex one at that. This would certainly have been the case had the post-war period been included, on which a whole volume could easily be written. Second, little work has been done on the earlier period, that is the eighteenth century and before, and the paucity of data would tend to limit either meaningful comment or comparison.[2] But perhaps the most important reason is that the period 1790–1939 does contain some degree of unity with regard to cyclical experience, though this statement, as we shall see, is subject to severe qualification. It could be claimed however that this was the period when the trade cycle, to use a now somewhat old-fashioned term, developed and flourished in its full glory and then finally reached its climax in the 'big bang' of the inter-war years. This is not meant to imply that the characteristics of cycles did not change over time. Almost certainly they did. The fluctuations of the first half of the nineteenth century, for instance, tended to be shorter and more frequent than those in the latter half, inter-war fluctuations were generally more severe than those before 1914, while each cycle possessed its own individual characteristics. Yet despite such obvious variations there was a degree of uniformity in the cyclical pattern which prevailed throughout these years. In short, the cycles of the inter-war era, together with the factors that caused them and the institutional setting in which they thrived, were not totally different

---

[1] The most notable exception being R. C. O. Matthews's excellent introduction *The Trade Cycle* (1959) in which some empirical data are incorporated.

[2] Despite the pioneering work by T. S. Ashton on the eighteenth century, *Economic Fluctuations in England, 1700–1800* (1959).

from those of the early nineteenth century. After the Second World War this no longer held since the nature of the business cycle altered substantially.[1] Post-war instability has taken the form of 'growth cycles' in which the slumps and contractions of earlier years have been replaced simply by retardations in rates of growth with the result that there are no clearly pronounced troughs as previously. In addition, cycles are now generally shorter and often dominated by, or at least considerably influenced by, government policy, an exogenous force which for the most part was either absent or exercised relatively little influence prior to 1939. These are not the only differences – note for instance the diminished role of exports – but they suffice to illustrate the point that post-war cycles are substantially different from those of the nineteenth and early twentieth centuries and as such deserve separate treatment.[2] Finally, fluctuations of the seventeenth and eighteenth centuries were shorter and came to an end more abruptly than those of the nineteenth. They were dominated to a considerable extent by harvest fluctuations associated with vagaries in climatic conditions and therefore do not bear much resemblance to those rooted in a maturing industrial economy.[3]

Given the present state of knowledge about business cycles it would be difficult to write a definitive and exhaustive account of the subject. But our knowledge is not so limited as to preclude a realistic overview of the position to date. We start first by discussing problems of definition and measurement and then proceed to delimit British cycles, their amplitude, duration and other relevant features. Next we look at some of the chief causal forces at work but do not at this stage attempt a rigorous explanation of observed cycles in terms of a formal model. For the most part the analysis concentrates on the standard business cycle or Juglar cycle of 7–11 years duration which featured most prominently in British cyclical history, though not to the complete exclusion of cycles of different duration, notably minor

[1] 'The experience of the control of the economy during the war and the effects of the teaching of Maynard Keynes have caused so great a discontinuity between the pre-1939 and post-1945 business cycles in the United Kingdom that any series or model purporting to combine the two has little, if any, meaning.' F. W. Paish, 'Business Cycles in Britain', *Lloyds Bank Review*, no. 98 (Oct 1970) p. 1.

[2] For a helpful long-term comparative analysis see R. C. O. Matthews, 'Postwar Business Cycles in the United Kingdom', in M. Bronfenbrenner (ed.), *Is the Business Cycle Obsolete?* (1969) esp. pp. 101–7, and 'Why Has Britain Had Full Employment Since the War?', *Economic Journal*, LXXVIII (1968).

[3] Ashton, *Economic Fluctuations*, pp. 172–3, and W. G. Hoskins, 'Harvest Fluctuations and English Economic History, 1620–1759', *Agricultural History Review*, XVI (1968). Harvest variations continued of course to influence the cycle after 1790 but the force of this factor naturally diminished over time.

cycles (3–4 years) and long waves (18–20 years) associated with the names of Kitchin and Kuznets respectively.[1] The former have been a much more characteristic feature of the U.S. economy than the British, but considerable effort has been devoted to establishing the existence of long waves in the British economy and for this reason we devote some space to discussing these cycles.

Problems of Definition and Measurement

It is not only the interpretation of cycles that presents complexities to students; a study of cycles also throws up severe problems of definition and measurement which require careful consideration.

Most writers would agree that business cycles can be defined quite simply as fluctuations in aggregate economic activity. One of the leading pioneers of business cycle research, W. C. Mitchell, used this very definition in 1927, though he questioned whether every fluctuation could be regarded as a cycle.[2] Later writers have followed this example though with qualifications. Thus Gordon sees them as comprising 'recurring alternations of expansion and contraction in aggregate economic activity, the alternating movements in each direction being self-reinforcing and pervading all parts of the economy'.[3] In order to get over the awkward problem of non-cyclic fluctuations caused by random irregularities it was felt necessary to specify some minimum time-period over which cycles could occur, say one year or more with a maximum of 10–12 years.[4] This of course does not rule out the possibility of random shocks or non-economic factors such as wars from generating a cyclical sequence, nor does it preclude the existence of cycles of longer duration. In other words, cycles are not characterised by their uniformity in duration or amplitude or by their initiating causes; the essential feature is the way in which the economy responds to a given set of stimuli by magnifying them into the cumulative movements which may or may not be self-sustaining.

Though the above definition may appear to be a relatively straightforward one there are certain conceptual and practical

---

[1] This does not exhaust the possibilities. Kondratieff noted the existence of very long waves (around 50 years or more) which Schumpeter later integrated into his monumental study of economic development and fluctuations. N. D. Kondratieff, 'The Long Waves in Economic Life', *Review of Economic Statistics*, XVII (1935); J. A. Schumpeter, *Business Cycles* (1939, 2 vols). For a summary of the views on these cycles see A. H. Hansen, *Business Cycles and National Income* (1951) chap. 4.

[2] W. C. Mitchell, *Business Cycles: The Problem and the Setting* (1927).

[3] R. A. Gordon, *Business Fluctuations*, 2nd ed. (1961) p. 249.

[4] Ibid., p. 249, and S. Bober, *The Economics of Cycles and Growth* (1968) p. 27.

difficulties which arise when attempting to measure business cycles. The most important of these is concerned with the relationship between the cycle and the trend. Any time series, whether of an aggregate or non-aggregate type, will normally comprise at least two elements, a cyclical component and a trend factor.[1] For purposes of studying cyclical magnitudes it would seem highly desirable to eliminate the trend component, otherwise we shall be observing composite movements of the trend and cycle. But the expediency of this approach has been questioned on more than one occasion.[2] The main grounds for this objection are as follows. First, it is contended that there is no really satisfactory statistical technique for decomposing time series in order to separate cyclical movements from other types of economic change. Ames suggests that the least squares method, or any other method for that matter, has the obvious defect of making cyclical behaviour largely dependent on the choice of trend and, in support of his argument, quotes Frickey's experience with the U.S. pig-iron series to which he fitted 23 different types of trend and thereby produced 23 types of cycles which varied in length from 45 to 3·3 years.[3] In addition, smoothing operations may transpose cycles; they can produce artificial cycles or exaggerate turning-points which are merely summations of random factors in the basic series. The dangers of producing spurious cycles by using smoothing techniques are particularly marked in the case of long cycles, a point stressed with some force by Irma Adelman.[4] For this reason some students of long waves prefer to work with untreated data.

A second criticism, though in many respects an extension of the first one, concerns the interdependent nature of cyclical and secular movements. Some writers argue that because the two are so inextricably linked together it is impracticable to make any distinction at all. Cyclical forces influence trends and vice versa, and since the shape of the resulting cyclical fluctuations will depend very much upon the type of trend chosen for elimination, there is a grave risk of distorting the shape of the cyclical movements. Schumpeter was the leading exponent of this view. He rejected the notion that cycles

---

[1] Time series also comprise irregular fluctuations which we shall ignore in this study, and, for data on less than an annual basis, a seasonal component.

[2] J. A. Estey, *Business Cycles*, 3rd ed. (1956) pp. 31–2.

[3] E. Ames, 'A Theoretical and Statistical Dilemma: The Contribution of Burns, Mitchell and Frickey to Business-Cycle Theory', *Econometrica*, XVI (1948).

[4] '... it is likely that the long swings which have been observed in the U.S. economy since 1890 are due in part to the introduction of spurious long cycles by the smoothing process, and in part to the necessity for averaging over a statistically small number of random shocks'. Irma Adelman, 'Long Cycles: Fact or Artifact?', *American Economic Review*, LV (1965) 459.

could exist without growth, a notion which carried with it the implication that any attempt at trend removal would eliminate the cycles as well. This was perhaps something of an extreme view – theoretically it is possible for cycles to exist without growth[1] – but the Schumpeterian position has not lacked supporters in more recent years.[2]

While recognising the force of these criticisms, and in particular the view that similar forces affect both trend and cycle, it is clearly unrealistic, when studying cyclical movements, to ignore trend factors altogether. If we do so we run the risk of facing equally serious problems in another direction. The very concept of fluctuations becomes somewhat meaningless if divorced from the yardstick of the trend line. By not eliminating the trend we are inevitably forced to mark off cycles from the basic time series and this may well produce distortions in the cyclical pattern and will certainly alter the amplitude of fluctuations. Moreover, serious practical difficulties can arise from using the untreated time series. The raw data may exhibit few or no fluctuations which are visible to the naked eye, merely a continued upward drift, and it is only after some smoothing technique has been applied that cyclical contours become apparent. This point is particularly relevant to post-war (1945) time series but it also applies to nineteenth-century income statistics for certain periods. One way to get round this difficulty, and at the same time avoid the process of smoothing the time series, is to mark off cycles from a diffusion index. This method, used extensively by the National Bureau of Economic Research, simply gathers together a large number of different indicators and combines them into a composite series known as a diffusion index. The index measures the percentage of indicators rising or falling at any given point in time and it is possible to trace the course of the cycle by marking off the peaks and troughs when most of the series stop rising or stop falling as the case may be.[3] Unfortunately this procedure is of limited utility in the present context. While the index is satisfactory for the purposes of delineating turning-points of cycles it is clearly of no use for measur-

---

[1] Theoretically possible but in practice unlikely. A multiplier-accelerator model with a marginal propensity to consume of 0·5 and an accelerator coefficient of 2 would produce regular cycles of unchanged amplitude around a static trend. See P. Samuelson, 'Interactions Between the Multiplier Analysis and the Principle of Acceleration', *Review of Economic Statistics*, XXI (1939).

[2] See for instance Goodwin, 'The Problem of Trend and Cycle'; also B. Higgins, 'Interactions of Cycles and Trends', *Economic Journal*, LXV (1955).

[3] It may well be the case that the diffusion index would never show a majority of the indicators declining. In this situation, demonstrably one of modern growth cycles, the lower turning-point would have to be marked off as soon as the percentage of components declining began to fall. Ideally the components in the index should be weighted.

ing their amplitude. Second, and more relevant from our point of view, to construct a satisfactory index requires a large number of individual time series, preferably on a monthly or quarterly basis. The limited amount of data available on nineteenth-century Britain would certainly not permit the compilation of a viable index.

Despite the criticisms made about trend elimination and the techniques employed, most business cycle analysts have continued to use some form of smoothing process. Here we adopt the same procedure. However, once a decision has been made in favour of treating the data there still remains the problem of deciding what technique to use to eliminate the trend. The practice of trend elimination may be defective in itself but the choice of a wholly inappropriate method for the elimination of the trend is even worse. For example, it would be clearly unsatisfactory to fit a linear trend line to a long-run series of which the trend function was anything but linear. Most of the long-run series that we have for the nineteenth century do exhibit a certain degree of linearity but probably not sufficient for a straight line trend to be of very good fit. However, to avoid the laborious calculations involved in fitting non-linear trend curves to the time series we have used the moving average technique as a reasonable sort of compromise. This gives a fairly accurate approximation of the trend and has the added advantage that it can be quickly calculated. A nine-year moving average appeared to give the best fit and this was therefore used for the data up to 1913. It was impossible to follow the same procedure for the inter-war years because the shortness of the period would have meant the loss of recorded values for about half the years in question. In this case it was necessary to eliminate the trend by means of a straight line regression function. Clearly the accuracy in the latter case leaves something to be desired, but since the turning-points of the cycles are fairly well established and amplitudes certainly greater than before 1913 it was easy to check whether the results were grossly distorted.

Any student of British business cycles has to confront the problem of severe data limitations. Short of fabricating new series to suit his purpose he must be content to make the best of the available material. There are no really reliable series extending back to the early nineteenth century. In fact the only continuous series are those for industrial production and exports, neither of which is completely satisfactory.[1] They do however enable us to mark off the turning-

[1] As in W. G. Hoffmann, *British Industry, 1700–1950* (1955) and A. H. Imlah, *Economic Elements in the Pax Britannica* (1958). The more recent index of industrial production, compiled by Lomax, only goes back to 1860: K. S. Lomax, 'Growth and Productivity in the United Kingdom', *Productivity Measurement Review*, XXXVIII (1964).

points for earlier years though they are not ideal for purposes of calculating the amplitude of cycles at the national level. From the early 1830s it is possible to work with national income estimates which have recently been made available by Phyllis Deane. These have been used in preference to those of Feinstein since the latter do not begin until 1870.[1] For the inter-war period the Feinstein estimates have been used.[2]

Duration and Amplitude of Cycles

The trend values of the income series were calculated in the manner described and then divided into the actual values to give the detrended ratios for each year.[3] It was then possible to plot the course of the cycles by marking off the peaks and troughs on the ratio series. The results are given in Table 1. Measured from peak to peak there were 11 full cycles between 1836 and 1913 with durations ranging from 3 to 11 years. The range is wide but it should be noted that a majority of the cycles fall in the 6–10-year range. The average duration for all cycles was exactly 7 years, though it would be slightly higher if the rather ill-defined cycle of 1856–9 were eliminated. Thus the Juglar pattern of cycles of between 7–11 years is confirmed in the British data. Rather surprisingly, the average duration of the upswings was only slightly greater than that of the downswings, 3·8 as against 3·2 years, while in the former case the range of the durations was considerably greater. For the inter-war years we have used the conventional dates for the turning-points, though our estimating procedure tended to shift the second and third peaks one year forward. The results produced two full cycles of slightly longer duration than those before 1914, but ostensibly in no way breaking the Juglar sequence.[4] This time however the upswings were very much longer than the downturns, a fact which seems to strike counter to popular impression of the period.

The cyclical pattern outlined above agrees reasonably closely with those of other observers though there are inevitably some differences in timing and duration. Matthews, for example, finds 8 cycles between 1856 and 1913 (peak to peak) which is exactly the same,

[1] Phyllis Deane, 'New Estimates of Gross National Product for the United Kingdom, 1830–1914', *Review of Income and Wealth*, XIV (1968).

[2] C. H. Feinstein, 'National Income and Expenditure of the United Kingdom, 1870–1963', *London and Cambridge Economic Bulletin*, L (1964).

[3] All calculations have been made on the basis of constant price data.

[4] Though see below.

TABLE I

Duration and Amplitude of Cycles in Gross National Product,
U.K., 1836–1937

Peak to peak	Trough year	Duration in Years Downswing	Upswing	Total	Amplitude
1836–9	1837	1	2	3	2·67
1839–46	1843	4	3	7	4·52
1846–56	1850	4	6	10	2·14
1856–9	1858	2	1	3	1·98
1859–65	1862	3	3	6	1·36
1865–74	1869	4	5	9	1·49
1874–83	1879	5	4	9	1·81
1883–90	1886	3	4	7	1·28
1890–1901	1894	4	7	11	1·88
1901–7	1904	3	3	6	1·55
1907–13	1909	2	4	6	–
Average duration		3·2	3·8	7·0	
Average amplitude					2·07
1920–9	1921	1	8	9	5·02
1929–37	1932	3	5	8	2·90
Average duration		2	6·5	8·5	
Average amplitude					3·96

Source: Based on G.N.P. constant price estimates as described in text.

though 4 of the peaks fall in different years.[1] For the inter-war years of course the sequence is exactly the same. On the other hand, Burns, using the National Bureau's findings, records 9 cycles between 1857 and 1912 (an additional one being added between 1903 and 1907), with only two of the upper turning-points, 1890 and 1907, corresponding to our own, though it should be noted that the National Bureau has attempted a more precise location of turning-points on a monthly basis which may account for one or two of the discrepancies.[2] After the war 4 cycles are located, the peaks occurring in March 1920, November 1924, March 1927, July 1929 and

[1] Matthews, in Bronfenbrenner, *Is the Business Cycle Obsolete?*, p. 102, n. 5. Rostow gets a similar number starting with a peak in 1857, W. W. Rostow, *British Economy of the Nineteenth Century* (1948) p. 33 and reprinted below, Essay 1.

[2] A. F. Burns, *The Business Cycle in a Changing World* (1969).

September 1937. On the face of it this would seem to suggest a break in the Juglar pattern and possibly a return to the shorter type of cycle characteristic of the early nineteenth century.[1] However, both the intrusions which break the pattern occurred in the 1920s and it is doubtful whether these should be regarded as cycles in the real sense of the term.[2] The downturn of 1927–8 was very weak and barely shows up in the annual data; real income and consumers' expenditure continued to rise, while the moderate dip in industrial production was largely the result of a recession in one or two sectors, notably construction, shipbuilding and textiles. The setback of 1925–6 was more severe but can be explained largely in terms of the General Strike; had there been no strike the recession would have been no greater than that of the later 1920s. If we then regard it as a minor interruption to the Juglar upswing of the 1920s caused by a non-recurring erratic shock it is possible to preserve the Juglar pattern for the inter-war years.[3]

The pattern emerging so far is that of a major cycle with an average periodicity of around 7 years extending from the 1830s through to the Second World War. Though cycles varied in length there is no evidence that they were getting either shorter or longer over the period. Nor is there any firm evidence that any other type of cycle existed, that is apart from the two short cycles in the 1830s and 1850s, the last of which was very weak indeed. These may be regarded as a throwback to earlier years, but since the lack of income statistics prevents an analysis on the same basis for the years up to 1830 we shall defer comment and judgement for the moment. At this point it is more convenient to consider the amplitude of cycles in income from 1836 to 1937.

Amplitude is generally used with reference to the severity of cyclical movements though the term has its ambiguities. Strictly speaking amplitude measures the total change in the time series through the entire cycle, that is the change during expansion added to the amount of decline in contraction. To measure the true severity of the cycle we really need to take into account both the amplitude and duration of the cycle. To do this we have calculated the standard deviations of the percentage deviations from the trend values for the number of years in each cycle. For any given deviation from the trend this method tends to increase the severity the shorter the cycle.

---

[1] See below, pp. 11–13.
[2] The Bureau has a penchant for listing all fluctuations, however modest their magnitude, a practice which at times is more a source of confusion than of illumination.
[3] D. H. Aldcroft, *The Inter-War Economy: Britain, 1919–1939* (1970) pp. 28–34.

It therefore approximates to a measure of intensity per unit of time. Other measures are possible which place greater emphasis on the length of the cycle in relation to deviations from the trend values.[1]

The amplitude values, calculated in the manner described, are recorded in Table 1 for each cycle in national income from 1836. The average for 10 cycles to the peak of 1907 works out at 2·07 but this encompasses a range extending from 1·28 to 4·52. However, apart from early on in the period, when cycles were fairly intense, there is no apparent tendency for the amplitude of cycles to increase or decline through to the early twentieth century. As one might expect inter-war cycles were far more severe: the average amplitude was about twice that of pre-war and the cycle of 1920–9 was more intense than any recorded in the nineteenth century.[2]

We now come to the problem of pushing back the analysis to the late eighteenth century. The absence of long-run income estimates obviously makes impossible exact comparison with the previous findings and we shall have to make do with a survey based on the industrial production index constructed by Hoffmann. To facilitate long-term comparison we have marked off the turning-points on the ratio scale calculated from the Hoffmann industrial production index excluding building for the whole period from 1785 to 1913. These results are presented in Table 2.

The turning-points do approximate fairly closely to those given by previous writers in the field though a few of the datings differ slightly.[3] Over the whole period, 1785–1913, 24 cycles are recorded (measured from peak to peak) with an average duration of 5·33 years and a range extending from 2 to 10 years. The average duration is now lower than before because of the inclusion of a number of short cycles of about 3–4 years in length. Most of these occurred in the first half of the nineteenth century; by the 1840s, when the major cycle was asserting predominance, they had all but died out and in the latter half of the century there is virtually no trace of a minor cycle. Thus if we take the period 1836–1913, corresponding to the years covered by the income cycles, we find only one additional cycle in production and the average periodicity works out at 6·4 years compared

---

[1] Cf. Matthews, in Bronfenbrenner, *Is the Business Cycle Obsolete?*, p. 102. A number of alternative methods are given in G. J. Staller, 'Fluctuations in Economic Activity: Planned and Free Market Economies, 1950–60', *American Economic Review*, LIV (1964).

[2] It is possible that the severity of the cycle of the 1920s is exaggerated since a proxy value for national income in 1920 had to be used.

[3] A. D. Gayer, W. W. Rostow and Anna J. Schwartz, *The Growth and Fluctuation of the British Economy* (1953, 2 vols); Rostow, *British Economy*; and W. H. Beveridge, 'The Trade Cycle in Britain Before 1850', *Oxford Economic Papers*, III (1940).

TABLE 2

Duration and Amplitude of Cycles in Industrial Production, U.K.,
1785–1913

Peaks	Troughs	Duration (*peak to peak*)	Amplitude	Major peaks	Duration	Amplitude
1785	1788	—	—	1785	—	—
1792	1793	7	4·53	1792	7	4·53
1796	1797	4	6·07			
1800	1801	4	7·43	1800	8	7·12
1802	1803	2	3·93			
1805	1808	3	1·26			
1811	1814	6	3·60	1811	11	3·63
1815	1816	4	4·04			
1818	1819	3	2·72	1818	7	3·86
1825	1826	7	3·39	1825	7	3·39
1828	1829	3	5·12			
1830	1832	2	2·92			
1836	1837	6	2·91	1836	11	3·81
1839	1842	3	4·30	1839	3	4·30
1845	1847	6	5·54	1845	6	5·54
1853	1855	8	3·30	1853	8	3·30
1857	1858	4	2·63			
1860	1862	3	3·70	1860	7	3·23
1866	1869	6	3·98	1866	6	3·98
1874	1879	8	2·78	1874	8	2·78
1883	1886	9	5·43	1883	9	5·43
1889	1893	6	5·71	1889	6	5·71
1899	1904	10	4·13	1899	10	4·13
1907	1909	8	3·0	1907	8	3·00
1913		6	—	1913	6	—

Average duration	5·33			7·53	
Average amplitude		4·02			4·23

Source: Based on Hoffmann industrial production index excluding building as
described in text.

with 7 years for the income cycles. On the other hand, the period
1785–1836 yields 12 cycles with an average duration of only 4·25
years. In column 5 of Table 2 the peaks of the major cycles have been
listed. In one or two cases the years differ slightly from those selected
by Rostow,[1] while four additional peaks have been added, one at the
beginning of the period (1785) and the other three at 1839, 1860 and
1907. The last two warrant inclusion on the grounds that unemploy-

[1] *British Economy*, p. 33, and below, Essay 1, p. 77.

ment was low in these years,[1] while the trend deviation for 1839 turned out to be very high and could hardly be ignored. In effect this produced 17 major cycles over the period 1785–1913 with an average periodicity of 7·53 years. Although the length of the major cycles varied considerably, ranging from 3 to 11 years, the average periodicity did not alter significantly over time. Up to 1836 there were 6 major cycles with an average duration of 8·5 years, between 1836 and 1874 a further 6 averaging 6·3 years, and 5 from 1874 to 1913 with an average periodicity of 7·8 years. Minor cycles were almost solely confined to the first of these sub-periods when there were 6 altogether. After 1836 there was only one minor cycle with a peak in 1857, though if 1839 is discarded as a major turning-point there would be two.

The amplitudes of industrial production cycles have been calculated in the same way as before. As might be expected they are more severe than those of income cycles and there is considerable variation between successive cycles. On the other hand, there is no noticeable trend in amplitude over the period as a whole. In fact the most remarkable feature is the stability in amplitude when cycles are placed in successive time groups. The average amplitude between 1785 and 1818 (8 cycles) works out at 4·2, for the period 1818–57 (8 cycles) it is 3·76 and for 7 cycles in the period 1857–1907 it rises again slightly to 4·10. This compares with an average amplitude for 23 cycles of exactly 4·0. The values for the major cycles are very similar, the average being 4·23 for the 16 cycles between 1785 and 1907. Likewise, a breakdown into sub-periods gives a value of 4·39 for 6 cycles between 1785 and 1836, 4·07 for 5 cycles between 1836 and 1866, and 4·21 for the last 5 cycles through to 1907.

The statistical analysis clearly indicates some degree of consistency in cyclical patterns. A major cycle of 7–8 years duration can be traced back to the late eighteenth century. During the first part of the nineteenth century the major cycle was punctuated or interrupted by shorter ones of about 3–4 years duration, but these gradually fade away by the middle of the century as the standard business cycle becomes dominant. If we discount the minor interruptions in the 1920s the Juglar pattern continues without check through to 1937.[2]

---

[1] As given by the trade union returns in B. R. Mitchell and P. Deane, *Abstract of British Historical Statistics* (1962) pp. 64–5.

[2] No doubt it would be possible to find other cycles especially if sub-aggregate series were used as the basis of analysis. But the more micro-indicators we cover the greater the possibility of discovering different cyclical patterns, and eventually the whole exercise gets out of hand and becomes somewhat meaningless. Hence, when examining cyclical movements in the economy as a whole it is important to work with aggregate data or the nearest approximation.

There is no tendency for the amplitude of cycles to become either stronger or weaker up to 1913, though amplitudes do vary considerably from one cycle to the next. However, the most remarkable feature is the stability in amplitudes through successive time-periods. The only exception to this statement is for the inter-war period when fluctuations were considerably more intense than before 1914.

International Comparisons and International Synchronisation

Britain of course was not the only country to experience fluctuations. Cyclical movements were a common feature of major industrialising countries of the nineteenth century. Though the precise pattern of fluctuations tended to vary from country to country one would expect, given the complex and increasingly interlocking relationships between western Europe and North America, some similarity in the phasing of fluctuations of the chief industrial powers. The presence of strong trade and monetary connections would seem to rule out the possibility that cycles in each country were independently generated. The process by which fluctuations were transmitted from one country to another and the theory of international business cycles have been very inadequately studied. The following comments do not repair this deficiency but are simply designed to place British fluctuations in an international context.

Earlier writers laid considerable stress on the apparent international unity of cyclical movements. In 1926 W. L. Thorp found a fairly close agreement in cyclical phasing for 17 countries.[1] Similarly Forchheimer, in a relatively little-known article published in 1940,[2] suggested that cycles in the leading industrial countries were not unrelated phenomena and that there were certain well-defined peaks common to the U.K., France, Germany and the United States. He also noted that most major cycles were interrupted by minor ones and that the peaks of the latter tended to occur simultaneously in all four countries. But opinion was by no means unanimous on this matter. Somewhat earlier, in 1913, Mitchell had come to the conclusion that, because the length of the cycle differed from country to country, the degree of international synchronisation of fluctuations must have been rather low.[3]

Such conflicting views are not as difficult to reconcile as might be expected. The main reason for the difference probably arises from the rather imprecise way in which analysis was conducted. Mitchell,

---

[1] W. L. Thorp, *Business Annals* (1926).
[2] K. Forchheimer, 'The "Short Cycle" in its International Aspects', *Oxford Economic Papers*, VII (1945).
[3] W. C. Mitchell, *Business Cycles* (1913).

for instance, averaged the length of all cycles for each country and discovered that the major discrepancy in periodicity lay between the United States and the three European countries, Britain, Germany and France. The fact that the U.S. cycle turned out to be considerably shorter than the others was not very surprising given the fact that the United States was more prone to minor fluctuations. Conceivably it would have been better to eliminate short cycles from consideration (both in the case of the U.S. and other countries where necessary) on the grounds that these were less likely to be of international significance. Some minor cycles were quite shallow and of purely domestic origin or were caused by some random factor of a rather specific type, and in consequence their international transmission effects were very weak. Thus to include all cycles in the analysis would certainly tend to reduce the degree of international correspondence. Had the minor waves been excluded, at least from the U.S. data, this would have left 17 cycles for the period 1795–1937 with an average duration of 8·35 years. This major cycle, which according to Hansen could be regarded as the international cycle,[1] appears to fit more closely with the phasing of British and western European cycles.

Discrepancies in cyclical periodicity between countries does not necessarily make for a low degree of synchronisation on an international basis. A variation in average periodicity of one or two years between countries over a time-span of 100–150 years only requires the difference of one or two cycles, but it does not follow that low covariation will result except in the unlikely event of corresponding phasing being destroyed completely by the small differential in the number of cycles between the countries. Of course, as the discrepancy in average periodicity increases and the number of countries is raised, so the degree of international synchronisation will diminish, but the orders of magnitude in which Mitchell was dealing were fully compatible with a reasonably high degree of international covariation in cyclical phasing. In any case, if, as Forchheimer maintained, short as well as major cycles were international in scope, there would seem to be even less justification for Mitchell's thesis. But Forchheimer's inquiry, if not misconceived, is a misleading one. The attempt to impose the American cyclical pattern on countries such as Britain, France and Germany was far from convincing. The basis of his analysis of short cycles rests on the evidence of sub-aggregate data of a very dubious nature, for example iron production and timber prices, the drawbacks of which were noted earlier.[2] As

[1] A. H. Hansen, *Fiscal Policy and Business Cycles* (1941) pp. 18–19.
[2] See above, p. 13, n. 2.

we have already seen, there is no sign that a short cycle existed in Britain after the middle of the nineteenth century and, after 1870 at least, fluctuations in France and Germany were by no means as frequent as those in the United States. Thus whatever the position in the first half of the nineteenth century we should be wary of any notion of a common short-wave movement throughout the century as a whole.

The upshot of this inquiry would seem to indicate that international comparisons could be most profitably pursued on the basis of the major cycle of 7–8 years. Certainly many of the writers who emphasize the international sweep of cycles have followed this practice after a fashion in as much as they have based their narrative around the well-known peak or crisis years which were common to a number of countries. They make familiar reading – 1825, 1836, 1847, 1857, 1866, 1873, 1882, 1890, 1900, 1907, 1912–13, 1920, 1929, 1931, 1937. Earlier business cycle writers in particular had a penchant for dealing with crisis years as though these were the be-all and end-all of cyclical analysis,[1] though the practice has not completely died out.[2] Superficially the listing of these key dates gave some strength to the notion that there was a fair degree of similarity in cyclical phasing between countries. Closer inspection however gives cause for some doubt about the faith placed in this type of exercise. For one thing some of the years have little meaning in terms of reference cycle dates. The most obvious case is 1931, a year which does not appear in a reference cycle pattern of any country. Secondly, the crises often occurred after the true reference cycle peaks and were associated with financial operations. Finally, even if these years were common to all reference cycle patterns they do not tell us anything about phasing at other points of the cycle. The peaks may tally but if the troughs tend to be dispersed the degree of similar phasing will obviously be reduced.

Fortunately the results of a more modern investigation by Morgenstern help to clarify some of the points at issue.[3] Though concerned primarily with international monetary relationships among the countries of Britain, France, Germany and the United States, as a preliminary to his study Morgenstern had to analyse the cyclical phasing of the four countries in question. From our point of view the work has two drawbacks; it only extends from 1879 to 1938, and the

---

[1] W. O. Henderson, 'Trade Cycles in the Nineteenth Century', *History*, XVIII (1933–4) and the bibliographical note on earlier works.

[2] Indeed, one recent work is very much in the old tradition. See M. Flamant and J. Singer-Kérel, *Modern Economic Crises* (1970, first published in French in 1968).

[3] O. Morgenstern, *International Financial Transactions and Business Cycles* (1959).

analysis includes both major and minor cycles, the expediency of which we have questioned in this context. However, it is by far the most sophisticated study to date in the field and the findings are worth considering.

Taking the three European countries we find that, for the 419 months between September 1879 and August 1914, they were in the same phase of the cycle for 83·1 per cent of the time, with the co-variation of expansions higher than that for contractions. The inclusion of the United States reduces sharply the percentage of similar phasing to 53·5 per cent (expansions 31·3 per cent and contractions 22·2 per cent), reflecting the shorter periodicity of the U.S. cycle. After the war the degree of international synchronisation diminishes significantly. Between June 1919 and July 1932 (157 months) the three European countries were in the same phase of the cycle for only 45·2 per cent of the time, and 35·6 per cent when the U.S. is included. But post-war the United States was less out of step with the European countries than before 1914, while the latter became less in step with each other but more in line as a group with America. Morgenstern himself is cautious about acknowledging the existence of an international cycle.[1] Clearly for the post-war period the degree of correspondence is too low to justify it, while pre-war it is high for the European countries but considerably lower when the U.S. is admitted.[2] He also points out that there is no generally agreed list of international reference dates. If then it is difficult to speak of a truly international cycle in this period, it is even less likely that one existed before the 1870s since the degree of international synchronisation could scarcely have been greater than it was in the late nineteenth century and early twentieth. We would question however whether it is so vital to have a very high element of covariation in cyclical phasing to warrant the nomenclature 'international cycle'. The international transmission of fluctuations inevitably involves some leads and lags and until we know more about the precise nature of the process it is perhaps premature to rule out altogether the concept of an international cycle.

Characteristics of the Cycle

It is hardly necessary to outline the way in which an economy generates business cycles. The path is so well trodden that it would

[1] Ibid., pp. 45–51, 53, 67.
[2] Cf. M. Simon, 'New British Investment in Canada, 1865–1914', *Canadian Journal of Economics*, III (1970) 252–3, who finds a greater congruence of British, Canadian and American business cycles after 1900.

be rather futile to cover the ground yet again. Nearly every book written on the subject devotes ample space to the subject and past research has yielded a rich store of empirical information which tells us what happens during business cycles.[1] In this section therefore we shall simply note a few of the main features of cycles and comment briefly on the movements of some of the key variables.

From what has already been said it will be obvious that no two cycles are the same. One cycle differs from the next in both duration and amplitude for a start. Differences such as these and others have led some students of the subject to regard all cycles as historical individuals. Mitchell, for example, considered each cycle to be a unique series of events which has its own particular explanatory forces and its own particular effects on the economy.[2] Yet while it may be important to underline the unique features of each fluctuation, it must not be forgotten that cycles do have many common characteristics and that they are subject to similar impulses and causal forces. As Burns has observed: 'Diversity and individuality are no less characteristic of business cycles than the family resemblance among them . . .'[3] If this were not the case it would be easy enough to abandon the search for any conformity and leave each cycle to be analysed and explained independently without reference to the others.

Most people, in so far as they ever think about business cycles, are probably aware that they consist of upswings and downswings bounded by peaks and troughs. Their very existence necessitates such simple attributes. It is possible to subdivide the two main phases. The upswing will generally consist of a recovery phase from the lower turning-point which occurs below the trend line, followed by a prosperity or boom period above the trend. The rate of expansion in the initial part of the upswing is usually more rapid than in the second stage when growth begins to slacken off or flatten out towards the peak. Similarly, the downswing may comprise a recession phase, when the cut-back in activity is quite marked, followed by a

---

[1] The literature is indeed vast but nearly all American. There is nothing to compare in this country with the work on business cycle indicators carried out in the United States. It is difficult to be selective but the work of Burns, Mitchell and Moore should certainly be consulted by readers interested in the sequential mechanics of cycles. There are plenty of short accounts; one of the most useful can be found in R. A. Gordon, *Business Fluctuations*, 2nd ed. (1961).

[2] W. C. Mitchell, *Business Cycles and Their Causes* (1950). Though Mitchell did not regard cycles as independent entities such that they had no influence whatever on one another.

[3] Burns, *Business Cycle in a Changing World*, p. 24.

depression below the trend line when the rate of decline tapers off before culminating in the lower turning-point.[1]

While for some purposes this terminology may be useful it does have its drawbacks. Not all cycles can be marked off so neatly into four stages and it is often more practical to use the two-stage system of upswing and downswing. The four-stage rotation can lead to ambiguities in meaning. For example, it is particularly incongruous to speak of a boom or prosperity phase in America during the 1930s when unemployment remained high and output had a struggle to get back to the pre-depression level. Moreover, the four stages, even if they can be identified exactly, will not normally be of the same length either within a cycle or between successive cycles. A more serious objection to the four-stage schema is that for part of the time the cyclical component will be growing at the same rate as the trend and in effect it will have no curvature at all. It is for this reason that Evans feels it is more appropriate to adopt a three-stage model as follows: the first consists of a period of rapid growth, greater than the trend rate, and beginning with an upturn; the second, a decline in the rate of growth relative to trend, which culminates in the upper turning-point; the third phase occurs when the decline in economic activity sets in and ends at the lower turning-point.[2]

Criticisms can be raised about this pattern as well. Presumably if the trend rate were falling or even horizontal it would be necessary to introduce an additional stage in the downswing. Not a great deal is to be gained, however, by pursuing this debate on stages. For all practical purposes it is more convenient to stick to the two-phase scheme since it gives rise to less ambiguity.

Even if each cycle could be regarded as a unique set of events this would in no way preclude a certain similarity in the pattern of movement of different economic variables between cycles. Most economic indicators of an aggregate or semi-aggregate type, whether income, consumption, production, investment, profits, prices or employment, tend to move pro-cyclically, that is they rise in the up-swings and fall during contractions. There are exceptions to this general rule. Prices, for example, have been known to move against the cycle. In the modified boom of the later 1920s prices were declining, while through the cycle of 1883–90 they fell almost continuously. Residential construction has a strong tendency to fluctuate counter-cyclically. Trade balances also exhibit some contrasts, though in general these have been more a question of fundamental long-term changes rather than short-term variations. Since the

---

[1] This would require some modification for modern growth cycles.

[2] M. K. Evans, *Macroeconomic Activity* (1969) pp. 418–19.

Second World War the balance of payments has tended to deteriorate in booms and improve in recessions, whereas in the nineteenth century the reverse was generally the case. Moreover, the more we disaggregate the more likely we are to get conflicting movements, some indicators rising while others are falling, both within and between cycles. Nor for that matter do all indicators turn at the peaks and troughs simultaneously.

At the same time there are significant differences in the behaviour of even the main variables throughout the course of the cycle. To take the most obvious, consumption, which accounts for the greater part of income, experiences milder fluctuations than investment. This is partly because most consumption is made out of current income or that received in the immediate past and partly because the consumption function possesses built-in stabilising properties. Thus for a given increase in income, consumption does not rise proportionately since in the short run the marginal propensity to consume is less than the average resulting in a decline in the latter and a rise in the average propensity to save. Conversely, in contractions consumption falls by less than the decline in income as the average propensity to consume rises and savings fall. In fact in some recessions, especially in more recent times with consumption being bolstered up by Government transfer payments, consumption may hardly fall at all, and it may even continue to rise. Even in the slump of 1929–32 real consumption in Britain continued to rise through to 1931 and only fell slightly in the last year of the downswing.[1] Investment, on the other hand, is by far the most volatile element of aggregate demand and has been accorded a central role in business cycle theory. The durability of capital goods and the fact that the level of investment demand is partly a function of the rate of change in the level of income or consumption (acceleration principle) means that investment tends to rise and fall quite sharply through the cycle. Moreover, because of reaction lags and the gestation period involved in constructing capital goods, investment may well lag the cycle and for part of the time act in a stabilising manner.

Not all the components of aggregate demand behave in the same way, however. Expenditure on durables, for example, is a much more volatile element of G.N.P. than expenditure on non-durables and services since it reacts more quickly to changes in income and is also subject to an accelerator and stock adjustment effect. Expendi-

---

[1] A useful empirical study showing the relative stability of the consumption function and its resistance to deflationary pressures is that by S. H. Hyman, 'The Cyclical Behaviour of Consumers' Income and Expenditure, 1921–1961', *Southern Economic Journal*, XXXII (1965).

ture on imports also fluctuates more than other types of consumption. Different categories of investment demand also vary quite markedly over the cycle. Inventory investment is probably the most volatile of all types of expenditure and it is generally accepted to be an important leading indicator at the turning-points. Investment in plant and machinery reacts more slowly to changes in income and lags at the turning-points and for this reason the accelerator effect is weaker. Residential construction has generally experienced larger swings than business investment in the past and for various reasons it has often moved in a contra-cyclical manner.

Other indicators may be mentioned briefly. Industrial production fluctuates more sharply than the output of services or total income and has generally coincided with the turning-points, though the experience of individual industries varies considerably. Exports are extremely volatile and in the past they have been an important leading indicator at the turning-points. Profits and stock prices tend to lead at the turning-points, while employment and unemployment coincide, though in the case of the former there is also a tendency for it to lag behind.

Business Cycle Theory

There are a large number of different business cycle theories ranging from the vague and eclectic models of earlier writers like Mitchell to the more formal and mathematical models of leading theorists in the subject. It would be neither practical nor very fruitful to examine or even list all the alternatives. It is possible however to simplify matters by classifying theories into two broad categories as follows: (1) endogenous theories which show that the internal structure of the economy is such that it will generate fluctuations once the equilibrium has been disturbed; and (2) exogenous theories which assert that forces outside the economic structure are responsible for producing fluctuations in economic activity. These two sets of theories represent opposite extremes though they are not mutually exclusive. In reality it is likely that cycles reflect a compromise between the two.

Most modern theories of business cycles, especially the econometric, are of an endogenous nature. They lay stress on the systematic movements arising from the internal mechanism of the economy as a result of specified relationships between economic variables, and they rely heavily on some form of acceleration or capital stock adjustment principle. They show how, once initial equilibrium is disturbed, the constant relationships between the variables can produce a fluctuating response as a result of reaction lags inherent in the system. Exogenous theories, on the other hand, contain no lagged response mechanisms. Economies are inherently stable and fluctuations are seen as 'nothing but a purely arbitrary and random succession of changes'.[1] The economy oscillates because it responds at once, that is without a lag, to any fluctuations or change in exogenous forces such as wars, climatic disasters or political events. These forces may be random or periodic; if they are random and the system responds immediately then there would be no cyclical pattern but merely a series of random fluctuations in the economy. A purely exogenous theory of the cycle would demand that the exogenous forces were of a periodic nature and that the system reacted at once to such shocks. Once a lag is introduced endogenous features come back into play again.

There are several awkward problems relating to the application of these theories in their rigid form. Indeed it is doubtful whether they are very realistic or whether a fine distinction can be made between exogenous and endogenous theories. It is difficult to conceive of a purely exogenous cyclical pattern emerging in practice for it is unlikely that all the variables in the system will react in an unlagged manner and it is even less probable that the pattern of shocks will be such as to generate a regular cyclical movement. Moreover, it is also difficult to determine exactly what are the exogenous forces which are relevant to the situation. Such factors as wars and climatic disasters can clearly be listed as autonomous influences but it is less easy to decide to what extent innovations or long-term investment can be regarded in the same manner since both are sensitive to economic change.

On the face of it endogenous theories would seem to contain a greater degree of realism. It seems plausible to assume that the economy reacts in a lagged manner to disturbances so that there would be a tendency for fluctuations to perpetuate themselves, once started. But it has proved virtually impossible to produce a satisfactory endogenous model to explain persistent business fluctuations. There are versions of multiplier-accelerator models which produce self-generating fluctuations, but except under certain conditions they tend either to become explosive or to remain damped. In the former case, therefore, restraints need to be imposed to limit the boundaries of fluctuations. The non-linear models of Hicks, Kaldor and Goodwin[2] are derived by imposing systematic parameter changes – e.g. shifts in the accelerator coefficient and in the marginal propensity to

---

[1] J. Tinbergen and J. J. Polak, *The Dynamics of Business Cycles* (1950) p. 253.
[2] J. Hicks, *A Contribution to the Theory of the Trade Cycle* (1950); N. Kaldor, 'A Model of the Trade Cycle', *Economic Journal*, L (1940); R. M. Goodwin, 'The Non-linear Accelerator and the Persistence of Business Cycles', *Econometrica*, XIX (1951).

consume – at the peaks and troughs of the cycles which result from the ceilings and floors inherent in the system. Thus in the most famous of the models – the Hicksian – oscillations take place on the backdrop of a growing economy. The non-linear constraints are imposed by a full employment ceiling and a floor determined by the secular rise in the level of autonomous investment. These serve to check the explosive nature of the process. 'Thus confined, the multiplier-accelerator process bounces from floor to ceiling and back again tracing out a secularly rising, cyclically fluctuating time series of income similar to that achieved by modern industrialised economies.'[1] In the case of damped cycles it was found necessary to introduce exogenous shocks to rejuvenate the process. Frisch, for example, believed that the system was disposed to produce damped fluctuations and that they were prevented from dying away by erratic shocks of one form or another.[2]

In both cases the conditions required to produce a systematically fluctuating system are fairly rigorous and somewhat unrealistic. The determination of the ceilings and floors in the explosive version has been the subject of much debate, while the relative constancy in the magnitude of observed cycles would seem to impose rather rigid constraints on the value of the parameter changes. The damped model kept alive by random disturbances would in fact presuppose a more orderly pattern of shocks of the right magnitude than are likely to occur in practice. Recently, however, an attempt has been made to test the validity of the shock theory. A sophisticated econometric model of the United States economy (the Klein–Goldberger model) was found to be relatively stable in its behaviour and could absorb large isolated shocks without producing fluctuations. But when it was subjected to a series of random shocks of a realistic order of magnitude, the cyclical fluctuations derived were very similar to those observed in the American economy. That the shocked Klein–Goldberger model offered close agreement with the facts strengthens the case for reassessing the role of shocks, but the authors of the study take care to point out that it does not prove that it is a good representation of the basic interactions among the sectors of the economy or that random shocks are the prime cause of cycles.[3]

[1] R. N. Waud, 'An Expectations Model of Cyclical Growth: Hicks on the Trade Cycle Revisited', *Oxford Economic Papers*, XIX (1967).

[2] R. Frisch, 'Propagation Problems and Impulse Problems in Dynamic Economics', in *Economic Essays in Honour of Gustav Cassel* (1933); cf. M. Kalecki, *Theory of Economic Dynamics* (1954) pp. 137–41.

[3] Irma and Frank L. Adelman, 'The Dynamic Properties of the Klein–Goldberger Model', *Econometrica*, XXVII (1959) 619–21, and Irma Adelman, 'Business Cycles: Endogenous or Stochastic?', *Economic Journal*, LXX (1960).

The issue between exogenous and endogenous theories of the cycle still remains a central theme of debate in business cycle analysis. Even if we could resolve the problem one way or the other we would still be left with a large number of different theories to choose from. The possible variations on the two plausible endogenous models, that is those producing damped and explosive cycles, is almost limitless. And whether any particular one would fit the facts all the time is very questionable. It is not therefore surprising that some economists have expressed doubts as to whether it is possible to develop a pure theory of the cycle. Models may be justified by the light they throw on some aspects of the cycle, but, as Wilson has pointed out, generally speaking most stylised models do not adequately reflect the facts.[1] Indeed, given the wide variety of cyclical experience, even within the confines of one country, it is scarcely to be expected that one formal model could do justice to the facts all the time. Quite probably a true representation of the facts in theory would require a series of models or one that was being continually adapted over time.

Most of the early writers on business cycles plied their trade without resort to rigorous theories. Even today, after years of formal model building, it is rare to find an author who is able to integrate theory and fact successfully. That facts often fly in the face of theory may be a well-worn phrase but it still bears a great deal of truth. Faced with reality the student of business cycle behaviour may prefer not to be constrained by the rigidities of a formal model but to rely on a more general analytical framework which provides a reasonable degree of flexibility. Hickman, for example, in his study of post-war U.S. business cycles, employs this type of framework which combines the best of both worlds in that it recognises the need to integrate or at least utilise both endogenous and exogenous theories of the cycle.[2] This procedure certainly lacks precision since it is sufficiently vague and general to be adaptable in any circumstances, but this may be a necessary requirement given the wide diversity of cyclical experience. Many writers, of course, employ no theory at all and are content to analyse the data and let the facts speak for themselves, while others test the validity of known hypotheses.

We should not, by implication from the above comments, conclude that models serve no useful purpose, or that it will not be possible to construct more viable theories in the future. Recent progress in econometric model building suggests that realistic models of

---

[1] T. Wilson, 'Cyclical and Autonomous Inducements to Invest', *Oxford Economic Papers*, v (1953) 87–8.

[2] B. Hickman, *Growth and Stability of the Postwar Economy* (1960) pp. 5–6.

cyclical behaviour are within the bounds of possibility. But future prospects are not of any help in the present context. Apart from Tinbergen's study for the period before 1914,[1] much of which is now out of date as regards the facts, there has been very little attempt to test the validity of particular theories as far as the U.K. is concerned. Most of the work carried out has been strictly empirical in content with almost no effort being made to reconcile theory with fact.

This is not a very impressive progress report and it clearly circumscribes our range of action in this introductory survey. It would of course be quite easy to specify a model which *might* fit the facts but there would be little point to the exercise unless we could test its validity, and to do this would require a complex and lengthy period of research. And in any case, there is no reason to suppose that one model would serve our purpose. However, the absence of the ordered precision of a verifiable model or theory of the cycle should not inhibit us from examining the causal significance of some of the factors which appear to have played an important part in business cycles. We first analyse the role of two variables which have featured prominently in business cycle discussions and then turn to some of the more important indirect influences such as innovations, monetary factors and harvest fluctuations.

The Role of Exports and Investment

Students of British business cycles have consistently emphasised the crucial role played by investment and exports, particularly the latter, in fluctuations. From a random perusal of the literature one cannot fail to note the overwhelming importance attached to these two variables.[2] Gayer, Rostow and Schwartz, in their mammoth study of cycles before 1850, place primary emphasis on movements in the volume of exports and domestic investment. Major cyclical upswings were dominated by movements in exports and investment while minor cycles were propelled largely by changes in export volumes. Exports rarely moved against the cycle and they were an important initiating force in revival from recession.[3] Somewhat earlier, Beveridge, in a series of studies, drew attention to the high correlation between movements in industrial activity and export

[1] J. Tinbergen, *Business Cycles in the United Kingdom, 1870–1914* (1951).

[2] Ilse Mintz, *Cyclical Fluctuations in the Exports of the United States since 1879* (1967) chap. 1, for a useful summary of the views on the role of export changes in business cycles.

[3] Gayer, Rostow and Schwartz, *Growth and Fluctuation of the British Economy*, vol. 2, pp. 532–5.

values and noted that exports led at the turning-points of cycles.[1] Other studies have reaffirmed the cyclical nature of domestic investment[2] and the primacy of export fluctuations. Ford, for example, has argued that the proximate cause of income fluctuations between 1870 and 1914 was fluctuations in merchandise exports the pattern of which was indirectly affected by shifts in British overseas investment.[3]

This apparent unanimity of opinion should not deter us from taking a further look at the influence of exports on fluctuations. The method of approach used in some of the studies mentioned above was not such as to produce conclusive results. Beveridge was forced to confine his analysis to exports and industrial activity. That he found a close association between the two was not very surprising given the fact that the exports absorbed a large share of industrial production. But since the latter accounted for less than half the total output of the economy it is unlikely that income fluctuations would be affected to the same extent by changes in exports. Nevertheless, it would be difficult to deny that exports did not influence the cycle. Throughout the nineteenth century and into the twentieth exports accounted for around 15–20 per cent of national income, while some industries, notably textiles, were heavily dependent on export markets. Exports, moreover, were noted for their volatility; short-run changes in exports were often very severe and they could exert a considerable impact on the economy. In part these wide swings in export volumes and values could be ascribed to the increasing internationalisation of the business cycle and to Britain's dependence on the markets of primary producers whose incomes were noted for their instability.

Similar considerations apply to investment though here the issue is a little more complex. Data limitations have circumscribed the analysis of this variable, and most of the discussion relates to the

---

[1] W. H. Beveridge, 'Unemployment in the Trade Cycle', *Economic Journal*, XLIX (1939); 'The Trade Cycle in Britain Before 1850: A Postscript', *Oxford Economic Papers*, IV (1940); and *Full Employment in a Free Society* (1944) p. 294. Beveridge's findings were supported for the inter-war period by E. H. Phelps Brown and G. L. S. Shackle, 'British Economic Fluctuations, 1924–38', *Oxford Economic Papers*, II (1939).

[2] See J. S. Pesmazoglu, 'A Note on the Cyclical Fluctuations of British Home Investment, 1870–1913', *Oxford Economic Papers*, III (1951).

[3] A. G. Ford, 'Notes on the Role of Exports in British Economic Fluctuations, 1870–1914', *Economic History Review*, XVI (1963–4), and 'Overseas Lending and Internal Fluctuations, 1870–1914', *Yorkshire Bulletin of Economic and Social Research*, XVII (1965); see also below, Essay 3. Paish (*Lloyds Bank Review*, Oct 1970, p. 1) attributes every major decline in business activity between 1845 and the outbreak of the Second World War largely to developments in the rest of the world.

later nineteenth century. A cyclical pattern in investment has been observed, it is true, but the situation is complicated somewhat by long swings in some sectors, e.g. residential building, transport and foreign investment, and these have tended to generate long cycles in total investment as well. Because of this and also the fact that investment is prone to gestation lags, it has been said that investment does not always synchronise very closely with general cyclical movements. However, since many theories of business fluctuations accord a critical role to the instability of investment, any empirical study must take account of this variable. In most of the models the determinants of investment are usually taken to be the rate of change in total output (acceleration principle) or the level of output in relation to the size of the capital stock (capital stock adjustment principle). Such formulations have been the subject of much criticism and generally they do not represent the facts very adequately.[1] Empirical tests have also cast doubt on the validity of the acceleration principle in explaining fluctuations.[2] Nevertheless, these criticisms of the theory do not necessarily mean that investment was not an important source of income fluctuations.

There are several ways of assessing the impact of investment and exports on income fluctuations. In particular, we wish to know the severity of cycles in these variables and relate it to that in national income. Secondly, the turning-points in exports and investment may be compared with those in income to see how closely they synchronise. And thirdly, it is useful to determine the degree of conformity between movements in income and other variables through the cycle as a whole. The following exercises provide some degree of quantification of these points. They are confined to the period for which income estimates are available.

A glance at Table 3 confirms the frequent assertions made about the magnitude of fluctuations in exports and investment. They were both very much larger than those in income and consumption for every cycle through to 1937. Averaging over successive cycles for the years 1836–1907 reveals an amplitude of just over 2 for income and

[1] Thus Gordon: 'They are unable to account for the important differences among past cycles; they abstract from most of the complexities of economic growth; they ignore some features of the cumulative process which observation suggests may be important in shaping the course of the cycle; and they yield explanations of investment behaviour which, as often as not, do not seem to fit the facts.' R. A. Gordon, 'Investment Behaviour and Business Cycles', *Review of Economics and Statistics*, xxxvii (1955) 23.

[2] J. Tinbergen, 'Statistical Evidence on the Acceleration Principle', *Economica*, v (1938). Tinbergen later found that there was little evidence of it being of great value for explaining investment fluctuations in the U.K. between 1870 and 1914. See his *Business Cycles in the United Kingdom*, p. 96.

TABLE 3

Cyclical Amplitude of Components of National Income,
1836–1937

Cycles from peak to peak	G.N.P.	Consumption	G.D.F.C.F.	Exports
1836–9	2·67	1·76	10·13	7·74
1839–46	4·52	3·06	22·57	4·43
1846–56	2·14	1·51	15·20	7·05
1856–9	1·98	0·92	3·29	2·45
1859–65	1·36	0·72	11·35	6·73
1865–74	1·49	1·35	9·60	4·72
1874–83	1·81	1·70	8·08	5·29
1883–90	1·28	0·83	8·50	5·09
1890–1901	1·88	1·37	8·79	4·85
1901–7	1·55	0·81	2·65	4·52
1920–9	5·02	1·86	5·34	14·34
1929–37	2·90	1·27	8·13	10·24

Note: For sources and methods of calculation see Table 1 and the text.

1·4 for consumption as against 10 and 5 for investment and exports (see Table 4). Of course the absolute amplitudes do not indicate the relative contribution of these variables to income fluctuations since the weighting of each variable in total income varies considerably. The value for each variable has therefore been multiplied by its weight factor in G.N.P. (for each cycle and then averaged) to show the approximate contribution to G.N.P. fluctuation. As might be

TABLE 4

Aggregate Amplitude of Cycles in Components of National Income

Absolute amplitudes

	G.N.P.	Consumption	G.D.F.C.F.	Exports
1836–1907	2·07	1·40	10·02	5·29
1920–37	3·96	1·57	6·74	12·29

Amplitude corrected for weighting in G.N.P.

	G.N.P.	Consumption	G.D.F.C.F.	Exports
1836–1907	2·07	1·19	0·69	0·79
1920–37	3·96	1·40	0·65	1·66

Percentage contribution to G.N.P. amplitude

	G.N.P.	Consumption	G.D.F.C.F.	Exports
1836–1907	100	57·5	33·3	38·2
1920–37	100	35·4	16·4	41·9

Note: For sources and methods of calculation see Table 1 and the text.

expected, the amplitudes for investment and exports are now very much reduced and lower than those for consumption, which accounted for the bulk of income, though there was considerable variation in the relative importance of each variable from cycle to cycle. Nevertheless, the percentage contributions given in the last panel of Table 4 show that export and investment fluctuations were still of considerable importance. Though exports accounted for 20 per cent or less of G.N.P. they accounted for 38 per cent of G.N.P. fluctuation before 1914 and a slightly larger amount in the inter-war years. G.N.P. fluctuation due to investment, which absorbed 10 per cent or less of total income, was about one-third before the war and rather less afterwards. Consumption,[1] which absorbed 85 per cent or more of G.N.P., accounted for very much less of its fluctuation.[2] Unfortunately, we cannot break down consumption expenditure to find out which items fluctuated most. But it seems fairly certain that the most unstable item was expenditure on imports. Total imports fluctuated almost as severely as exports and the two moved in close harmony over the course of the cycle. Between 1836 and 1909 imports and exports, and G.N.P. and imports, moved in the same direction for just over 78 per cent of the time. Thus it could be argued that export fluctuations were indirectly the source of fluctuations in consumption. A rise in exports boosted investment and incomes at home and part of the consequent increase in consumption spilled over into imports which in turn led to a further expansion of exports. A fall in exports would of course reverse the process.

As far as synchronisation of turning-points is concerned it is significant that the peaks and troughs in exports either coincided with or preceded those of income. This was true in practically every case through to 1937, the major exceptions being the income peaks of 1859 and 1865 when exports lagged by one year or less. The behaviour of domestic investment was more erratic but it did not, as might be expected, generally lag at the turning-points. Of the 11 peaks in income between 1836 and 1907 investment preceded on 5 occasions, coincided on 3 and lagged twice, and on the remaining occasion, that of 1859, there was no definite peak in investment. At the troughs there was no lagging at all: in 7 cases investment turned before income and on the remaining 4 occasions it coincided. Thus the turning-points in income, investment and exports did

---

[1] The amplitude of fluctuations in consumption may be on the high side since indirect taxes have not been excluded in the calculations.

[2] The percentages in the last panel of Table 4 do not sum to 100 since several items have been left out of account. These include public expenditure, foreign investment and imports, the last of which being the largest leakage.

approximate fairly closely, but with a tendency for investment and exports to change direction before income at both the upper and lower turning-points.

It does not necessarily follow from this that exports and investment moved pro-cyclically all the time, that is throughout the course of the cycle. Even though there was a degree of correspondence at or around the turning-points, there was still considerable scope for divergent fluctuations within cycles averaging 7 years duration without upsetting the cyclical conformity at the peaks and troughs. As a preliminary check on this we paired income, exports and investment alternatively and from the detrended ratio series determined what proportion of the time movements were in the same direction. For this purpose and for the correlation estimates which follow the current price estimates were used since it was suspected that the deflated series were not entirely reliable for observing year-to-year changes. The results in Table 5 show that for about three-quarters of the time the cyclical movements in exports and investment were

TABLE 5

Signs of the First Differences of the Detrended Ratio Series for Selected Pairs of Variables, 1836–1909

	Similar phasing	Opposite phasing	Percentage of similar phasing
1836–1909			
G.N.P. and exports	54	19	74
G.N.P. and investment	54	19	74
Exports and investment	46	27	63
1870–1909			
G.N.P. and exports	32	7	82·1
G.N.P. and investment	29	10	74·4
Exports and investment	28	11	71·8

in the same direction as those in income, while the correspondence between exports and investment, though still high, was somewhat lower. The breakdown given in Table 5 also suggests that the conformity was greater after 1870 than before, especially as regards G.N.P. and exports. During the inter-war period the degree of conformity, particularly between exports and income, declined somewhat.

Correlations between the selected pairs of variables gave relatively high values, especially for the period after 1870, though the correlation coefficient between income and exports for the whole period (1836–1909) was surprisingly low (0·4929). A multiple linear regression model of the form $Y_1 = a_{1·23} + b_{12.3} X_2 + b_{13·2} Z_3$, where Y_1, X_2 and Z_3 stand for the cyclical values of income, exports and domestic investment, gave better results. The multiple correlation coefficients were higher than the simple correlation coefficients for both periods, while the coefficients of determination ($R_{1·23}^2$) were significant at 0·659 and 0·729 respectively. The results for the partial coefficients of determination also indicated that exports were a more important determinant of income fluctuations for the years after 1870, whereas for the whole period the investment variable was more powerful.[1] Though a more sophisticated statistical analysis might have produced more precise results the exercise does appear to substantiate the visualistic impressions noted above.

In sum, therefore, these findings confirm the general opinion that exports and investment were important sources of fluctuations in British incomes in the nineteenth and early twentieth centuries. The lack of income data before 1830 precludes a statistical verification of this point for earlier years though at the moment we have no reason to dissent from the testimony of Gayer, Rostow and Schwartz. To hazard an opinion, it might be suggested that exports were the chief element of instability and were partly responsible for fluctuations in investment, though of course the latter was influenced by purely domestic forces as well. Export fluctuations were both large and consistent in frequency throughout the whole period and their synchronisation with the cycle was such that it would be difficult to believe that they did not play a determining role in income fluctuations. It would be wrong, of course, to suggest that exports and investment were the only sources of instability; further study of other variables, especially stocks and the components of consumption (data for which are not available for the nineteenth century), is required before we can form a completely accurate picture. It should be also borne in mind that the method of analysis adopted here has involved considerable averaging and compression of the data in order to bring out the salient features, which does mean that the

[1] The results are as follows:

	1870–1909	1836–1909
Coefficient of multiple correlation		
$R_{1·23}$	0·8115	0·8537
Coefficient of multiple determination		
$R_{1·23}^2$	0·6585	0·7288
Partial coefficients of determination		
$r_{12·3}^2$	0·3894	0·3454
$r_{13·2}^2$	0·2209	0·6416

intricate relationships between variables have been glossed over to some extent. The derivation of export fluctuations is a case in point. Did they respond indirectly to forces in the British economy such as changes in imports or British overseas investment, or were they a product of autonomous forces arising in the main markets? This is an issue which we cannot take up here but it is treated in some of the selected readings which follow.[1] The reader should also not be surprised to find that for particular cycles or phases of cycles the above conclusions have limited relevance. There was a marked variation in the degree of influence which exports had on fluctuations both within and between cycles. The cycle of 1839–46 owed comparatively little to exports, being dominated largely by domestic influences, notably railway building; by contrast the cycle of 1859–65 appears to have been very much affected by export activity. Similarly, the boom of the later 1890s was closely associated with domestic activity, especially construction, and in fact exports experienced a secondary wave with peaks and troughs in 1896 and 1898 which barely showed up in the income data. By the inter-war years the influence of exports was beginning to disintegrate, at least in the early phases of upswings. Though the downturns in economic activity were very much precipitated by unfavourable movements in export-sensitive industries, exports lagged at the lower turning-points, especially that of 1932, and contributed little to the early phases of recovery.

Although exports and investment were the major elements of instability in the economic system, this does not mean that fluctuations in income were not conditioned by other factors. The determinants of the fluctuation in these variables requires fuller analysis than we can afford here, but it is important to discuss the role of some of the chief indirect influences which affected the character of the cycles in the period under review. The most widely known of these are innovations, monetary factors and harvest fluctuations. All of these could be classified as partly autonomous in that their movements were not determined primarily by the interrelationships of the economic system,[2] though their influence was felt, in varying degrees, throughout the course of cyclical history. In addition, random shocks, such as wars, political disturbances, etc., occurred from time to time which again had some influence on the pattern of certain cycles. Thus an upswing might be cut short or damped by monetary stringency or through a check to exports arising from the outbreak of

[1] See below, Essays 2 and 3.
[2] Though see below, pp. 57–8.

war.[1] Alternatively, a boom might be inspired or prolonged by a renewed burst of innovation, while recovery from a recession could be facilitated by easy money conditions. These of course are only a few of the ways in which such forces could affect the system, though it does not necessarily mean that they were of critical significance at the turning-points. They can be incorporated into either exogenous or endogenous models of the cycle without much difficulty. In the former case these factors would act as periodic disturbances necessary to maintain a fluctuating system, while in the case of endogenous cycles they would either serve to restrain the parameter values, thus giving rise to the ceilings and floors, or they would operate as reinvigorating influences, depending on whether or not cycles were explosive or damped. Fortunately, it is possible to discuss the manner in which these influences worked without being committed to any particular model of the cycle.

Schumpeter's Innovations

There are at least two reasons for examining the role of innovations in business fluctuations. Recent theoretical and empirical studies have placed a great deal of emphasis on the importance of technical progress as a source of growth. In so far as growth and cycles are subject to common stimuli, it would seem plausible to postulate that innovations do have some bearing on fluctuations. Secondly, Schumpeter, in his classic study of business cycles, made innovation the centrepiece of the process. In his opinion economic development is propelled largely by the force of innovation which gives rise to waves of progress and the consolidation of that progress. Innovations are prone to clustering and expansion stems from the bunching effect of swarms of imitating businessmen following the lead of the pioneer innovator. Eventually, when innovation or technological opportunities are exhausted, the peak of expansion is reached. This gives rise to a period of retrenchment and consolidation, and not until a new equilibrium is reached, after the initial recovery from the lower turning-point, do conditions become favourable for a renewed burst of innovating activity. Schumpeter employs a complex cyclical pattern the basis of which is the Juglar with the points of inflection located at the neighbourhoods of equilibrium. The Juglar pattern is punctuated by minor waves while the whole scheme is set against the backdrop of the long-wave Kondratieff.

It is one thing to say that innovations influence business cycles but

[1] Exports may well be regarded as an autonomous force and in many econometric models they are written in as such.

quite another to infer, as Schumpeter did, that they are of crucial significance. This is not to deny that the theory does have certain attractions – for example, an innovations theory of fluctuations could explain why cycles rarely have the same magnitude or periodicity since the character of each cycle would depend upon the magnitude of the innovating impulse. But such merits scarcely make up for the defects of the theory. It is imprecise and vague and very difficult to quantify or substantiate empirically.

One general problem concerns the type of cycle with which Schumpeter was concerned. It is not immediately clear whether he thought in terms of exogenous or endogenous mechanisms, and later writers on Schumpeter have not done much to clarify this issue. If the former, this could explain the need to discover innovatory impulses for each cycle. On the other hand, if the system were inherently unstable the only justification for pushing innovation relentlessly to the forefront would be to maintain support for his obvious desire to find a uni-causal explanation of cycles. It does appear likely that he considered innovation to be an endogenous element, an unfortunate decision since it meant straining the facts. Had he chosen to regard innovation purely as a random external force acting upon an oscillatory system it would have been possible to produce a more plausible theory,[1] though inevitably it would have meant abandoning the central role accorded to innovation. Whatever his stance on this matter, however, it still remains that he strove hard to show that innovations provided the key to business cycle analysis.

Schumpeter took greater pains to define what he meant by innovation, though the end result was not a happy one. At one point he insists on a wide definition, so broad and vague as to be somewhat meaningless. The definition runs in terms of the setting-up of new production functions which cover not only new technology and new commodities, but also include among other things new forms of business organisation, the opening-up of new markets, and new sources of supply of materials.[2] In other words, it is a catch-all definition to cover every conceivable situation. But it is difficult to believe that all these changes are directly relevant to business cycle phasing. Changes in business organisation or the opening-up of new markets or raw materials supplies may well be relevant to long-term develop-

---

[1] Bober, *Economics of Cycles and Growth*, p. 161, appears to regard innovation in the Schumpeterian sense as being an external force necessary for the continued stimulation of the cycle and quotes Frisch's pendulum analogy. But this only relaxes slightly the necessity to find recurrent innovatory impulses.

[2] Schumpeter, *Business Cycles*, vol. 1, pp. 87–8.

ment, but it is unlikely that they would have much influence on the cycle unless they led to a sudden surge in investment opportunities – not an impossibility but in practice improbable. Later, however, he suggests that disturbances to equilibrium can only come from 'big' innovations that upset the system and enforce adaptation,[1] while throughout the study he is concerned very much with new technologies and sometimes with quite minor innovatory influences.

The theory that innovations tend to bunch together appears to have greater credibility. It is not uncommon for innovatory experience in leading growth sectors to be transmitted to other sectors of the economy, thus giving rise to a clustering effect. But innovational opportunities cannot be turned on and off like a tap and for this reason it is difficult to visualise them as being of great significance at the turning-points of cycles. Many major innovations, e.g. steam, iron and steel, electricity and the internal combustion engine, ranged over lengthy periods of time, their application was diffused and as a result they cut across standard business cycles. Hence, if anything, they would appear more relevant to cycles of longer duration than that of the Juglar. Furthermore, the supposition that innovatory impulses have a periodic sequence which fits the cyclical pattern is not very convincing. It may well be true that an element of regularity occurs through the repeated appearance and exhaustion of important innovations, but as Goodwin has pointed out, the time shape of innovation will have a specific historical context which is not repeated. 'A certain tendency to "bunching" is about all there is in common between the expenditures incident to the railroads, the Napoleonic Wars, the Civil War, steamships, the internal combustion engine, etc.'[2]

It would be easy to add to this list of criticisms but it is important to move on to the practicalities of measurement. Defining innovations was one thing, measuring them and their influence was quite another. Schumpeter did little to clarify this issue; in fact rather the reverse. The main body of the treatise contains very little statistical analysis designed to quantify the effects of innovations. In the absence of quantitative verification the main burden of proof lay in descriptive analysis by example. This made it relatively easy to generalise on the basis of selected innovations.[3] Thus Schumpeter could point to cotton innovations and canal construction as the key

[1] Ibid., pp. 94, 101.

[2] R. Goodwin, 'Innovations and the Irregularity of Economic Cycles', *Review of Economic Statistics*, XXVIII (1946) 100.

[3] On this point see S. Kuznets, 'Schumpeter's Business Cycles', *American Economic Review*, XXX (1940) 266–7.

to the first Juglar beginning in 1787, that railways were important in the Juglar prosperity that preceded the crash of 1837, and dominated the first Juglar in the second Kondratieff wave (1843–97); in the third Juglar which began in 1861 the iron steam-freighter appears to have been the distinctive innovation, while the fourth and fifth Juglars of the second Kondratieff were ascribed to steel.[1] Often, however, it was not very clear what were the important innovations, if any, and in some cases it was necessary to scrape the bottom of the barrel. The last Juglar of the second Kondratieff (1890s) was one 'of odds and ends that mainly summed up and completed'. According to Schumpeter the great developments of the following period in electricity and chemistry began to show; there was the shadow of a building boom; from 1894 onwards investment in breweries and distilleries; a boom in bicycles around the mid-1890s; new gold discoveries asserted themselves especially in exports to South America, and so on; all these contributed to the prosperity phase of the cycle.[2]

But what did it all mean? Despite the impressive effort put into the proof it reads more like a catalogue of the changes occurring as the process of development continued. Often industries or sectors were included because they were growing and not because they were subject to significant innovational activity. The vagueness of the description and the absence of quantification make it difficult to determine what importance to attach to innovational impulses at any particular time.[3] All Schumpeter was really concerned with was to find enough new developments of one sort or another which would give the weight of respectability to his thesis. Had he tried to measure their quantitative impact he might have been disappointed in the results.

Possibly we ought not to criticise Schumpeter unduly for failing to tackle this problem, for no satisfactory method has since been devised by which to measure the cyclical impact of innovations. Possible indicators such as patents, investment or productivity movements provide very imprecise guides. Some writers have urged that the number of patents sealed can be used as a rough index of innovation. Ashton, for instance, found that in the later eighteenth and early nineteenth centuries patents, though on an upward trend, responded in a cyclical fashion with peaks in 1766, 1769, 1783, 1801–2, 1813 and 1824–5, nearly all of which were years of low interest rates and

---

[1] Schumpeter, *Business Cycles*, pp. 297–8, 341, 369, 379–80.
[2] Ibid., pp. 381–2.
[3] In so far as Schumpeter had at the back of his mind a very wide definition of innovation it was possible to explain almost anything in terms of it.

active trade. From this he concluded that invention (and by implication innovation) was not a force operating more or less casually
outside the system, but was an integral part of the economic process.[1]
But the number of patents taken out scarcely provides a very satisfactory index of the rate of innovational activity. There is a world of
a difference between the patenting of an invention and its commercial application and the time-lag from the one to the other may be
very large indeed. Moreover, many patents are granted but never
exploited, while large and small inventions are weighted equally
irrespective of their commercial importance. For these reasons alone
it is very unlikely that such an indicator would tell us anything very
useful about the role of innovations in the business cycle. Nor is it
possible to derive much satisfaction from looking at the investment
data, since it is practically impossible to determine that part of
investment which arises from new innovational opportunities as
distinct from that which is purely a response to rising demand or the
needs of replacement.[2]

It is easy to be critical rather than constructive. While Schumpeter's theory has not been proved, neither is it completely dis-
proven. It certainly has many weaknesses as a general theory and it
is difficult to give it proper empirical clothing without straining at
the facts. Yet this does not mean that we can completely disregard
the force of innovation. Business cycles were influenced by innovations and one can easily point to the examples of the railways in the
1830s and 1840s,[3] steel in the later 1870s and 1880s and new industry
developments in the 1930s to substantiate the point. But this is far
from arguing that they are the prime cause of fluctuations. There
were many occasions in the past when innovational impulses were
very weak and the notion that the cyclical turning-points were
determined by the ebb and flow of innovations is hard to corrobo-
rate. While therefore we would not subscribe to an innovations
theory of the cycle, it is none the less true that cycles were influenced
to a lesser or greater degree by erratic spurts in the rate of innovation.

[1] T. S. Ashton, 'Some Statistics of the Industrial Revolution in Britain', *Manchester School*, XVI (1948) 216–18.

[2] See D. H. Aldcroft and H. W. Richardson, *The British Economy, 1870–1939*
(1969) pp. 36–8, for a brief discussion on the difficulties of measuring innovational
activity.

[3] The boom of the 1860s was also closely associated with the railway sector. There
was a tendency for railway construction to lag the cycle especially at the peaks, thus
acting as a stabilising factor for part of the time. G. R. Hawke, *Railways and Economic
Growth in England and Wales, 1840–1870* (1970) pp. 208–10, 364–8, 376.

Harvest Fluctuations

If we were dealing solely with cycles in a fairly mature economy it would be possible to ignore the influence of agricultural fluctuations. In Britain after the middle of the nineteenth century agriculture accounted for a relatively small and rapidly declining share of national income – 17·8 per cent in 1861, just over 10 per cent in 1881, and a mere 6·4 per cent by the turn of the century.[1] So long as the supply of imported food remained relatively elastic and there were no really serious harvest failures such as in 1879, variations in the magnitude of the domestic harvest were unlikely to have more than a very limited influence on fluctuations in the economy as a whole.[2] By contrast, for most of the eighteenth century and before agriculture bulked large in the total economy; it accounted for some 35–50 per cent of the national income and probably for a higher share of total employment. Under such conditions any analysis of fluctuations must inevitably devote considerable attention to the activities of this sector. Writing of the eighteenth century Ashton commented: 'Among the causes of instability of economic life in this century variations in the yield of the soil must be given first place.'[3] The period between the end of the eighteenth century and the middle of the nineteenth forms something of an intermediate stage when the agricultural component of the economy was in decline and no longer dominated the course of fluctuations, but yet was still large enough to have a considerable influence on the business cycle generally. It is this period with which we shall be mainly concerned in this section.

The role of agricultural fluctuations in the business cycle is perhaps the least satisfactorily treated aspect of the subject. This is not due to lack of agreement regarding the nature of agricultural fluctuations *per se* but rather to the failure to reach a consensus about the interactions between changes in agricultural production and business activity. Few writers have sought to establish an independent cycle in agricultural production itself. Timoshenko once argued the case for specific agricultural cycles but did not show why they occurred,[4] while a more explicit theory based on sunspot cycles has been associated with the names of W. S. Jevons and H. L. Moore.

[1] Figures from Phyllis Deane and W. A. Cole, *British Economic Growth 1688–1959* (1962) p. 166.

[2] This does not rule out the possibility that harvest variations in other countries may influence British fluctuations through the demand for exports.

[3] T. S. Ashton, *An Economic History of England: The Eighteenth Century* (1955) p. 62.

[4] V. P. Timoshenko, *The Role of Agricultural Fluctuations in the Business Cycle* (1930).

This postulated an association between metereological conditions (changes in which were activated by sunspots) and economic activity, the connecting link being provided by changes in agricultural output. But for the most part business cycle scholars have been content to regard agricultural fluctuations as non-cyclic in character and more in the nature of random shocks which occur at irregular intervals and upset the pattern of business fluctuations. This seems sensible enough given the fact that crop variations are caused largely by climatic factors.

On the second point however there has been much keener debate. Few would deny that harvest fluctuations affect the cycle but there is considerable difference of opinion both as to the extent of the influence and the mechanism by which it is effected. Both Pigou and Robertson stressed the importance of harvests as a causal factor in economic fluctuations, though the latter was more concerned with indirect influences stemming from crop fluctuations abroad.[1] Others, notably Keynes, J. M. Clark and Gordon, have taken the view that agriculture, though not without influence, was an entirely passive element,[2] while Hawtrey maintained a rather extreme position by declining to accept that agricultural fluctuations had any impact on trade except in cases of acute famine.[3]

The impact of agriculture will obviously vary according to the weight of that component in the total economy. Some divergence of opinion on the matter was probably inevitable since not all commentators were alluding to the same country or time-period when advancing their hypotheses. Robertson, for example, was thinking very much in terms of the indirect influences on Britain flowing from crop fluctuations abroad, while Gordon was referring to the United States mainly after the First World War. Much will also depend upon the assumptions and conditions on which any analysis is based, so that any conclusion about the role of agriculture may only have relevance in a specific historical context. Gould has warned against the hazards of trying to postulate a uniform significance of harvest fluctuations for the level of economic activity which will apply to any historical environment.[4]

Yet even within a specific historical context the position is not altogether clear-cut. With reference to the British case it has

[1] A. C. Pigou, *Industrial Fluctuations* (1927) pp. 37, 40, 41; D. H. Robertson, *A Study of Industrial Fluctuation* (1915) pp. xi, 110 ff., 137, 156, 170.

[2] G. Haberler, *Prosperity and Depression* (1958) pp. 153–4; and Gordon, *Business Fluctuations*, p. 386.

[3] See Robertson, *Study of Industrial Fluctuation*, p. 156.

[4] J. D. Gould, 'Agricultural Fluctuations and the English Economy in the Eighteenth Century', *Journal of Economic History*, XXII (1962) 319.

frequently been asserted that an increase in agricultural production had a stimulating influence and a decrease a depressing effect on economic activity, which put simply means that good harvests would be associated with boom periods and bad harvests with recessions. 'One emerges', says Rostow, 'simply, with the impression that an abundant harvest was a good thing for the non-agricultural community; a very mixed blessing for agriculture; and, in net, clearly a good thing for the country taken as a whole.'[1] The case has been argued forcibly by Ashton mainly for the eighteenth century.[2] A good harvest raised the return to human effort in agriculture, it increased the demand for labour to gather the harvest and it resulted in higher real wages through a decline in the price of agricultural products thereby boosting the demand for industrial products and services. Furthermore, an abundant harvest reduced or eliminated the need for imports of grain and might even produce a net export to the subsequent benefit of the balance of payments and the money market. Conversely, a bad harvest would lead to reduced investment in agriculture, high food prices and lower real wages and hence a cut-back in the demand for non-agricultural products. In addition, if the harvest was seriously deficient it would lead to increased imports (assuming that the external supply of farm products was elastic) which would put pressure on the balance of payments and money market resulting in higher interest rates and tighter credit and possibly a contraction in domestic activity.

It is possible, however, to argue the case, albeit somewhat less convincingly, for the reverse sequence – that abundant harvests were bad for the economy and vice versa. The low prices of plenty would lower the profits and incomes of the farming community and in so far as wages were flexible in terms of the price of farm products it would lead to a reduction in the money wages of both agricultural and industrial workers. The total effect might be an overall reduction in aggregate demand. Moreover, a drastic reduction in farm prices brought about by a succession of good harvests could lead to a deflationary set of consequences resulting in a cut-back in farm investment, a reduction in the demand for labour, the collapse of estate prices, mortgage foreclosures and bankruptcies. Such a train of events could scarcely fail to exert a considerable impact on the economy as a whole. In the same way bad harvests need not necessarily spell disaster either for the farming community or the economy as a whole. In fact bad harvests meant compensation in the form of higher prices for the farmer, so much so that it was he 'who prayed

---

[1] Rostow, *British Economy of the Nineteenth Century*, p. 51, and below, p. 90.
[2] Ashton, *An Economic History of England*, pp. 60–1.

for the high prices of a bad harvest or a bloody war'.[1] If high prices
were sufficient to more than offset the effect of reduced sales and the
increase in harvesting costs, profit margins would be raised, an outcome more likely to lead to an increase in farm investment than the
low prices of abundance.[2] Since bad harvests tend to require careful
attention the demand for labour would be increased, money wages
would rise and the agricultural worker might fare better than his
industrial counterpart.[3] If wages generally were flexible in terms of
price the net effect might be a rise in aggregate purchasing power,
though the redistribution of income towards the farming community
might lead to a decline in aggregate demand because of the lower
marginal propensity to consume of this sector.

There is a further point to bear in mind. The tendency to associate
good and bad years in agriculture with the state of the harvest is
somewhat misleading since farming fortunes do not depend upon
grain production alone. 'The changeability of the weather and the
great diversity of farming practice thus set limits to the real damage
done even to the physical production of English agriculture.'[4] A wet
summer and autumn could play havoc with the grain yields but at
the same time produce ideal conditions for root and fodder crops.
On the other hand, livestock farmers who depended on grain for
fodder were unlikely to welcome a deficient harvest. Clearly not all
branches of agriculture reacted in the same way to climatic conditions or to any other stimuli, so that one must be careful in equating
good and bad harvests with the measure of the harvest yield alone.

It is obviously not easy to make firm generalisations about harvests
and their impact on the economy. The position is complex since
there are many variables to be taken into account about which we
know very little. On balance, a more convincing case can be made
for the proposition that good harvests are favourable to the economy
and vice versa. And in particular, as the importance of the agricultural component of the economy diminishes, the greater the likelihood is that good harvests will favour economic activity and bad
harvests depress it. This is because good harvests will raise the real
incomes of the majority of consumers and hence boost aggregate
demand. Poor harvests will lower real wages and because of the
diminishing role of agriculture it is unlikely that any gains accruing

---

[1] E. L. Jones, *Seasons and Prices: The Role of the Weather in English Agricultural
History* (1964) p. 131.

[2] This assumes a closed economy or an inelastic external supply of farm products.

[3] In Britain the real incomes of industrial workers were partially stabilised by the
poor relief system. See M. Blaug, 'The Myth of the Old Poor Law and the Making
of the New', *Journal of Economic History*, XXIII (1963) 155.

[4] Jones, *Seasons and Prices*, p. 49.

to the farming community will be sufficient to offset losses elsewhere. Moreover, if deficient harvests are made up through high imports, then the unfavourable effects will be intensified through balance of payments and money market pressures.

Empirical study for the period with which we are concerned lends some support to the sequence outlined above. Agriculture's share of national income declined from just over one-third at the end of the eighteenth century to about 20 per cent by 1851, and by the latter date wheat imports constituted 25 per cent of the nation's supplies. In these circumstances there would be an increasing tendency for harvest variations to exert their influence through the external account rather than directly on domestic incomes. Thus the high wheat prices and heavy imports of 1795–6, 1800–1, 1810, 1817–18, 1824–5, 1836–7 and 1846–7 put pressure on the balance of payments and money market and exerted a general deflationary effect, while the low prices arising from the good harvests of 1791, 1797–8, 1820–3 1832–5 and 1843–4 no doubt helped to foster the major cyclical expansions.[1] At first sight this might suggest support for a theory of the cycle based on the periodicity of harvests, that is good harvests setting in motion the expansions which were cut short by pressures on the money market as a result of later harvest failures. But the evidence is far more equivocal than it appears. First, it is not always possible to determine years of good and bad harvests very precisely since there is a considerable difference of opinion among authorities on this score. For example, Jones suggests that the year 1801 gave an excellent harvest and wheat prices fell sharply in the autumn, that 1844 produced a very large grain harvest but a near total failure of fodder crops resulting in a bad year for cattle farmers, while the 1846 wheat crop was good.[2] The reader will notice that these interpretations conflict somewhat with those of Gayer, Rostow and Schwartz given above. Secondly, it is also evident that some of the cyclical downturns occurred before rising imports had brought pressure to bear on the economy. This was certainly the case in 1836–7, 1846–7, and to a lesser extent in 1800–1.[3] In any case grain imports were not the only source of pressure on the external account near the top of the boom. Finally, as Matthews has noted,[4] factors other than the weather were responsible for influencing the behaviour of corn im-

---

[1] Gayer, Rostow and Schwartz, *Growth and Fluctuation of the British Economy*, vol. 2, p. 563.

[2] See the annual summary in Jones, *Seasons and Prices*, pp. 137 ff.

[3] On the 1847 experience see C. N. Ward-Perkins, 'The Commercial Crisis of 1847', *Oxford Economic Papers*, II (1950) 83.

[4] R. C. O. Matthews, *A Study in Trade Cycle History: Economic Fluctuations in Great Britain, 1833–1842* (1954) p. 41.

ports and prices. Large stockpiles could keep corn prices down while the Corn Laws, by checking imports until prices reached a prescribed level, could exert a considerable impact on the pattern of imports. These two factors undoubtedly helped to keep imports at a low level for several years after 1832, and in turn led to the high imports of 1837–8, while much of the increase in imports in 1842 resulted from a lagged response to earlier high prices rather than to a deficiency in the domestic supply.

While the evidence on harvest variations is not sufficiently firm or consistent to support an agricultural theory of the cycle for this period, it is none the less apparent that the degree of conformity between harvest fluctuations and cycles was close enough to be of some significance. Years of good and bad harvests did bunch together and they tended to be associated with certain phases of the cycle. Good harvests usually occurred during the main upswings while bad harvests tended to predominate around the peaks or just after. Either way they contributed to the particular phase of the cycle, though it is unlikely that they can be regarded as a major causal factor, given the fact that exports provided a much more positive determinant. In any case, as time progressed their influence waned. By the middle of the nineteenth century the impact of harvest variations was much weaker than it had been earlier and in the 1850s the earlier pattern of association was clearly breaking down.[1] With the dwindling role of agriculture in the economy, improved communications, the free availability of imports after the abolition of the Corn Laws in 1846, and better techniques in agriculture, harvest fluctuations become of negligible importance to the study of the business cycle in the latter half of the nineteenth century.[2]

Monetary Factors

Some years ago it might have been possible to deal relatively briefly with monetary aspects of the cycle. The Keynesian revolution in economic thinking and its aftermath led to a somewhat contemptuous dismissal of earlier theories, such as those of Hawtrey, which

[1] For example, the good harvest of 1854 was followed by low imports but high prices, the moderate and good harvests of 1855–8 by falling prices but large imports, though the bullion drain of 1857 cannot be attributed to the effects of a deficient harvest and high imports. J. R. T. Hughes, *Fluctuations in Trade, Industry and Finance: A Study in British Economic Development, 1850–1860* (1960) pp. 63–4.

[2] Beveridge found no significant correlation between industrial activity and wheat prices between 1856 and 1913. W. H. Beveridge, 'The Trade Cycle in Britain before 1850', *Oxford Economic Papers*, III (1940) 99.

sought to emphasise the role of monetary forces in the cyclical process. Modern theories of the cycle now concentrated on real forces and monetary influences were at the most permissive in nature. To all intents and purposes the quantity theory of money was dethroned; in so far as the demand for goods and services was connected with the quantity theory it was only indirectly, inasmuch as variations in the supply of money, by inversely affecting interest rates, caused aggregate demand, more especially for investment goods, to change. Whether expenditure decisions were sensitive to changes in interest rates was a matter on which Keynes himself was not fully committed, but empirical studies made shortly after the appearance of the *General Theory* suggested that business investment did not respond readily to shifts in interest rates.[1] The upshot of this revision in economic thinking meant that monetary policy came to be regarded as a very weak regulator of economic activity and attention was shifted to fiscal instruments.

Almost inevitably however the wheel had to turn a full circle. Work across the Atlantic by Professor Milton Friedman and his disciples has brought a 'monetary' counter-revolution, to use Kaldor's phrase,[2] and although his followers may still not be in the majority his persuasive message is forcing many economists to undertake a rethink of the way in which money matters influence growth and cyclical change. Apart from the new money supply school, who stress the direct relationship between the money supply and expenditure, the credit school of thought has also gained some ground in recent years. They believe that the main impact of a change in the money supply falls on interest rates which determine the cost and availability of credit, and in turn the changes in financial conditions influence expenditure and hence economic activity. These developments in monetary thought seem to justify a more extensive discussion of the role of monetary factors than might once have been the case.

The new money supply approach has been outlined on numerous occasions, mainly of course by the chief protagonists, and only a brief summary need be given here.[3] Basically the revamped quantity theory posits a direct link between money and income. Variations in

---

[1] See in particular the series of articles by Andrews, Henderson and Meade in *Oxford Economic Papers*, I (1938) and III (1940).

[2] N. Kaldor, 'The New Monetarism', *Lloyds Bank Review*, no. 97 (July 1970) p. 1.

[3] See H. G. Johnson, 'Monetary Theory and Policy', *American Economic Review*, LII (1962); and M. Friedman, 'The Role of Monetary Policy', *American Economic Review*, LVIII (1968) and the references below. There is an excellent summary of the new developments in this field in A. D. Bain, *The Control of the Money Supply* (1970) esp. chaps. 3 and 4.

the money stock are thought to determine income and expenditure flows directly and not via interest rates and investment as in Keynesian models. Thus for the United States Friedman and Schwartz found that there was a close relationship between cyclical movements in the money stock and incomes and business activity. The rate of change in the money stock regularly reached a peak before the reference cycle peak and troughed before the lower turning-point, with a lead of money stock over income changes which ranged between three months and eight quarters. Though the authors recognised that the two variables were mutually interacting, money was regarded as an autonomous and determining factor. They therefore concluded that the stock of money was a much better predictor of economic activity than were investment or autonomous expenditures.[1] On the basis of these findings it would be possible to formulate a monetary theory of the cycle; a partly self-generating cyclical mechanism, for example, could be rejuvenated or kept alive by successive changes in the money stock.

These results are, of course, derived from U.S. data. Much less work has been done in this country, partly because of the statistical limitations. Long-period analysis is being undertaken by the National Bureau for the years 1880–1965 and the preliminary results suggest a fairly high correlation between movements in money and those in income.[2] Walters has conducted an investigation into the effect of changes in the money stock on incomes but the results are not particularly conclusive. In fact for the inter-war years and the post-war period the monetary equation did not provide statistically significant results at all, and for the first period a Keynesian formula produced a far better fit. On the other hand, for the period before 1914 (1880–1914) the monetary model performed somewhat better. Although only 29 per cent of the variation in income could be explained by money, the coefficients of the equations proved to be similar to those of a quantity theory model involving a lagged reaction. In other words, a 1 per cent increase in the money stock gave rise to approximately a 0·9 per cent increase in income, about half of which occurred in the current year and the rest in the year following.[3]

[1] M. Friedman and Anna J. Schwartz, *A Monetary History of the United States, 1867–1960* (1963) pp. 678, 695, and 'Money and Business Cycles', *Review of Economics and Statistics*, XLV (1963) 63–4.

[2] Anna J. Schwartz, 'Why Money Matters', *Lloyds Bank Review*, no. 94 (Oct 1969) p. 14.

[3] A. A. Walters, 'Monetary Multipliers in the U.K., 1880–1962', *Oxford Economic Papers*, XVIII (1966), and *Money in Boom and Slump* (1969, Hobart Paper 44); also C. R. Barrett and A. A. Walters, 'The Relative Stability of Keynesian and Monetary Multipliers in the United Kingdom', *Review of Economics and Statistics*, XLVIII (1966).

The results so far, at least those for the U.K., are not such as to urge the necessity for exploring the possibilities of a monetary theory of the cycle, though they do suggest that monetary influences may have been more important than previously supposed. But even the more statistically significant U.S. findings do not provide a convincing demonstration of the superiority of monetary models. Several criticisms can be made about the methods of analysis and the conclusions drawn therefrom which weaken the validity of the new approach. The new approach has given rise to fierce controversy which is very far from being settled.

In the first place there has been considerable debate and disagreement over the definition of the money supply. The Chicago School (the main centre of the money supply approach) uses a narrow definition, covering currency in circulation and bank deposits, which is determined by the high-powered monetary base, that is currency in circulation and bank reserve assets. But it is by no means certain that this is always the case; a broad definition which, in addition to the above two items, includes deposits at savings banks and the Post Office, deposits held at accepting houses, overseas banks and discount houses, and the deposits and shares of building societies, may produce somewhat different results.[1]

A more difficult problem is the question concerning the autonomy of the money supply. A line of causation running from money to income rests on the assumption that the money supply is exogenously determined. It does not matter how it is determined – it could be done, as Walters says, by 'tossing a coin'[2] – so long as it has an independent origin. The model then takes the money supply as given and provided that the multiplier effect is lagged it can predict what income will be in a later period. Since the determination of the money supply is crucial to the new theory, it is important to decide whether the assumptions on which it is based are valid. If, as the proponents claim, it is exogenously determined then it is straining the bounds of credibility to be asked to believe that the stock of money could have consistently peaked and troughed before the cyclical turning-points for so long a period as appears to be the case in the United States. In the unlikely event of any divine act of providence we conclude that the monetary authorities were responsible for manipulating the money supply. Now granted that they, in their infinite wisdom, might have been capable of producing such a result in the post-war

---

[1] Judith A. Waters, 'Money Supply and Credit: Theory and Practice', *National Westminster Bank Quarterly Review* (Nov 1969) pp. 21–2; A. D. Cramp, 'Does Money Matter?', *Lloyds Bank Review*, no. 98 (Oct 1970) p. 33.

[2] Walters, *Money in Boom and Slump*, p. 39.

years, it seems highly improbable that the techniques of monetary control were geared to producing such a systematic behaviour of the money supply before 1939, though it might be possible to get round this by invoking appeal to the variable lag structure. But it is difficult to believe that money has always been an autonomous variable; there have certainly been times, e.g. in Britain during the 1930s, when changes in the money supply have been induced by prior changes in economic activity.[1] Even Cagan, an adherent of the new money school, admits that 'It seems highly probable that cyclical fluctuations in business activity account for most of the cyclical variations in growth of the money stock although many variations in particular years can be traced to special developments largely unrelated to concurrent business conditions'.[2] This seems a more reasonable line of thought though it does not fully resolve the problem of the systematic movement of money at the turning-points. But if correct, then the case for the money to income sequence is very much weakened, though not destroyed because of the mutual interaction effect between the variables.

The supporters of the money approach perhaps too readily conclude that the high correlation between money and income together with the time-lag point to a clear one-way causal relationship. The relevance of the time-lag is open to debate. Kaldor has pointed out that with a Keynesian model of income determination it would be possible for money peaks and troughs to precede those of the reference cycles.[3] Moreover, in some cases the time-lag is so short that it is doubtful whether the desired transmission effects to income would have time to operate.

Finally, it should be noted that the theory of income determination is one based almost exclusively on monetary forces. Monetary changes generate income changes and cycles and there is little scope for the operation of real forces. In other words, both impulse and propagation mechanisms have a monetary origin, whereas it is more likely that money acts in a propagating capacity. In any case, to prove the dominant influence of money it would be necessary to show conclusively that other variables, particularly autonomous expenditures, had not an equal generating power.

These are only a few of the criticisms that can be made about the new money supply theory but they are sufficient to cast doubt on the

[1] Cramp, 'Does Money Matter?', p. 31.

[2] P. Cagan, *Determinants and Effects of Changes in the Stock of Money, 1875–1960* (1965) p. 272; though Cagan himself is not altogether consistent on this matter.

[3] Kaldor, 'The New Monetarism', p. 10. This is a severely critical article and needs to be read cautiously. See the debate between Kaldor and Friedman in the October 1970 issue of *Lloyds Bank Review*.

validity of the conclusions. Money has some importance but its superior predictive power has not yet been demonstrated. Because of the large number of variables in the system and the complex inter-acting mechanisms it seems highly improbable that a convincing model of the business cycle could be constructed in which the main causal and propagation roles were assigned to the one variable – money. For Britain at any rate there is insufficient data and analysis even to contemplate the prospect.

We are not forced from the above discussion to conclude that monetary factors are unimportant. The notion that developed in the 1930s that monetary forces had an indirect and very weak effect on incomes reflected the extreme end of the spectrum, and no doubt sprang out of the peculiar conditions of those years. Today we should probably acknowledge that the credit approach has greater relevance; that changes in interest rates and the availability of credit brought about by changes in the money supply do have some influ-ence on economic activity. The impact of these forces depends very much upon how sensitive borrowers and lenders are to changes in the cost and availability of credit, and the psychological effect such changes produce. But assuming for the moment that there is some sensitivity, monetary forces of this type can influence the cycle in a number of ways. For example, external considerations might force on the monetary authorities a policy which was actively destabilising, especially in recessions when drains on reserves might necessitate high interest rates and a tightening of the credit situation. Alter-natively, monetary instruments may move in a counter-cyclical manner thus acting as a stabilising force; rising interest rates and tighter credit conditions may serve to moderate a boom or even check expansion altogether, while cheap money and easy credit may help to facilitate recovery from depression. In practice monetary policy is more likely to be effective in checking or at least moderating a boom than in inducing recovery from a recession. If severe enough, monetary controls can be successful in damping an overheated economy; but to be effective such measures need to be implemented quickly and vigorously, and probably backed up by other policies, and the danger is that this will create an emergency and precipitate a slump. At the trough it is more difficult to activate changes through monetary controls. There is a floor below which interest rates cannot fall and it may be difficult to induce businessmen to invest if profit expectations remain depressed. Moreover, if banks refuse to use their resources to grant loans and advances cheap money may have little effect in prompting revival. In general, an easy money policy will no doubt facilitate a recovery once it has got under way but by itself it will be insufficient to halt a downswing or initiate recovery from the trough.[1] Even Hawtrey, who was a firm believer in the ability of the monetary authorities to stabilise business activity, conceded that if action was not taken promptly a credit deadlock could develop which would not yield to a low Bank Rate.[2]

However, to appreciate the importance of monetary controls it is necessary to understand the historical context in which they operated and the way in which they operated. There was a considerable difference in the structure and behaviour of monetary institutions of the late eighteenth and early nineteenth centuries and those of the later nineteenth century.

Until around the middle of the nineteenth century the banking and monetary structure of the U.K. was very fragmented. There was a large number of country banks, a number of private London bankers, joint-stock banks later on in the period, a loosely controlled money market and the Bank of England which exercised limited direction over the whole system. Though the supply of money and credit tended to vary with the state of trade there was no one agency which decreed credit restriction or relaxation. The Bank of England exercised only a weak control over the market; it had limited influence over interest rates and more often than not it tended to follow the market rate rather than lead it. The outcome of this system was a fairly elastic supply of credit, at least in boom periods, but one which, in the absence of unified direction, often resulted in the constituent parts pulling in opposite directions.

The second half of the nineteenth century saw the development of a much more closely unified and integrated system. The decline of the country banks, the rise of large joint-stock banks with numerous branches, legislation, the product of which was to improve the structure of banking and establish the central position of the Bank of England, together with an improvement in the Bank's techniques of operation, paved the way for a more efficient and orderly system. Although it was to be some time before the Bank of England was

[1] According to Bain, *Control of the Money Supply*, p. 124, 'Monetary policy as a medicine taken in good time and in moderation has a part to play in regulating the trade cycle; but if taken to excess and at the wrong time may wreak effects which are worse than the disease!'

[2] L. W. Mintz, *A History of Banking Theory in Great Britain and the United States* (1945) p. 278. Hawtrey of course only believed that monetary control could be exercised via the short-term rate of interest which affected the willingness of traders to hold stocks and hence set up an acceleration response. Long-term rates, he believed, were very insensitive to the cycle and had little influence on the level of economic activity. R. G. Hawtrey, *A Century of Bank Rate* (1938); and J. R. Hicks, 'Mr Hawtrey on Bank Rate and the Long-Term Rate of Interest', *Manchester School*, x (1939).

fully recognised as a central bank with power of direction over the market – for twenty years after 1858 Bank Rate was following rather than leading the market[1] – by the 1880s it had more or less established its supremacy and market rates now tended to reflect changes in Bank Rate rather than vice versa. Thus although the supply of credit was possibly less elastic than it had been earlier, the monetary system as a whole responded very much more quickly to actions of the Bank of England. By contrast, there was little marked change in the set-up during the inter-war years apart from the closer contact developed between the Bank of England and the Government over monetary policy.

There was one unifying theme throughout the period, however. The Bank of England's policy was dominated largely by the state of its reserves. The Bank's primary objective was to safeguard its gold reserves and the main weapon of control was the Bank Rate. When its reserves fell, either through an internal or external drain, the rate was raised to attract funds back. Conversely, with an influx of gold and exchange the rate would be lowered. Fortunately, except for short periods, there was no great conflict between external and domestic needs during the nineteenth century. The reserves tended to move inversely with the cycle so that Bank Rate moved counter-cyclically and was therefore potentially stabilising. It was only after the war that domestic and external needs came into conflict, a situation which eventually contributed to the collapse of the gold standard.[2]

Thus up until the 1930s monetary policy was the single established instrument of economic policy. The chief weapon of control was Bank Rate, though open market operations were being employed increasingly from the later nineteenth century. Stability of domestic economic activity was not regarded as an objective; monetary policy was used primarily to protect the reserve and secure external equilibrium. But by the later nineteenth century Bank Rate was regarded as synonymous with monetary policy and it was generally felt that movements in the rate reflected the current state of credit and the money supply.[3]

[1] R. S. Sayers, *Central Banking after Bagehot* (1957) p. 12.

[2] There are numerous writings on the monetary system as i t had developed by the later nineteenth century; see in particular A. G. Ford, *The Gold Standard, 1880–1914: Britain and Argentina* (1962); A. I. Bloomfield, *Monetary Policy under the International Gold Standard, 1880–1914* (1959); W. M. Scammell, 'The Working of the Gold Standard', *Yorkshire Bulletin of Economic and Social Research*, XVII (1965); on the post-war period see D. Williams, 'Montagu Norman and Banking Policy in the 1920s', ibid., XI (1959), and D. H. Aldcroft, 'The Impact of British Monetary Policy, 1919–1939', *Revue Internationale d'Histoire de la Banque*, III (1970).

[3] Thus troughs in interest rates would tend to coincide with peaks in monetary growth and credit availability and vice versa. See P. Cagan, 'The Influence of

The way in which interest rates and Bank Rate in particular affected domestic activity is another matter, and one that is difficult to determine exactly since evidence on the subject is very scanty. The general impression one gets is that economic activity was not particularly responsive to variations in rates of interest. It is unlikely that long-term domestic investment was very responsive to small changes in the cost of accommodation, especially as much industrial finance by-passed the market,[1] though penal rates might deter confidence. In any case, changes in rates were often so frequent – in one year alone (1873) there were no less than twenty-four changes in Bank Rate – that it is difficult to believe that businessmen could react sensibly to such fluctuations. Many empirical studies suggest that the influence of interest rates on investment activity is at best modest and in fact more likely to be very weak,[2] though more recently it has been observed that this may not be the case.[3] But interest-rate changes may have been important in the short term, by affecting the willingness of traders to hold stocks or the readiness of businessmen to raise loans for minor extensions or renewals. In the former case the main influence was probably transmitted via the trade balance. A rise in rates would encourage merchants to reduce stocks; this would affect imports adversely and eventually it would lead to a check in exports and domestic production. But even in this context we must be careful about being too dogmatic. The rates on overdrafts and loans from the banks were fairly sticky in a downward direction; the usual charge in the later nineteenth century was 1 per cent above Bank Rate with a minimum floor of 5 per cent, so that it was only when Bank Rate was above this level that traders became sensitive to the cost of credit.[4] Much therefore depended upon the availability of accommodation rather than its price. Nevertheless, rates of interest might act as an important psychological barometer as regards the state of trade. As Sayers has noted, 'There is some reason to believe that both lenders and borrowers looked to Bank Rate as an important "Index" of economic prospects, and both

Interest Rates and the Duration of Business Cycles', in J. M. Guttenberg and P. Cagan (eds), *Essays on Interest Rates* (1969) vol. 1, p. 18; and 'Changes in the Cyclical Behaviour of Interest Rates', *Review of Economics and Statistics*, XLVIII (1966).

[1] On the theoretical assumption that interest-rate changes will be more influential the greater the reliance on outside sources of finance.

[2] The findings are summarised in Ford, *The Gold Standard*, pp. 43–7.

[3] M. K. Evans, *Macroeconomic Activity*, p. 138; Bain, *Control of the Money Supply*, pp. 105–22. The evidence is conflicting and it seems likely that the interest-elasticity of investment demand has more relevance for the long term than short-term cyclical changes.

[4] Sayers, *Central Banking*, p. 17.

sides would probably become more wary when Bank Rate rose, more adventurous when Bank Rate fell'.[1]

The available evidence suggests that monetary forces varied in their impact from cycle to cycle and that for this reason it is difficult to make sweeping generalisations. It is true that studies have shown that interest rates and Bank Rate have behaved in a systematic way, that is rising and falling with economic activity. Thus for the first part of the nineteenth century Beveridge found a fairly close agreement between interest rates and industrial activity with a lag of up to one year in Bank Rate.[2] For more recent years, from the 1870s to the 1930s, Morgenstern noted a similar correspondence between short-term rates, Bank Rate and reference cycles, with Bank of England discount rate lagging at the troughs and leading at the peaks.[3]

Such findings are not, however, very illuminating. Although Bank Rate tended to move in a counter-cyclical manner it would be mischievous to conclude that monetary control was always a stabilising influence. In fact several points can be put forward to show the fallacy of this type of deduction. For one thing, interest rates are not necessarily an accurate indicator of the elasticity of supply of credit, while even when they move in a contra-cyclical fashion they may still exert a destabilising influence in specific instances. For example, a sharp rise in Bank Rate and credit restriction near the peak of the boom may well precipitate a loss of confidence and aggravate the downturn. It has in fact been argued that monetary policy may be destabilising because of the lagged effect of its impact,[4] in which case a contra-cyclical Bank Rate may not be the most desirable situation. Secondly, the Bank itself often helped to aggravate expansionary tendencies and it was not until the reserves were threatened, by which time the position had got out of hand, that it took firm action. And since the reserve position took time to rectify, the discount rate usually remained at a fairly high level in the early stages of the downturn. Thirdly, a rise in Bank Rate could do nothing to initiate a credit restriction if banks were already fully loaned up, though the absence of traders' complaints in this respect suggests that the supply of credit was normally fairly elastic.[5] Finally, in the early part of the

[1] Ibid., p. 64.
[2] W. H. Beveridge, 'The Trade Cycle in Britain Before 1850', *Oxford Economic Papers*, III (1940) 89–90.
[3] O. Morgenstern, *International Financial Transactions and Business Cycles*, pp. 96, 396, 397.
[4] T. Mayer, 'The Inflexibility of Monetary Policy', *Review of Economics and Statistics*, XL (1958) 374.
[5] Sayers, *Central Banking*, p. 64.

period when the structure of monetary institutions was disorganised and the Bank of England had little control over the credit market, its policy did little to stabilise the level of economic activity, except in so far as it came to the assistance of business and other bankers at times of credit strain generated by falling markets. In this sense, as a lender of last resort, it could act as a cushion to the market when a crisis of confidence arose.[1]

These reservations make any broad generalisations about the role of monetary forces very difficult, and in consequence it is necessary to look more closely at the actual historical record. It is evident that monetary influences varied from cycle to cycle and between different phases of cycles, though probably their influence was felt most around the peaks of the boom when monetary forces could affect the cycle either way, and during the upswings. Thus the expansions of the 1840s and 1850s were certainly helped along by monetary developments. The speculative activity and rail boom of the 1840s were spurred on by easy credit conditions and the cheap money policy of the Bank of England, and the latter was later criticised for its aggressive policies which fanned the flames of speculation.[2] Even more so, the monetary system, backed by a large influx of gold, financed the expansion of the mid-1850s, and the Bank found itself powerless to control the credit boom which eventually culminated in the crisis of 1857.[3] Cheap money and easy credit also played a part in other upswings; in 1862–5 cheap money and the new limited

[1] N. J. Silberling, 'British Prices and Business Cycles, 1779–1850', *Review of Economic Statistics*, v (1923) 241. Hughes, in an interesting study of monetary forces before 1914, raises another point which is perhaps of more relevance to long-term development. He argues, on the basis of Wicksellian theory, that the influence of interest rates depends on the relationship between market rates and the natural rate of interest (the natural rate being the equilibrium rate for price stability). Thus high market rates could be low if the natural rate was high enough and vice versa. He suggests that the relationships were such as to foster development between the mid-1840s and early 1870s whereas afterwards (until the end of the century) the natural rate fell faster than market rates thus exerting a compression effect. The argument is not altogether convincing since it depends on the rather abstract concept of the natural rate and also because the links between rates of interest, prices and investment are not made very explicit. J. R. T. Hughes, 'Wicksell on the Facts: Prices and Interest Rates, 1844 to 1914', in J. N. Wolfe (ed.), *Value, Capital and Growth: Papers in Honour of Sir John Hicks* (1968).

[2] C. N. Ward-Perkins, 'The Commercial Crisis of 1847', pp. 81, 84; E. V. Morgan, 'Railway Investment, Bank of England Policy and Interest Rates, 1844 –8', *Economic History* (supplement to *Economic Journal*), IV (1940); Hughes, loc. cit., p. 230.

[3] Hughes in fact suggests that the great expansion of this period need not have occurred had the monetary system acted in the way the theory of the Bank Charter Act of 1844 postulated. J. R. T. Hughes, 'Fluctuations in Trade, Industry and Finance', pp. 280–2.

liability provisions led to a crop of company promotions, the recovery of 1887–9 was facilitated by cheap money as were the initial
stages of the industrial booms which culminated in 1873–4, 1907 and
1913.[1] After the war monetary policy tended to exert a mildly
restrictive effect on the protracted upswing of the 1920s, but during
the recovery of the next decade it had a more powerful influence,
though it was not the critical factor prompting the initial upturn
from the slump.[2]

Around the peaks of the cycles monetary forces played a rather
ambiguous role. Generally interest rates moved upward in the later
stages of the boom, credit conditions became tighter, the Bank's
policy became more restrictive in the wake of its depleting reserves
and the net effect was stabilising. Unfortunately, the last twist of the
screw often came either at the very point when the boom was about
to break, thus tending to clinch the turning-point, or very shortly
after the real peak in economic activity, thereby aggravating the
subsequent downturn.[3] Financial crises, especially in the first half of
the nineteenth century, had a habit of occurring just after the cyclical
peaks, which forced monetary institutions to tighten credit conditions
at an awkward time. Moreover, because of the fear that premature relaxation might endanger the financial situation, it was often
some time before easier credit conditions were realised. A good case
in point is the boom of the 1840s; not until near the reference cycle
peak did the monetary authorities really begin to restrict facilities,
and the financial crisis came after the peak in the autumn of 1847
when Bank Rate was pushed up to 8 per cent (October 1847). Subsequently monetary conditions were only eased slowly and it was not
until the end of January 1848 that Bank Rate got down to 4 per cent,
by which time the economy was very much recessed. A similar
situation occurred in the next decade. The Bank, as noted earlier,
was unable to control commercial credit in the boom, and the
financial panic came after the reference peak in the autumn of 1857,
when Bank Rate was raised to 10 per cent and cash payments were

[1] E. V. Morgan, *The Theory and Practice of Central Banking, 1797–1913* (1965 ed.)
pp. 178, 203; Robertson, *Study of Industrial Fluctuation*, p. 214.

[2] Aldcroft, 'The Impact of British Monetary Policy, 1919–1939', pp. 53, 64;
H. W. Richardson, *Economic Recovery in Britain, 1932–9* (1967) chap. 8.

[3] Thus for the decades before 1914 Sayers suggests that 'the rise in interest rates
often waited until the boom was already cracking, and merely ensured that the
depression should be severe'. R. S. Sayers, 'Monetary Thought and Monetary
Policy in England', in R. L. Smyth (ed.), *Essays in Modern Economic Development* (1969) p. 192. This essay was previously published in the *Economic Journal* for
1960.

suspended once more. Again it was some time before the crisis was checked and monetary conditions were relaxed.[1]

Financial crises were much less common in the second half of the nineteenth century. The last major one was in 1866 but it coincided closely with the peak in the cycle and the harsh monetary policy that it entailed was soon relaxed. But the cheap money policy which followed did little to moderate the downswing and it was not until 1869 that the trough was reached. In the boom of 1873–4 monetary forces had little influence, probably not surprising in view of the frequency with which Bank Rate was changed. It is noticeable however that once the immediate threat to the reserve was past, the Bank lowered its rate, an indication that it was anxious not to press too hard on sagging activity at home.[2] But greater sensitivity to domestic needs was not to deflect the Bank from its prime objective of protecting the reserve. In general, Bank Rate tended to move with the cycle though the timing of the changes was not always the most propitious from a domestic point of view, and on occasions there was open conflict. Moderate or even low rates were not conducive to damping the strong boom of 1900–1, while in April 1907 the Bank lowered its rate to 4 per cent just prior to the peak in activity. Not until November did it reach the ceiling of 7 per cent and dear money certainly hastened the downward trend in activity which had then set in, and it was only in the spring of 1908 that cheap money again prevailed.[3] An almost parallel situation occurred in the boom of 1919–20. Monetary restraint was imposed at the peak of the cycle, and though it is doubtful whether it activated the turning-point it certainly intensified the downswing since relaxation was very belated. In 1929–30 money conditions were actually eased soon after the upper turning-point, but in the situation obtaining at that time they were powerless to halt the downward spiral.

During the early years of the nineteenth century, when the monetary structure was more chaotic, less responsible, and growing rapidly, monetary forces probably played a more significant part in cyclical fluctuations. Even so, the major money market crises were generally a product of the booms rather than the cause of them and it would be difficult to argue the case for a monetary theory of the cycle.[4] Nevertheless, monetary forces were a significant influence

---

[1] J. R. T. Hughes, 'The Commercial Crisis of 1857', *Oxford Economic Papers*, VIII (1956) 215–17. He notes however that the 1857 crisis was not caused solely by excessive speculation and the abuse of credit.

[2] Morgan, *Theory and Practice of Central Banking*, p. 184.

[3] Ibid., pp. 222–3.

[4] Gayer, Rostow and Schwartz, *Growth and Fluctuation of the British Economy*, pp. 561–2.

during upswings and at the upper turning-points and they frequently operated in a destabilising manner. The indiscretionary activities of the country banks and their inherent weaknesses certainly contributed a great deal to aggravating the booms and subsequent crises in the quarter-century or more down to 1825, and on occasions the Bank of England added fuel to the flames by its liberal discounting policies. During the upswings credit inflation was aggravated by the operations of a vast number of largely unregulated provincial banking institutions, and then brought to an abrupt halt around the upper turning-points. '. . . it was the vast, almost wholly unregulated, flood of inconvertible country-bank credit which mainly caused the inflation, or at any rate greatly facilitated the successive "booms" of the war years; while the severe price reactions both produced, and were in turn intensified by, heavy country-bank failures.'[1] Nor were the early joint-stock banks much better in this respect. Matthews has observed how the joint-stock banks, by relaxing their security requirements and pressing loans on customers, actually intensified the boom of the mid-1830s by expanding the supply of credit. Then when recession occurred they were forced to contract their operations.[2]

In sum, therefore, monetary forces varied in their influence from cycle to cycle, sometimes acting in a stabilising manner, sometimes the reverse, but rarely did they initiate the turning-points. In general, they operated in a passive manner, by aggravating or intensifying cyclical tendencies already present. Monetary restriction was probably more effective in damping boom tendencies than easy money conditions were in releasing the economy from recession. We have not exhausted all the possible repercussions of monetary control in the above discussion, however,[3] and in view of the recent developments in monetary theory and history it is doubtful whether this will be the last word on the subject.

Random Shocks

A number of writers have drawn attention to the influence of random shocks in economic fluctuations. Frisch, for example, felt that they served the purpose of rejuvenating damped cycles, while Burns has recently re-emphasised their importance in terms of cyclical indi-

---

[1] Silberling, 'British Prices and Business Cycles', p. 243.

[2] Matthews, *Study in Trade Cycle History*, pp. 198–9.

[3] Little has been said, for instance, on the way monetary forces affected the external account. A rise in Bank Rate would check overseas lending and depress income growth abroad and in turn this would react on the demand for British exports. For these reactions the reader should consult the writings of A. G. Ford.

viduality. 'The ragged contours of most business cycles testify to the role of random disturbances and so too does the strong individuality of successive business cycles.'[1] However, many business cycle students have found some difficulty in coping with the problem of shocks and for this reason they are often accorded rather cursory treatment. The existence of random disturbances does pose something of a problem for model builders since they enhance the difficulty of constructing a model or theory of the cycle which has universal applicability. Self-generating models of the cycle may be badly upset by random disturbances of high magnitude and their predictive power thereby reduced. On the other hand, purely shocked theories of the cycle have not had widespread appeal for obvious reasons, though the recent tests on the Klein–Goldberger model of the U.S. seem likely to offer more promising prospects in this direction in the future. A further difficulty has centred around the definition of random shocks. A broad definition might conceivably include such things as innovations, monetary factors and even exports. But this approach would seem unrealistic for two reasons. These factors are neither wholly random in their occurrence nor are they entirely exogenous in origin. Indeed, in some cases, notably monetary factors, it could well be argued that they have a periodic sequence and are partly determined within the system itself. Therefore, a more plausible definition of random shocks would include only such items as are determined exogenously and occur at irregular intervals. On this basis the classification would cover wars, political disturbances, climatic upsets,[2] strikes, disturbances caused by events abroad, e.g. financial crises or tariff changes, and possibly the discovery of new resources or unexploited territories. Such factors exhibit no cyclical or periodic tendencies and for the most part they are determined quite autonomously outside the system.

It is not necessary to subscribe to a shocked version of the cycle to recognise that random disturbances can influence the pattern of fluctuations. Large random disturbances may present something of a problem for precision model builders but it is possible to incorporate most shocks into self-generating models without too much difficulty. Thus shocks might simply lengthen or reduce the periodicity of cycles and/or alter their amplitude. They can serve to keep damped cycles running or contain explosive ones. Only at the very worst will they upset the prevailing cyclical pattern.

The most influential type of shock has undoubtedly been that of war, the only one of sufficient strength to upset cyclical patterns sub-

---

[1] Burns, *Business Cycle in a Changing World*, p. 8.
[2] These have already been dealt with in the section on harvest fluctuations.

stantially. The French and Napoleonic Wars certainly distorted the cyclical pattern in Britain up to 1815,[1] though precisely in what way is more difficult to say because we have only a hazy notion of what went before. The impact of the First World War was even greater since it was global in its effects and had repercussions for many years afterwards. Yet it did not alter the basic cyclical pattern. This is because just before the outbreak of war the economy had been moving into a recession which the war reversed, and on normal expectations a Juglar peak could have been anticipated around 1920 when in fact it occurred. What the war did was to intensify and prolong the upswing which culminated in the post-war peak of 1920, and provoke a sharp reaction, but it did not destroy the basic pattern. Apart from these two instances the influence of war was relatively small. The Crimean War intensified and lengthened the upswing of the mid-1850s, as did the Spanish–American and Boer Wars at the turn of the century, but neither had a really dramatic impact in terms of claims on resources. Other external wars such as the Indian Mutiny, the American Civil War, the Franco–Prussian War and the Balkan Wars were of even less significance. In general their effects were felt only in a few sectors of the economy and very often there were offsets elsewhere. Perhaps more important than these was the threat of war in the 1930s which boosted the heavy sectors of industry and helped to lift the economy out of the minor recession of 1937–8.

Non-war disturbances did not generally have very widespread repercussions on the British economy. There were exceptions to the rule, however. The gold discoveries of the 1850s and 1890s had a more general if somewhat indirect influence on the British economy.[2] The impact of the General Strike of 1926 was more direct since it caused a sharp interruption to the protracted Juglar upswing of the 1920s. It would also be possible to point to events abroad, e.g. domestic disturbances in the U.S. in 1836–7 and 1907, which checked the flow of British exports at the upper turning-points of the cycle. But to go this far raises the risk of confusion between the impact of purely autonomous shocks and those of interrelated cyclical forces; though, on the other hand, it does serve to illustrate the difficulty involved in drawing fine distinctions between the two.[3]

Apart from these examples, most other disturbances tended to affect particular sectors of the economy and their influence was often

---

[1] Gayer, Rostow and Schwartz, *Growth and Fluctuation of the British Economy*, p. 568.

[2] See W. Fellner, *Trends and Cycles in Economic Activity* (1956) pp. 81–8, for a discussion of the relationship between gold production and cycles.

[3] See Aldcroft and Richardson, *British Economy, 1870–1939*, p. 59, for discussion as to whether export fluctuations can be regarded as the product of random forces occurring abroad.

swamped by stronger forces pulling in the same or opposite direction. For example, in the 1890s the export trade of the wool textile industry was kept in 'a continual state of upheaval by the antics of the U.S. tariff'; harvest fluctuations abroad affected the fortunes of a number of industries, notably cotton and shipbuilding, from time to time;[1] while strikes sometimes damped activity in certain sectors. Such minor disturbances came in endless succession and could be listed *ad infinitum*. For the most part their repercussions were felt only in particular branches of the economy and their force was far too weak to alter the basic cyclical pattern.

Long Cycles in Economic Activity

It has been recognised for some time now that economies have experienced cycles of longer duration than the standard Juglar. We refer here not to the long-wave Kondratieff, the evidence in support of which is rather flimsy, but the long cycles which have been associated with the name of Simon Kuznets. It was Kuznets who before the war exposed their reality in the American economy and later studies by Kuznets and others have confirmed their existence both in the United States and Great Britain.

Since much of the analysis on long swings has been based on American experience it is pertinent to comment briefly on the basic findings. Long swings, averaging around 15-20 years, have been discerned in a number of variables as far back as the early nineteenth century. They appear most prominently in investment, capital flows, population, migration, building and transport, though some writers (Kuznets in particular) have claimed that they also show up in the growth of output and industrial production and in the time series relating to particular industries. Demographic factors have generally been regarded as a major element in U.S. long swings. Kuznets, for example, emphasises the crucial role of population growth (both through natural increase and migration) which generated inverted waves in population-sensitive capital formation (in particular residential building and transport) and 'other' capital formation and this in turn affected the pattern of aggregate growth.[2]

[1] Robertson, *Study of Industrial Fluctuation*, pp. 74, 78, 86–7, 103, 105–7.

[2] The literature on U.S. long swings is too lengthy to quote in full. For a concise statement of Kuznets's thesis see S. Kuznets, 'Long Swings in the Growth of Population and in Related Economic Variables', *Proceedings of the American Philosophical Society*, CII (1958). For a useful review of the evidence for long swings in various indicators see M. Melnyk, *Long Fluctuations in Real Series of American Economy* (1970, Printed Series No. 9, Bureau of Economic and Business Research, Kent State University, Ohio). The relationship between transport and building was developed

Several variations on this theme have been put forward but basically population factors still remain the important causal link.[1] However, two criticisms have been raised, one methodological and the other interpretive. It has been argued that the methods adopted for smoothing the data may produce artificially created long swings. Irma Adelman, using the new techniques of spectral analysis, finds no evidence of long swings in the U.S. data since 1890 and suggests that the long swings that have been observed are nothing more than spurious cycles resulting from the smoothing processes employed.[2] However, her analysis was somewhat limited in its scope and a valid counter-objection to her thesis has been put forward, namely that some of the time series, especially residential construction, transport and population, do exhibit long swings when the data remain untreated. Secondly, there has been little attempt made to explain long swings in terms of a self-generating mechanism. Kuznets, it is true, maintained that the swings were self-perpetuating but so far analysis has not revealed the factors which yield a systematic or cyclical response and explain the turning-points of the cycles.[3]

Long swings have also been identified in Britain. Hoffmann, as early as the 1930s, claimed that long waves of 15–23 years in industrial production could be traced back to the eighteenth century, while more recently Parry Lewis has revealed a similar phenomenon in building activity.[4] However, because of the paucity of reliable data few other writers have been prepared to press the case so far back in time, and for the most part the analysis and debate on long swings in Britain have centred on the latter part of the nineteenth century.[5] The main claims put forward can be summarised briefly. Long swings have been charted in a number of variables, notably population-sensitive investment, though not apparently in income and industrial production. In particular, long swings have been observed

---

in two articles by W. Isard, 'Transport Development and Building Cycles', *Quarterly Journal of Economics*, LVII (1942), and 'A Neglected Cycle: The Transport–Building Cycle', *Review of Economics and Statistics*, XXIV (1942).

[1] See M. Abramovitz, 'The Nature and Significance of Kuznets Cycles', *Economic Development and Cultural Change*, IX (1961); R. A. Easterlin, *Population, Labor Force, and Long Swings in Economic Growth: The American Experience* (1968).

[2] Irma Adelman, 'Long Cycles: Fact or Artifact?', *American Economic Review*, LV (1965) 459. See also R. C. Bird *et al.*, '"Kuznets Cycles" in Growth Rates: The Meaning', *International Economic Review*, VI (1965).

[3] A. C. Kelley, 'Demographic Cycles and Economic Growth: The Long Swing Reconsidered', *Journal of Economic History*, XXIX (1969) 634.

[4] Hoffmann, *British Industry*, and J. Parry Lewis, *Building Cycles and Britain's Growth* (1965).

[5] Though there is still some dispute as to the temporal origin of the long swing in Britain.

in home and foreign investment. Those in domestic investment were associated with swings in population-sensitive investment and they moved inversely to those in the United States. This inverse relationship with the United States forms the basis of the famous Atlantic economy thesis developed by Cairncross and Brinley Thomas.[1] The connecting link was the demographic factor. When economic conditions in the U.S. were booming British capital and British and European emigrants flowed to that country which boosted population-sensitive investment in America and damped it at home. Conversely, when economic activity slackened in the U.S. the flow of capital and migrants was reduced and this paved the way for an upsurge in population-sensitive investment in Britain. The theory is an appealing one but it has its limitations and in recent years greater emphasis has been laid on the domestic determinants of residential building. Finally, it has been suggested that the 7–10-year cycles in income were largely the product of long and unsynchronised waves in foreign and domestic investment between 1870 and 1914.[2]

All this provides the basis for a further lengthy research inquiry and here we can do no more than comment briefly on some of the salient features of the long swing. First, the data are examined to see what support there is for a long swing in Britain. The mechanisms by which long cycles might be generated are then discussed, and the case for and against the Atlantic thesis is debated. Finally, reference is made to the relationship between the long cycle and the business cycle.

The Long Cycle in Britain

The two variables which have received most attention in studies on long swings in economic activity are building and transport. They are important because of their sheer weight in economic activity, particularly in the nineteenth century when housebuilding accounted for about 19 per cent and railway construction 12 per cent of total gross fixed capital formation between 1870 and 1913.[3] J. Parry Lewis[4] has suggested that long waves in building activity show up much earlier than this. Using such indications as timber imports,

---

[1] A. K. Cairncross, *Home and Foreign Investment, 1870–1913* (1953), and Brinley Thomas, *Migration and Economic Growth* (1954). For a more recent statement of Thomas's thesis see 'The Historical Record of International Capital Movements', in J. H. Adler, *Capital Movements and Economic Development* (1967).

[2] Matthews, *The Trade Cycle*, pp. 220–1.

[3] Investment figures used in this section are drawn from data kindly supplied by Dr C. H. Feinstein.

[4] Lewis, *Building Cycles and Britain's Growth.*

glass output, stained paper and the yield on Consols, he finds that building emerged from depression in the late seventeenth century to peak in 1705. From that date building declined into a trough in 1711 and subsequently peaked again in 1724. With the imperfect data at his disposal Lewis is able to show that there are plausible grounds for accepting the existence of building cycles long before the advent of railways, steamships, sustained population increase and mass migration. However, because of data limitations findings for this earlier period must remain very tentative, and there does not appear to be very much evidence for long swings in other variables.

Much of the debate about the long swing has centred on the latter part of the nineteenth century. It is only then that the data became sufficiently reliable to enable analysis to be carried out. From Weber's Index of Building Activity[1] it is possible to discern a peak and trough in residential construction in 1852 and 1857 respectively. Subsequently Feinstein's figures for investment show the course of dwelling construction rising to a new peak in 1876 with two slight checks in 1864 and 1872. Then a decline set in to a low point in 1886 with the industry as a whole stagnant till the early nineties. From 1892 housebuilding activity expands rapidly and exhibits twin peaks, separated by the Boer War, in 1899 and 1903. After this residential construction declines through to 1913 though with a temporary interruption in 1908. In the inter-war years, however, the long swing disappeared from building. Richardson and Aldcroft in their analysis of the building industry between the wars found residential building peaked in 1921, 1927 and 1934, while troughs occurred in 1923 and 1928. The authors also point out that fluctuations in the building industry at this time differed from those experienced in the rest of the economy both in amplitude and periodicity.[2]

In the second half of the nineteenth century transport also exhibited a long swing, though this was not as distinct as the one in housing. Annual net increments to railway mileage reached a peak in 1863, while annual increases in rail and tram mileage peaked in the late 1870s and at the turn of the century. A trough in rail and tram mileage is visible in 1891 and after 1905 the series declined till 1914. The periodicity of transport fluctuations works out at 16 years and 24 years, measured from peak to peak. In the next section the relationship between transport and building cycles will be examined more thoroughly.

It has frequently been noted that population and migration have

---

[1] In Lewis, op. cit., Appendix 4.

[2] Harry W. Richardson and Derek H. Aldcroft, *Building in the British Economy between the Wars* (1968) chap. 10.

experienced long secular movements. In England and Wales the figures for additions to population per annum show no evidence of a long swing in the first half of the nineteenth century. There then followed a period of remarkable stability in the series, during the 1840s and 1850s, until population started to rise in 1861. A peak in net additions to population was reached in 1880 after a short interruption in 1870. After 1880 the series declined till 1882 and moved to a new peak in 1900, followed by a trough in 1902. From then on till the outbreak of the First World War population growth moved in an erratic manner. Thus the evidence to show that there was a long cycle in Britain's population is very scanty, though it is tempting to distinguish two long waves between 1861 and 1902. Long swings are more pronounced in the emigration figures. Troughs occur in 1861, 1875 and 1898; the peaks are not so pronounced as emigration rises to a peak in 1863 then falls away before rising to a new peak in 1873. The eighties were a period of high emigration, with a peak in 1883, and so was the period after 1905 until growth was checked by the outbreak of war. Thus the movements in emigration and other variables are, to some extent, inverse. Troughs in 1875 and 1898 occur at times of peak building activity and the peak emigration periods of the eighties and the decade before 1914 are highly coincident with recession or stagnation in building. The building peak in 1853, however, does not fit this pattern nor does the trough in emigration in 1861 coincide with a building boom. Indeed quite the reverse. This divergence is probably caused by the abnormally high emigration of the early 1850s resulting from the Irish famine which grossly distorted the peak and trough in emigration. Furthermore, if we believe that both the building cycle and the migration cycle in the second half of the nineteenth century were at least partly the product of the Atlantic economy, the forces which were at work from the late sixties were not so evident in the fifties and early sixties.

Total new long-term British capital exports from the 1860s to the outbreak of the First World War show two long swings with peaks in 1872, 1889 and 1913. Troughs occurred in 1877 and 1901.[1] There are obvious similarities, therefore, between the swings in foreign investment and the swings in some of the other variables noted above. Troughs in overseas capital flows and migration coincide with peaks in the building cycle, while peaks in these two variables coincide with stagnation in building. The fluctuations in British

---

[1] Matthew Simon, 'The Pattern of New British Portfolio Foreign Investment, 1865–1914', in John H. Adler (ed.), *Capital Movements and Economic Development* (1967) pp. 48–50.

foreign investment are largely due to the variations in the demand for capital from North America and other regions of recent settlement. However, investment in practically every other area – South America, Europe and even the tropics – peak and trough very close to the turning-points of total overseas investment. Finally, J. G. Williamson[1] has found evidence of a long swing in deflated imports to Britain and suggests that long cycles in Britain's exports are caused by fluctuations in American demand.

Other examples of the long swing in British economic growth are hard to find. There is no evidence of a long swing in coal or iron output, for example, and there is little trace of Kuznets cycles in national income.[2] The main point about most of the long cycles we have isolated is that their movements can be seen in the untreated data. This overcomes any objection that might be raised about smoothing methods inducing the long swing. The nature and availability of the data mean that there is a concentration on the late nineteenth and early twentieth centuries as statistics before this date are unreliable and two world wars after 1914 so distort the British and international economies that the long waves were broken up and dispersed. With this in mind we can now examine the factors which may have generated the long swings.

The Generation of the Long Swing

Building is important in the economy not only because of its substantial contribution to fixed investment but also because of its relatively unstable nature and the special character of its fluctuations. In most countries building cycles have tended to be longer and more severe than those in general economic activity. The forces which influence the course of building are numerous and complex; they include not only those forces relevant to the business cycle but also a number of special factors which explain why fluctuations in building activity, especially residential construction, should be of longer duration than those in business activity.[3] These latter influences are largely independent of the business cycle and in the main they derive from the specific features of the industry, namely durability of product, reaction lags and speculation in house construction. In addition, demographic factors and large random shocks such as war also determine the course of fluctuations in construction.

---

[1] See below, Essay 8.

[2] However, as noted earlier, Hoffmann identified long waves in Britain's industrial production.

[3] Matthews, *The Trade Cycle*, chap. vi.

One of the most important reasons for the length of the building cycle is the durability of bricks and mortar, a factor which means that obsolescence takes place more slowly than for other types of capital. During a slump most forms of capital equipment begin to deteriorate and must soon be replaced, but a slump in housing leads to very little depletion of the stock of houses through obsolescence. Thus durability of houses not only lengthens the slump but lengthens the boom as well. Once builders try to repair any deficiency in the stock of houses this shortage will be difficult to overcome quickly as any new dwellings will add only a small percentage to total stock. The industry is not geared to a level of output that would substantially raise the stock of houses in a short time.

Market reaction lags may also serve to accentuate the process. Any shortage of accommodation takes time to make itself known as rents are often fixed for a long time and are not subject to immediate changes in sympathy with the market. There is a further check as builders take time to decide whether any shortage of accommodation which has manifested itself is real or imaginary, a decision which is made more precarious because the structure of the trade, with its many small units, does not help the dissemination of information. The structure of the industry is also responsible for delays in building at the start of a boom. During the previous slump a fair proportion of building firms will have disappeared owing to bankruptcy and workers moved to other trades. Thus when a building firm wants to expand it will be held back not by a shortage of capital equipment but by a shortage of labour.[1] Until that shortage is overcome the building boom cannot get under way at full pace. Building, moreover, is an industry which is susceptible to changes in the cost of borrowing as its working capital requirements are relatively high. Consequently changes in the rate of interest are important, along the margin, in persuading builders to work or not to work. This speculative aspect of the industry also helps to bring about the long swing.

On the demand side the fortunes of the building industry will be influenced particularly by changes in taste, income and population. The last named is the most relevant variable for the long swing and includes not just increases in population but also migration and emigration. In a slump emigration is encouraged and internal migration discouraged, causing regional surpluses in housing. During a boom the reverse happens and regional shortages of accommodation appear in areas which attract migrants. Family size is important because it influences not only the amount of available

[1] The building industry is labour-intensive.

income which can be spent on housing but also the type of house desired. Easterlin[1] points out that decisions to marry, to set up a household, to have children or to migrate are important economic actions. Once taken they involve individuals in a new pattern of expenditure as they set up house, provide for their children and so on. It is during this period of their life cycle that families are most heavily in debt – for example to institutions like building societies. This pattern of expenditure, this high propensity to consume, will last for several years and will be relatively insensitive to short-run changes in the economy. The key to the Kuznets cycle could be this bunching of long-term spending in a relatively short phase in the life cycle, say some time in the age group 20–40 years. A relatively large number of persons in this age group will raise the demand for houses and transportation in this country or, if they emigrate, in another. This bunching effect can arise if there is some disturbance to the population trend such as the effect of emigration, war or economic prosperity. The echo effect of this disturbance will be felt a generation later when the offspring of this population change reach marital age, thus raising the number of persons in the 20–40 age group. The echo effect may repeat itself through successive generations though its impact is lessened as time goes on. The bunching of spending and the echo effect are other reasons why housebuilding, transport and migration cycles exhibit swings not only longer than but also independent from the trade cycle.

Another suggestion put forward to explain long waves in building activity is the erratic occurrence of transport innovations. Some years ago Isard[2] maintained that the United States experienced long cycles in building as the result of the irregular emergence of transport development. From 1825 to 1933, according to Isard, the United States saw four major transport innovations, namely the canal, the railway, electric traction, and the motor-car. These innovations, by altering passenger transport and industrial location, preceded building booms and a pattern of six transport/building cycles emerged with an average duration of just over eighteen years. Isard stresses the leading nature of transport with building being the culmination of the relationship between the two variables. Thus the United States building peak of 1836 was preceded by a canal boom which reached a peak some four years earlier. However, the building peak of 1853 predates a railway peak in 1856 while in 1871 both transport (railways) and building coincide. The three transport

---

[1] Richard A. Easterlin, 'Economic–Demographic Interactions and Long Swings in Economic Growth', *American Economic Review*, LVI (1966) 1071–2.

[2] See above, p. 59, n. 2.

peaks in 1887 (railway building again), 1906 (electric traction) and 1923 (the motor-car) all precede building peaks by two or three years. In Britain, on the other hand, the sequence was partly reversed. Net additions to railway mileage peak in 1863, a time of increased building activity but no obvious building peak. Net additions to rail and tram mileage peak three years after the building peak of 1876 and a trough in rail and tram mileage occurs between 1889 and 1891 at the tail end of a building trough. The transport series peaks again around the turn of the century to coincide with the second of the twin building peaks in 1899 and 1903. Thereafter both variables decline to 1914. There is, therefore, some relationship between transport and building in the British economy at this time but transport plays a secondary role since increases in building tend to be followed by extensions of the transport system. If we want to discover the origins of the long swing it will not be found in transport which is very much a dependent variable.

One of the most striking phenomena of the long swing is the inverse nature of British and American building cycles. It is well known that building cycles in the United States had a similar periodicity to building cycles in the United Kingdom and that when building in the United States was booming the industry was stagnant in the United Kingdom. The reverse is true when a building slump hit the United States. This relationship holds for the period 1870 to 1914 though there is some dispute about the starting-point.[1] The reason given for this inverse relationship is the development of the Atlantic economy with its consequent migration of labour and capital.

If the reciprocal character of the British and American long swing is not entirely fortuitous then its mechanism is quite clear. After the middle years of the nineteenth century emigration occurred on a great scale and major flows of people into the United States helped to create the ideal conditions for a housing boom. For Britain this meant a large number of people leaving this country, resulting in less labour for housebuilding and a lower demand for houses which gave rise to vacant accommodation, lower rents, lower profit and consequently poor expectations for landlords and builders. Eventually, when the American building boom declined, emigration fell and internal migration in the United Kingdom increased. This change put pressure on the housing sector which, after a suitable lag, led to a rise in rents. With the collapse of the American boom money which could otherwise have gone abroad remained at home. As expectations of profit in housing increased, some of this money could

[1] See below, Essay 6.

find its way into the building industry; then conditions were ripe for a domestic building boom.

Brinley Thomas, the main proponent of the Atlantic economy thesis, points out that increases and decreases in emigration from Great Britain were accompanied after a short lag by inverse movements in building. Also spurts of building in the United States were preceded by incoming population.[1] Cairncross found a similar pattern in his investigation of Glasgow. At times of high emigration the Glasgow economy was stagnant but the reverse was true when emigration was low. He concluded that 'the building cycle was little more than a migration cycle in disguise'[2] brought about by the powerful forces of the Atlantic economy. In other words, international movements of capital and labour determined the shape of economic development and in particular they influenced the growth of population-sensitive capital formation. A long swing is also apparent in the overseas investment series. Between 1860 and 1914 British investment in the United States described peaks in 1872, 1890 and 1913. These peaks were separated by troughs in 1877 and 1900.[3] These turning-points coincide very closely with those in U.S. residential construction and other population-sensitive capital formation. On the other hand, too much emphasis should not be laid on the strength of the Atlantic economy through to 1914. First, because by the early twentieth century the force of the Atlantic economy was already beginning to weaken; the great bulk of America's immigrants came now not from Britain but from eastern Europe and second-generation Americans were becoming more important in the labour market; so too was the importance of internal sources of finance with the result that British overseas investment to America contributed proportionately less to U.S. capital formation.[4] Second, because the timing of the turning-points in British investment in the United States corresponded closely with those in total British overseas investment. For example, the latter series peaked in 1872, 1889 and 1913 while troughs occurred in 1877 and 1901. Although it can be argued that the pattern of timing of the total series is weighted heavily by the U.S. component, especially in boom periods, it is also noticeable that flows of capital to countries other than the United States (or North America) show a similar pattern of fluctuation. Conceivably this could arise through the operation of similar forces to those in the Atlantic economy but, as

[1] Thomas, *Migration and Economic Growth*, pp. 175–9.
[2] Cairncross, *Home and Foreign Investment*, p. 25.
[3] Simon, in Adler, *Capital Movements*.
[4] John H. Dunning, *Studies in International Investment* (1970) pp. 169–70.

we shall show below, it would be difficult to verify this proposition.

Before 1914 the largest proportion of British capital invested in the United States went to finance the development of social overhead capital, in particular transport, and very little was invested in manufacturing industry. In other words, much of the overseas investment was in population-sensitive capital formation and each wave of labour to the United States was accompanied or followed by an expansion in the flow of capital. Thus emigration and overseas lending peaked together in the early seventies while high emigration in the eighties and in the decade before the First World War preceded investment peaks by a few years. The timing of the troughs in these two variables, which occurred in the late seventies and at the turn of the century, was also similar. The Atlantic economy thesis would suggest, therefore, that the relationship between home and overseas investment is to be found in changing patterns of migration which influence the growth of population-sensitive capital formation. Consequently in the United States population-sensitive capital formation exhibits a long swing which is coincident with immigration, while in Britain long swings in domestic investment were inverse to those of population-sensitive capital formation in the United States.

Cairncross has suggested that British foreign investment in the long term was undertaken largely at the expense of domestic investment.[1] When foreign investment was booming domestic capital formation fell away and when foreign investment subsided, as it did in the 1870s and 1890s, domestic investment expanded. These flows, he suggested, were the product of Britain's changing terms of trade. When the terms of trade moved against Britain there would be an incentive to invest in countries like the United States which provided Britain with imports. When the terms of trade moved in the opposite direction domestic investment could be more profitable. British investors were able to switch from domestic to overseas investment because of the great freedom which the multilateral trading system allowed.

The Cairncross thesis encounters problems in the foreign investment booms of 1868–72, 1883–90 and 1910–13. In the early phases of these booms the terms of trade were against Britain, but in the later stages, when capital exports were heaviest, the terms of trade moved in Britain's favour. Cairncross's attempts to explain this paradox by falling shipping and railway freight rates which depressed Britain's import prices are not very successful. More recent work in this field tends to cast doubt on the terms of trade hypothesis. Dunning finds that there is no significant relationship

[1] Cairncross. *Home and Foreign Investment*, chap. vii.

between movements of capital from the United Kingdom to the United States and the United Kingdom's terms of trade. Nor does he find any relationship between the same movements and the United States terms of trade.[1]

Brinley Thomas offers an alternative explanation. He suggests that movements in the terms of trade were not a causal factor determining the ebb and flow of international capital movements, rather they were the consequence of these movements.[2] In the early stages of a capital export boom unused and underutilised resources in the domestic sector were attracted to the growing export sector. The result of this movement enabled the export sector, initially, to meet increased demand and at the same time prevent rapid price increases. However, after some period of time bottlenecks began to appear in the export sector which ultimately forced up export prices. This relative movement of export prices rising faster than import prices brought about a change in the terms of trade. Therefore the key to capital flows is to be found in migration.

The Atlantic economy thesis leaves unexplained why capital exports from Britain to countries other than North America tended to move in long waves. For example, overseas capital flows to South America, where there were no waves of emigration, peaked in 1871, 1889 and 1912 with troughs occurring in 1877 and 1902. This pattern is not very different from that of British investment in the United States. It seems unlikely that this pattern of movement would be explained entirely by forces similar to those operating in the Atlantic economy. If so, perhaps more emphasis will have to be placed on conditions in the domestic economy in the generation of the long cycle. Indeed, many scholars have expressed doubts about the validity of the Atlantic economy thesis because they feel it places far too much emphasis on external factors and consequently domestic factors are brushed aside. Habakkuk, for example, suggests that the alternations in British and American building activity reflect, among other things, the different rates of application of electricity to traction in the two countries.[3] A. C. Kelley also questions the emphasis on emigration. Emigrants from Britain and immigrants to the United States formed only a very small proportion of the total population in each country and it is doubtful whether the magnitudes involved were sufficient to influence the ebb and flow of capital

---

[1] Dunning, op. cit., p. 175.

[2] Brinley Thomas, 'The Historical Record of International Capital Movements to 1913', in Adler, *Capital Movements*, pp. 28–9. See also G. M. Meier, 'Long Period Determinants of Britain's Terms of Trade 1880–1913', *Review of Economic Studies*, xx (1952–3).

[3] See below, Essay 7.

formation in a way the adherents of the Atlantic economy thesis suggest.[1] In a more detailed study of housebuilding between 1890 and 1914 Saul stresses forces of domestic origin and suggests that migration could only have accounted for a small part of the fluctuations in housebuilding.[2] Obviously it would be impossible to account for the long swing in purely domestic or external terms. The difficulty lies in trying to establish to what degree either factor is responsible.

Perhaps the answer to this problem can be found in the interaction between the long cycle and population growth. As has been pointed out, population growth in the second half of the nineteenth century was subject to fluctuations from the early 1860s. It is not possible to say what caused this fluctuation after two decades of stability except to suggest that the relatively recent growth of emigration might have influenced it. The building boom which terminated in 1876 was accompanied by a growth in net additions to population evident from 1861 and lasting till 1880. This period of rising births and marriages was coincident with a trough in emigration and overseas lending in the late seventies. A population bulge such as this must have had a dramatic effect on the demand for accommodation just as the heavy emigration of the eighties depressed demand. An echo effect of the seventies bulge was felt in the nineties when net additions to population rose again to coincide with building expansion. The nineties was a period of low emigration and high marriage rates. However, the rate of natural population increase was greater in the eighties than in the nineties but the net increase in the nineties was higher by half a million. Lewis's examination of the housing boom of the nineties shows that this increase was due to a fall in emigration from its high level in the eighties.[3] The high marriage rate led to a third of a million new married couples looking for houses in the nineties, and since emigration is most prevalent in the 20–40 age group a large part of this increase in married couples must be attributed to the fall in emigration. As expenditure is bunched in this age group it is the most important element in generating the long cycle.

If this analysis is correct the housing booms of the seventies and nineties can be explained largely by low emigration. Therefore the demand for housing at home was influenced to no small degree by conditions abroad, particularly in the United States. So for this

---

[1] Kelley, 'Demographic Cycles and Economic Growth', p. 647.

[2] S. B. Saul, 'Housebuilding in England 1890–1914', *Economic History Review*, xv (1962) 131.

[3] Lewis, *Building Cycles and Britain's Growth*, pp. 203–8.

period at least, overseas factors are as important as domestic factors in generating the long swing. Emigration, however, cannot explain all building cycles. There were building cycles long before mass migration, even before the sustained increase in population growth. The cause of these must await more detailed regional studies on housing and population. After 1918 the forces of the Atlantic economy no longer operated so we must seek other reasons for the building booms between the wars. The pattern of residential building in this period was conditioned by a wide variety of factors, some of which were quite new. They included the severe housing shortage created by war, the advent of state assistance and local authority building on a substantial scale, rising real incomes, low interest rates (in the 1930s), changes in consumer tastes and shifts in the rate of family formation and regional migration. These housing booms took place without great expansion of population and also without a long swing. The conclusion that must be drawn for the half century before 1914, when there is adequate statistical evidence relating to the long swing, is that demographic movements are of prime importance in the origin of Kuznets cycles.

Notwithstanding the theoretical and empirical evidence that exists, not everyone is convinced that building cycles exist as a separate entity. Habakkuk,[1] for example, suggests that the long swing is induced by the behaviour of the shorter cycle. This view is in some ways feasible as we know from the investigations of Parry Lewis and others that there are regional building cycles whose course was determined by local economic conditions. Thus in the Manchester area housebuilding closely reflected the fortunes of the cotton industry, and building in South Wales was influenced by fluctuations in the coal trade. However, local building moved fairly closely with the national trend during the nineteenth century, with the exception of London and South Wales. London's building pattern was different because there was no dominant industry in that town while South Wales construction reflected the instability of the export trade. Building obviously moved in the same direction as the trade cycle at times, but was building dominated by the business cycle?

The growth of residential building which reached its peak in 1876 partly coincided with an upswing in the economy from the late 1860s through to 1873–4. After 1876 the decline in building comes at a time of upswing in the economy from 1879 to 1883. Then residential building shares in the general upswing of the economy from the later 1890s but falls steadily through the upswings of 1904–7 and 1909–13. As Parry Lewis points out, the movements of the long

[1] See below, Essay 7. Cf. Matthews, *The Trade Cycle*, pp. 220–1.

swing in building both with and against the trade cycle can create a statistical illusion.[1] The opposite movements often cancel each other out so that a coefficient of correlation over a long period would suggest that building and the trade cycle are more closely connected than they are. Residential building can and did move in the opposite direction to short-term fluctuations, while non-residential building was more closely influenced by the trade cycle. There is, therefore, a strong case for arguing that residential building does have a cycle of its own during the half century before 1914 which is different in amplitude and periodicity from the standard business cycle.

[1] Lewis, *Building Cycles and Britain's Growth*, pp. 359–60.

1   Cycles in the British Economy: 1790–1914*

W. W. ROSTOW

I

THE previous chapter sought to outline the broad pattern of growth
to which the British economy conforms, over the century and a
quarter from about 1790 to 1914. Within the framework set by the
expansion of population and total production, an attempt was made
to establish and briefly to explore five periods during which the
nature of new enterprise, in Britain and throughout the world, is
judged to have given a distinctive cast to the movements of real
wages, commodity prices, interest rates, and the terms of trade. The
present chapter seeks to move an approximation closer to the pattern
of economic events as they actually unfolded, by examining short-
period fluctuations in total industrial output and employment.

A reading of the evidence, statistical and qualitative, on the movements within the British economy in modern times, taken year by
year, month by month, or week by week, leaves two enduring impressions. First, one is impressed with the uniqueness and variety of
the story of economic life. The combinations of forces within the
moving economy are, like those in political life, in an important
sense always new and fresh. No year is quite like another year; and
after a time one gets to know them like old friends. Contrast the
lively impression to be derived from Tooke and Macpherson and the
Annual Register, in the early days, and later the *Economist* and *Bankers
Magazine*, with the story presented in conventional texts, or the view
from the statistics alone. Second, one is impressed with the solid
reality of the cyclical pattern which steadily recurs in Britain, and
then gradually widening throughout the world from the end of the
American Revolution to the outbreak of the First World War. No
two cycles, of course, are quite the same; and one can trace, as well,
certain long-period changes in the character of cycles. But it is evident that the whole evolution of modern society in the West occurred
in a rhythmic pattern, which had consequences for social and political as well as for economic events.

* This essay first appeared as Chapter II in *British Economy of the Nineteenth
Century* (Oxford University Press, 1948).

II

Table 1.1 sets out annual dates for the turning-points in British trade fluctuations from 1788 to 1914. For the whole of this era it is possible, on evidence available, to set down monthly turning-points, of reasonable accuracy, although that refinement is unnecessary for the level of analysis pursued here.[1] The annual dates do not necessarily define the year within which recovery or depression began.[2] The years are taken as analytic and statistical units, and are weighed as a whole. For example, it is likely that recovery, after the decline from 1792, began at about June 1794; on the whole, however, 1794 was a year of greater prosperity than 1793; and so the latter is marked as a trough year.

It should be emphasised that the year designated in this table is, in many cases, a matter for judgement. The processes involved in the cyclical turning-points are complex; and they are woven in each case into unique historical circumstances. Perhaps more important, there are no accurate, continuous, and sensitive indexes of production, national income, or employment which might singly, or in some aggregate, be regarded as definitive of general trade movements throughout these years. Hoffmann's indexes of production, and Beveridge's, until 1850, however valuable they may be, are, because of their constitution and weighting, dubious instruments for

---

[1] A. F. Burns and W. C. Mitchell, *Measuring Business Cycles* (1946) p. 79, present turning-points in British trade cycles annually from 1792, quarterly and monthly from 1854–5. Monthly turning-points were established from 1790 to 1850 in the course of the study directed by A. D. Gayer, *The Growth and Fluctuation of the British Economy, 1790–1850* (1953). In the annual dates presented in Table 1.1, the author has deferred to the Homeric researches of Burns, Mitchell, and their staff in several instances where his earlier calculations diverged from theirs. The setting of these dates is a matter of judgement; and little would be gained by opening this specialist sport to public controversy. Something, in fact, would be lost; for in the technique of measurement developed by the National Bureau of Economic Research these dates serve as the framework against which other statistical data are measured. Alterations in the framework involve laborious new calculations which are most unlikely to yield results of analytic significance. Unless new data are adduced, it is likely to prove useful and proper to accept the National Bureau dates as standard. The author, however, has retained the decline in 1801 as a cycle; and he has not judged the movement from 1901 to 1903 as, in net, an expansion.

The most serious error that might arise from the use of turning-point tables would be the assumption that, analytically, the cycles were of the same order, or represented necessarily comparable phenomena. As the National Bureau has been careful to emphasise, the definition of turning-points constitutes merely a preliminary working stage in the process of analysing cyclical phenomena.

[2] For an authoritative discussion of the problems involved in the setting of turning-points the reader should consult Burns and Mitchell, op. cit., especially chap. iv.

turning-point analysis.[1] And the invaluable statistics for unemployment within the trades unions, available from 1850, represent for much of the period so partial a sample of the total working force as

[1] Lord Beveridge's index, to 1850 (*Full Employment in a Free Society*, Appendix A; also *The Trade Cycle in Britain before 1850*, and a subsequent emendation, *Oxford Economic Papers*, 1940), invites two basic criticisms, both of which stem from the role of the brick production and shipbuilding figures in his calculations. First, because of their large amplitude of movement, they tend to dominate the general movements of his index as a whole. Second, because they represent capital investment, of considerable period of gestation, they lag what are regarded here as the general movements of the economy, at both troughs and peaks, as follows:

	Turning-points, Table 1.1		Turning-points, Beveridge Index
Trough	Peak	Trough	Peak
1793		1795	
	1802		1803
1803		1804	
	1806		1805
1811		1812	
	1815		1813
1819		1821	
	1828		1827*
	1839		1838–40
1842		1843	
	1845		1846

* In the case of 1828 the fall in the indexes of capital goods' production used by Beveridge outweigh the rise in the volume of exports; on the judgement here the latter movement was the more significant. A decline in indexes of investment in the course of a minor cycle expansion is not inconsistent with our definition of a minor cycle.

These criticisms imply the view that the Beveridge index underestimates the role of the volume of exports, in cyclical fluctuations of the first half of the century, and overestimates the significance, for the economy as a whole, of brick production and shipbuilding, as well as certain other series reflecting capital construction. Hoffmann's index of production is subject to similar criticism. Both indexes, and any possible formal index constructed on the basis of known statistical data alone, for this period, suffer from the poverty of consistent quantitative evidence on production. For the eighteenth century, as well, and for earlier periods, it is likely to prove more satisfactory to exploit the quantitative evidence fully, whether in continuous series or covering a limited number of years, and to muster in addition all relevant forms of qualitative evidence, in the setting of turning-points.

It should be pointed out, however, that Beveridge's central purpose was amply served by his index; namely, to indicate the existence of a persistent trade cycle in Great Britain from the close of the eighteenth century. The result of its deficiencies, however, is to obscure the existence of minor cycles, to 1850, as well as to distort somewhat the timing and shape of the major cycles.

TABLE I.I

Annual Turning-points, British Trade Cycles, 1788–1914

Trough	Peak	Trough	Peak
1788	*1792	1842	*1845
1793	1796	1848	*1854
1797	1800	1855	1857
1801	*1802	1858	1860
1803	1806	1862	*1866
1808	*1810	1868	*1873
1811	1815	1879	*1883
1816	*1818	1886	*1890
1819	*1825	1894	*1900
1826	1828	1904	1907
1829	1831	1908	*1913
1832	*1836	1914	...
1837	1839	...	...

Note: An asterisk (*) indicates that the cyclical expansion thus marked was characterised by substantial long-term investment, at home and/or abroad; and that conditions of virtually full employment were reached. Of these, the most ambiguous case is that of 1907, where capital exports occurred, during expansion, on a considerable scale, but home investment was not sufficient to create conditions of full employment. In the case of most other cycles not marked by an asterisk (e.g. 1796, 1806, 1810, etc.) the primary impulse towards expansion lay in foreign trade. The cycle marked by a peak in 1800, a trough in 1801, is to be regarded as an interruption in the expansion from 1797 to 1802, rather than as a minor cycle confined to foreign trade. Similarly, the setback of 1861–2 is to be regarded rather as an interruption in a major cycle expansion than as a minor cycle contraction, being affected by the outbreak of the American Civil War.

to require cautious use.[1] The years given here are derived from an examination of a wide body of both statistical and qualitative evidence; but no absolute validity attaches to them. One might conduct fairly even-balanced, if not very fruitful, debate as to whether 1794 rather than 1793 was a trough year, or 1809 rather than 1810 a peak, and so on.

[1] The extent to which the pre-1914 trades union unemployment figure may be regarded as representative was raised before the Royal Statistical Society in February 1923 (*J.R.S.S.*, 1923, pp. 154–205) by J. Hilton, in the course of an examination of the unemployment statistics derived from the Unemployment Insurance Acts. See especially pp. 154–5, 181–7, 197–8 (Pethick-Lawrence), 200–3 (Ramsbottom). On the basis of comparative behaviour in the period of overlap between the trades union figures and the more modern official compilation of insured workers unemployed, Hilton concluded that the trades union figure appeared to be representative of general unemployment in years of low unemployment, but overestimated unemployment in years of severe depression due to the heavy weighting of the engineering, shipbuilding, and other cyclically sensitive industries. See also A. L. Bowley, 'The Measurement of Employment: An Experiment', *J.R.S.S.* (July 1912); and Colin Clark, *National Income and Outlay* (1937) p. 232.

Leaving aside the technical problem of establishing turning-point years, or months, there is a prior issue of conception. How big a movement, in what indicators of production and employment, justifies the marking off of a formal trade cycle? The criterion employed here is that the movement be one which is evidenced by a significant change in direction of overall indexes of industrial production and employment, or such other reflections of those variables, covering particular segments of the economy, as are available. There are occasions, such as 1823, when the volume of exports declined; and in the twenties the volume of exports must be regarded as an extremely important element in the trade cycle. On the other hand, the evidence relating to total employment and production suggests that, in net, they increased in 1823. The mild downward impulse imparted from the export markets was overwhelmed in stronger domestic forces making for expansion; and thus no cycle is recorded between 1819 and 1825. An obverse case is that of the decline from 1800 to 1801, where the movements indicated in the various forms of data available are diverse, some indicating expansion; some contraction. On the whole, however, it has been thought proper to mark off a downturn in that year, with recovery following in 1802, during the brief Peace of Amiens. The analyst of cycles, like other historians, cannot be relieved of the burden of making arbitrary judgement, no matter how large or superficially comforting the mass of statistics with which he is able to surround himself.

III

Table 1.1 distinguishes 24 cycles, over the period of 126 years. Both the initial and terminal dates are untidy points of demarcation. The year 1788 marks a mild trough in a long sequence of expansion begun after the end of the American War of Independence. There was a brief post-war slump; then revival started in foreign trade, gathered momentum from the middle of the decade, but was set back briefly in 1788; recovery then moved on to a considerable and general boom, reaching its peak in 1792. On the other hand, 1914 was the first year in a cyclical decline which would have continued, almost certainly, for several further years had war not intervened. The average duration of these 24 cycles, taken as a whole, and thus regarded implicitly as comparable units, is about 5·25 years.

The average figure for the duration of all cycles distinguished is not particularly meaningful, since these cycles differed significantly in character among themselves. The most important of these differences has been indicated in the accompanying table by distinguishing fourteen of the cycles with an asterisk, and designating them major cycles. A major cycle is defined by two related criteria: first, that, at its peak, conditions of relatively full employment were attained; second, that in its latter stages at least, persons and institutions proved willing to enter into long-term investment commitments, at home and/or abroad, on a large scale. In most cases an application of these criteria to the evidence clearly and satisfactorily distinguishes the major cycles.

Some problem is raised, however, by the cases of major cycles before 1825. On the whole, long-term investment played a lesser part in the economy in the earlier than in the later years of the era; and in addition, the economic requirements of war, to 1815, diverted resources abnormally into foreign trade and agriculture. Nevertheless, the behaviour of brick production, as well as other indicators of long-term investment, justify the distinction of cycles reaching their peaks in 1792, 1802, and 1810. The not very impressive, but nevertheless real, post-war cycle, reaching its peak in 1818, also falls in this category of lesser major cycles.

Perhaps the most ambiguous of the cycles, however, lies not in the early years, but is that which reached its peak in 1907. Average unemployment in Britain in the peak year was almost 4 per cent, a considerably higher figure than for any of the other major cycle peaks after 1850; and, looked at closely, it is evident that domestic long-term investment was on a depressed scale throughout the upswing from 1904 to 1907.

The minor cycles were characterised by limited general expansion which, for various reasons, gave way to depression before conditions of relatively full employment were reached. In most cases the primary impulse sustaining expansion, in the minor cycles, was confined to foreign trade; and although multiplier effects undoubtedly operated to spread the increase in production and employment, the economic system failed to move continuously upward to full employment. In some cases the downward movement can be traced, in part, at least, to an external event; e.g. the coming of Civil War in 1861. In other cases (e.g. 1828), the timing of decline appears in large part to proceed from a virtually autonomous short rhythm in foreign trade itself; although some of the minor cycles were supported by the completion of acts of investment, with long periods of gestation, undertaken in the peak years of the previous major cycle, and their end was accompanied by the final collapse of these waves of long-term investment.

In general, this dual distinction among cycles appears useful so long as the individual cycles are so well understood that their abstraction into categories is not compounded to advanced abstract conclusions which the raw historical evidence does not support.

Taking the major cycles apart, we find a consistent duration of about nine years;[1] and this duration does not vary significantly through time. From 1792 to 1900 the major cycles may be associated in 4 successive groups, of 3 each.[2] Although the individual cycles vary in length, the average for each of the 3 groups is remarkably similar: 8·7 years for the period up to 1818; 9·0 years to 1845; 9·3 years to 1873; and 9·0 years to 1900. The author can adduce no simple and persuasive reason why the rhythm of fluctuations in long-term investment should have remained so stable, at about 9 years, through the nineteenth century; but there seems little doubt concerning the reality of the phenomenon.

The minor cycles, of which ten are distinguished over these years, are consistently about four years in length; and these too exhibit no very significant change in their average duration over the century. It will be noted in Table 1.1, however, that the minor cycles tend, virtually, to disappear from the array of trade cycles after 1860, excepting, of course, the special case of 1907. This characteristic of cyclical behaviour proceeds from the nature of the two types of cycles, as they have been defined, and from the character of the basic changes in the British economy over the century and a quarter: four minor cycles are in the first trend period, to 1816; three are in the second;[3] two in the third; none in the fourth; and one in the fifth. The euthanasia of the minor cycle presents, in fact, no great analytic mystery.

---

[1] The average duration of major cycles varies with the form of measurement. Measured from peak to peak (1792–1913) their average duration is 9·4 years; measured from trough to trough (1788–1914) their average duration is 9·0 years. The consistency of the duration is indicated, in the latter case, by an average deviation of 1·29 years.

[2] Measurement is here taken from 1792 to 1900, dropping, in effect, the first and last major cycles, because the major cycle trough preceding 1792 is not established; and because the final trend period, 1900–14, includes by our definition only one major cycle, that reaching its peak in 1913. Economically, as noted above (p. 78), the trough in 1914 is almost certainly artificial. The major cycle trough preceding 1792 probably falls in 1784–5; and the expansion to 1787 and the decline to 1788 would be accounted a minor cycle movement.

[3] A secondary cycle, after the peak in 1845, can be detected in the monthly data, running from a trough in Sep 1846 to a peak in Apr 1847. Analytically it shares some of the characteristics of the secondary peak (after 1836) in 1839, involving stimulus from both the completion of railway projects, earlier initiated, and from the export trade; but it is too slight a movement to justify inclusion among the annual dates. Such inconclusive secondary movements, among others, can also be detected in the course of the downswing of the seventies, the upswing of the later nineties, and the downswing following 1900, the latter movement having attained the dignity of a separate cycle in the calculations of the National Bureau.

IV

The minor cycles are distinguished here by the fact that they involved increases in production and employment arising preponderantly, but not exclusively, from increases in exports. In the first half of the nineteenth century textiles and other consumers' goods constituted the dominant element in British exports. Against the background of a rising world population and real income, and cheapened real costs of production, the amounts capable of being sold in world markets increased steadily, year after year: the demand curve for British exports shifted steadily to the right, and the supply curve as well. The markets through which British exports were sold abroad, however, were speculative in the sense that more or less was sent abroad, by individual merchants, depending on their information and judgements concerning stocks and prices in foreign markets at future times. In addition, because time-lags were involved at various stages in the process of trade, current and expected conditions with respect to the price and the availability of credit entered the calculation.

Acting, in fact, on similar or identical intelligence, British merchants tended, roughly, to behave in the same manner. When inventories fell off, and prices rose abroad, word was received from overseas agents and fully circulated; and more goods were shipped from Britain. Such actions, individually taken, tended to reverse the conditions in foreign markets which justified the increased shipments, in the first instance; and the reversal could not be reported instantaneously, nor the production decisions which stemmed from it instantaneously reversed within Britain. And so the curve of British exports did not rise smoothly, in continuous accord with market conditions abroad. It moved upward, with occasional setbacks, fluctuating about the imaginary line which, at any moment of time, would have represented the equilibrium volume of exports. There was, undoubtedly, a tendency for British foreign trade to fluctuate cyclically, in what we might call an inventory cycle.[1]

[1] Thomas Tooke's *History of Prices* (1838) is the best source of data on the course and the mechanics of short cycles in foreign trade, his account deriving vitality and authority from a long merchant's experience. The institutional arrangements, with their time-lags, credit arrangements, and dependence on expectations, are described by N. S. Buck, *Anglo-American Trade, 1800–1850* (1925): for the system of credit advances on consignments, and the 'interlacing of credits' and speculation with foreign trade operations, see especially pp. 12–14, 23, and 39; for reference to the inventory nature of the foreign trade crises of 1816 and 1831 see pp. 138–9. For a recent analysis of the nature and possible causes of inventory fluctuations, partially relevant to this problem, despite its application to a closed economy, see L. A. Metzler, 'The Nature and Stability of Inventory Cycles', *Review of Economic Statistics* (1941), and 'Factors Governing the Length of Inventory Cycles', ibid. (1947).

The rhythm of that cycle was, of its nature, relatively short; and, in times of peace and normal market relationships, the amplitude of its movement relatively mild. There are several reasons why this should have been so:

First, while there was undoubtedly an element of judgement about future markets, and future costs involved in the export trade, the period of time between a change in market conditions and the receipt of intelligence in London was not very great, even before the introduction of the cables.

Second, the flow of exports could be altered quickly and sensitively, with changed knowledge and judgement about future market conditions; a commitment to build a railway is binding over a number of years; commitments to manufacture and to ship textiles were capable of review and alteration in a matter of weeks or months.[1]

Finally, the demand for consumers' goods from peoples abroad was under fairly steady impulse to enlargement; the purchases of foreign merchants were, of course, sensitive to changes in British prices, and to general movements of demand within their own market regions; but behind them were enlarging populations, with increasing real incomes; and they were trading in consumers' goods.[2]

Together these forces made for a relatively short cycle, of mild amplitude, in the basic British exports of the first half of the century. And it is this type of inventory cycle which one could, almost cer-

---

[1] Buck, op. cit., p. 102, notes: 'As it generally took from a month to six weeks to manufacture the goods and prepare them for shipment, merchants, who purchased from the manufacturers, were required to place their orders for goods fairly early.' To establish what Metzler, in his articles cited above, calls 'the planning period' one would, presumably, have to take into account the length of time from the placing of the order by the merchant to the receipt of the manufactured goods. This would include the period from transmission to receipt of orders, from overseas, as well as the period for shipment and delivery of the finished British products. In fact, shipments from Britain to the United States tended to be concentrated in two periods of the year: 'There were the spring shipments, from the middle of January until the middle of April, and the fall shipments, during the months of July and August' (idem). It is not unlikely that 'the planning period', fully analysed in this trade, would work out to something close to six months.

[2] The economies to which Britain sold its exports were themselves subject to cyclical fluctuations, as well as to secular growth: fluctuations in harvests, in their income from exports, and in their domestic industry. These fluctuations undoubtedly affected the demand for British exports; and they were both affected by, and influenced the course of, British cycles. Probably the optimum form in which to analyse these foreign trade fluctuations would be as an aspect of inter-regional trade, within a single economy moving to the rhythm of fully interrelated, if not synchronous, cyclical forces. What is essential to the argument here, however, is that, until about the fifties, the principal British exports were consumers' rather than capital goods.

tainly, trace back into the eighteenth century; and perhaps even back to medieval times. Its character stems from the nature of the merchant's trade.

From the late 1780s at least, however, this rhythm is woven into the longer and deeper rhythm of fluctuations in long-term investment. In the latter stages of the boom reaching its peak in 1792, for example, there was an expansion in canal- and road-building, agricultural inclosures, and an increased building of ships, houses, and factories. This element of long-term investment grew relatively as the economy became increasingly industrialised; and it grew notably after the ending of the French wars had lifted the burdens and removed the distorting pressures which war had imposed. Until the sixties, however, the short cycle can not only be detected but, on the judgements which entered the compilation of Table 1.1, it had sufficient power to produce distinguishable general movements in total production and employment.

As industrialisation progressed, however, and the metallurgical and engineering industries began to play an increased proportional role in the economy, the long-term investment cycle became increasingly dominant. This was the trend not only for Britain, but for certain key British markets on the Continent and in the United States; and thus the longer rhythm – the nine-year average – infected not only British domestic activities, but foreign trade as well. In 1808 to 1810, when Britain enjoyed a boom focused on Latin America, freed for trade by the Spanish Revolution of 1808, the goods sent out, as recorded in the famous quotation from McCulloch, were: textiles, cut glass, chinaware, hammers, and the inevitable skates for Rio de Janeiro.[1] From the fifties onward not only did railway-iron and other capital equipment go abroad, but the further industrial development of certain of the importing economies probably made their demand for British consumers' goods more sensitive to cyclical fluctuations than had been the case in earlier, more pastoral times.

The net effect of the British and world-wide transition towards capital development and industrialisation was to overwhelm, in a sense, the minor cycle as an independent cyclical phenomenon. Its rhythm, however, can still be detected in the export figures for British textiles. Whereas, between 1848 and 1914, ten trade cycles can be marked off, there are some fifteen cycles which can be detected in the value of exports of cotton goods and yarn, with an average duration of somewhat over four years. In the early decades of the century the movement of textile exports might have been decisive to

[1] Quoted in Tooke, *History of Prices*, vol. I, pp. 276–7.

the contour of fluctuations in the economy as a whole; in the latter year it was simply one determinant of general fluctuations, and by no means the most powerful. But the short rhythm of its movement persists.

Thus, the statistical conclusion that the average duration of trade cycles increased after 1860 is to be understood in general as the shifting from a secondary to a primary position of the rhythm of long-term investment;[1] and a reduction in relative status within the world economy of the shorter rhythm which, for Britain, took the form notably of textile exports. From the beginning to the end of the era, however, the two rhythms are detectable in the evidence.

The two types of fluctuations did not pursue their course in separate and discrete channels. They were linked in at least four ways:

First, both partially depended, in their timing, on the state of the capital market; and their course related to conditions in the interwoven complex of credit markets in London and the provinces.

Second, and more broadly, the consumers' goods industries and capital-goods industries competed for labour and raw materials in common markets; cost calculations which affected decisions in both stemmed from, partially, identical data.

Third, a part of British exports depended on the export of capital; and in most cases waves of capital exports occurred at the same time, and under the same general impulses that led to long-term domestic investment.

Fourth, a source of the confidence and the funds for long-term investment were the increases in profits and in general income derived directly and indirectly from prior increases in the export trade.

For these reasons, among others, fluctuations within the British economy must be examined and understood as a whole, no matter how useful or illuminating the abstraction of elements within them may be for special purposes.

The shift in the balance and structure of the British and world economies, and thus the changed character of cyclical fluctuations, had consequences for the relative impact of the trade cycle on the economy and the society as a whole. At the beginning of the era

---

[1] 1860 in no sense constitutes a sharp analytic line of demarcation with respect to the relative role of the two types of cycles. The coming of the railway on a very large scale in Britain in the forties affords a sharper conceptual breaking-point. Indeed, the minor cycle of the late forties is so slight a manifestation that it is not recorded in the annual turning-points; and that of the fifties (peak 1857) would, perhaps, not have stood out so strongly, but for the distortions imposed on the pattern of the decade by the Crimean War.

Britain was, in agriculture, virtually self-sufficient, with only minor capital industries, and a foreign trade mainly in consumers' goods. By the end of the era Britain was heavily deficit in agriculture, with its industries closely tied, in both their domestic and foreign markets, to long-term capital development. Undoubtedly a larger proportion of the population felt the impact of the trade cycle on their lives and fortunes in 1910 than in 1790.

There is, further, good evidence for concluding that the amplitude of trade cycles, in both their expansion and contraction phases, increased after the French wars. From 1819 to 1848, however, covering the three great major cycles of the twenties, thirties, and forties, there appears to be no clear trend increase in the amplitude of cyclical movements.[1] From 1850 there is available the trades' union unemployment figures, which cover a gradually larger proportion of the labour force. It is difficult to judge whether the changing constitution of that index gives it a bias towards greater or lesser average unemployment, over time, and greater or lesser amplitude of fluctuation. The greater coverage in terms of industries which are less sensitive to cyclical movements may well be compensated for by its greater coverage of, and the weighting given to, industries with a high sensitivity to cycles.[2] If one regards the unemployment figures as a uniformly representative sample, one is led to the conclusion that, while the trade cycle undoubtedly affected an increasing proportion of the population, the relative amplitude of cyclical move-

---

[1] In the course of the study *The Growth and Fluctuation of the British Economy, 1790–1850*, directed by A. D. Gayer, an index of trade fluctuations was constructed which, while not fully satisfactory for the definition of turning-points, is judged reasonably to reflect the amplitude of the cyclical movements. It exhibits the following behaviour from 1797 to 1848, for major cycles:

	Trough to Peak		Peak to Trough	
	%		%	
1797–1802	15·1		4·2	1802–3
1808–10	12·7		10·8	1810–11
1816–18	24·6		11·3	1818–19
1819–25	45·7		39·7	1825–6
1832–6	41·8		29·0	1836–7
1842–5	49·3		50·0	1845–8

Unfortunately, data available to the author do not permit the extension of this index at the present time. Regarded analytically, the measurements from peak to trough for the last three major cycles are not comparable. Due to the lag at the peak, the waves of long-term investment took some time to subside. After 1825 and 1836, only one year of decline, measured by turning-points, occurred; after 1845, on the other hand, the trough is measured to 1848.

[2] See above, p. 77, n. 1.

ments in employment did not change in a systematic and significant way from 1850 to 1914.[1]

Unfortunately, the data are not now in such a form that the important gap from the forties to the fifties can be bridged by a continuous and satisfactory general index of cyclical fluctuations; nor have the measurements of particular series made by the National Bureau of Economic Research yet been fully mobilised on this problem. Tentatively, however, it would appear that the percentage movements in total employment and production do not exhibit a significant long-term trend variation, paralleling the growing industrialisation of the British economy from, roughly, the 1820s to 1914.

A separate but related question concerns the possible relationship between the character of trade cycles and the trend periods. It has long been believed that the trend periods after 1815 and 1873 were, in some sense, more depressed than the other three, whether that depression was associated with trends in the price-level or the more complex inner rationale of Schumpeter's Kondratieff process.[2]

There are many possible tests of this hypothesis of which two appear tractable within the limits of present data:

(a) the dubious test, of comparing the proportion of years of increasing prosperity to years of increasing depression for cycles within the trend periods;

(b) a superior test, where possible, of comparing the average level of unemployment for cycles within the trend periods.

The first test is of doubtful value because, if applied directly to this issue, it implies that all cycles designated by turning-points were comparable analytic units, of similar amplitude, and similar rates of expansion and contraction. In particular, the gradual disappearance of the minor cycle influences the measurements over this era in a

---

[1] This is not to imply, of course, that all cycles, or even all major cycles, were of similar amplitude. The cycles varied among themselves in intensity; and there is, from the seventies to 1914, an apparent trend towards a diminished amplitude of cyclical movement in the unemployment index, which can be seen in the successive figures for peak unemployment in the various cycles: 1879, 11·4 per cent; 1886, 10·2 per cent; 1893, 7·5 per cent; 1908, 7·8 per cent. Leaving aside the margins of error and biases that may exist within the unemployment series, it seems preferable to analyse these cases in terms of their particular environment than in terms of an indicated trend change in the nature of the trade cycle. See below, pp. 87–9.

[2] See Schumpeter, *Business Cycles* (1939) pp. 161 ff.; also J. Viner, *Studies in the Theory of International Trade* (1937) p. 218; and W. C. Mitchell, *Business Cycles* (1927) pp. 407–12. For a recent interesting but inconclusive and partial test of this hypothesis see Burns and Mitchell, *Measuring Business Cycles*, chap. ii, esp. pp. 431–40.

manner such as to diminish the proportion of prosperous to depressed years.

This phenomenon occurs because the characteristic pattern of the minor cycle, based on the course of foreign trade, was one of a preponderance of years of prosperity to years of depression. The trend was strongly upward, and a single year of setback was usually sufficient to bring down inventories sufficiently to permit the resumption of an upward movement: e.g. 1819, 1826, 1829, 1832, etc. As this element loses its power to affect what are judged to be general movements of employment and production, the rhythm of long-term investment, more evenly balanced between expansion and contraction phases, stands forth, and the proportion of years of prosperity to years of depression tends to fall. This factor does not affect comparative measurements significantly as between the first two trend periods, to the mid-century. After that time, however, it becomes significant.

From 1793 to 1816 inclusive, 67 per cent of the years are years of rising prosperity; from 1816 to 1848, 64 per cent.[1] The impropriety of drawing any distinction between the two periods on the basis of this calculation is indicated by the fact that if, for example, the single year 1847 is regarded as one of rising prosperity, as the monthly data suggest might well be done,[2] the prosperity proportions become identical, as between the two trend periods.

Applied to the period after 1848, however, the measure yields a less steady result, as follows:

Period	Prosperity Proportion %
1848–68	67
1848–79	59
1879–94	50
1879–1904	54
1904–14	73

From these overlapping measures one might firmly draw the conclusion that in the seventies the relative periods of prosperity fell away, and rose again after the middle nineties. The evidence appears unambiguous, and the orders of magnitude substantial. And, indeed,

---

[1] In all such measurements a problem exists of establishing periods which both fall within the trend intervals being compared, and which represent an equitable balance of cyclical phases. The years chosen here are regarded as representing a fair comparison, although the fact that the trough years are counted at the beginning and the end of each period somewhat underestimates the 'proportion of prosperity' in each case.

[2] See above, p. 80, n. 3.

such is the result one obtains if the cycles are regarded as analytically comparable units over the period 1848–1914.[1]

These measures of the 'prosperity proportion' should be contrasted with measures of the average level of business activity and of unemployment. For the period up to 1850 an index of general business activity has been constructed, on the basis of all available evidence, in which each year is rated from 0, a year of deep depression, to 5, a year of virtually full employment. The average standing of years within each trend period was then calculated. The fairest measure, analytically, runs from 1793 to 1816; and from 1816 to 1848, all years of demarcation being cyclical troughs. The average standing of years in the first period is then 2·10, in the second, 1·95. Given the nature of the data, any very firm conclusions do not appear justified from this distinction in average standings.

An examination of the unemployment data from 1850 yields a similar inconclusive result. The most satisfactory measuring periods, analytically, are the following: 1855–73; 1874–1900; 1901–13.[2] For

[1] This is the conclusion drawn, in more generalised form, by Burns and Mitchell, *Measuring Business Cycles*, pp. 437–40, from Table 167; although they regard their results as preliminary and tentative.

[2] These periods are taken because 1850 comes after the beginning of revival, in 1848; and 1914 is the first year of what would, almost certainly, have been a more protracted depression. The lack of any very great distinction between unemployment in the Great Depression period, as opposed to the trend periods which lie on either side, is indicated in the following supplementary calculations:

Average Unemployment by Decades

	%
1850–9	5·03
1860–9	5·16
1870–9	3·83
1880–9	5·61
1890–9	4·35
1900–9	4·83

Average Unemployment by Cycles

	%
1850–5	4·0 (1849, year of depression, lacking)
1856–8	7·5
1859–62	4·8
1863–8	4·9
1869–79	4·1
1880–6	5·9
1887–94	5·1
1895–1904	3·8
1905–8	5·3
1909–14	4·1 (downswing interrupted by war)

The overall average for unemployment, 1850–1914, is 4·69 per cent.

the first, the mid-Victorian period, average unemployment is 4·8 per cent; for the second, the Great Depression, it is 4·9 per cent; for the third, the pre-1914 period, it is 4·5 per cent. These figures, or any other reasonable analysis of the unemployment data, do not appear to justify the view that the Great Depression period was marked by significantly higher unemployment than the average from the mid-century to the outbreak of war in 1914.

The traditional conception, which associates falling-price trends with high secular unemployment, probably stems from a quantitatively inaccurate picture in our minds of the cyclical depression of the seventies and of the expansion of the early eighties, so far as the Great Depression is concerned; and, for the three decades after the French wars, from the imprint of the falling price-curves of Peterloo, the Irish famine, the Chartists, and Engels on the forties.

In the seventies a surprisingly high level of activity was sustained from the beginnings of the downswing in 1873 to 1878–9. From 1874 through 1877, all regarded as years of 'depression' in the earlier measurement, average unemployment was only 3·1 per cent, as opposed to the 1850–1914 general average of 4·7 per cent; and the behaviour of statistics of production, and other evidence, support this view of the period. Prices, to be sure, were falling, and interest rates and profits as well; but the impact of depression, for Britain after 1873, like the preceding prosperity, came largely from abroad; and the country turned promptly, after 1873, to housing, shipbuilding, and other domestic enterprise of low expected yield; while the quantity of sales abroad, at lower but still profitable prices, was surprisingly maintained.

The years from 1879 to 1883 are regarded, usually, as a minor upward movement in a period of general depression. But the expansion in production was very real indeed; and unemployment was down close to 2 per cent in 1882 and 1883. This expansion did not move, in its latter stages, into a phase of new adventurous investment. A flotation boom in electricity companies was about the best it could summon; and the economic system was not pushed, as in the special circumstances of the early seventies, to a phase of almost absolute full employment and rapidly rising prices. Moreover, in its muted character the expansion of the early eighties is related to what we have defined as the central quality of the Great Depression period, namely, the lack of high-yield outlets for new investment. The years 1884–7 were probably the worst continuous sequence, from the point of view of unemployment, of any throughout this era. The expected yield on new investment was not as high as it had been in the seventies, or the fifties, although the position was in many ways similar to that in the sixties. The volume of investment was, however, sufficiently high over the Great Depression period as a whole to avoid a significantly greater average level of unemployment than in the trend periods which preceded or followed.

This judgement, based on materials and an analysis that are patently subject to later refinement, is advanced not only because of its intrinsic interest in cyclical history, but also because it relates to an important implicit assumption that runs through much of the discussion of trends.[1] If it is possible to assume, roughly, that resources were about equally employed, on the average, in the various trend periods, then the emphasis on the importance of the different types of investment outlay, as the decisive factor determining the trend course of the principal variables, is thereby the more legitimate.

v

It is impossible, within the compass of the present essay, to examine systematically the typical cyclical behaviour of the major elements within the economy, and to explore the sort of trade cycle theory which appears best to account for their course. It may be useful, however, to present some interim observations on the cyclical behaviour of the British harvests, commodity prices, long-term investment, and the Bank of England.

For the period to 1850, clearly, and probably to the seventies, the domestic harvests played a significant part in British trade fluctuations. Theoretically, a good harvest, with a consequent fall in the price of bread, could be assumed to increase real wages, and thus to increase the demand for commodities other than bread; or, less likely, and mixed in its effects, it might reduce the resistance to a decline in money wages, making possible lowered marginal costs for entrepreneurs. On the other hand, an abundant harvest might be regarded as reducing the money incomes of the agricultural community, and thus decreasing its demand for non-agricultural commodities; for the demand for grain was highly inelastic, over this period. Undoubtedly fluctuations in the yield of the harvests did shift the demand curves for non-agricultural commodities within the community, although it is impossible on present evidence to trace those shifts in detail. One emerges, simply, with the impression that an abundant harvest was a good thing for the non-agricultural community; a very mixed blessing for agriculture; and, in net, clearly a good thing for the country taken as a whole.

There is, however, a more solid approach to the effects of harvests

[1] See W. W. Rostow, *British Economy of the Nineteenth Century* (1948) chap. i.

in these years, and a more clearly definable set of effects, namely, those which operated through the foreign balance and the money market. A good harvest reduced the requirements for imports of grain; a bad harvest increased those requirements. The orders of magnitude of the outlays in a poor harvest year, as opposed to those in a time of domestic abundance, were very considerable. And an increase in grain imports served to put pressure on the money markets, to raise interest rates, and thus to discourage other forms of foreign trade, domestic commerce, and long-term investment. In addition, it set in motion strong forces in the labour market making for higher wages. A good harvest, on the other hand, tended to reduce the pressure on the foreign balance, to ease the money markets, to lower interest rates, and to free funds for other purposes.

The good harvests of 1797-8, 1820-3, 1832-5, 1843-4, and 1850-2 undoubtedly helped foster the major cycle expansions which were set in motion in those years; conversely, the high wheat prices and increased imports of 1795-6, 1800-1, 1810, 1817-18, 1824-5, 1836-7, and 1846-7 undoubtedly contributed to the pressure on the money market in those years of strain or crisis. The evidence is not such, however, as to justify the conception of a trade cycle detonated into its upward phase by a good harvest, operating through the foreign balance and the monetary mechanism, and brought to its close by an inadequate harvest and monetary stringency. Nevertheless, the harvests must be accounted, to the seventies, a significant permissive and contributory factor, which affected the timing of recovery, and which counted among the various strains within the economy which helped bring on the downswing. As Britain's harvest came to contribute a decreasing proportion of the total food supply, however, and foodstuffs were drawn from an increasingly large number of sources, this factor appears to diminish in importance within the trade cycle.

It is a potent heritage of the quantity theory of money, in its less sophisticated applications, that commodity prices are believed to move in close conformance with trade cycles.[1] There is no very good theoretical reason why this conformity should have been assumed. The quantity theory provides that an increase in MV can result in an increase in T, the volume of trade, as well as in P, the level of prices. In fact, the early stages of most trade cycles in Britain in this era were accompanied by stagnant or falling prices: the early twenties, thirties, forties; the periods from 1848 to 1852, 1868 to 1871, and so on. Later in the era the conformity somewhat improves; but prices

---

[1] For a late example of this view see Beveridge, *Full Employment in a Free Society*, Appendix A, pp. 286-7.

are, in general, a very inadequate index of British trade cycles before 1914.

The periods of falling or stagnant prices were, normally, the intervals when the largest increases in production occurred, and the greatest declines in unemployment. From 1868 to 1871, for example, an index of total production (1900 equals 100) rises from 52 to 60; while unemployment falls from 7·9 per cent to 1·6 per cent. Prices, however, rise from 132 to 133, the rise being confined to the last quarter of 1871, to which point prices had, in net, fallen from 1868. From 1871 to 1873 production rises from only 60 to 64; unemployment falls only from 1·6 per cent to 1·2 per cent; but prices rise from 133 to 148. Thus, in the first phase, to 1871, a rise of production of eight points was accompanied by a one-point rise in prices; in the final years of expansion a rise of four points in production was accompanied by a price rise of fifteen points. And for the nineteenth century in Britain this relationship of prices to production and employment, in the course of cyclical upswings, is not exceptional.

The principal explanation for this phenomenon is, of course, that the early stages of expansion represent a condition of partially unemployed resources; and the latter stages represent more nearly full employment. But it is also worth emphasising that, while it is often useful in business cycle theory to assume Marshallian short-period conditions and to ignore changes in fixed factors, the historian concerned with actual events, as they occur in time, cannot permit himself the luxury of that abstraction. The late Lord Keynes, in one of the stories on which we are now all brought up, is reported to have remarked that in the long run we are all dead. It is, however, a clear lesson of economic history, including the recent history of war economies, that the long period, in the Marshallian sense, can be very short indeed. Thus, in studying the movements of prices, even over relatively short periods in time, it is necessary to look at the changes in productive capacity and technique, and the productivity of labour, as well as at the supply of money, the state of effective demand, and the extent of unemployed resources. Changes in real costs undoubtedly served to restrain the tendency of prices to rise in the early stages of cyclical expansion.

One of the most consistent cyclical phenomena, throughout this era, is the tendency for long-term investment decisions to concentrate in the latter stages of the upswing of the major cycles. This appears to be true, not only of formal flotations in the capital markets, but to a considerable extent, also, of other forms of investment. From 1790 to 1850, over which period a great many statistical series have been subjected to analysis, with respect to their cyclical behaviour, brick production exhibits a significant average rise only in the latter stages of expansion of major cycles.[1] The cyclical behaviour of shipbuilding is similar, except that there were, on the average, declines in shipbuilding during the early stages of both major and minor cycles; and as befits the tie between minor cycles and foreign trade, there was a substantial rise in shipbuilding during the latter stages of minor cycles, although a lesser rise than in the latter stages of major cycles.

With respect to the expansion of industrial plant, the evidence available is less systematic and must be pieced together industry by industry, cycle by cycle, from diverse forms of evidence. On the whole, the impression one receives is that the Industrial Revolution, regarded as a process of plant expansion and the installation of new industrial methods and techniques, lurched forward in a highly discontinuous way, with a high concentration of decisions to expand, or to improve technique, occurring in the latter stages of the major cycles.[2]

There are, of course, exceptions to this general pattern, some of considerable importance. The modern iron industry in Scotland, for example, based on Neilson's hot-blast, was founded in 1828 and grew steadily, for a considerable time, with apparently little relevance to the trade cycle.[3] Moreover, in several instances the result of the withdrawal from the capital market of the high-yield new investment, which had dominated the latter stages of expansion, and which

---

[1] These measures are presented in the study directed by A. D. Gayer, referred to earlier. For brick production, the measures are as follows. Stage I–III constitutes the early phase of expansion; III–V the late phase of expansion; V–VII the early phase of contraction; VII–IX the late phase of contraction.

Averages and average deviations of per month rate of movement in the reference cycle stages of major and minor trade cycles

		I–III	III–V	V–VII	VII–IX
Production of	Major	+0·1 (0·2)	+1·6 (0·4)	0·0 (1·6)	−0·5 (1·8)
bricks	Minor	−0·7 (0·7)	0·0 (0·4)	−0·6 (0·5)	−0·7 (0·4)

[2] An interesting but extremely limited example of this pattern can be derived from figures given by E. Baines, *History of Cotton Manufacture* (1835) p. 395. Baines gives the number of cotton mills in the Manchester district at three-year intervals between 1820 and 1832 as follows:

1820	.	.	.	.	.	66 factories
1823	.	.	.	.	.	72 ,,
1826	.	.	.	.	.	92 ,,
1829	.	.	.	.	.	95 ,,
1832	.	.	.	.	.	96 ,,

The greatest increase occurred in the latter stages of the major cycle expansion reaching its peak in 1825 (1823–5). Increase in the two subsequent minor cycle expansions (1826–8, 1829–31) was negligible.

[3] H. Hamilton, *The Industrial Revolution in Scotland* (1932) pp. 179–83.

had been discredited in the course of the turning-point and crisis, was to bring promptly into the market the low-yield type of investment which had been, as it were, starved out in the course of expansion.

It was the decision to undertake long-term investment, rather than the consummation of these acts, which has been noted as a particular but not exclusive characteristic of the latter stages of major cycle expansions. In fact, the period of gestation of many types of investment was such that projects undertaken in the boom were not completed until some time after the turning-point. And, as a result, the impact of depression, in its early stages, was cushioned by the necessity for completing projects earlier begun. A notable, but by no means unique, instance of this was the period 1845 to 1847. The mileage of new railway lines actually opened reached its peak in 1848, although the cyclical downturn came, clearly, in 1845. As noted earlier, this element of lag at the peak is quite generally typical of brick production and of shipbuilding.

In general, the nature of the trade cycle would suggest the likelihood that decisions to undertake long-term investment be concentrated disproportionately in the latter stages of expansion, rather than spread evenly throughout its course. One would expect a gradual growth in confidence concerning the future, as incomes rose, and a willingness to make commitments over increasingly long future periods. The first impact of recovery, for Britain, came normally through an increased demand for exports, especially of consumers' goods. This involved only short-term financing, usually from London, and thus relatively minor hostages to fortune. Then, gradually, one can trace the growth of daring, often leading to a concentration of interest in a particular line of new investment, at home or abroad, in the final stage of expansion. Mr Hicks's elasticity of expectation increases.[1] The process is real, and can be quite sharply, if not quantitatively, delineated, stage by stage, in the evidence of cyclical expansions.

We turn, finally, to the behaviour of the monetary system in the course of cyclical fluctuations, and especially to the position of the Bank of England. The early stages of revival were normally marked by easy money conditions, and by falling rates of interest, short and long, inside and outside the Bank. To this tendency, as noted earlier, abundant British harvests contributed in several important instances. Credit advanced in all forms outside the Bank, for which evidence is poor, probably increased mildly in most such early stages; but the falling tendency of prices made it possible to finance an increased volume of transactions with a given supply of money. Within the

[1] J. R. Hicks, *Value and Capital*, 2nd ed. (1946) p. 205.

Bank, bullion increased, bills and notes discounted decreased, and the Bank Rate fell, or remained steady at a low level.

In the latter stages of expansion there was a gradual tightening in the market, and a tendency first for the market and then for the Bank Rate to rise. Credit advanced outside the Bank rose sharply, and an increased amount of business came to the Bank as well, as other credit resources became more fully employed.

After the peak, interest rates continued to rise, but credit advances outside the Bank fell off. The Bank's discounts rose, often rapidly, as it fulfilled more or less adequately its role as *dernier resort*. Up to the turning-point the Bank had been gradually coming to share a proportion of the burden of financing expansion; after the turning-point it was meeting a crisis in confidence, an increase in liquidity preferences. The great financial crises of this era occur, almost without exception, after the downturn of the cycle; and in fact they result, largely, from the change in expectations which can be taken, analytically, if not statistically, to define the beginnings of the downturn. The nature of financial crisis, with its hasty liquidations and spreading of panic, accelerated the course of the decline in production and employment. It would, however, be incorrect to regard the financial crises of the nineteenth century as the mechanism by which prosperity was turned to depression.

The question still remains, nevertheless, as to whether the gradual tightening of the money markets, and the rise in interest rates, in the latter stages of expansion, well before financial crisis, played a decisive part in causing a changed view of the future, and the downturn. A full exploration of the mechanics of the upper turning-point is outside our present scope. The evidence suggests, however, that rising interest rates, like rising prices, symbolised an approach to an unstable position of full employment, in the major cycles. They made cost conditions different from those which had been expected when various commitments were undertaken, and they carried psychological overtones as well; and the situation was also being altered by the completion of acts of investment, previously undertaken. From these basic alterations in the complex of forces determining the volume of investment, rather than from a short-term credit shortage, the turning-point appears to occur.[1] Like the supply of labour, or commodities, or fixed capacity, the short-term money supply set a limit to the extent to which expansion could proceed. But that limit was elastic, so far as money was concerned, more elastic, certainly,

[1] For a discussion of the upper turning-point in Britain in 1920, in terms similar to these, see A. C. Pigou, *Aspects of British Economic History, 1918–1925* (1947) pp. 188–97.

than for other factors of production. So long as confidence prevailed the money supply for domestic purposes appears to have been ample. In no cycle, over this period, does inelasticity in the supply of money appear to have been the decisive factor in determining the moment of the downturn.

It is, indeed, possible that the powers held by the Bank of England, in different hands, with different conceptions of central banking function, might have been so manipulated as to alter somewhat the timing and intensity of general cylical fluctuations. In fact, however, playing a consistently passive role, the Bank more or less adequately fulfilled its function as protector of the reserve and as *dernier resort*; but in meeting the 'legitimate demands of trade', as conceived at different points in the cycle, the Bank, and the monetary system as a whole, would appear to have been an essentially negative element in the British trade cycles of this era.

2 The Trade Cycle in Britain, 1790–1850[*]

R. C. O. MATTHEWS

I

WITH the long-delayed publication of the results of the work on British business cycles from 1790 to 1850 carried out under the auspices of the Columbia University Council for Research in the Social Sciences,[1] students are provided with what is perhaps the fullest picture that has yet been made available of the evidence relating to fluctuations in the British economy in any period of its history. The work was carried out under the direction of the late A. D. Gayer between 1936 and 1941. Various obstacles have caused its publication to be delayed till now, and in an addendum to the preface Professor Rostow and Mrs Schwartz, who were Professor Gayer's chief collaborators, briefly review contributions to the field that have appeared since the work was completed.

The book falls into four clearly defined divisions. The first (Vol. I, Part I) is a chronological survey of the period. The second (Vol. I, Parts II and III) presents and discusses two new groups of index numbers. The first of these groups relates to share prices. This section of the work has already been published in part.[2] The indices of share prices are accompanied by a chapter on their institutional background, which contains material on the history of the various types of joint-stock enterprise launched during the period. This chapter has been condensed from a much longer original text which has been microfilmed but is not to be published in full. The second group of index numbers relates to commodity prices. These indices are likely to become the standard ones for use by students in the future, superseding Silberling's index, of which the authors have some pertinent criticisms to make. The third division of the work (Vol. II, Part I) is the one which is likely to have the greatest number of readers. It contains a general theoretical analysis of the nature and causes of the

---

[1] *The Growth and Fluctuation of the British Economy, 1790–1850*, by A. D. Gayer, W. W. Rostow, and A. J. Schwartz, assisted by I. Frank (Oxford University Press, 1953, 2 vols).

[2] A. D. Gayer, A. Jacobson, and I. Frank, 'British Share Prices, 1811–1850', *Review of Economic Statistics* (1940) pp. 78–93.

---

[*] This essay was first published in *Oxford Economic Papers*, VI (1954).

fluctuations chronicled in Vol. I, Part I, followed by a briefer discussion of trend movements over the period. Finally, in Part II of Vol. II, the chief statistical series available are charted and subjected to measures of average cyclical behaviour according to the technique of the National Bureau of Economic Research. The results indicated by these measures are discussed in a running commentary accompanying the charts. The statistical tables on which this part of the work is based are not included, but form part of the ancillary microfilmed material.

The principal purpose of the present article is to describe and criticise in as constructive a manner as possible the leading theses advanced in Part I of Vol. II. These theses are reflected at many points in the discussion of the average measures of cyclical behaviour, and they also influence both the arrangement and the substance of the narrative section of the work. Despite its title, the book is much more concerned with fluctuations than with growth, and we shall pass over without discussion the brief but interesting and, to the present writer, largely acceptable suggestions about trend movements over the period that are put forward in Chapters IV and V of Vol. II, Part I.

Both the narrative section and the theoretical analysis are based on the distinction drawn by the authors between major and minor cycles. The application of this distinction to the period 1790–1850 has become familiar from Professor Rostow's *British Economy of the Nineteenth Century*, which was, of course, written after the present work had been completed. The major cycles are (trough–peak–trough) 1788–92–3, 1797–1800–1, 1808–10–11, 1816–18–19, 1819–25–6, 1832–36–7, and 1842–5–8; the minor cycles are 1793–6–7, 1801–2–3, 1803–6–8, 1811–15–16, 1826–8–9, 1829–31–2, and 1837–9–42.[1] Major and minor cycles thus usually occur alternately, and the major cycles are on the average of longer duration. The contraction phases of both major and minor cycles in most cases last for only one year.

In accordance with the customary National Bureau procedure, the dates given for turning-points are intended to show turning-points in 'general business activity', as emerging from the consensus of statistical data, rather than turning-points in any particular magnitude such as national income. General business activity is not defined. The authors suggest, however, that the ambiguity in this respect is

---

[1] For certain purposes the years 1797–1803 are treated as a single major cycle. A further minor cycle 1846–7–8 is recognised when dealing with monthly as distinct from annual data. The years 1819–21 also partake of some of the characteristics of a minor cycle.

more apparent than real, on the grounds that the consensus of the chief statistical series shows that fluctuations were both pervasive and persistent. This view is, of course, not without its difficulties, and some of these will be discussed presently.

The distinction between major and minor cycles depends partly on the amplitude of the fluctuations involved; but the main basis of the distinction is that major cycles are those which included a period of substantial domestic investment. The authors' thesis is that the minor cycles arose chiefly from fluctuations in exports, whereas the expansion phases of major cycles, although initiated by increases in exports, depended at their later stages on domestic investment. This pattern they consider to have persisted in essentials even during the war period, although at that time capital export to some extent took the place of domestic investment.

Space does not permit discussion of the many interesting points that arise out of the narrative section of the book and out of the average measures of cyclical behaviour. The statistical and other material which the authors have passed in review is very extensive, and some of it is little known. This does not mean that there are not some sources which might have been more fully used,[1] and specialists in particular fields will find a fair number of minor misstatements. The presentation of some of the statistical material is also open to criticism.[2] The narrative is arranged in standardised form, the

[1] In particular, many of the relevant Parliamentary Papers, especially those dealing with money and banking, appear not to have been very carefully worked through. No use is made of the weekly *Circular to Bankers*, which is a mine of information for the second quarter of the nineteenth century.

[2] Certain particular faults may be enumerated for the benefit of those who wish to use the volumes for purposes of reference. (*a*) The figures given in the narrative section as those of the official values of imports, exports, and re-exports are, in fact, not the official values but Schlote's calculations of volume, which are computed on a different basis. (W. Schlote, *Entwicklung und Strukturwandlungen des englischen Aussenhandels vor 1700 bis zur Gegenwart*, 1938; English edition, *British Overseas Trade from 1700 to the 1930s*, trans. W. O. Henderson and W. H. Chaloner, 1952.) These are also the figures that are charted and analysed in Part II of Vol. II. Schlote's estimates and the official values behave broadly similarly, but their movements are not identical. In the case of imports there are 4 years in which the direction of change of the two are different, in the case of exports 2 years; and there are also a good many differences in the relative magnitudes of movements as between different years. In the case of exports, moreover, the difference of base causes the official values to exceed Schlote's index throughout by a factor of about two. (See also below, p. 118, n. 2.) (*b*) The figures given for consumption of raw cotton – regarded as an index of production of cotton textiles – are derived from a variety of sources and are, as the authors remark, unsatisfactory. 'It is claimed that the series was derived by correcting net cotton imports for changes in stocks; but the series seems to partake of the nature of inventory rather than production variations. . . . It is virtually identical, in its short-period movements, with total cotton imports. It is clear from the history of the period that, for example, cotton production did

treatment of each cyclical period consisting of six sections, dealing respectively with prices, foreign trade, investment, industry and agriculture, finance, and labour. This arrangement greatly facilitates reference, but it tends to hamper the development of any sustained argument, and on occasions threatens to degenerate into a scrap-book. Criticism is partially disarmed by the authors' admission (p. 5) that the narrative has deliberately been kept on a more or less 'journalistic' plane so as to make it independent of the more speculative hypotheses contained in Part I of Vol. II. The result is, however, that many of the most interesting and difficult questions about particular periods go unanswered or even unasked.

The measures of cyclical behaviour in Vol. II, Part II, follow the standard National Bureau technique, as described at length in A. F. Burns and W. C. Mitchell's *Measuring Business Cycles* and conveniently summarised in Chapter 3 of Mitchell's posthumous *What Happens during Business Cycles*.[1] This technique has been subjected to various criticisms in the past, and the results it yields certainly require to be handled with great caution; but much that is interesting emerges. For certain selected series separate measures are given for major and minor cycles, and it would have been interesting to see this done on a larger scale. Since the minor cycles are to be regarded from certain points of view as part of the contraction phase of the preceding major cycles, it might also have been valuable for some measures to have been given on the basis of one major plus one minor cycle as the cyclical unit – as it would have been to have had separate measures of average cyclical behaviour during the war and during the rest of the period.

The arrangement of the remainder of this article is as follows. Section II contains a general discussion of the behaviour of invest-

---

not fluctuate from 1819 to 1826 in the highly irregular manner that the cotton consumption series would indicate' (pp. 700–1). The figures in T. Ellison's *Cotton Trade of Great Britain* (1886), which cover the years after 1811, are much more plausible than those which the authors have used, and might with advantage have been given instead. (*c*) The so-called 'Kondratieff index of money wages in the textile industry' is merely G. H. Wood's index of money wages in the cotton industry, adjusted during the Bank Restriction period by a gold conversion factor that is likely to mislead the unwary. Wood's figures (*History of Wages in the Cotton Trade*, 1910) are themselves a weighted average of two series relating respectively to the wages of factory operatives and of hand-loom weavers, and the diminishing weight accorded to hand-loom weavers' wages as the period advances contributes substantially to the upward trend of the composite series. It would surely have been better to have given separately Wood's two series, the movements of which are largely dissimilar.

[1] A brief description of part of the National Bureau's technique of measurement is given below, p. 116, n. 1.

ment, which, as has been said, provides the criterion of major cycles as defined by the authors. Section III concerns certain offsets to investment which were of importance especially, though not exclusively, during the war period. Section IV is devoted to foreign trade. Foremost among the issues which we are passing over for reasons of space are those that relate to monetary aspects of fluctuations and their connection with the balance of payments.

II

It may be well to begin by describing briefly the evidence available on investment. Much the most important statistical series is that recording the number of bricks produced annually, a series which starts in 1785 and does not cease until the repeal of the duty on bricks in 1850. From 1829 to 1849 (and to a limited degree for part of the earlier period) figures of brick production are available on a regional basis, but these regional series are not used in the present work. Further evidence on the level of building activity comes from the figures on timber imports, which move in a pattern broadly similar to that of the brick index. Almost the only other continuous and unambiguous series relating to investment is that recording the tonnage of new ships constructed annually. The remaining evidence, though important, is heterogeneous. We have particulars of the annual number of private Acts of Parliament sanctioning the construction of railways, canals, and various other public utilities, and the amount of capital authorised in each case; but the proportion of the sums authorised that was actually spent and the timing of this expenditure are not always easy to ascertain. Much the same applies to the inferences that may be drawn about investment in agriculture from the number of bills of enclosure. Evidence on the number of joint-stock company prospectuses issued exists for certain years and may be compared with the figures of private Acts of Parliament. Finally we have a good deal of evidence which is non-continuous or non-quantitative or both on investment in manufacturing industry and other branches of the economy. It will be seen that the evidence is thus very heterogeneous and, such as it is, is biased in favour of that part of investment consisting of construction.

The account given by the authors of the time pattern of investment and the designation of particular cycles as major and minor are based chiefly on the brick index, but the other measures of investment quoted give broadly consistent results. Brick production was low or declining during each of the minor cycles, with the exception of 1837–42, and, less clearly, 1801–8 (years during which the cyclical pattern as a whole is rather confused). It rose during every major cycle, with a marked tendency to lag at both upper and lower turning-points behind other indicators of the level of activity. In the case of contraction phases limited to one year in duration, this lag sometimes appears as a net rise during the contraction phase. The lag at the lower turning-point is one of the considerations that gives rise to the thesis that major expansions were *initiated* by causes outside the sphere of investment, such as increases in exports.

Most of the quantitative evidence on investment relates, as has been seen, to building and public utilities. The theoretical treatment of fluctuations in investment in Vol. II, Part I, of the work is, however, cast mainly in terms of manufacturing industry. This theory will now be described.

It is based in essence on two concepts: the gestation period of investment and the secular growth of demand. Let us start at the beginning of the expansion phase of a major cycle. There is excess capacity, and the time is not yet ripe for a renewal of domestic investment. A lapse of time is necessary before investment will rise, partly in order for demand to catch up with the existing level of capacity, partly because a decent level of profits will have to be maintained for some while before entrepreneurs can be persuaded to take a sufficiently optimistic view of the future to engage in long-term commitments, and partly because investment cannot be done unless entrepreneurs and investors have accumulated sufficient capital to finance it.[1] The catching-up process is going on the whole time on account of the secular growth of demand; and the rise in profits, which is the second necessary condition, is brought about by the increase in exports which is the characteristic of the early stages of major expansions. (Whether the authors regard this increase in exports as something distinct from the secular growth in demand or merely as part of it is not entirely clear.[2]) Other favourable factors may also make a contribution, such as good harvests, which were in fact present at the beginning of almost all major expansions. At length the various conditions are satisfied which are necessary for a large amount of investment to be set on foot, and the expansion moves into its second and culminating stage. Now additions to capacity must, for technical reasons, be made in fairly large indivisible units, and the investment involved has an appreciable gestation period. All firms are operating under the influence of broadly

---

[1] The most obvious application of this is to investment financed out of ploughed-back profits; but it is relevant also to projects like railways, financed by public subscription, since investors commonly had to go on paying calls on shares for quite a long time after buying them, and so would not be ready for some while after one boom to assume fresh obligations and so help start another.

[2] See below, p. 126.

similar stimuli, and the working of competition thus causes capacity to be expanded beyond that justified by the current level of demand. It is this which keeps investment low in the years after the major peak. However, this is not what brings about the recession in the first place. The authors say:

> The upper turning-point came, in fact, before all the acts of new investment were complete; and the level of employment in several minor cycles was supported by the completion of projects inaugurated in the preceding boom. Our theory of the upper turning-point does not depend, then, on a fall of profits brought about by the actual introduction of new equipment; although knowledge of the scale of investment in certain lines could, and did, affect expectations of profit from further investment, even though the investments already undertaken were not yet in full operation. *Our view is dependent on this latter factor combined with the consequences for costs of relatively full employment, partially created by the domestic industrial investment. . . .*[1]

The minor cycle that follows on the major cycle is essentially part of the contraction phase of the latter, and its upswing, such as it is, is based on factors other than domestic investment. When the minor contraction phase is completed, a new major expansion begins, and we are back to the beginning again.

This outline statement of the theory is capable of modification in various respects to suit individual cycles. It will have been observed, for example, that fluctuations in the level of final demand are not essential to the explanation of fluctuations in investment just described; but the authors are perfectly willing to concede that some sort of multiplier-accelerator interaction was at work as well and that the high level of consumers' demand in the boom helped to account for the high level of investment then, and conversely in the slump. Likewise although monetary stringency is not regarded as the basic cause of the upper turning-point, it is freely admitted that rises in interest rates were a regular feature of these periods and that they may have contributed to a greater or less degree to bringing the boom to an end on various occasions.

Apart from possible disagreements about matters of emphasis, on which the authors are quite undogmatic, certain more fundamental difficulties about this theory suggest themselves.

1. Reference to the gestation period makes it easy to understand why investment should have lagged behind the decisions giving rise

[1] p. 557. Italics added.

to it. But the fact that investment (as measured chiefly but not exclusively by the brick index) should have continued to rise in the early stages of the recession and should even sometimes have risen during the whole of the contraction phase of the major cycle raises a difficulty which the authors appear not to have sufficiently considered. If investment expenditure continues to rise after the peak, what is it that does decline at the beginning of the recession? What is the recession a recession of? A decline in investment decisions does not lead to a recession in the normal sense of the term until the decisions come to be translated into action. And if the recession originates outside the sphere of investment, some revision in the theory would appear to be required.

2. The thesis that investment decisions decline partly because entrepreneurs foresee that the current rate of construction will presently bring into existence an excessive amount of capacity in the industry is obviously a plausible one, even though the authors do not cite much evidence that can be considered to support it directly. That expectations should to some degree operate in this way may perhaps be taken as sufficiently obvious to make specific evidence to that effect unnecessary. (That this factor was the *decisive* one at the upper turning-point is, of course, not obvious in this sense.) But the same cannot be said of the suggestion that investment decisions were checked by rising costs attributable to the approach to full employment. As far as I have been able to discover, this suggestion as applied to 1790–1850 is a piece of pure theorising, unsupported by any evidence whatever.[1]

The authors' treatment of this subject is also unsatisfactory on other grounds. In the first place, it may be questioned whether the concept of full employment is really a very helpful one as applied to an economy such as Britain's in the early nineteenth century, when the chief occupations were agriculture and domestic service, and the labour force of the leading manufacturing industry consisted largely of juveniles.[2] In the second place, although the term 'full employ-

---

[1] Unless one considers as such the rise usually shown in the later stages of major expansions by the available price indices, which in any case relate mainly to the prices of food and raw materials and are not very relevant to the cost of investment.

[2] An interesting example of the difficulties involved in the concept of full employment arises from some little-known statistics which the authors have unearthed from a Parliamentary Paper of 1890–1 (1890–1, xcii), pp. 522–3. These figures show the proportion of unemployed to total members of the Friendly Society of Ironfounders of England, Ireland, and Wales, beginning with the year 1831. The movements in this proportion show a very close negative conformity to the normally accepted dates of business cycles, as also do those in payments by the Society for unemployment benefit (also, surprisingly, for sick benefit). On looking up the reference one finds that it also contains figures for the total membership of the

ment' is often on the authors' lips, especially in the narrative section of the book, there seems to be some lack of clarity in their minds as to what is the factor of production involved. At some points they appear to have in mind the full employment of capacity – yet on their own account it is the approach to this situation which *starts* investment booms. At other times they talk as if all factors of production – labour, capacity, and even monetary facilities – were likely to approach full employment at the same time – a position not easy to defend theoretically. The best case in *a priori* terms could be made for the supposition that full employment either of capacity or of labour in the investment-goods industries was the bottleneck – for example, the capital equipment of textile machinery manufacturers, or the labour force attached to the building industry. This, however, is not made clear, and in any case, as has been said, it remains at best no more than an interesting conjecture unsupported by evidence.

3. The theory is stated chiefly with reference to investment in manufacturing industry. It can, however, evidently be applied in principle to investment in such lines as housebuilding and shipbuilding. The authors do not attempt to apply it to investment in agriculture, which was an important item during the war period. The principal factor here was clearly the price of wheat, which in turn depended on harvests and the availability of foreign supplies.[1] More important, however, is the question to what extent the theory is applicable to investment in the transport industries. Canal construction played a leading part in the boom of the 1790s; railway building was of great importance in 1836 and absolutely dominant in 1845. In the case of railways, a national network was built up from virtually nothing in the course of little more than a decade, and while the

---

Society, which the authors do not quote. There are no doubt certain objections to taking the Society's membership as indicative of the total number of workers attached to the industry; but if they are taken as an approximate indication of this, the unemployment proportion appears on several occasions in rather a different light. A notable instance is in 1838–40. In these years the number and proportion of unemployed men were much higher than in the general peak year 1836; but the rise in membership in the meanwhile had been so great that the number of employed members of the Society was much higher also, not declining substantially till 1841. It is interesting to compare this with the rather similar picture shown by the statistics relating to active and idle blast-furnaces in the industry at the same period; see R. C. O. Matthews, *A Study in Trade-Cycle History: Economic Fluctuations in Great Britain, 1833–42*, pp. 158–9.

[1] It is possibly true that the extension of agricultural capacity undertaken in years of high prices during the war influenced prices even in the short run, and that the significance of this has often been underrated. But harvest fluctuations remained the dominant factor.

development of the canal system was a more gradual process, it was of the same innovatory nature. It follows therefore that in both cases the concept of the rate of investment being governed by the secular rate of growth of demand is inapplicable. It is most implausible to maintain that the principal reason for the delay between the railway promotion booms of 1836 and 1845 was that time had to elapse before traffic on the older lines became sufficient to justify building new ones, and one could not even begin to apply the theory to the first railway boom. In its chief features, therefore, the theory propounded by the authors is inapplicable to these highly important branches of investment, although the subsidiary parts of the theory – those relating to finance and to confidence – remain broadly relevant.

4. There are certain special problems about the behaviour of investment during the war. These bring into some doubt the validity of the distinction between major and minor cycles as applied to that time. This question is discussed later (section III). For the present our discussion will be confined mainly to the years of peace.

In the light of these criticisms, it must be concluded that the theory in its simple form is open to serious objections. It must be said in fairness, however, that, particularly in their summing-up (pp. 571–6), the authors do qualify the theory by reference to a wide range of complicating factors. Many of the points discussed in the following pages are touched on with greater or less emphasis at various stages in the book. It may be useful, however, to try to bring some of the more important factors into clearer perspective.

Perhaps the most important deficiency of the theoretical statement described is its insufficient emphasis on the speculative character of major booms in this period. This character is seen in the invariable tendency of peace-time major expansions to culminate in what contemporaries called 'manias'. These manias were closely connected with the institution of the joint-stock company, the development of which during the period left an important imprint on the character of business fluctuations. Speculation in the shares of newly formed joint-stock companies played a part in British business cycles at this period somewhat similar to that played in the United States then and later by speculation in real estate. The violent outbursts of joint-stock company promotion in 1792, 1807, 1825, 1836, and 1845 cannot be explained entirely with reference to objective calculations of profit in the enterprises proposed. At least as important were, in the promoters' minds, the desire for commissions and profit by the sale of shares at a premium, and, in the minds of investors, the desire for quick gains by the resale of shares on a rising market. The speculative nature of the whole proceeding was enhanced by the novel and untried character of the undertakings usually canvassed. The development of a boom of this sort was essentially dependent on the creation of a general expectation that the market was rising; once under way it proceeded by its own momentum. Naturally such an expectation was in the normal way unlikely to take hold unless trade was in a generally prosperous state to start with. For this reason speculative manias usually came towards the end of a period of business expansion, and thereby contributed to the concentration of investment in the later stages of major expansions. But the basis of the mania remained largely irrational, and the nature of the schemes canvassed was governed rather by the type of enterprise in which the joint-stock principle was acceptable than by consideration of which sectors of industry had been particularly favoured by any preceding business expansion.[1] Many of the joint-stock companies so begun did not, it is true, ever lead to the creation of any physical capital; yet those that did were sufficient to account for a large part of the nation's railway and canal network, and much else besides.

The part played by pure speculation at the culmination of the upswing helps to explain many of the features of cyclical fluctuation which appear from the evidence collected by Professor Gayer and his associates, including some of the features that are not satisfactorily explained by their own simplified model. In particular it helps to explain the nature of the upper turning-point and the difficulty about the lag of the brick index and other indicators of investment at that stage. Any purely speculative movement is a highly unstable phenomenon, liable to be halted by a comparatively slight obstacle like a small rise in interest rates and incapable of avoiding collapse when once a halt has occurred. Tooke's admirable description of events in 1825 could be applied with only slight modifications to 1836 and 1845 as well:

> The recoil from speculations in loans and shares . . . was inevitable. The process by which the fall took place is simple and obvious: As regarded the schemes, a more accurate appreciation of a greater outlay, and of smaller returns, than had been before anticipated; and a limitation of the demand for investment in

[1] An extreme example of this may be seen in the years 1807–8, when an outburst of a series of 'new projects of various kinds, such as canals, bridges, fire offices, breweries, distilleries and many other descriptions of joint-stock companies' (T. Tooke, *History of Prices*, vol. i, pp. 277–8) apparently owed its origin largely to the speculative feeling engendered by the rise in import prices brought about by the development of the war!

them, to such persons only as could afford to depend upon remote contingencies for an income, where any income was to be expected above all, a general deficiency of means among the subscribers to pay up the succeeding instalments, as they had relied for the most part upon a continued rise, to enable them to realise a profit before another instalment should be called for, or upon the same facility as had before existed, of raising money for the purpose at a low rate of interest. ... A pause naturally ensued: and, under such circumstances, a pause is generally fatal to projects that do not proceed on solid grounds.[1]

Readers of Schumpeter's *Business Cycles* will be familiar with the distinction Schumpeter draws between the recession and the depression.[2] The recession is the contraction phase of the 'primary wave', and is the period during which are felt the logical consequences of the preceding boom in innovatory investment. National income declines as investment projects come to completion, and older firms are driven to bankruptcy by the lowering of prices which the expansion of capacity has brought about. The depression, which immediately follows on the recession, is the contraction phase of the 'secondary wave'. It reflects the reaction from the non-innovatory commitments which are likely to have been irrationally – or at least optimistically – undertaken during the boom and which can be supported only as long as boom conditions continue. The magnitude of the secondary contraction depends on the extent and character of these commitments and on the amount of damage done to expectations and commercial confidence by the price falls and business failures (including failures of banks) in the recession phase. Now the course of events at the upper turning-points of many of the major cycles in the period under discussion may perhaps best be summarised by saying that the speculative character of the concluding stages of the boom caused a severe secondary contraction, in Schumpeter's sense, to come before or, at least, not later than the primary contraction. The more extreme speculative manifestations of the boom – often including some elements of criminal fraud – bred their own reaction before investment had proceeded to the point where the increase in the capacity had become really damaging to profits. An important part in this secondary contraction – as in the preceding mania and subsequent minor recovery – lay in the sphere of foreign trade; this aspect of the matter will be considered later on. Falls in prices of shares and commodities led to bankruptcies and discredit, bringing with them on some occasions widespread bank

[1] T. Tooke, *History of Prices*, vol. II, pp. 158–9.
[2] J. A. Schumpeter, *Business Cycles* (1939) vol. I, pp. 145–61.

failures. This was the essence of such crisis years as 1826 and 1837. The advent of this secondary contraction itself brought about a downward revision of investment decisions in sectors of the economy that were not yet feeling any great pressure on profits from previous increases in investment.

The expansion phase of the ensuing minor cycle consisted essentially of recovery from the extremes of discredit that prevailed at the trough of the secondary contraction. No increase in investment in fixed capital was as yet normally forthcoming, since the effects of the *primary* contraction were felt in their full force throughout the length of the minor cycle. Investment planned during the mania period continued to be carried out after the mania had come to an end, and the burden of this became plain as soon as the dust raised by the crisis had settled. The precise pattern of the minor cycle depended largely on the gestation period of the investment planned during the preceding major boom. Thus the investment preponderating in 1825 was apparently of short gestation period, and although the immediate cause of the recession was of a 'secondary' nature, it was not long before the full effects of the primary contraction were also felt. Hence a bottom was reached as early as 1826, and after some recovery in 1827 the years 1828–32 were not marked by any conspicuous further deterioration. In 1836, on the other hand, the investment projected (largely railways) was of much longer gestation period. Important categories of investment continued to rise during the minor expansion after 1837, and the full force of the primary contraction was not felt until 1841–2. The years 1820–1 were broadly comparable to 1827–32, and 1846–8 to 1837–42.

It should not, of course, be supposed that the speculative forces described above were the only or even necessarily the most important cause of fluctuations in investment. The factors affecting the level of investment were numerous and diverse, and there are many unsolved problems relating to particular industries and periods. In the case of the beginnings of the railway boom of the 1830s, I have suggested elsewhere[1] that the Schumpeterian concept of the clustering of innovations is fairly exactly applicable. Likewise the great railway boom of the 1840s can certainly not be treated exclusively in terms of speculation, although the most appropriate theoretical categories in which to describe it are not altogether obvious. In many branches of investment the interaction of an upward trend in demand and a gestation period, as described in the Columbia authors' model, was no doubt of paramount or at least substantial importance. Fluctuations in housebuilding, for example, lend them-

[1] Matthews, *Study in Trade-Cycle History*, pp. 108–10, 204–5.

selves well to analysis in these terms, though one might add that there is evidence that the industry was also a good deal influenced by fluctuations in the rate of townwards migrations of labour. At the same time our knowledge of the structure of the building industry makes it difficult not to believe that in the periods of most intensive activity, like 1825, prospects of high rents were not often less to the fore in the minds of builders than the speculative hope of quick sale on a temporarily rising market. Manufacturing industry was not yet normally a field of joint-stock enterprise and on that account was, like housebuilding, less directly affected by manias than was investment in transport and public utilities. Fluctuations in investment in the cotton industry, for example, are no doubt largely to be explained in terms of the authors' model, though a more explicit recognition of the innovatory element of investment in this as in other industries (such as iron) might call for certain modifications in the model. Yet in this case, too, the mania element cannot be entirely neglected, if only because there is evidence that investment in manufacturing industry, as also in trade, was on a number of occasions (1792, 1825, 1836) stimulated to an important degree by the mushroom growth of banks and the relaxation of conventional standards of caution on the part of existing banks that were a feature of mania periods.

III

Reference has been made to the special problems raised by the behaviour of investment during the war period. Throughout the war the Government's expenditure exceeded its revenue by a large though fluctuating margin. Calculations can be made on the lines indicated by Professor Morgan[1] to show which parts of the Government's deficit can be reckoned to have had a direct inflationary impact on the British economy (excluding the effects of expenditure by the Government abroad in stimulating exports, which can better be taken account of along with other factors affecting exports). The movements in the series which result from such calculations are very substantial, and although Professor Gayer and his collaborators do make regular allusion to the figures of the excess of Government expenditure over Government revenue, they hardly appear to give the matter sufficient weight. In their view the chief significance of Government deficit spending during the war lay in the encouragement given to exports by military expenditure abroad and loans to allies. Under the influence of this encouragement, and also that of

[1] E. V. Morgan, *The Theory and Practice of Central Banking, 1797–1913* (1943) pp. 32–34.

private capital export, exports, as they see it, played a larger part relatively to domestic investment in the major cycles of the war than in later major cycles. Yet Professor Morgan's calculations show that the effect of Government deficit spending at home must also have been very great, and the movements involved are often larger than those in exports.[1]

Now the interesting thing is that during the war there is, on the one hand, a marked direct correlation between fluctuations in the size of the Government's deficit and fluctuations in the yield on Consols, and, on the other hand, a marked inverse correlation between these two and the brick index (with a tendency for the brick index to lag by about a year). The steep decline in brick production in the mid-1790s and in 1811–14 coincided with steep rises in Government deficit spending and Consol yields, while the years from 1798 to 1810, during which brick production had a strong upward trend, were a period over which the Government's revenue increased more rapidly than its expenditure and Consol yields tended to fall.

Two related issues are involved. In the first place, in what sense is it legitimate to describe such periods as 1793–6 and 1811–14 as merely minor expansions? They were characterised by low and declining levels of private investment, but also by mountainous increases in the Government's deficit. Likewise can we be sure that 1810 really deserved the name of major boom, in view of the curtailment of consumption that must have been involved by the Government's belated success in raising taxation to the level where it at last approximately equalled the enormous amount of the Government's current account expenditure? Was not what was involved a switch in productive resources from one use to another rather than a variation in the degree of utilisation of productive resources?

It may be remarked in parentheses that a similar problem of interpretation arises in other connections with regard to the war period. Different sectors of the economy often enjoyed very different fortunes at the same time. The magnitude of fluctuations in corn prices brought about tremendous shifts in real income from one class to another, and the prosperous condition of agriculture that stimulated agricultural investment in the years of high corn prices was not prosperity for the country in the sense normally understood. Rises in the prices of imports and re-exports caused by real or anticipated

---

[1] In any systematic study of the effects of the war on the level of effective demand, account would, of course, have to be taken not merely of fluctuations in the Government's deficit but also of fluctuations in the absolute amount of its expenditure.

war-time shortages had favourable effects on profits and confidence amongst merchants and hence perhaps in City circles generally, but rising import prices were the reverse of beneficial to the consumer. Prices of different classes of goods, moreover, as Tooke delighted to point out,[1] often moved in opposite directions according to the effect of the war on the conditions under which they were supplied or demanded. With so many magnitudes moving diversely, the concept of 'the general level of business activity' (and hence of peaks or troughs in same) is evidently one to be used with great caution. In addition to the periods mentioned in the last paragraph, the years 1799–1802 and 1807 may be quoted as examples of times when the course of events in different sectors of the economy was more than usually diverse. The task of marking off the dates of peaks and troughs in such cases and of distinguishing between major and minor cycles consists essentially of balancing one thing quantitatively against another – a purpose for which the available evidence is peculiarly ill-adapted. For this reason doubts may be entertained whether, if we had figures for money national income – let alone real national income – they would during the war period always conform to the reference peaks and troughs marked by the authors.

The issue just discussed concerned the *nature* of fluctuations during the war; the other related issue concerns the *causes* of fluctuations in investment at that time. It is natural to ask whether the low level of investment in the so-called minor cycles of the war was not at least as much referable to competition for resources brought about by Government expenditure as it was to the overhang of excess capacity from the previous major boom. In their treatment of trends the authors give full weight to this,[2] but they seem to regard it as less important from the short-period point of view.[3]

---

[1] See, for example, *History of Prices*, vol. 1, pp. 189–90, 235, 344–5.

[2] The point is, of course, similar to the idea familiar in Professor Rostow's later writings and elsewhere that, particularly in the period 1870–1914, capital export and domestic investment stood in a competitive rather than a complementary relation to each other *as between* different cycles (or longer periods), though not necessarily *within* cycles.

[3] Those who are sceptical about the meaningfulness of trend drawing may be amused to recall that, while the Columbia authors find no upward trend in brick production during the war years, Professor Shannon, in his original article on the brick index ('Bricks – a Trade Index', *Economica*, 1934, pp. 300–18), found a scarcely less rapid upward trend for the war period than for 1815–49. He referred in corroboration to evidence from Mrs George's *London Life in the Eighteenth Century* (1930 ed., pp. 79–80) to the effect that the Napoleonic Wars after 1802 constituted a departure from the experience of previous wars by being accompanied by vigorous activity in the building trades – the contrast being explained with reference to the restriction of cash payments.

Further study is clearly needed of the whole question of the rela-tion between fiscal policy, monetary policy, and private investment during the war period.[1] But whatever the exact mechanism involved, if it is agreed that the high level of Government spending did some-how inhibit private investment, presumably chiefly through lessen-ing the availability of finance, the question arises why a similar check was not present in ordinary commercial booms in peace-time. If, when Government deficit spending rose, the result was not an especially violent boom – for the evidence does not suggest that the periods of highest Government war deficit were marked by more than moderately high business activity – but instead was, at least in part, a curtailment of private investment, why was it that increases in private investment in peace-time[2] were not likewise halted by shortage of funds before they had brought about a real boom? Evidently there can be no simple answer to such a question, but it may be suggested that broadly the reason was that increases in private investment were able to a large degree to create their own finance by breeding an atmosphere of confidence conducive to an expansion of credit media of all sorts. Government demands for credit did not evoke any such response; when the Government required to raise particularly large loans from the public or from the Bank of England to pay for the war, business confidence was not thereby enhanced but rather the reverse.

But there was nothing automatic about the availability of funds for private investment, and there is reason to believe that, particu-larly in the case of investment expenditure carried out during periods when confidence was not at its peak, this expenditure was partly at the expense of consumption, just as during the war Govern-ment expenditure was partly at the expense of private expenditure even when it was not paid for out of taxation.

A case can be made for this view in connection with the aftermath of several booms, notably 1792 and 1836; but much the most import-ant case in point is the great railway boom of the 1840s. The Colum-bia authors accept without question 1845 as the date when the boom of the 1840s reached its peak, but add (p. 318): 'There is little doubt

---

[1] For example, to what extent should the fall in interest rates between 1798 and 1802 be attributed to greater monetary ease brought about by the Bank Restriction, and to what extent should it be attributed to the greater success of the Government in balancing its budget in these years? This is important in so far as the contrast between the fall in private investment in 1793–8 and its rise in 1798–1803 was caused by interest-rate movements rather than by a normal cyclical fluctuation in the marginal efficiency of capital following upon the boom of 1792.

[2] And also in 1798–1801, when the Government deficit was still very large, though tending to decline.

that railway construction continued for a considerable period after the flotation bubble had burst. The general decline induced by a falling off in the export trade in 1845 was thus considerably cushioned'. In the light of the statistics, this is a notable understatement. The amount of money raised and spent by railway companies was more than £20 million higher in 1846 than in 1845, and there was a further rise of £3 million in 1847.[1] To indicate the orders of magnitude, the fall in the value of exports in 1846 amounted to less than £2½ million, followed by a rise of £1 million in 1847. On the face of it, therefore, it is more than a little anomalous to regard 1846 and 1847 as recession years. The undoubted evidence of declining activity in many sectors of the economy in these years can surely be made intelligible only if one accepts Newmarch's view (not mentioned by the authors) that railway building was paid for largely at the expense of consumption on the part of those who had bought railway shares for a small deposit during the mania period and were then obliged to pay up repeated calls.[2, 3]

The arguments of the last few pages have tended to cast some doubt on the validity of the concept of the general level of business activity, especially though not exclusively as applied to the war years, since there is good reason to believe that on certain occasions the movements of different parts of the national income diverged to an important extent. And in this connection it should also be borne in mind that even in years when the overall level of effective demand did unquestionably fall, the effect on the volume of production was probably often no worse than to cause a slackening in rate of growth,

[1] For the figures (not quoted by the authors) see Tooke, *History of Prices*, vol. v, p. 352.

[2] It is probable that the same sort of thing took place on a smaller scale after the canal boom of 1792–3 and the railway boom of 1836. In the former case the difficulty of raising funds was aggravated by the increase in the general level of costs and prices brought about by the war in the interval between the mania period and the completion of the schemes then initiated.

[3] This seems much more plausible than the line adopted by *The Economist* and other contemporaries, and accepted by the Columbia authors, that the finance of railway building by converting 'floating capital' into 'fixed capital' starved the rest of industry of credit. The theoretical basis for this is extremely dubious, and the comparison of discount rates and calls on railway share capital by months does not support the statement that 'it was the progressive calling up of short-term funds, earlier committed to the railways, that impoverished the money market' (p. 335). The process of railway finance effected a transfer of loanable funds from the country banks to the London money market rather than a reduction in the total supply of loanable funds. Cf. E. V. Morgan, 'Railway Investment, Bank of England Policy and Interest Rates, 1844–8', *Economic Journal* (*Economic History*) (1940) pp. 331–6; idem, *Theory and Practice of Central Banking, 1797–1913*, pp. 152–5; C. N. Ward-Perkins, 'The Commercial Crisis of 1847', *Oxford Economic Papers* (Jan 1950) pp. 84–7.

since in many branches of manufacturing industry the downwards inelasticity of supply was very pronounced. This applies particularly to the latter part of the period.[1]

IV

The important place assigned by the authors to exports, both in their narrative and in their analysis, has already been mentioned. Exports were, in their view, one of the two chief sources of fluctuations in the economy (the other being domestic investment). They were, it is claimed, the most important dynamic force in starting off the major expansions, preparing the way there for the subsequent increase in domestic investment; and their fluctuations caused, and indeed to a large extent comprised, the fluctuations designated as minor cycles. The forces governing the short-run behaviour of exports were, the authors point out, numerous and complicated. Of these forces, two are singled out as having the greatest and most general significance. These are, first, changes in the amount of British capital export, and, secondly, fluctuations in foreign demand caused either by inventory movements or by autonomous fluctuations in the incomes of foreign consumers. As the authors point out, exports at this period consisted very largely of textiles, and investment goods like iron accounted for only a small proportion of the total.

On first consideration of these views, there are two doubts that come to mind. In the first place there is an obvious danger of the historian of this period being biased in the direction of overrating the importance of exports, since the statistical evidence on them is so much more ample than that relating to production for the home market. In the second place the authors' neglect of imports both in their theoretical statement and in their treatment of particular periods must be considered a distinct fault. The consequences of large imports in bringing about drains on the Bank of England's bullion reserve and so raising interest rates are ably discussed, but it is nowhere made clear that movements in imports have a direct effect on income levels through the foreign trade multiplier exactly analogous to those caused by movements in exports. It will not do to say without qualification that a rise in exports was responsible for a given improvement in business activity, if we find, as we often do, that it was accompanied by a not smaller increase in the value of imports; in such circumstances the increase in exports can, on the face of it, at least not have been the only inflationary factor at work.[2]

---

[1] See below, p. 121.

[2] This statement is subject to qualification in so far as the recorded movement in imports was attributable to fluctuations in the level of stocks rather than to fluctuations in the amount consumed. This point is discussed at length below.

For this reason it will be well in our ensuing discussion of the part played by foreign trade to take both sides of the balance in turn, beginning with imports.

The authors' conclusions about foreign trade are heavily dependent on the average cyclical behaviour of exports, imports, and their different components, as revealed by the National Bureau measures given in Part II of Vol. II. The technique of measurement is the standard one devised by the National Bureau, with certain simplifications and omissions called for by the annual rather than monthly or quarterly basis of most of the series analysed.[1] The standard National Bureau technique divides the cycle into nine stages from trough to trough; with annual data only five are used, these being designated, however, I, III, V, VII, and IX.[2] Stage IX of one cycle is identical with stage I of the subsequent one.

Imports

The behaviour of imports does not at first sight present any features of great note. The following are the figures given by the authors of the average monthly rates of change of the value and volume of imports (reckoned as a percentage of the cycle average) between the different stages of the cycle.[3] (Figures in parentheses represent the average deviation from the average.)

	I–III	III–V	V–VII	VII–IX
Volume	+0·7 (0·5)	+0·7 (0·6)	−1·0 (1·0)	−1·1 (1·0)
Value	+0·5 (0·8)	+0·8 (1·3)	−1·7 (1·6)	−1·7 (1·6)

[1] The technique may be briefly summarised for the benefit of readers unfamiliar with it. Reference dates are first established for peaks and troughs in general business activity. Each series is broken up into segments on the basis of these reference dates, and the seasonally adjusted data within each segment are expressed in terms of 'cycle-relatives', i.e. as percentages of their average value over the given reference-cycle. Each reference-cycle is then divided into nine stages, and an average is computed of the cycle-relatives in the different reference-cycles at each of these stages. The result gives the reference-cycle pattern. Calculation is also made of 'specific-cycle' measures on exactly similar lines, the time unit here being, instead of reference-cycles, cycles in the individual series considered in isolation. The measures of average behaviour over reference-cycles and specific-cycles are accompanied by measures of the average deviation from the average at each of the nine stages, and by measures of conformity, which relate to the proportion of all reference-cycles to which the series in question is found to respond.

[2] In practice there are often only four really distinct stages, since in the numerous one-year contraction phases figures for stage VII are obtained by interpolation.

[3] The figures for import values used by the authors are Schlote's, since their work was completed before the publication of Imlah's more elaborate calculations on the subject. Schlote's and Imlah's series on the whole behave very similarly, though occasional differences of substance are to be found.

The authors call attention to the increased rate of growth of values between stages III and V as having a bearing on the regular tendency for the balance of payments to become adverse towards the end of the boom, and suggest that, compared with exports (see below), the demand for imports does not seem to have been too much checked by the rise in prices that might be expected to occur in III–V.

Reference to prices raises the first puzzle about imports. The rate of growth of values shown above increases appreciably in III–V, but that of volume does not. Comparison of the figures yields the implication that import prices on the average fell in I–III and rose in III–V. But on turning to the authors' own new index of prices of imported commodities, we find the following figures of average monthly rate of change:[1]

I–III	III–V	V–VII	VII–IX
0·0 (0·4)	−0·1 (0·4)	−0·3 (0·5)	−0·3 (0·6)

So far from import prices turning up in III–V after a decline in I–III, they remain constant in I–III and actually fall slightly in III–V.[2] It is not clear what conclusion is to be drawn from this surprising inconsistency (not commented upon by the authors) beyond the obvious one that National Bureau average measures of cyclical behaviour are slippery things to handle, especially when the deviations from the average are large. The presence of some fault in Schlote's estimates of values may perhaps be indicated. It seems probable that one important source of the trouble lies in the omission of corn from the commodities represented in the import price index, corn being treated as a domestic commodity in the construction of the price indices. Both the price of wheat and the quantity of wheat imports on the average rose steeply in III–V. The average monthly rates of movement of the quantity of wheat imports over business cycles are as follows:

---

[1] The figures quoted relate to the movement of the index in its annual form. The monthly rates of movement of the series in its monthly form are as follows:

I–II	II–III	III–IV	IV–V
+0·4 (0·7)	+0·3 (0·6)	−0·1 (0·4)	+0·1 (0·7)

V–VI	VI–VII	VII–VIII	VIII–IX
−0·3 (0·7)	−0·7 (0·9)	−0·7 (0·6)	+0·1 (0·7)

[2] The import price index is not, of course, derived by dividing volume into value, which would make this result impossible, but is an index of prices of individual imported commodities with constant weights.

I–III	III–V	V–VII	VII–IX
−0·2 (3·9)	+2·6 (4·9)	−1·4 (6·9)	−2·5 (6·7)

Since wheat imports, on account of their dependence on harvests, must be regarded as on a different footing from the generality of imports, one is led on by these reflections to wonder how the average measures of cyclical behaviour of imports would be affected if corn imports were subtracted from the total. This calculation is not performed by the authors.[1] It is evident, however, that in such a calculation the acceleration in the rate of growth of import values in III–V would be reduced and might disappear, and that the rate of growth of volume might be found to show some slight deceleration in III–V. In any case it becomes clear that one must not think of accelerated growth in value in III–V as the *typical* behaviour of imported commodities.

The authors' explanation of the cyclical behaviour of wheat imports – to digress for a moment to this important subject – is a sensible one. As they point out, the large deviations from the average in the figures quoted above show that no sweeping general conclusions can be drawn.[2] In so far as the movement is significant, one should probably think of the direction of causation proceeding from corn imports to the state of trade rather than the other way round.

---

[1] The statistics available to the authors would not have enabled this calculation to be made for values, but it could have been done for volumes. In this connection a complaint is in order about the way in which statistics of corn imports are presented in the narrative section of the book. In each chapter of this section Schlote's index figures for the volume of imports for the years involved are tabulated (see above, p. 99, n. 2), and a footnote is appended to the table giving the quantity in each year of wheat and wheat-flour imported, measured in physical units (quarters). Because of the difference in units, it is difficult to assess the importance of the contribution made by corn to the movement of the total. It would surely have been more useful either to have given alongside the official values of total imports the official values of corn imports (which are available in the annual *Finance Accounts* in the Parliamentary Papers), or else, if Schlote's figures were to be given for the total volume, to have accompanied them with his series for the volume of grain imports, for the years which this series covers.

[2] In the case, moreover, of a series subject to such enormous erratic fluctuations as corn imports, there is a certain danger of being misled by the method of averaging reference-cycle relatives and the practice of plotting all time-series on a logarithmic scale, which is its counterpart. For example, in such years as 1821–4 the absolute level of corn imports was little above zero, and the fluctuations occurring at this low level had no economic significance; but proportionally, and relatively to the low average for that reference-cycle, these fluctuations were substantial, and they therefore produce an appreciable effect on the average measure for all cycles. There is reason to believe that the authors have themselves occasionally been misled by this; they are inclined, for example, to speak of the increase in corn imports in such years as 1824–5 and 1836–7 as if they had an importance which is belied by the absolute amounts involved.

That is to say, the tendency of corn imports to fall in VII–III may be taken as some indication that recovery in business was fostered by a preceding period of good harvests – as the authors point out, there was only one major cycle (1816–19) during the first stage of which wheat imports increased substantially. And on the occasions when the later stages of the expansion were marked by high wheat imports, these imports may have contributed to the failure of the boom to last much longer.[1]

The conclusions so far reached about the behaviour of imports do not contain anything very striking. Both value and volume fluctuate in line with the cycle, and it seems that, if corn is abstracted from, there is no clear quickening or slackening of growth as the expansion proceeds. A comparison of the movements of imports in major and minor cycles, however, yields rather more interesting results. The following figures show the monthly rates of change of the volume of imports[2] between the different stages of major and minor cycles respectively:

	I–III	III–V	V–VII	VII–IX
Major cycles	+0·8 (0·4)	+1·4 (0·8)	−1·6 (1·0)	−1·7 (1·1)
Minor cycles	+0·7 (0·3)	+0·3 (0·3)	−0·8 (0·8)	−0·9 (0·7)

The rate of growth of the volume of imports thus increases in III–V of major cycles and diminishes in III–V of minor cycles.

The explanation of this raises matters similar to those discussed in section II above with respect to 'manias'. At or near the peaks of all major cycles in the period except 1845, there took place speculative or semi-speculative booms in the markets for some or all of the chief imported commodities. Steep rises in prices were followed by very large increases in quantities imported and then by equally steep declines in prices. In some cases pure speculation was apparently the chief force at work – imports providing, apart from corn, the chief objects of speculation in the commodity markets; but sometimes the

---

[1] Alternatively, one could seek to explain the tendency for wheat imports to rise in III–V by arguing (a) that the early stages of recovery tended to follow and be accompanied by good harvests and low wheat imports, and (b) that periods of high and low wheat imports tended to alternate with some regularity (on this see Matthews, *Study in Trade-Cycle History*, pp. 30–42). The joint result of these two conclusions would be that, by the time the upswing of the cycle had proceeded some way, a spell of higher wheat imports would be about due.

[2] The authors do not carry out separate calculations for major and minor cycles in the case of the value of imports.

expansion of activity in the earlier stages of the upswing seems to have outstripped the supply of imports in such a way as to create a real need to increase stocks. In these circumstances prices naturally rose, and speculation added fuel to the flames to a greater or less extent on different occasions. The large imports thus stimulated put an end to any real or imagined shortage, and prices inevitably slumped, bringing bankruptcy to the speculators in the process. The volume of imports thereupon declined heavily and fell below the level of current consumption. This reaction in turn was frequently excessive (largely because of the general state of discredit prevailing immediately after the upper turning-point of major cycles) and so prepared the way for a subsequent pronounced increase in imports, even if trade was not yet particularly prosperous. The volume of imports would then remain at a more even level until the next major boom approached its peak.

The element of inventory fluctuations in the behaviour of imports is one which the authors emphasise in many passages. The broad outline of events stands out clearly from the sections on the commodity markets in Tooke's *History of Prices*. More information about the movements of stocks might be gleaned from the statistics of the volume of imports entered for home consumption. The authors do not subject these to methodical study; but observation of the comparative mildness or even contra-cyclical character of the fluctuations in consumption of such commodities as sugar and coffee, and also of raw cotton, strongly suggests that in the peak years imports substantially exceeded consumption and that in the ensuing crisis stocks were a good deal drawn upon.

The relevance of this to the measures of rates of movement of imports over major and minor cycles quoted above is as follows. Normally major and minor cycles occurred alternately, and normally major cycles were accompanied by a speculative import boom and reaction of the sort described and minor cycles were not. Hence normally major cycles started in a period of comparative quiescence in commodity markets and ended in a speculative boom and reaction; whereas minor cycles started in the aftermath of such a boom and reaction but did not themselves culminate in one. The more rapid rise in imports in I–III of minor cycles as compared with III–V is explicable by the need to rebuild stocks from the low levels to which they had fallen in the commodity market slump that followed the major boom. Major expansions did not normally start with any such arrears to make up, and the acceleration in III–V reflected the speculative boom with which they concluded. The absence of any clear pattern of acceleration or deceleration in the average behaviour of import volume over all cycles now become intelligible as the result of the averaging out of majors and minors.[1]

Exports

The average monthly rates of change of the value and volume of domestic exports between the different stages of the cycle are as follows:

	I–III	III–V	V–VII	VII–IX
Volume	+1·0 (0·5)	+0·4 (0·2)	−0·8 (0·8)	−0·6 (0·9)
Value	+0·8 (0·5)	+0·5 (0·4)	−1·3 (0·9)	−1·3 (0·9)

The broad cyclical movement is very clear, but the variety of factors at work makes the explanation of the behaviour of exports in any particular period or to any particular market inevitably complicated.

Inspection of the chart showing the volume of domestic exports over the period indicates clearly that fluctuations were much smaller and less frequent in the 1830s and 1840s than they had been during the war, with the 1820s intermediate in this respect. The disappearance of arbitrary war disturbances on the demand side is evidently part of the explanation; but in view of the much less marked extent to which the amplitude of fluctuations in export *value* diminishes over the period, supply-side factors may be inferred to have played a part as well. With factory production progressively replacing outwork, there was a stronger incentive to entrepreneurs to maintain a

---

[1] The above statement is, of course, cast in very general terms. In practice not all major cycles were accompanied by speculative import booms, and such a boom did not occur in one cycle designated as minor (1811–16). Moreover, there is one instance of two major cycles occurring in succession (1816–19 and 1819–25) and one or two instances of two minors occurring in succession (1826–9 and 1829–32, and 1801–3 and 1803–8 if one does not include 1801–3 in the same cyclical unit as 1797–1801). What one is led to expect by the argument in the text is this: that there will be acceleration in the rate of growth of the net volume of imports in III–V if a cycle is not immediately preceded by an import boom-and-reaction but contains one; that there will be deceleration in III–V if it is preceded by one but does not contain one; and that the rate of growth will be roughly constant between I–III and III–V if there is one *neither* before nor during the cycle or else *both* before and during the cycle. (In the latter case, one would, to be precise, expect a rapid rise at the beginning and end of the expansion phase, with a less rapid rise in the middle. When only three stages are distinguished, I, III, and V, this would yield a roughly equal rate of growth in I–III and III–V.) Examination of the cases shows that apart from occasional irregularities caused by corn imports and the events of the war, this hypothesis fits every cycle in the period very well, except 1819–25. For some reason the crisis of 1819 was not followed by an immediate increase in imports by way of reaction, but instead dragged out, with the volume of imports low, for several years.

steady flow of production, even during periods when prices were unremunerative.[1]

The authors begin their general treatment of the behaviour of exports by arguing that the expansion of world population and real incomes, together with the secular fall in British export prices, created a strong upward trend. They then go on to enumerate the following as the chief factors liable to bring about short-run interruptions in this trend:

1. Military factors and other arbitrary obstacles, obviously of prime importance during the war.
2. Changes in the competitive power of foreign producers, caused by tariffs or otherwise.
3. Stringency in the London money market, making difficult the discount of bills drawn on account of exports.
4. Fluctuations in the level of demand from British consumers for exportable commodities.
5. Fluctuations in inventory holdings of British exports abroad, traceable to time-lags.
6. Autonomous fluctuations in the level of incomes abroad, relevant chiefly to exports to the United States.
7. Fluctuations in the amount of British capital export.

Of these factors the last three are held to be most important in the explanation of regularly recurring cycles. Naturally the different factors interact and shade into one another; for example, military events favourable to exports on certain occasions led to an excessive response on the part of exporters and hence to the accumulation of inventories and a recession.

The factors enumerated no doubt go a long way to explain the short-run movements in exports during the period. The authors do not, however, mention one factor which, as I have argued elsewhere,[2] appears to have been of great importance for the period after 1830. This is the fluctuation in the availability of sterling to overseas countries brought about by fluctuations in the value of British imports. In British trade with such areas as the United States and northern Europe, short-period tendencies to deficits or surpluses in the balance of payments could up to a point be met by accommodating capital movements or by shipments of specie. But in the case

---

[1] It may be observed that the amplitude of fluctuations in the volume of imports also diminishes after the war, but not so pronouncedly as is the case with exports. The *frequency* of fluctuations in imports does not diminish.

[2] See Matthews, *Study in Trade-Cycle History*, pp. 75-83, where the question is discussed at greater length.

of overseas areas where financial facilities were not so well developed, sales of British goods appear to have been more closely governed by the availability of bills on London earned by sales in Britain of goods exported from the areas in question. Hence as the value of British imports fluctuated over the cycle, the value of British exports to such areas tended to fluctuate also. This factor helps to explain the regular covariation of export values and the state of trade in Britain. This would otherwise be difficult to explain in the case of exports to remote areas in years when the chief causes of fluctuation in activity in Britain lay in domestic investment.

In so far as fluctuations in exports were due to this cause, the level of exports is to be regarded as a dependent variable, determined by the state of activity in Britain. But the relationship was not, of course, rigid or clear-cut. In some cases fluctuations in exports, even to entirely underdeveloped countries, undoubtedly involved independent inventory fluctuations in the foreign markets (factor 5 in the list on p. 122 above). But fluctuations in this class of exports can to a large extent be explained even on the assumption that all the goods exported passed more or less smoothly into consumption, if regard is had to changes in the availability of sterling.[1]

On the analogy of imports, one might expect to find exports increasing their rate of growth in stages III–V of major cycles and diminishing it in stages III–V of minor cycles, especially if it is accepted that the value of imports had a direct bearing on that of exports. In fact, however, although the pattern is as expected in minor cycles, major cycles, contrary to expectation, also show deceleration in both value and volume in III–V. The following are the average monthly rates of change:

	I–III		III–V		V–VII		VII–IX	
Volume of exports:								
Major cycles	+0·9	(0·9)	+0·2	(0·3)	−1·4	(1·1)	−1·4	(1·1)
Minor cycles	+1·0	(0·5)	+0·4	(0·2)	−0·2	(0·5)	−0·1	(0·4)
Value of exports:								
Major cycles	+0·7	(1·0)	+0·4	(0·5)	−1·6	(0·8)	−1·8	(0·7)
Minor cycles	+0·9	(0·5)	+0·2	(0·4)	−0·6	(0·6)	−0·6	(0·6)

The deceleration in volume is not especially surprising, if one

---

[1] The significance of the factor under discussion was undoubtedly much less during the war than it became later. During the war British Government expenditure abroad constituted an enormous erratic element in the supply of sterling. Moreover, the chief fluctuations in exports at that time were to the continent of Europe, where, as stated above, the availability of sterling was always less important in determining the level of demand for British goods than it was in parts of the world where financial facilities were less advanced.

supposes that either demand or supply or both were fairly inelastic; but the deceleration in value is rather contrary to what one would expect. This result, however, is an average of very different patterns in individual cycles – note the large average deviations shown in parentheses in the table – and its explanation probably lies in the greater variety and complexity of the factors affecting exports as compared with those affecting imports.[1]

From this review of the cyclical behaviour of imports and exports, what conclusions are to be drawn about the role of foreign trade in the mechanism of the cycle?

Movements in imports and exports at the upper turning-points of peace-time major cycles seem to follow a fairly clear pattern. As the boom moved towards its peak there usually came to be felt a real or imagined shortage of some or most imported commodities, and this led to a speculative rise in their prices.[2] Commodity speculation thus accompanied the speculation in joint-stock company promotion which was a regular feature of mania periods. The rise in prices presently stimulated a large increase in the volume of imports, which then outran consumption and caused stocks to accumulate. Exports, in the meanwhile, were stimulated by the increased availability of sterling brought about by the rise in import values, and further stimuli to exports were often present at the same time from investment in foreign securities – a feature of several mania periods – from over-confidence on the part of exporters bred by general boom conditions, and from such other sources as autonomous or partially autonomous booms in the United States.

The rise in the value of exports was not normally so general or on so large a scale as the speculatively induced rise in imports, and a drain of gold from the Bank of England and rises in discount rates were the result. On the other hand, since the increase in imports largely represented stock accumulation and so did not necessarily involve any deflection of consumers' expenditure away from home-

---

[1] The only two major booms in which the deceleration of export values in III–V is unequivocal are 1808–10 and 1842–5. The decline in rate of growth in 1810 was due to Napoleon's tightening of the blockade. In 1845 the retardation was due primarily to a minor recession in the United States, and secondarily to a reaction from the boom in exports to the Far East which had followed the conclusion of the Opium War.

[2] This statement, as a general description of what happened at major peaks, need not be regarded as inconsistent with the equivocal behaviour of the index of import prices between stages III and V (see above, p. 117 and n. 1 there), since (a) the latter reflects minor as well as major cycles, and (b) the rise in import prices might be of quite short duration, either anticipating the general peak (as in 1809 and 1814) and being followed by a fall in stage V, or coming only at the very end of the upswing following upon a fall or absence of rise in stage IV (as in 1824–5).

produced goods, the combined effect on incomes of the movements in imports and exports was quite likely to be strongly favourable, even though the balance of payments was moving adversely. Moreover, so long as the rise in import prices continued, it bred confidence in mercantile circles, notwithstanding that its direct impact on the level of effective demand was probably unfavourable.

It was not long, however, before the combined effect of increasing supplies and dearer money caused import prices to fall. This might occur while exports, as well as investment were still rising, and in this way it served to hasten the end of the period of mania. The fall in prices formed part of the process of pricking the bubble, and had its counterpart in the more or less contemporaneous collapse of joint-stock company speculation. Both were reflected in an early rise in bankruptcies, which frequently preceded the turning-point in business as a whole.[1] These bankruptcies and the associated discredit added an internal drain of gold from the Bank of England to the external drain from which it had for some time been suffering, and there resulted a general crisis of greater or less magnitude. The ensuing fall in the volume and value of imports itself led directly to a reduction in exports, and exports were also likely to be reduced in the course of the reaction from the other abnormal circumstances that had been responsible for their previous rise. The movement in the balance of payments in this phase of the cycle was usually favourable; but as this was achieved largely by drawing on stocks of imports, the net direct effect on incomes was most likely to be adverse. The fall in exports and in the prices of imports formed a large part of what was earlier called the secondary contraction process.

The subsequent recovery in import and export values was also an important element in the expansion phase of the ensuing minor cycle.[2] This expansion consisted essentially of two related elements: a general revival of confidence, accompanied by a fall in discount rates from their crisis levels, and a rebuilding of inventories. Exports were a branch of production particularly affected, (a) because exports were affected by import values, and the import trade was

---

[1] This explanation of the tendency for bankruptcies to rise in advance of the general turning-point – an interesting fact to which the authors call attention – is no more than a suggestion. Analysis of the bankruptcy returns by trades and localities might cast further light on this, and would be a useful piece of research.

[2] It is interesting to note that in the aftermath of the one major boom that was not accompanied by any speculative rises in import prices, namely 1845, there was after the initial recession no immediate recovery sufficiently pronounced to justify by the authors' criteria the marking off of a minor cycle in the annual data. The relatively moderate rise in the number of bankruptcies in 1846, compared with such years as 1826 and 1837, is also to be noted in this connection.

specially subject to large inventory fluctuations, and (*b*) because exports were subject to inventory fluctuations on their own account, particularly in the earlier part of the period. In the absence of evidence about the movements of inventories of goods for sale in the home market, however, it would be wrong to assume that restocking in that sphere did not also play an important part in the expansion phases of minor cycles.

This account of the typical minor recovery phase does not provide any explanation for the subsequent contraction. As the Columbia authors rightly point out, the various minor contractions recorded do not in fact seem all to be explicable in the same terms. The minor contraction might represent the delayed primary contraction process of the preceding major cycle (see above, p. 109); it might result from the continuation and reversal of the previous inventory movements in exports or imports; or it might be due to such accidents as a bad harvest. If none of these factors was present, the minor recovery might not be followed by a recession at all, but might instead pass straight into the next major upswing (as in 1819–21).

Naturally every minor cycle had its own peculiarities which caused it to depart to a greater or less extent from the pattern which may be thought of as typical. Moreover, not all the fluctuations designated as minor cycles by Professor Gayer and his associates are necessarily to be interpreted along the lines described. For example, the minor cycle 1829–32 lends itself much more readily to explanation in terms of harvest vagaries than in terms of fluctuations in confidence or in inventories, and the minor cycles of the war period were influenced in varying degrees by the special circumstances affecting foreign trade at that time.

It remains now to discuss the part played by foreign trade in the initiation of major expansions. It will be recalled that the Columbia authors, basing their case on the rapid increase in exports in stages I–III of major cycles as compared with the small increases in domestic investment until stage V, regard the increase in exports as the chief stimulant to major expansions in their early stages. This hypothesis is clearly an important one. It is capable of two rather different interpretations, both of which appear to be present in the authors' minds to some degree. According to the first interpretation, the long-run upward trend of demand (referred to earlier in the discussion of investment) was strongest in the field of exports, and it was this trend which brought the economy into a position from which expansion of investment could follow. According to this view, the growth of overseas outlets for the produce of British industry appears as of critical significance for the whole process of the economy's development. The second interpretation does not involve such far-reaching implications as this. According to it, at the opening of major expansions, exports, on account of inventory fluctuations, were as a rule rising at an abnormally rapid rate and so provided a shock which, in the circumstances then prevailing, was sufficient to start a cumulative expansion. This would imply that the origins of major upswings were similar to those of minor upswings.

In order to test the hypothesis conclusively – whichever way it is interpreted – a great deal of information would be necessary which we do not possess. One would have ideally to compare the movements in exports with those in the value of investment, taking account as well of any changes in the propensity to consume and the propensity to import, and one would also have to distinguish between the changes in these magnitudes that were autonomous and those that were induced by fluctuations in income. In practice, of course, this cannot be done, and we do not even have figures for the money value of investment. Instead a rough-and-ready test may be provided by considering movements in the balance of those items in the overall balance of payments that have a direct inflationary or deflationary effect on income. If this balance does not move favourably in the early stages of major expansions, it follows that the expansion can at least not have been caused exclusively by increases in exports. The balance of trade is not precisely the relevant magnitude to consider, partly because account must be taken of certain of the invisible items in the balance of payments, and partly because fluctuations in recorded imports reflect movements of stocks as well as of consumers' expenditure. For the same reasons comparison of the average rates of growth of imports and exports is inconclusive. Professor Imlah has recently provided us with estimates of the invisible items,[1] and by using these and the available indications of the direction and order of magnitude of inventory movements in imports, it is possible to get some idea of what we want for the post-war years. Let us consider the opening years of each of the major post-war cycles briefly in turn, beginning at the end of the period.

1. In 1843 the net effect of movements in foreign trade on income through the foreign trade multiplier was unquestionably very favourable. Of this effect, more than half was attributable to a reduction in the rate of consumers' expenditure on imported corn. There does appear, however, to have been a net favourable movement in the other items in the balance of payments, and this can best

[1] A. H. Imlah, 'British Balance of Payments and Export of Capital, 1816–1913', *Economic History Review*, v 2 (1952) 208–39.

be explained with reference to fluctuations in export inventories, along the lines suggested by the authors. In 1844 the net effect of movements in foreign trade on the level of income was apparently more or less neutral.

2. In 1833 the net effect was favourable, but more than all of the improvement was accounted for by reduction in consumers' expenditure on foreign corn. In 1834 the net effect was slightly adverse.

3. In 1820 and 1821 the value of imports declined while that of exports remained roughly constant. Professor Imlah's calculations accordingly show an improvement in the balance of payments on current account in both years. It appears, however, that in both years appreciable disinvestment in import stocks was taking place; and in the absence of quantitative information on this it is not clear whether the net effect of the movements on the two sides of the balance was favourable or unfavourable.

4. The year 1817 presents a case exactly opposite to the last one. The increase in the value of exports was negligible and that in the value of imports was large; but much of the latter represented rebuilding of stocks after the depression of 1816. The result is again unclear, but is on the face of it unfavourable to the hypothesis that movements in the sphere of foreign trade initiated the recovery.

Professor Imlah's balance-of-payments estimates have not been carried back earlier than 1816. Comparison of the figures for import and export values, however, gives a picture for 1809 similar to that for 1817, with the rise in imports outstripping that in exports but containing probably a substantial element of stock accumulation. The picture for the upswing 1797–1801 is confused, with apparently an adverse net effect in 1798 but a small favourable one in 1799. It is not till we go right back to the first major upswing of the whole period, that of 1788–92, that we really find unequivocal support for the thesis under discussion. For these years there are only volume figures to go on, but there certainly is an impressive expansion of exports compared with imports.

From a review of these cases it is plain that, since the deflationary effect of increases in imports (especially if corn imports are abstracted from) was so often apparently equal to or greater than the inflationary stimulus received from increases in exports, a substantial contribution – to put it no more strongly – to the initiation of major expansions must normally have been made by factors other than exports.[1]

---

[1] To guard against misinterpretation, it may be useful to state in more explicit theoretical terms what may and what may not be inferred from the movements discussed in the text. Suppose that there take place equal rises in imports and exports (abstracting from inventory movements), accompanied by some rise in the

In this connection the importance of good harvests in reducing expenditure on imports has stood out at several points already; and there are many categories of investment, especially but not exclusively investment in stocks, which are not reflected in the available statistical evidence and which may have started rising at an early stage in major expansions.

How, then, should we sum up the part played by exports in the cyclical process? There is no doubt that the value of exports was subject to wide fluctuations. But it is not proved that fluctuations in exports were wider than those in the value of goods consumed at

---

national income. It follows, as stated in the text, that the rise in income cannot be entirely attributed to the rise in exports, except in the limiting case where the marginal propensity to save is zero. It does not, of course, follow that the rise in exports is not partly responsible for the rise in income. It is even possible under certain conditions that the rise in exports is the chief cause of the rise in income – that is to say, that it is greater than the rise in investment.

The matter may be analysed in terms of foreign trade multiplier theory thus. We write Y for income, X for exports, M for imports, I for investment, m for the marginal propensity to import, and s for the marginal propensity to save. What we want to consider is what may be inferred about the relative magnitude of the change in exports and the change in investment, in the case where there is an equal rise in imports and exports.

If there are no autonomous changes in M, we have $\Delta Y = \dfrac{\Delta M}{m}$ and also $\Delta Y = \dfrac{\Delta X + \Delta I}{s+m}$. Since we are considering the case where $\Delta M = \Delta X$, it follows that $\dfrac{\Delta X}{m} = \dfrac{\Delta X + \Delta I}{s+m}$. This reduces to $\dfrac{\Delta X}{\Delta I} = \dfrac{m}{s}$. That is to say, the rise in exports may be inferred to exceed the rise in investment if the marginal propensity to import exceeds the marginal propensity to save.

If there is an autonomous increase of amount k in imports, we may write $\Delta M = k + m\Delta Y$. The basic equations then become $\Delta Y = \dfrac{\Delta M}{m} - \dfrac{k}{m}$ and $\Delta Y = \dfrac{\Delta X + \Delta I - k}{s+m}$. Where $\Delta M = \Delta X$, it follows that $\dfrac{\Delta X - k}{\Delta I} = \dfrac{m}{s}$. This means that the increase in exports is *pro tanto* more likely to exceed the increase in investment if the increase in imports is partly autonomous. If, on the other hand, k is negative so that the increase in the total of M occurs notwithstanding some autonomous fall in M (e.g. lower corn imports following upon a harvest improvement), it is *pro tanto* less likely that the increase in exports exceeds the increase in investment (and, *a fortiori*, that it exceeds the sum of the increase in investment and the autonomous fall in imports, the other two factors which contribute to raising income).

It is obvious that if the increase in exports is itself partly induced – e.g. induced by the increased British demand for imports that occurs during the boom, as suggested on p. 122 above – it is *pro tanto* less likely that the autonomous element in the increase in exports exceeds the increase in investment.

Similar reasoning can be applied to cases where the rises in imports and exports are unequal. Plainly if the rise in imports exceeds the rise in exports, it is less likely that the rise in exports is the main cause of the increase in income, and conversely.

home,[1] nor is it proved that it was exports which controlled the state of business activity as a whole in the periods when the recorded evidence on investment does not show much fluctuation. If it is accepted that short-run movements in exports were partly dependent on those in imports, the way is open for a view of exports which would regard their movements as in some cases more a symptom than a cause of general prosperity, at least after 1815. On some occasions export values did no doubt fluctuate a good deal more widely than other components of the national income. Such occasions occurred not merely during the special circumstances of the war but also in peace-time under the influence of such causes as capital exports, the state of trade in the United States, and inventory fluctuations both in exports themselves and in imports. On other occasions, however, exports and the value of home consumption most probably marched roughly in step, as when both expanded under the influence of general prosperity springing from an investment boom. On yet other occasions, as, for example, when there were particularly good or particularly bad harvests, home consumption was liable to fluctuate violently while exports remained comparatively stable.

A word may be said in conclusion about the contribution made by exports to the upward trend of the economy over the period (see above, p. 126). The rate of increase in the value of exports between 1790 and 1850 was comparatively moderate (0·9 per cent per annum). Even in the case of cotton textiles, the rate of growth of the volume of exports after 1797 was only very slightly more rapid than that of total production. If any one factor is to be singled out as having made the greatest contribution to the upward trend in the value of the national income over the period, it should surely be technical progress rather than the opening-up of foreign markets. Whether and how and to what extent population growth is to be regarded as an independent factor itself creating the expansion of demand necessary for its own absorption remains an obscure and difficult question always in the background.

[1] Compare the estimates of sales of cotton textiles abroad and in the home market between 1826 and 1842 in Matthews, *Study in Trade-Cycle History*, p. 128.

Postscript (1971): Without withdrawing any of the specific points made in this paper, I now feel on rereading it that as a review it was ungenerous. More tribute should have been paid to what was without question a major and pioneering contribution to the application of economics to economic history.

R.C.O.M.

3 British Economic Fluctuations, 1870–1914[1*]

A. G. FORD

THE intention of this paper is to survey British economic fluctuations in this period and to seek to derive some underlying patterns which might clarify the causes of the fluctuations. Furthermore, it may indicate possible lines of development for trade cycle theories and it may suggest the structure that an econometric model should perhaps have.

The procedure adopted has been to take the raw data in terms of current prices (rather than in real terms) from which trends in the form of 9-year moving averages have been calculated so that attention can be directed to the comparative behaviour of absolute deviations from these. These deviations and their interactions are then the economic fluctuations or 'trade cycles' which are to be examined and explained. As basic reference points the peaks and troughs of the deviations from trend of British money national incomes are employed. In so far as expenditure in money terms influences output, incomes and employment it seems legitimate to treat the trade cycle in terms of fluctuations in money incomes provided that we remember that price as well as output fluctuations are involved.[2] It will also avoid deflation of data originally recorded in current price terms by price indices whose reliability is open to question, and will enable direct links with the balance of payments and monetary flows. It is clear from Fig. 3.1 that fluctuations in money incomes reflect pretty accurately movements in trade union unemployment and industrial activity in Britain, more so than fluctuations in incomes at 1900 prices. It should be noted that all troughs have the same turning-points for money incomes, unemploy-

---

[1] An earlier version of this paper was read at the University of Manchester, *Advanced Economics Seminar*, for whose helpful comments I am indebted.

[2] At peaks of booms money incomes were on average some 5 per cent greater than trend values, and a similar amount less in troughs of slumps, while retail prices varied above and below trend by roughly half that amount on average so that the amplitude of fluctuations in real output was of the order of 5 per cent relatively to trend, and this was of the same order as fluctuations in employment. See R. C. O. Matthews, 'Why has Britain had Full Employment since the War?', *Economic Journal* (1968) pp. 564, 567.

---

* This essay was first published in the *Manchester School*, XXXVII (1969).

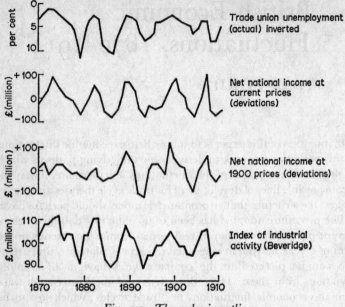

Fig. 3.1. The cycles in outline

ment and industrial activity, but that there is some tendency for
unemployment to turn at peaks before money incomes (e.g. 1872–3,
1899–1900), although the turn is very gentle on these occasions.
Thus it seems reasonable to adopt the peaks and troughs in deviations of money incomes from trend as reference points, while it
should be pointed out that the use of moving averages has not
caused any important shift in turning-points as compared with those
indicated by the raw data. All the peaks are the same, while troughs
are advanced one year in the cases of 1886, 1893, 1909 and from the
evidence of unemployment and industrial activity, the moving average figure would seem better for 1886 and 1893.

It is instructive to look at the behaviour of trends of some of the
series (Fig. 3.2) where the alternation of home and overseas investment in 18–20-year swings contrasts with the smoother behaviour of
money incomes. For overseas investment by its effects on exports
(visible and invisible) tended to influence effective demand and
money incomes in the same way as home investment spending but
perhaps not to the same extent,[1] so that a large trend rise in home

[1] See A. G. Ford, 'Overseas Lending and Internal Fluctuations: 1870–1914',
Yorkshire Bulletin of Economic and Social Research (1965) p. 24, where it is argued that
£100 worth increment in home investment produced a larger increase in effective

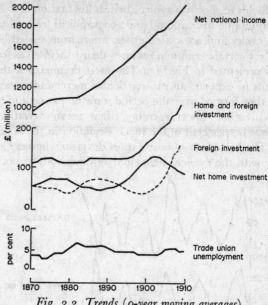

Fig. 3.2. Trends (9-year moving averages)

investment was partially offset by dull exports, and a large trend fall offset by rising exports (under the influence of rising foreign investment) as far as their effects on effective demand and money incomes were concerned. The behaviour of the trend of home plus foreign investment appears similar to the trend of money incomes for the periods 1870–85 and 1895–1910, but for 1885–95 the money income trend rises whereas the home plus foreign investment remains constant. However, I do not wish to discuss these swings, which it may be a mistake to divorce from the short-run (7–10-year) fluctuations in this 'trend/deviations from trend' fashion. Indeed, Matthews, referring to the U.K. cycle, has suggested '. . . but the main cause of the seven- to ten-year cycles in income seems to have lain in the alternation of two much longer waves in home and foreign investment respectively, unsynchronised with each other'.[1] In contrast, I wish to concentrate on the patterns and interrelationships of the deviations, since the addition of home and foreign investment trends provides a smooth trend, and it would seem that the cyclical factors are to be found in the deviations.

---

demand via the multiplier than a similar increment in foreign investment, and it is pointed out that from 1879 to 1909 the trend of unemployment tends to be higher when trend foreign investment is high than when trend home investment is.

[1] R. C. O. Matthews, *The Trade Cycle* (Cambridge, 1959) p. 223.

It is difficult to specify a typical British fluctuation or cycle; there are certain unique institutional and geographical features to each of the main cycles and associated crises, apart from varied behaviour patterns, yet certain common features thrust themselves forward in the series presented in Fig. 3.3. The most dominant is the role of fluctuations in exports, and in particular merchandise exports, for although they formed over the period some 60 per cent of merchandise and invisible export earnings, their mean deviation (£17·4 million) was 80 per cent of the mean deviation in the latter (£21·9 million). The behaviour of both export deviations agrees closely and positively with the cyclical behaviour of deviations in net national

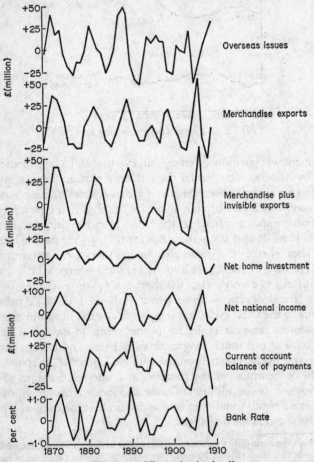

Fig. 3.3. The cycles in detail
(absolute deviations from 9-year moving averages)

income (mean deviation £43·9 million): indeed, to the eye exports play a more dominant role in influencing the behaviour of net national income than net home investment (mean deviation £7·0 million) and in closeness of turning-points. This visual impression is borne out in Table 3.1 where signs of first differences of the deviations of selected pairs of variables are compared.

TABLE 3.1

Signs of First Differences of Deviations in National Income, Exports and Home Investment, 1870–1909

	Similar	Opposite
Merchandise exports and national income	34	5
Merchandise and invisible exports and national income	31	8
Net home investment and national income	27	12
Merchandise exports and net home investment	24	15
Merchandise and invisible exports and net home investment	22	17

Although this table gives a qualitative impression and neglects the quantitative strength of similar and opposite groupings, it does suggest a simple Keynesian model to explain deviations in incomes in terms of the 'worked-out' multiplier effects of deviations in exports and in net home investment. In so far as a constant 'multiplier' is envisaged, this does assume constant marginal propensities to consume and import – or at least that their sum is constant. Accordingly a linear regression equation of the form (standard errors in brackets):

$$y_t = a_1 x_t + a_2 i_t$$

where y, x, i stand for the deviations in net national income, merchandise and invisible exports, and net home investment respectively was fitted by least squares for the period 1870–1909 and yielded the following significant result:

$$y_t = 1·635 x_t + 1·228 i_t$$
$$(0·136) \quad (0·391)$$

$$R^2 = 0·829$$
Durbin-Watson d 1·141

This bears out the visual impression, but also suggests that there are some difficulties arising from autocorrelation of the residuals. One interesting result is the difference in the values of the regression coefficients a_1 and a_2 which one might have expected to have been of very similar magnitude since they represent the 'multiplier' influences of export and investment fluctuations. If we assume that their difference is significant, certain possible explanations present themselves. On the one hand it might be that the initial effects of variations in exports and investment made themselves felt on groups with different marginal propensities, or that exports and investment have different import contents at the margin with investment having the greater import content. Again, if it is recalled that much home investment was financed from undistributed profits and personal loans, a rise in investment might be accompanied by a fall in the proportion of profits paid out as dividends or taken by partners for personal spending, or by a fall in consumption of people making personal loans, so that, for example, a given £100 of extra home investment might be accompanied by a £25 cut in consumption spending and would have a net primary effect on effective demand of £75. (In the case of a £100 rise in exports the primary effect would be £100[1]). This is perhaps making too much of the difference in coefficients. What should be noted is the small size of these 'multipliers'.

All this is what one might expect from an economy where export proceeds (both visible and invisible) formed from 30 to 40 per cent of national income. Another feature of an export economy is the tendency for the balance of payments current account to improve in export-generated booms and to worsen in slumps, provided that the marginal propensity to save is greater than zero, and that imports are clearly related to incomes and that this function does not shift about too drastically. Although not plotted, deviations in British import values were positively associated with deviations in net national income (30 similar and 9 opposite for 1870–1909) and thus exhibited a broadly similar cyclical pattern as exports (29 similar and 10 opposite for 1870–1909) with a mean deviation of £14·2 million. A linear regression equation of the form:

$$m_t = by_t$$

where m and y are the deviations of U.K. import values and net national income respectively, was fitted by least squares for the period 1870–1909 to yield:

$$m_t = 0.2802y_t \qquad R^2 = 0.6425$$
$$(0.0335) \qquad \text{Durbin-Watson } d\ 1.287$$

Better results would perhaps have been obtained if a price term had been introduced and if imports had been split into foodstuffs and

---

[1] In so far as we are including net income from abroad in export receipts, this is not strictly true, as some part of this would be saved, thereby lessening its impact on effective demand. However, the deviations in this item were relatively slight as compared with merchandise exports.

industrial raw materials. However, the working assumption of this paper that the deviations of import values were dependent on deviations in money incomes with a given marginal propensity to import is shown to be reasonably satisfactory.

However, the expectation that the British current account balance of payments would improve in booms and worsen in slumps is too simple since it only pays attention to the behaviour of exports, and account must be taken of the behaviour of home investment, which exhibited varying patterns over the cycles. When exports and home investment tended to move together, as in the period 1879–1901, theory would suggest that the improvement in the current account in booms would be curtailed as the rise in imports was accentuated, or it might even turn into a deficit, and vice versa in slumps. On the other hand when exports and home investment moved in opposite directions, the swings in the current account should be larger than if exports alone fluctuated, as in 1904–9 for example.

These expectations appear to be borne out. For in the period 1879–1901 when home investment was reinforcing the effects of exports, net national income and current account deviations showed no clear-cut association (13 similar and 10 opposite movements) while the mean deviation of imports was £15·6 million as compared with the 1870–1909 figure of £14·2 million and the mean deviation of the current account was £8·3 million as compared with the 1870–1909 figure of £13·2 million. Again, in the years 1870–8 and 1902–9 when movements in exports and home investment were, if anything tending to offset each other, there was a strong positive association between deviations in incomes and the current account (13 similar and 3 opposite), while the mean deviation of imports dropped to £12·3 million and the mean deviation of the current account rose to £19·6 million.

Hence, it is not possible to be so categoric and assert generally that the U.K. current account balance of payments improved in booms and worsened in slumps, so far as deviations are concerned, but it is fair to say that there was a general tendency in the periods 1870–9, 1886–93, 1902–9. Likewise it is not possible to assert any general tendency for the behaviour of cyclical movements of home investment and overseas investment (taking the behaviour of the current account as an approximation to movements in realised overseas investment), for there are 18 similar and 21 opposite movements so that it cannot be said that they moved either together or in opposite directions cyclically over the period.

The behaviour of deviations in average annual Bank Rate is of interest in that it displays considerable similar cyclical fluctuations

with national income, although there was no thought of using monetary policy for income stabilisation. It was a fortunate accident that
Bank Rate tended to be high in booms, low in slumps, as a result of
the needs of convertibility. Despite Bank Rate's cyclical connection
with incomes (30 similar, 9 opposite, as well as the visual impression
of Fig. 3.3) and a similar but less pronounced connection between
the current account and national income (26 similar, 13 opposite)
there is no such clear-cut relationship between deviations in Bank

TABLE 3.2

Signs of First Differences of Deviations in National Income, Exports,
Current Account Balance of Payments and Home Investment,
U.K., 1870–1909

	1870–1909		1870–8 1901–9		1878–1901	
	Similar	Opposite	S	O	S	O
Net national income and current account balance of payments	26	13	13	3	13	10
Merchandise exports and current account balance of payments	30	9	15	1	15	8
Merchandise and invisible exports and current account balance of payments	28	11	14	2	14	9
Net home investment and current account balance of payments	18	21	7	9	11	12
Net home investment and merchandise exports	24	15	8	8	16	7
Net home investment and merchandise and invisible exports	22	17	6	10	16	7

Rate and in the current account (22 similar, 17 opposite). In Fig. 3.3,
however, for certain periods Bank Rate and the current account are
associated positively – 1870–8, 1885–92, 1898–1909. Other things
equal on the capital account, this conjuncture would not be expected
and the behaviour of Bank Rate over the cycles needs explanation
and evaluation as a potentially disruptive force.

Now Bank Rate was raised by the Bank of England when its
Reserve was experiencing strain or was felt to be inadequate and, if
necessary, additional measures were taken to make it effective on the
London market rate of discount which influenced international

short-term capital transactions: it was lowered when the Reserve was felt to be more than adequate. It is worth suggesting that the magnitude of an 'adequate' Reserve might vary over the cycle in the Bank's eyes – for example, in the later stages of a boom it might revise upwards its notion of 'adequate' when all around there was evidence of growing speculation, reports of malpractice abroad, and the likelihood of international monetary strains. The basic aim of its monetary policy was to maintain convertibility of its notes into gold on demand at face value, and as its Reserve was not usually very big (approximately equal to 2–3 weeks' import payments), speedy action was necessary. Bank Rate, indeed, was adjusted frequently, far more so than for other central banks' rediscount rates, and a distinct seasonal pattern emerged with rising rates in the autumn and falling rates in the early spring.

One source of strain, which tended to grow in booms and lessen in slumps, was the internal drain, as rising home incomes brought increased transactions demand for sovereigns and notes to be supplied from the Bank, while in the ensuing slump came the internal reflux to help replenish the Reserve. In upswings the extra internal demand (relatively to trend) averaged some £2–3 million a year over several years, while the reflux (relatively to trend) was of the same annual order, but usually concentrated in one slump year. Furthermore, there was a seasonal pattern with a net reflux every spring, and a net drain for the rest of the year.

The second and quantitatively more important source of strain was provided by external drains through adverse balances of payments. One would expect this to be the prime reason for a rise in the rediscount rate in a gold-standard economy experiencing a home investment boom, as the current account moved into deficit, assuming no change in autonomous capital account transactions, but not in an 'export' economy such as Britain. Here export fluctuations were the major proximate cause of the cycle, and could be expected to bring favourable balances of payments in booms, unfavourable in slumps, with external movements in gold more than sufficient to offset internal movements so that the actual positive cyclical pattern of Bank Rate would not be that expected – other things equal.

However, other things were not equal. In some cycles, as already noted, home investment movements reinforced fluctuations in exports and caused a greater rise in imports so that the expected improvement in the current account was diminished or even turned into a deficit in booms, and in slumps the deterioration was less marked or even became an improvement (relative to trend). This, together with the internal movements, provides one strand of explanation of the cyclical pattern in Bank Rate, especially for the years 1879–1901.

Of more importance, in my view, were the capital account items in the British balance of payments in explaining monetary stringency in booms in Britain and monetary ease in slumps. In upswings the Bank of England was subject to external drains because of the tendency for British lending abroad (both short-term and long-term) with a given interest-rate structure to exceed the emergent current account surplus so that the basic balance moved into deficit. Strain was thrust on the Reserve and Bank Rate was increased. In slumps (with falling exports), even though the current account tended to worsen relatively to trend, the fall in lending abroad with a given interest-rate structure exceeded the deterioration in the current account so that the basic balance moved into surplus again. The Reserve position became more comfortable so that Bank Rate could be cut speedily in the downswing.

The behaviour of overseas issues on the London Stock Exchange is taken as evidence of the behaviour of intentions to lend abroad, since it was the principal vehicle of British overseas capital formation, and it is noteworthy in Fig. 3.3 that peaks and troughs in this precede peaks and troughs in incomes and in Bank Rate – for example, in 1872, 1881, 1889, 1905 – so that the suggestion above appears well borne out. Indeed, before 1893 the cyclical movement in overseas issues which leads the cyclical movement in incomes by 1–2 years is particularly marked, and later will be treated as of great importance.

What, then, were the effects of Bank Rate whose rise and fall have been explained in general terms? Did monetary forces choke off the boom? Will such forces help to explain turning-points? These matters may be worth more attention, perhaps, than has been accorded them in recent years.

The main immediate influence of Bank Rate (when effective) was on international short-term money flows by narrowing the differential between yields on bills in London and in other monetary centres to encourage profit-seeking bankers to switch their funds to London and perhaps to deter short-term borrowing by foreigners. In Fig. 3.4 the differential between the Bank bill rate in London and the short-term interest in the rest of the world is plotted against Bank Rate (all annual averages) and it is clear that the differential (negative) narrows when Bank Rate rises, especially at some of the main crises, and that too despite similar rises elsewhere.

This mechanism provided quick defence of the Reserve and the sensitivity of such capital movements to British short-term interest rates was the reason why the Bank and London could do so much on such a small Reserve. However, it is important to note that the manipulation of Bank Rate and the changed flows of funds had secondary effects elsewhere. The flow of funds to London, when Bank Rate was raised effectively, naturally thrust monetary difficulties and rising short-term rates on to other developed monetary centres (Berlin, New York, and Paris especially) as they increased their rediscount rates in a protective as well as a rather immaturely imitative fashion. Further, the same pressures which prompted the rise in Bank Rate might of their own be causing strains in these centres and bringing increases in rates. The parallelism in monetary

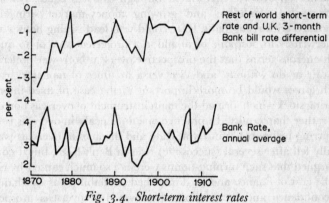

Fig. 3.4. Short-term interest rates

conditions (especially in short-term markets) which occurred in these developed monetary centres can be explained thus, for international forces and the maintenance of convertibility dominated banking policy. Certainly, the main centres were 'together in behaviour' at each of the main crises of the period, and all this may help somewhat to explain elements of the cyclical parallelism between Britain and other (developed) economies. In so far as the funds moving to London were withdrawn from much less developed monetary markets and banking systems (for example, from parts of Latin America, or parts of the Empire), these centres experienced liquidity troubles and possible checks to activity as commercial banks with no 'lender of last resort' facilities sought to restore desired cash ratios by cutting lending.

The direct cost effects of Bank Rate on domestic investment spending have generally been thought to be weak; certainly variations in Bank Rate brought changes in short-term interest rates to which investment spending was insensitive, but did not influence substantially longer-term rates to which such spending might be

more sensitive.[1] Furthermore, the nature of finance of home investment from undistributed profits and private loans rather than the
Stock Exchange would lessen sensitivity to interest-rate changes and
their associated cost effects. Of more significance were the effects
which changes in Bank Rate had on profit expectations (the 'confidence' effect) and perhaps the liquidity effects.[2] In the period 1870-
1909 there are 22 similar movements in first differences of deviations
of Bank Rate and net home investment and 17 opposite, so that no
clear-cut relationship is apparent.

However, the effects of variations in Bank Rate might have more
influence on overseas investment through overseas issues. Difficult
stock-market conditions and growing money-market stringency
associated with rising Bank Rate could well lead issuing houses and
underwriters to postpone or abandon a projected issue or to quote
such onerous terms that the prospective overseas borrower preferred
to wait or do without, and vice versa at times of monetary ease.
Such forces would be more important in the case of fixed-interest
bearing stock which formed the main instrument of overseas borrowing rather than equity. In practice one finds peaks in overseas issues
occurring before peaks in Bank Rate and incomes as overseas issues
finally fell after several (successive) rises in Bank Rate, but it could
be argued that such turning-points were not so much caused by rises
in the cost of finance and its diminished availability, as by changes
in confidence and by revisions downwards of overseas prospects
with fears of crisis abroad. Perhaps, the same factor which caused
a fall in overseas issues caused the continuing rise in Bank Rate.

If the first differences of deviations of Bank Rate and overseas
issues are compared for 1870-1909, there are 17 similar movements
and 22 opposite: in the first part of the period, 1870-92, there are 14
similar and 8 opposite (this was the period when the one-year lead
of overseas issues deviations over exports and incomes is so marked),
while from 1892-1909 there are 3 similar and 14 opposite movements. However, such comparisons are misleading because there are
two processes at work whose relative strength varied: (*a*) a surge of
overseas lending brings balance of payments strain and rising Bank

---

[1] Cf. 'We have already observed that the influence of interest rates on the course
of investment activity – which is the chief influence interest rates exert, according
to our results – is only moderate.' J. Tinbergen, *Business Cycles in the U.K. 1870-1914*,
2nd ed. (Amsterdam, 1956) p. 133. Cf. J. S. Pesmazoglu, 'A Note on the Cyclical
Fluctuations of British Home Investment 1870-1913', *Oxford Economic Papers* (1951)
p. 61.

[2] See 'Inquiry into the Effects of Dear Money on Home Trade', *Economist*, 23
and 30 Nov 1907, and A. G. Ford, *The Gold Standard 1880-1914* (Oxford, 1962)
pp. 44-6.

Rate; (b) the rise in Bank Rate may bring (or be associated with) a fall in overseas issues. In the early stages of an upswing we might expect to find (a) dominant with rising overseas issues and rising Bank Rate, but in the later stages (b) asserting itself with rising Bank Rate and falling overseas issues. Likewise in the downswing falling overseas issues would permit Bank Rate to fall and this pattern could well persist until overseas lenders recovered their nerve to yield the pattern of falling Bank Rate and rising overseas issues. I suggest that this sort of pattern is discernible, especially from 1870 to 1893 and after 1908 (where raw data have to be used). From 1870 to 1872 overseas issues and Bank Rate both rise, 1872–73 then yields a continued rise in Bank Rate and a fall in overseas issues; the same pattern is found for 1879–81 and 1881–2. In 1885 after continued falls in Bank Rate overseas issues recover and continue to rise with rising Bank Rate from 1886 to 1889, after which they decline with 1890 showing the Bank Rate peak. Both decline after the Baring Crisis, with overseas issues deviations showing some recovery in 1894. These joint patterns are less clear-cut after 1893 until 1909 onwards, and it would appear that the (b) relationship of opposite movements dominates in those years. Such happenings provoke the speculative thought of whether the trade cycle changed its character in the mid-1890s until 1910.

At these crucial times just before the peaks of 1873, 1882, 1890 and perhaps 1906, was it the final Bank Rate increases as the peak of the boom was reached which finally choked off overseas issues with monetary stringency deterring would-be borrowers and issuing houses, or were the marginal efficiency estimates of overseas investment cut sharply as news of speculative excesses, profligacy, blighted prospects and evidence of over-optimism and of myopic greed came into London? The answers given will have an important bearing on the mechanisms of the cycles and the view that monetary forces deserve a place. Certainly detailed study is necessary, which would perhaps be out of place in a general survey such as this.

This study has placed prime emphasis for the proximate causes of fluctuations in U.K. money incomes on fluctuations in export values, aided (or at times impeded) by fluctuations in home investment as a junior partner. Further, it has been suggested that changes in short-term interest rates had slight influence on home investment spending, but mainly made their impact on international capital movements. By implication the role of (autonomous) fluctuations in the stock of money as a causative factor has been relegated to insignificance. Rather, the opinion is taken that the stock of money, in particular bank deposits (and discounts and advances), adjusted to demands for accommodation and was thus a somewhat passive feature, although rising demands in booms led to rising bill rates (if the supply of finance was not perfectly elastic) and facilitated the Bank of England's task of making Bank Rate effective at times when strain on its Reserve was associated with upswings, ease with downswings. The Bank does not appear to have deliberately expanded its domestic assets as its international assets rose, or vice versa, as the Rules of the Game doctrine would demand[1] – such primitive open-market operations as the Bank undertook were purely to make Bank Rate effective The domestic monetary situation has been well summed up by R. S. Sayers:

> We may conclude, therefore, that within the banking system itself interest rates were substantially, but by no means universally, moved with Bank Rate, and that a movement of Bank Rate would probably be accompanied by some change in the availability of bank credit, though the absence of traders' complaints suggests that the latter effect cannot have been marked.[2]

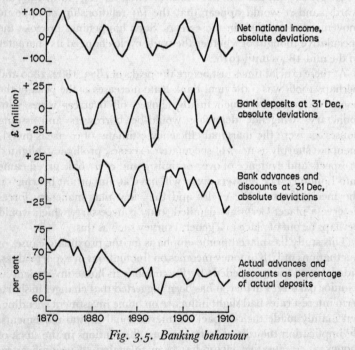

Fig. 3.5. Banking behaviour

[1] See A. I. Bloomfield, *Monetary Policy under the International Gold Standard: 1880–1914* (New York, 1959) pp. 47–51.

[2] R. S. Sayers, *Central Banking after Bagehot* (Oxford, 1957) p. 64.

TABLE 3.3

Signs of First Differences of Deviations in National Income,
Bank Deposits and Advances

		1870–1910		1870–1893		1893–1910	
		Similar	Opposite	S	O	S	O
Deposits and net national income	*	26	10	16	3	10	7
Deposits and Bank Rate	*	19	17	12	7	7	10
Advances and discounts and net national income	*	28	8	17	2	11	6
Advances and discounts and Bank Rate	*	23	13	13	6	10	7
Advances and discounts / Deposits and net national income		26	14	15	8	11	6
Advances and discounts / Deposits and Bank Rate		29	11	17	6	12	5

Notes: * 1874–1910.

Advances and discounts: first differences of actual figures.
Deposits

In Fig. 3.5 the behaviour of deviations in bank deposits and discounts and advances at 31 December of the years concerned and
national income are compared together with the movements in total
advances and discounts as a percentage of total deposits, while the
behaviour of first differences of deviations is presented in Table 3.3.[1]
Both deposits and discounts and advances display considerable
cyclical agreement with fluctuations in net national income with the
agreement being decidedly stronger in the period up to 1893, after
which the clear cyclical pattern becomes obscured. Less certain are
the relations between Bank Rate and deposit deviations, while
advances and discounts tended to rise and fall as Bank Rate rose and
fell. The ratio of advances and discounts to deposits is associated
positively more closely with Bank Rate fluctuations than with
national income, and more evenly over the whole period than the
other comparisons. It certainly appears that in booms bankers met
increased demands for accommodation by becoming less liquid,
while in slumps they became more liquid (interpreting 'less liquid'
as a rise in this ratio). The deviations in deposits and in advances and

[1] The banking statistics are taken from Tinbergen, *Business Cycles in the United
Kingdom 1870–1914*. They are not very satisfactory in terms of compilation, but
their behaviour perhaps gives a rough idea of actual banking behaviour. See R.
Higonnet, 'Bank Deposits in the U.K. 1870–1914', *Quarterly Journal of Economics*
(1957) pp. 329–67, for a critical account.

discounts have roughly similar turning-points as net national income, particularly before 1893. The patterns of behaviour displayed in these series, together with the diminished size of deviations after 1895, would appear to fit in with earlier opinions that fluctuations in the money stock were not an important feature of the cycles in Britain.

Fluctuations in export proceeds (both merchandise and invisible) were a main cause of fluctuations in British money incomes and much of the absolute deviation in the former was attributable to fluctuations in merchandise exports which were more volatile than deviations in service earnings and in income from abroad.[1] What, then, caused them to behave thus?

Merchandise export values fluctuated as a result of similar fluctuations in prices and volumes with the volume fluctuation exceeding the price fluctuation in percentage terms. The mean deviation of export values amounted to some £17 million over the period, while the mean deviation of export volumes (valued at 1880 prices) was £13 million. One important element in this was that the rising world demand for British goods brought increased demand for raw materials whose prices rose, thus causing industrial costs and prices to rise, so that Britain in booms experienced rising export and raw material import prices, and on the other hand in slumps falling export and import prices. A by-product was the dampening of movements in the British terms of trade over the cycle.

A geographical breakdown of British merchandise export values into Europe, North America, Central and South America, Asia (mainly India), and Australia and New Zealand provides evidence of varied trends and varied cyclical behaviour of the component series, although as the period wears on more complete accord is found between the deviations. The importance of various areas differs in the cycles, except that the European market dominates in providing the chief source of absolute fluctuations in export values and of showing the closest accord with cyclical turning-points in British activity (see Fig. 3.6 and Table 3.4).[2] It should be pointed out that the 'Europe' category comprises a large group including Turkey, Egypt and North Africa, but one close-knit with trade ties, in which British export sales to France, Germany, Holland and

---

[1] Much of the services earnings (shipping and financial) were closely linked to the course of British and world trade, and these latter fluctuated together so that services earnings moved closely with British export sales. Income from abroad was linked both to the pace of overseas activity *and* to the flow of British overseas lending. Bearing in mind its fixed-interest element, the comparatively small deviations in income from abroad are not surprising.

[2] See also Table 3.7 for mean deviations.

Belgium comprised over half total British export sales to 'Europe'. By the turn of the century Germany was proving a better customer for Britain than the United States, though a poorer customer than India. From this it is clear that the role of the 'Atlantic' economy in generating economic fluctuations in Britain needs reassessing in the light of the influence of Europe on British exports and incomes, even though the volatility of deviations of North American exports was greater than European (expressed as percentage of trend). It is possible to lump the Americas together to try to preserve the role of the Atlantic economy but this is mistaken, in my view, since direct trade and finance connections between them (especially the United States with Argentina and Brazil) were weak in this period.

TABLE 3.4

Signs of First Differences of U.K. Export Deviations, 1870–1909

	Similar	Opposite
Total U.K. exports and U.K. exports to Europe	32	7
,, ,, ,, ,, ,, ,, ,, N. America	30	9
,, ,, ,, ,, ,, ,, Central and S. America	30	9
,, ,, ,, ,, ,, ,, Asia	27	12
,, ,, ,, ,, ,, ,, Australia/ N.Z.	29	10
U.K. exports to N. America and U.K. exports to Europe	25	14
,, ,, ,, ,, ,, ,, ,, Central and S. America	31	8
,, ,, ,, ,, ,, ,, ,, Australia/ N.Z.	22	17
U.K. net national income and total U.K. exports	34	5
,, ,, ,, ,, U.K. exports to Europe	35	4
,, ,, ,, ,, ,, ,, N. America	29	10
,, ,, ,, ,, ,, ,, Central and S. America	29	10
,, ,, ,, ,, ,, ,, Asia	28	11
,, ,, ,, ,, ,, ,, Australia/ N.Z.	26	13

Between 1870 and 1885 North America appears of roughly equal importance with Europe in terms of absolute deviations, while South America becomes more volatile in 1885–91, and after 1890 Asia, North America and Europe all fall together. However, after 1890 Europe becomes more important, to be rivalled by Asia after 1900, and all series move up and down in unison for the upswing to 1907 and the subsequent slump. Further support for the demotion of North America as the source of the cycles is provided by figures for cyclical correspondence in 1879–1914 for Britain, the United States France and Germany: all four reference cycles were in the same phase in 53·5 per cent of all months, but if the United States is deleted, the three European reference cycles were in the same phase in 83·1 per cent of all months.[1] Certainly as the world economy developed and became more linked together with more multilateral settlement patterns, the speedy international transmission of fluctuations was facilitated, but this should not lead to the uncritical assertion that a slump or boom in one part meant automatically slumps or booms in other parts. Europe and North America were in opposite phases on several occasions as indeed has certainly happened in more recent times (for example, in the 1950s).

While it is necessary to recognise exogenous elements which influenced British export performance, nevertheless it is appropriate to investigate the extent to which British export sales were influenced by the variability of British overseas investment. Overseas issues, which were the principal vehicle of British investment abroad and were in this period in terms of raw data, of comparable magnitude to the calculated *ex post* investment abroad (from the balance of payments), are employed as an indicator of both relative and absolute variations in *ex ante* British overseas investment. For what is important here is how the decision to lend abroad affected the British economy as well as the borrower.

It is clear from Fig. 3.3 that turning-points in overseas issues deviations lead turning-points in British export deviations (and in net national income) especially in the period from 1870 to 1895 by one year, while after 1895 the lead lengthens and the relationship appears less close until after 1908, when the surge in overseas issues until 1913 was accompanied by rising exports but cannot be shown here because of the use of moving averages.[2] Furthermore, the absolute size of these deviations in overseas issues were of comparable magnitude to the size of export deviations, at least until the turn of the century. Table 3.5 reinforces the graphical conclusions by indicating that for the whole period the strongest qualitative association between merchandise export behaviour (and net national income) and overseas issue behaviour is obtained with a lead of one year of

[1] O. Morgenstern, *International Financial Transactions and Business Cycles* (Princeton, 1959) p. 43.

[2] Turning-points in British overseas issues also lead turning-points in the World Trade Index. See A. G. Ford, *Economic History Review* (1963–4) p. 335. In 1900 British trade was some 25 per cent of total world trade, and thus its movements had considerable influence on the behaviour of world trade.

issues over exports. Most noteworthy as well is the very strong relationship for the period 1870–93, and the marked change for 1893–1910 when the previous clear-cut relationship disappears. This, it should be recalled, was the period when overseas issues appeared more sensitive to Bank Rate changes in an inverse way, and when other countries were growing in relative importance in world trade so that the purely British influences were diminishing in importance. Furthermore, overseas issues for the years from 1893 to 1902 were secularly low.

TABLE 3.5

Signs of First Differences of Deviations in Overseas Issues, Exports and National Income

	1870–1910		1870–93		1893–1910	
	Similar	Opposite	S	O	S	O
Merchandise exports and overseas issues	26	14	17	6	9	8
Merchandise exports and overseas issues—1	28	12	20	3	8	9
Merchandise exports and overseas issues—2	24	15	16	6	8	9
Net national income and overseas issues	25	15	16	7	9	8
Net national income and overseas issues—1	27	13	21	2	6	11
Net national income and overseas issues—2	26	13	17	5	9	8

Secondly, much of the British overseas lending in the whole period was essentially developmental in character – public and private borrowing to finance the construction of railways, ports, public utilities, together with mines and land companies – and was frequently undertaken to increase the output of primary products for export in the borrowers. It was directed mainly to the 'empty' lands together with migration of labour from Europe (for example, to Canada, Australia, New Zealand, South Africa, the United States, Brazil, Argentina, Chile) to promote these ends, while diminishing amounts went to Europe and increasing amounts to India.

Thirdly, extra finance often formed a necessary precondition of a rise in economic activity in certain parts of the world, especially those which had rudimentary domestic banking systems, which possessed no central banks, or which relied for bank services on the Anglo-imperial or Anglo-foreign banks based in London, and which adhered to some variant of the gold standard.[1] Rising British overseas lending helped to supply this in the short run, but as the loans were used to finance extra imports, the reserve position weakened and more finance was needed to prolong the growth in activity. Furthermore, the drying-up of overseas investment by Britain could impose liquidity crises in such borrowing countries as well as other deflationary pressures as spending financed from overseas borrowings declined, which might easily spread to more developed monetary centres. Depressive tendencies could easily be initiated by the international spread of declining expenditure and through the collapse of excessively optimistic expectations, just as expansionary forces were spread in upswings of British overseas lending.

It is important to ask how the recipients of British overseas lending used the proceeds. The answers can be categorised as follows: (*a*) to buy directly imports of (capital) goods or materials needed for their construction; (*b*) to finance foreign debt service charge payments (both old and new); (*c*) to finance extra home spending, which through multiplier effects caused their purchases of imports of goods of all sorts to rise. Hence some (substantial) rise in British exports, invisible as well as merchandise, might be confidently expected to follow an increase in British overseas lending as a result of the borrowers' use of the proceeds, and the stronger the informal bilateral trading links the greater the stimulus exerted on British exports, with imperial links having particular importance. Likewise, when British overseas lending declined, a decline in British exports might be expected to follow shortly.

Before proceeding further, it is vital to ask how the loans were raised in Britain. For, if they were raised at the expense of home spending – as they certainly were in the long run in terms of trends – then the stimulative effects of improved export sales would be offset by the depressive effects of falling home (investment) expenditure and the multiplier influence on incomes might even vanish. If this were found in terms of the behaviour of deviations as well as trends, then one would expect cyclical patterns to be upset as the effects of a given rise in exports on incomes and imports were damped down. This is not so, in fact. As was shown earlier there was a tendency for deviations in home investment to reinforce the behaviour of exports in the years 1879–1901 especially, while in the other years when no

---

[1] The *commercial* banking systems in these circumstances certainly appeared to operate the 'rules of the gold standard game' – if only because their overseas balances (their foreign exchange reserves) and their gold holdings were their cash reserves as well, and the 'rules' fitted in with commercial prudence and the maintenance of banking solvency.

clear pattern emerged the size of fluctuations in home investment was quite outweighed by that of exports. Further, if anything, fluctuations in overseas issues were positively associated with net home investment fluctuations, as Table 3.6 would indicate, while the mean deviation of overseas issues is £18·5 million as compared with £7·0 million for net home investment. The cycle, then, is not obliterated, because in some cases the deviations in overseas issues and exports quite outweighed the opposite deviations in home investment, and in the other cases the investment deviations reinforced the

TABLE 3.6

Signs of First Differences of Deviations in Overseas Issues and Home Investment

	1870–1910		1870–93		1893–1910	
	Similar	*Opposite*	*S*	*O*	*S*	*O*
Net home investment and overseas issues	23	17	14	9	9	8
Net home investment and overseas issues—1	25	15	17	6	8	9
Net home investment and overseas issues—2	27	12	17	5	10	7

export deviations.[1] It also emerges that in the short run much of overseas investment deviations must have been financed by lenders from previously idle money holdings in booms, and in slums these were replenished.

It is attractive to consider that the fluctuations in exports were a direct result of the variability of *ex ante* British overseas lending which led them so distinctly in the years before the turn of the century. This assertion is, however, too simple and uncritical: on the one hand it neglects the differences which emerge for the periods 1870–93 and 1893–1909, while on the other it is framed at too aggregative a level. Reference to the geographical breakdown of deviations in British merchandise exports and overseas issues makes it clear that the influence of overseas issues fluctuations on exports could only have been partially bilateral since over the period British lending to Europe diminished to small figures whereas the behaviour of exports to Europe provided some considerable part (at least 40 per cent) of the explanation of absolute fluctuations in British export values.

This point is examined in more detail with the aid of Fig. 3.6 in which the series of overseas 'calls' compiled by M. Simon for particular geographical areas are plotted against the series of

[1] This is assuming reasonably stable consumption and import functions over the courses of the cycles.

merchandise export values for similar areas. Although the classifications may not be precisely the same, nevertheless it is felt that any errors arising from marginal classification discrepancies would be slight and thus the comparison would be worth-while. Initially there is close correspondence between deviations in overseas issues and in exports for the main areas both as regards size and timing (allowing for leads) until 1885. Thereafter the amplitude of fluctuations in British exports to Europe exceeds considerably the amplitude of overseas issues thence, while the case is reversed for North America, and to a lesser extent for South America and Asia, where the am-

TABLE 3.7

Mean Deviations in British Exports and Overseas Issues to
Selected Areas, 1870–1909
(£ million)

	British merchandise export values	Overseas issues
Europe	8·1	4·4
North America	3·4	8·4
South America	2·5	4·9
Asia	3·6	3·8
Australasia	2·3	2·3

plitude of issues exceeds that of exports. Some of the explanation may lie in the fact that funds for these areas were raised at concentrated times but spent gradually as the development projects required. Certainly there are tendencies for turning-points in issues to lead export turning-points by up to two years in the European, North American and Asian series. Nevertheless, Fig. 3.6 is also strongly suggestive of multilateral channels of influence and settlements involving particularly the Americas and Europe together with Britain.

In this period many of the underdeveloped borrowers purchased at least three-quarters of their imports from continental Europe and Britain with the British share being noticeably higher in the case of 'Empire' territories. Secondly, they paid almost all their foreign remittances of interest and profits to Britain, France and Germany, while a world trade boom (partially initiated by a surge in British overseas lending) increased the demand for shipping, and forced up both shipping rates and the price of coal, and on the other hand these prices declined in trade slumps. Hence variations in British overseas lending which reacted on British merchandise and invisible exports and incomes also affected European exports and incomes in the same way, so that repercussion effects influenced British exports to Europe and European exports to Britain. Furthermore, the value

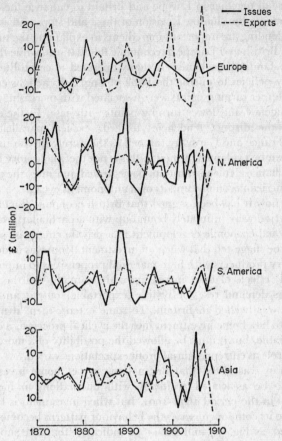

Fig. 3.6. British overseas issues and exports by areas
(deviations from 9-year moving averages)

of British coal exports to Europe (an important trading item in the later part of the period) were more variable because of the sharp cyclical variations in the price of coal. However, these repercussion effects in themselves were not likely to be strong enough to explain the observed cyclical parallelism.

Rising or falling activity initiated by the variability of British overseas lending could certainly touch off further expansionary or contractionary forces elsewhere, and the factors which attracted or repelled British interest abroad also likewise affected other (European) countries. This reinforced the earlier-mentioned trade effects in stimulating similar movements in activity in Europe and Britain, while psychological forces further helped to cause profit expectations to rise or fall together in Europe and Britain to enhance the booms and aggravate the slumps. Revision of these and stops and starts in overseas lending are important ingredients in explaining the turning-points in British and European economic fluctuations, while the way the gold standard mechanism actually operated to cause European monetary policies to mirror the Bank of England's actions ensured that the upper turning-points were associated with increasing monetary stringency and lower turning-points with ease. In these ways some of the distinct tendencies towards cyclical parallelism in Britain, France and Germany (as well as the purely British turning-points) can be explained, although this is not the whole story by any means. Chance elements must not be neglected, nor must the growth of the American economy and its own autonomous cycles.

Up to now it has been argued that British economic fluctuations in this period were intimately bound up with a particular process of international economic development in a private enterprise setting. It might be suggested that when an investment boom was under way in primary producers with high marginal propensities to import, the 'induced' effects of their increasing activity might well be felt in Britain as demand rose for British (exportable) output and extra capacity was needed in Britain. To some extent, then, it may be possible to link home investment into the cyclical process as a dependent variable, but it must be allowed the possibility of a more independent role as entrepreneurial profit expectations varied.

Earlier it was noted that fluctuations in net home investment tended to be associated positively with fluctuations in incomes, especially in the period 1879–1901, but when investment is broken down into its component series the behaviour patterns become more variegated, as Fig. 3.7 and Table 3.8 indicate,[1] than the sub-series for merchandise exports. Gross mercantile shipbuilding displays the strongest cyclical agreement, which is not surprising since the British cycle had a strong international root, and also has the largest mean deviation of £3·0 million.[2] and the greatest volatility. The next

---

[1] The series available relate to gross investment, whereas this paper has used net investment and net incomes in its earlier discussion. In total terms net investment was some 70 per cent of gross investment, and it is not unreasonable to suppose that in the component series 'gross' and 'net' moved together as in the aggregate series.

[2] Other mean deviations are:

Total gross investment	...	...	...	...	... £9·8 million
Gross building investment	...	...	...	...	... £1·8 million
Gross capital investment by railways		...	...	...	... £2·4 million
Local authority loan expenditure	...	...	...	...	... £1·9 million
Gross value of machinery for domestic use	...		...	...	... £1·9 million
Other gross capital formation		...	...	...	... £2·8 million

TABLE 3.8

Signs of First Differences of Deviations in Gross Investment and
its Component Series, National Income and Industrial Profits,
U.K., 1870–1910

	Similar	*Opposite*
Total gross investment and net national income	25	15
Gross building investment and net national income	23	16
Gross capital expenditure by railways and net national income	23	15
Gross mercantile shipbuilding and net national income	30	10
Local authority loan expenditure and net national income	16	24
Gross value of machinery for domestic use and net national income	19	21
Other gross capital formation and net national income	27	12
Total gross investment and industrial profits	19	20
Total gross investment and industrial profits—1	24	15

closest is 'other gross capital formation' and in terms of trend values
is the most important sub-component. However, other series display
considerable lack of agreement with fluctuations in net national
income and in some cases do not appear to have any well-defined
cyclical pattern at all, except that local authority loan expenditure
appears to have anticyclical effects.

The behaviour of the domestic investment series would suggest
that the influence of innovation and technical progress in Britain on
cyclical activity was quantitatively slight. For one would expect
these forces to make themselves felt through variations in home
investment. However, technical progress in primary producers
induced by British overseas investment, would be a different story.
Although fluctuations in home investment in this study have been
treated as an exogenous variable influencing effective demand and
incomes, but not more than a contributory feature to the British
trade cycle,[1] it is appropriate to inquire to what extent its fluctuations might be explained by such factors as international influences,
the behaviour of profits, incomes, and interest rates, though the
varied behaviour patterns of the component series would seem to
preclude any simple theoretical explanations. Earlier it was suggested that Bank Rate and short-term interest-rate fluctuations
hardly affected home investment decisions at all in terms of cost

[1] Cf. J. S. Pesmazoglu, 'A Note on the Cyclical Fluctuations of British Home
Investment, 1870–1913', *Oxford Economic Papers* (1951) p. 60.

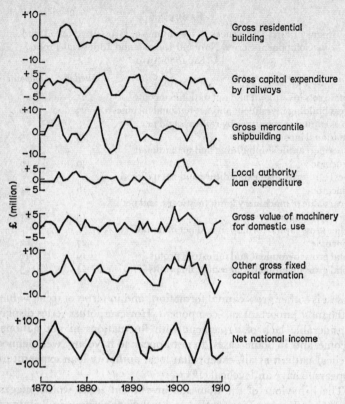

Fig. 3.7. Home investment behaviour
(deviations from 9-year moving averages)

effects, while the influence of the long-term rate of interest was at best only moderate.[1]

Fluctuations in realised profits could be expected to influence investment both in terms of providing the available finance – self-finance played an important role in Britain at this time – and in terms of affecting expectations of future profits. Certainly Table 3.8 indicates a moderate positive association between fluctuations in investment and in industrial profits of the previous year, but this may not be a direct causal influence.[2] Income fluctuations were mainly caused by export variations reflecting international influences, which

---

[1] This is in line with Pesmazoglu's findings (pp. 60–1).
[2] Pesmazoglu, indeed, found that all influences on investment through variations in aggregate net profits were probably of small importance.

also influenced shipbuilding and, perhaps, investment in export industries to yield the moderate cyclical pattern found in home investment. This could then be expected to show some cyclical agreement with the profit fluctuations, which were themselves strongly associated with variations in incomes. What, of course, may have been crucial were anticipated profits about which information is lacking. Profits certainly were related strongly to variations in incomes (30 similar and 9 opposite signs of pairs of first differences of deviations of the same year, which improved to 34 similar and 5 opposite when income deviations were compared with profit deviations of the previous year) with some tendency for turning-points in profits to lead turning-points in money incomes. Certainly in upswings this must have reflected full capacity working with rising short-run costs (the upward portion of the cost curve, plus rising money wages and input prices, and less efficient labour taken on) squeezing profits.

International influences on home investment have already been noted for particular kinds of capital formation, but influences through changes in short-term interest rates dictated by balance of payments needs could only have been very weak. Changes in business confidence in Britain may well have been related to changes in conditions abroad, particularly in the primary producers, but again this cannot be demonstrated. Indeed it would seem that the cyclical characteristics of home investment in aggregate, and its role in generating fluctuations in effective demand, were mainly imparted from shipbuilding and 'other' capital formation activities under the stimulus of international forces, and of their influence on expectations.

In the above survey a passive role has been allotted to the money supply in terms of initiating variations in British economic activity. In so far as domestic conditions were concerned, there was considerable elasticity in the supply of bank deposits in these years, as distinct from earlier periods when sharp contractions of liquidity had such sharp effects on spending before the business of central banking was clearly understood. Banks, it is felt, tended to meet the increasing demand for accommodation in upswings with rising short-term interest rates, and in downswings deposits and advances and short-term rates all fell with the declining demand for accommodation. Interest rates, however, had a more active role to play. Bank Rate, although it had little direct effect on home investment spending, made its influence felt on international capital movements and at times (especially near turning-points) did appear to influence long-term overseas lending, or at least was inversely associated then with movements in overseas issues. Its use to protect the Bank of England's Reserve was not without repercussions on borrowers *and* on their purchases of British goods. Hence the view that Britain by its use of Bank Rate in the context of the pre-1914 gold standard thrust the burden of readjustment on to others (the borrowing primary producers) is positively misleading, for once their activity was checked they ceased to purchase so many British goods and unemployment rose in Britain. Monetary forces by checking the pace of overseas lending, partly by cost and partly by confidence effects, had some influence in this roundabout way on British activity as well as on world activity.

The long-range effects of British overseas investment were dynamic. They increased the capacity of borrowers to produce primary products for which there were growing markets in Britain and continental Europe especially. The borrowers provided increased markets for British exports both in the construction period of the projects, and when their capacity to produce had expanded as their rising primary product exports increased their ability to import manufactured goods. Further, the rising demand for British exports influenced home investment. This interacting model of economic growth was naturally not bilateral, although there were strong trading ties between the primary producers and Britain, nor indeed did it produce smooth growth, for it was undertaken under conditions of private enterprise with speculative excesses and associated reactions, nor were chance features absent.

Accompanying this process two sorts of fluctuations can be discerned: (i) the 18–20-year waves in home and overseas investment and migration which 'trends' perhaps make smoother than they were and which did not seem to have great cyclical effects on money incomes; (ii) the 7–10-year cycles about the 'trends'. In the latter the variability of *ex ante* overseas lending must be incorporated in explanations of fluctuations which had a strong export root. One must relate these British economic fluctuations not only to world market conditions, but also to the varying pace of British overseas lending, itself dependent on expectations of profit and British monetary conditions, and its reactions on home activity. Further, it does seem that the British overseas lending was more dominant in the earlier period of 1870 to 1893, than the later one of 1893–1909 when other economies were growing relatively to the British and trade influences were more multilateral.

The conclusions of this paper would seem to agree with Keynes's stress on changes in confidence and expectations and with Robertson's view that British industrial fluctuations should be linked with affairs on far-off Prairies and Pampas. On the other hand they would be against the Hicks trade cycle model with its strong accelerator and its suggestion that the full-employment ceiling was responsible for ending booms by checking investment. Rather, it could support the use of a weak multiplier-accelerator model with erratic shocks (autonomous investment abroad would be one strong source) with emphasis on 'real' forces, although the monetary or interest-rate factor must not be neglected. The 'trade cycle' in this period for Britain is seen as inextricably linked with the growth and development processes not only of Britain but of the primary producers and borrowers. At the same time it must be recalled that there appears a distinct European contribution which has been undervalued and perhaps underexplained as compared with the American contribution.

Sources of Statistical Series Employed in Graphs
(for U.K. unless otherwise stated)

Index of industrial activity: W. Beveridge, *Full Employment in a Free Society* (London, 1944)

Trade union unemployment

Interest rate on three-month Bank bills

Subdivisions of U.K. exports

} Mitchell and Deane, *Abstract of British Historical Statistics* (Cambridge, 1962).

Net national income

Net home investment

Gross home investment

Components of gross home investment

Industrial profits

} C. H. Feinstein, 'Income and Investment in the U.K. 1856–1914', *Economic Journal* (1961).

Merchandise exports

Merchandise imports

Invisible exports

Current account balance of payments

} A. H. Imlah, *Economic Elements in the Pax Britannica* (Cambridge, Mass., 1958).

Overseas issues (calls) and subdivisions thereof

} M. Simon, 'The Pattern of New British Portfolio Foreign Investment 1865–1914' in J. H. Adler (ed.), *Capital Movements and Economic Development* (London, 1967).

Discounts and advances

Short-term interest rate abroad

} J. Tinbergen, *Business Cycles in the U.K. 1870–1914* (Amsterdam, 1956).

Average Bank Rate: W. Beveridge, *Unemployment, a Problem of Society* (London, 1930).

4 The Role of Consumption in Interwar Fluctuations*

H. W. RICHARDSON

I HAVE chosen to comment on economic fluctuations in Britain between the wars not by a sweeping survey of the period as a whole but by reprinting a more detailed investigation of the behaviour of consumption in the depression and recovery of the 1930s. A virtue of this approach is that it throws light on one of the most puzzling of the many paradoxes in the interwar economy, namely, the paradox of unemployment rising from 1·54 to 2·85 million in the depression and real consumption spending remaining unaffected. Careful explanation of paradoxes of this kind is necessary if the economic character of the interwar period is to be comprehended.

As a preliminary, however, it may be useful to present a minimal framework for understanding by way of background information on interwar fluctuations considered as a whole. There was nothing remarkable about the periodicity of the cycles. An immediate post-war boom reached a peak in 1920 and was followed by a sharp and severe slump. The upswing after 1921–2 was weak and unsteady, interrupted by a number of random shocks the most important of which was the General Strike of 1926 and the associated seven-month coal strike. This reversed the upward movement (industrial production fell by over 5 per cent), though the lost ground was more than made up in 1927. The upswing continued until late 1929, or a few months earlier depending on the indicators observed, when depression spread from abroad. The depression deepened until the third or fourth quarter of 1932, after which a recovery based on domestic impulses got under way. This was the beginning of one of the longest uninterrupted upswings in British economic history, fully five years in duration. The one-year recession of 1937–8 was as much due to the bursting of a domestic boom as to external factors. Although severe (the *Economist*'s index of business activity dropped by 11 per cent), the recession was quickly eliminated by increased spending on rearmament which carried the economy along vigorously up to and beyond the outbreak of the Second World War.

* This essay is adapted from Chapter 5 of *Economic Recovery in Britain, 1932–9* (Weidenfeld & Nicolson, 1967).

Apart from the exogenous shocks, the periodicity of fluctuations was not much different from that experienced abroad or from the pre-1914 United Kingdom pattern. What was striking, however, was the marked differences in amplitude in the British compared with the world cycle (world cycles were about $1\frac{3}{4}$ times more intense than the British). Although the post-1918 boom and the slump that followed it were, if anything, sharper in Britain than abroad, British fluctuations over most of the interwar period were 'damped'. The upswing of the later 1920s was weak, and the depression after 1929 relatively mild compared with the world slump. On the other hand, the recovery of the 1930s was more complete than in most overseas countries. The amplitude of fluctuations in the United Kingdom diverged from that found in United States cycles throughout the interwar period. This contrast calls for some comment, particularly since we would scarcely expect the most industrialised country in the world and the one most dependent on international trade to be one of the least affected by the world business cycle.

In the first place, the self-generating mechanism of the cycle itself is a relevant factor in the sense that the nature of one phase of the cycle determines the character of the next. On this view, the sequence 'weak upswing 1925–9 → mild depression 1929–32 → early and smooth recovery 1932–7' is explained as part of the natural course of events. This explanation throws a lot of weight on exports. Export sluggishness and the associated difficulties of the staple industries were important elements in the damped upswing of the late twenties. The depression that followed had few if any internal origins. Exports led the way into the slump in 1929, and although export collapse had severe effects on certain industries and certain regions and obviously had negative foreign trade multiplier effects on aggregate income, there were no autonomous internal sources of falling income. Similarly, and not surprisingly, the depression was much more obvious in the components of the balance of payments than in domestic activity. The fact that the downturn was not due to the bursting of a domestic boom had several favourable repercussions on the slump. There had been no overbuilding of capacity in manufacturing industry, and indeed a fair amount of excess capacity had been eliminated. Replacement investment could be undertaken sooner than would otherwise have been possible. Similarly, it could scarcely be argued that investment opportunities had been temporarily exhausted as in the United States; once expectations had revived (and they did not suffer a great deal compared with experience overseas) there was plenty of scope for investment. Some of the growth sectors had been able to expand in the later twenties without the disadvantages (e.g.

supply inelasticities) associated with an economy-wide boom. In such sectors, the temporary fall in demand was soon reversed by rising real incomes, and in some cases net investment was taking place even in the depression. Also, the lack of a boom in the 1920s avoided, despite the financial crisis of 1931, any collapse in monetary institutions of the kind that aggravated the slump in many overseas countries.

The mildness of the depression helped to make an early recovery possible. The weaker are depression impulses the smaller the impetus needed to induce recovery. The floor was reached long before the point of zero gross investment, and net investment was stimulated in some sectors by an early revival in demand and, in a few cases, by the opportunity to introduce cost-reducing innovations. In general, profits and share prices fell mildly enough not to make entrepreneurs and investors too pessimistic. Their expectations were kept reasonably buoyant from 1931 because the Government in power introduced measures that met with their approval. There was no serious stumbling-block to an investment revival once demand forces began to work (as is shown below, forces making for an upturn in consumer demand were already in existence during the slump). If anything damaged expectations this was the financial crisis of 1931, rather than the slump, and any fears on that score were alleviated by the abandonment of the gold standard and the consolidation measures following it.

There are several other factors that help to explain the better *cyclical* performance of the economy in the 1930s compared with the previous decade. These include the effects of monetary policy, the impact of building, and the interrelationship between secular growth trends and cycles. Monetary policy before 1931 was dominated by external considerations up to 1925 because of the strain on the exchange rate pending the return to the gold standard and after 1925 because of pressure on the gold and exchange reserves. In this period there are only two clear-cut cases of internally motivated actions: the deflationary measures of 1919–20 and the attempt to reflate in 1929–30. In the early 1920s the need to reduce the U.K./U.S. price ratio at a time when U.S. prices were falling forced drastic credit restrictions, while in the period 1925–9 monetary policy was used to try to reduce export prices in order to increase competitiveness and interest rates were also kept high to attract foreign funds. Over the decade as a whole, the effect of monetary policy was to dampen the cyclical pattern, though this was probably not a major depressant compared with the stagnation in exports and competition of imports. On the other hand, the cheap money policy adopted from the middle of 1932 was a lubricant to the economy and enabled the real cyclical forces at work to exert a natural and un-inhibited influence. It is doubtful whether monetary policy was a significant cause of the revival.

In the case of building too, its impact was to dampen cycles in the 1920s but to allow the natural cyclical pattern to assert itself in the 1930s. Building is an important component of general activity; residential construction accounted for more than 30 per cent of domestic capital formation between the wars. Moreover, it can be a major cyclical influence because building investment fluctuates more widely than most other types of investment, and is fairly insensitive to minor fluctuations in national income. Thus, the fact that there was a lack of correspondence between building and general activity in the first interwar decade and a broad similarity in movements in the second had a more than negligible impact on the course of interwar business cycles. The contrariness of the 1920s was accounted for largely by exogenous factors, particularly changes in the level of Government subsidies. The expansions of 1920–1, 1926 and 1927 were mainly due to high subsidies while the decline of 1927–8 (and to a lesser extent of 1931–2) is most easily explained by subsidy cuts. Only between 1922 and 1925 did building and economic activity in general move together. Accordingly, over much of the decade the economy followed a much more even, if a low-level, course than if residential building had not fluctuated in this way. Whereas public-sector housebuilding dominated the twenties, the private sector was much larger and more versatile in the thirties. Nevertheless, its influence on the cycle was on the whole a favourable one. Expansion in the private sector through the depression meant that total building activity was relatively well maintained, the acceleration after 1932 reinforced the recovery and the flattening out of the housebuilding curve after 1934 did not accentuate the late stages of the upswing.

It is difficult to understand the character of interwar fluctuations without giving some attention to secular growth factors and to the structural readjustments of the interwar period. I have referred elsewhere to the *structural growth influence* on cycles.[1] The growth of new industries (both manufacturing and services sectors) is predominantly a non-cyclical influence. If new industries are expanding rapidly, this could be described as a high rate of inter-industry structural readjustment. This rate of structural readjustment varies markedly over time and from one economy to another. If the timing is right, a high rate of structural readjustment may alleviate a slump, help to initiate a revival or strengthen the upswing.

[1] H. W. Richardson, *Economic Recovery in Britain, 1932–9* (1967) pp. 90–9.

Although introduced as early as in the United States, the new twentieth-century industries grew more slowly in Britain. Resources were transferred to the growth sectors at a low rate until after the First World War, and even then the early lag was only gradually overcome. The economy was subject to two successive trend influences: a depressive trend in the 1920s as market forces and stagnating exports forced the need for readjustment upon a reluctant economy, and an upward trend in the 1930s as the readjustments asserted themselves. These structural trends modified the course of fluctuations. There was a connection between the low rate of structural change and the weak upswings of the 1920s, while in the 1930s when faster structural change was influencing aggregate growth it was not solely coincidental that the depression after 1929 was mild and the recovery strong. Although it is possible to build an endogenous trend-cycle model, I prefer to treat the structural growth influence as a series of erratic shocks acting upon the endogenous cyclical mechanism. On this view, it is enough to argue that slow structural readjustment in the 1920s was an important element in the failure to develop a real boom, and that the acceleration in the growth of new industries and expanding service sectors in the early 1930s helped to bring the slump to a halt and set in motion a relatively vigorous recovery.

Random shocks of a quite different kind had some impact on the pattern of fluctuations. The repercussions of the First World War were of some consequence, particularly on certain sectors such as building (due to the complete cessation of housebuilding during the war and to the war's demographic consequences). The violent fluctuations of the first three or four postwar years were, in a real sense, a direct result of the war itself. The General Strike has already been mentioned; tariff increases abroad in the 1920s and even certain background events to the financial crisis of 1931 can also be treated as erratic shocks.

The foregoing provides merely the sketchiest of generalisations about interwar economic fluctuations. Although this background information may be a prerequisite for understanding, we need to descend to details to grasp the real character of business cycles. We now examine the behaviour of consumption at the lower turning-point in the early 1930s. This question is important because consumption was undoubtedly the most crucial cyclical determinant in the 1930s.

I

Whereas the relation of consumption to income tends to be stable in the long run, it varies quite markedly over the cycle. A given change in income results in a larger change in saving and a smaller change in consumption in the cycle than in the long run. The consumption component of income tends to act as a 'built-in-stabiliser' moderating both the contraction and expansionary processes. There is a wide variety of reasons why cyclical movements in consumption should be different from those in the long run, but they can be classified into two broad categories. The first group relates to the distribution of income. Various influences lead to shifts in the distribution of income during the depression with the result that although aggregate income is falling the real income of some sections of the community rises. Secondly, consumers may behave in such a way that the (marginal) propensity to consume of those with falling incomes such as the unemployed rises, not surprisingly since unemployed families faced with sharp falls in their income are very likely to spend more than they receive, while the propensity to consume of those with expanding incomes may remain (at least) stable. The likelihood of this latter possibility is debatable, and depends upon the validity of certain hypotheses about consumer behaviour.

The strong probability that consumption will fall proportionately less than income during the downswing can be matched only with the possibility that consumption will rise less during the upswing. Real wages, for instance, do not necessarily move inversely with the cycle. Studies of the relationship between factory wages and *wholesale* prices (the relevant prices, since these affect business profits) in the United States have shown that earnings have failed to fall as much as prices in slumps, but have risen as much or more in expansions.[1] There is therefore less risk in using the traditional theory in relation to consumption behaviour during depressions than over the cycle as a whole. This fits in with the purpose of this inquiry. What happened to consumption during the recovery in the 1930s is important, but less crucial than the behaviour of consumption at the bottom of the downswing since the early upturn in activity is more difficult to explain than the carriers of recovery once expansion had got under way.

Stable consumption was important during the depression because it helped to moderate the force of the contraction and set a relatively high floor to the level of income. But it can be argued that consumption played a more active role by helping to get recovery under way as well as by softening the depression. There are *a priori* objections to such an argument. First, even if the aggregate propensity to consume is rising it might be difficult to explain how this could induce a re-

[1] D. Creamer, *Behaviour of Wage Rates during Business Cycles*, N.B.E.R. Occasional Paper 34 (1950).

covery if total income is *falling*. Secondly, the depression of the early 1930s was of course characterised by heavier unemployment levels than any previously experienced. It might appear incongruous to account for the upturn in terms of high consumption at a time when between a quarter and a fifth of the labour force was out of work. Such objections stem from an over-emphasis of aggregates. Just as the falling income level was composed of people with rising incomes as well as with falling incomes, so a stable consumption level consists of reduced expenditure on some consumption goods and increased expenditure on others. The point is, however, that the effects of these additions and reductions of expenditure on the rate of economic activity do not cancel each other out. The industries which are affected by falls in sales will, of course, disburse labour and add to unemployment and will tend to disinvest, while the industries benefiting from increased demand for their products will have more workers and may (if expectations are favourable) invest in new plant. Whereas the increases and decreases in employment may tend to balance, this will not be true of the changes in investment. The industries facing a fall in demand will (if investment responds at all) undertake negative net investment, but as this can only take the form of scrapping obsolete plant as it wears out this will be a very slow process indeed. Unless the depression is very long, the fall in sales will not induce much disinvestment. What happens in the industries where demand is rising will, of course, depend on the view which businessmen in these industries take of the future course of demand. If demand is rising in the depression it is very likely that the industry was working at capacity in the previous boom (there would probably have been a transition period when demand fell slightly after the boom broke) so that there is not much excess capacity available to meet the rise in demand. There will be some elasticity in other directions, for example, the running down of stocks, but if long-term expectations are reasonably bright businessmen in some of these expanding industries will invest in response to the change in demand. This net investment is likely to be large because of the size of the capital–output ratio (in most industries considerably higher than unity). Such net investment may be crucially important, for its multiplier effects on the capital-goods industries may be reinforced by a psychological impact since a substantial if narrowly based dose of investment could initiate a revival in business confidence. Thus, the net investment which follows from a given rise in demand for certain consumer goods will almost certainly exceed the disinvestment resulting from a *similar* fall in demand for other consumer goods. The conclusion is that, although in macroeconomic terms induced investment is determined by the rate of *change* in consumption, a disaggregated analysis suggests a *stable* level of consumption can induce net investment. Such a disaggregated view is essential for understanding the role of consumption at the lower turning-point of the depression in Britain in the early 1930s.

II

As a starting-point it is convenient to look at the aggregate propensity to consume. The statistics are summarised in Table 4.1.[1] They clearly indicate the stability of consumption expenditure during the depression. Even in money terms consumption expenditure fell by only 7·9 per cent between 1929 and 1932, while real consumption expenditure expanded year by year up to 1938 except for a modest fall in the year 1931–2. At the same time, the aggregate propensity to consume G.N.P. rose continuously through the depression, reaching a peak of ·844 in 1932, then fell year by year thereafter, thus confirming the usual hypothesis about the behaviour of consumption over the cycle. It is misleading, however, to interpret the rise in the propensity to consume as meaning that consumers as a whole were consciously deciding to spend a higher proportion of their income. It must be remembered that the measure here refers to the relation between consumption and G.N.P. and not between consumption and disposable income. The difference between consumption and G.N.P. is made up of many heterogeneous factors, such as personal saving, depreciation, net business saving, taxes, social security contributions, and these do not necessarily behave in the same way as

TABLE 4.1
Aggregate Consumption, 1929–38

Year	Consumers' expenditure at current market prices	Consumers' expenditure at 1929 prices	Expenditure generating G.N.P. at current market prices	Aggregate propensity to consume G.N.P.
1929	4,062	4,062	5,040	·806
1930	4,006	4,206	4,915	·815
1931	3,865	4,290	4,590	·842
1932	3,743	4,267	4,435	·844
1933	3,751	4,329	4,492	·835
1934	3,864	4,482	4,689	·824
1935	3,995	4,554	4,949	·808
1936	4,145	4,601	5,175	·801
1937	4,356	4,661	5,500	·792
1938	4,457	4,680	5,826	·765

[1] Based on the estimates given in Appendix 3, Table 91, in P. Deane and W. A. Cole, *British Economic Growth, 1688–1959* (1962) pp. 332–3.

G.N.P. changes. Moreover, without any discretionary action activity by the public sector tends to boost disposable income. Firstly, because tax rates are graduated and assuming no change in the *rate* of taxation, receipts from both company and personal income taxes fall off as income declines, thereby reducing the amount by which consumers' expenditures would otherwise have to fall. Secondly, disposable income is maintained in depression by a rise in transfer payments such as unemployment benefit; revenue from social security contributions will drop while expenditure will increase. To some extent, it is as meaningful to regard consumers' expenditure as a large residual item left after automatic cyclical changes in other components of income have taken place as to regard it as the level of consumption relating to how consumers decide to allocate their income between consumption and saving.

The stability of aggregate consumption undoubtedly helped to moderate the depression, but on the argument presented above, that the net effect of balancing positive and negative changes in consumption expenditures for different commodities might be an expansion in investment, what happens to consumption at the sub-aggregate level is probably more significant. Comparing the distribution of the flow of goods and services to consumers in the 1930s with the distribution in the 1920s, the share of food and alcohol fell whereas the share of rents and rates, other services, tobacco and to a limited extent other goods increased. The proportion of durable goods, rent and services rose in the early 1930s relative to the proportion of perishable and semi-durable goods. Table 4.2 shows fluctuations in the pattern of consumers' expenditure in more detail.[1]

It is clear that expenditure on different items did not always move in the same way; expenditure on food rose steadily throughout the period 1929–38 with only minor interruptions in 1932–3 and 1934–5, expenditure on drink and tobacco fell sharply up to 1932 and rose thereafter fairly rapidly, while expenditure on clothing and footwear wobbled around the same point between 1929 and 1934, took a leap forward in 1935 and 1936 and then stagnated again. Expenditure on durable goods rose steadily throughout the depression, with very sharp rises indeed in 1931–2 and 1933–4, to a peak in 1936, then fell markedly. Finally, expenditure on cars and motor cycles fell by 18 per cent between 1929 and 1931 then more than doubled by 1937. Consumption of different kinds of goods, therefore, did not behave alike over the course of the cycle. Food and clothing purchases

---

[1] Data from J. R. Stone and D. A. Rowe, *Consumers' Expenditure in the United Kingdom, 1920–38* (1954) vol. I, and L.C.E.S., *Key Statistics of the British Economy, 1900–62* (1963) Table E.

showed no clear cyclical pattern and in fact there was a definite upward trend in expenditure on food. Expenditure on drink and tobacco moved strongly with the cycle, and expenditure on motor-cars too, to a lesser extent. In this case, however, the downswing was moderate and the upswing got under way very early (in 1931–2) leading the cycle in the economy as a whole. Expenditure on other durable goods followed a definite anticyclical course, expanding very fast in the later stages of the depression and falling rapidly in the later stages of recovery.

Expenditure on housing was another important expanding item of consumption. The rise in the number of houses built clearly illustrates this fact. Although houses are obviously consumer goods, most

TABLE 4.2

Indices of Real Consumption Spending, 1929–38 (1929 = 100)

Year	Food	Drink and tobacco	Clothing and footwear	Furniture, electrical and other durable goods	Cars and motor cycles
1929	100	100	100	100	100
1930	103	98	99	101	96
1931	107	93	101	103	82
1932	108	84	96	106	89
1933	107	88	100	111	103
1934	110	91	101	119	128
1935	110	95	105	126	154
1936	112	100	108	127	171
1937	113	105	108	121	175
1938	113	106	108	110	154

of them are akin to investment goods in that their construction is financed by institutions and paid for by the consumer over a large part of the good's life. How can the growth of the housing sector, therefore, be related to increasing consumption? In the first place, expenditure on rents (as well as on rents and rates taken together) rose steadily from year to year throughout the thirties in money terms, indicating a sharp expansion in real terms throughout the depression and early years of recovery.[1] Secondly, even when house purchases are financed through building societies as were most in the 1930s, the periodic repayments can be regarded as a part of consumption since unlike the initial deposit these almost certainly came out of current income rather than from saving. The expansion in

[1] Stone and Rowe, *Consumers' Expenditure in the U.K.*, p. 221.

repayments[1] points not merely to a rise in housing consumption but also to the emergence of a new class of consumers. This is because the rise in total repayments masks a significant fall in the average monthly repayment, due to lengthening of the mortgage term and later to reductions in building society interest charges. As the costs of housebuilding and house purchase fell, more and more people came within the ambit of potential house purchasers.

The stability of overall consumption at the lower turning-point hides, therefore, a rapid upsurge in individual categories, particularly houses and durable goods. Could the building and consumer durable industries respond to an increase in demand, and possibly have a critical effect in inducing recovery? Building had a low capital–output ratio, with the result that the impact of rising output on plant and equipment was very modest, while the substantially increased demands for materials affected in the main a narrow range of industries which had little contact with other sectors in the economy. Yet investment in construction adds up to a high proportion of total investment, so that the relative stability of housebuilding at a high level meant a firm base of positive gross and net investment going on at the bottom of the cycle. Moreover, the modest stimulus of rising building output to capital-goods industries was more than compensated by its direct effect on employment. The other consumer durable industries had been expanding steadily in the 1920s and output fell very little in response to the shock of depression so that they had little spare capacity. Also, they were on the whole very capital-intensive. The growth in demand resulted in a sudden and dramatic fillip to the capital-goods industries supplying consumer durable producers with plant and equipment. The combined effect of investment in these two sectors might well have been sufficient in itself to reverse contraction even in the absence of a rise in aggregate consumption.

The supplementary question of how this investment could be financed in view of the severe fall in both business and personal savings presents little problem. Building societies were able to finance the increase in the number of houses built because they were the principal beneficiaries of funds driven from the gilt-edged market by the lower yields associated with cheap money. Investment in the consumer durable industries was financed mainly out of undistributed profits. These industries had been reasonably profitable in the

---

[1] Mortgage repayments (excluding interest) to building societies rose from £46·5 million in 1931 to £71·6 million in 1934, while the annual total advances increased by over 50 per cent between 1932 and 1934. H. Bellman, 'The Building Trades', *Britain in Recovery* (1937) p. 418.

1920s and had retained high proportions (for the time) of their profit for reinvestment.[1] There is consequently little reason to doubt that the increase in demand for some items of consumers' expenditure, which the statistics suggest took place, could be made effective and could induce net investment and hence recovery.

III

Is the above argument reconcilable with the evidence of changes in consumers' disposable income and of consumer behaviour? If expenditure on certain important elements of consumption was rising at the lower turning-point, who were buying the goods? Is it reasonable to argue that many people were more prosperous in the depression than they had been before? The reason why contemporary explanations played down the role of consumption in the recovery is that they were unable to give satisfactory answers to these questions. For example, one observer wrote:

> It is sometimes argued . . . that the fall in retail prices left the bulk of the population with increased purchasing power . . . it does not appear convincing as a major explanation: can it be maintained that a substantial portion of the population was better off in 1931 and 1932 than in 1926? Even those who did gain through the fall in the cost of living would have hesitated to enter into new commitments.[2]

Of course, the trouble went deeper than that. It was difficult for interpreters of the scene in the 1930s to accept that, assuming purchasing power increased, rising consumption could induce recovery. The *Economist*, which by 1935 was arguing that expanding real income was one of the main factors in the growth in output of houses and motor-cars,[3] heavily criticised Keynes in 1931 for arguing that increased spending was the solution to depression:

> Every pound saved, according to Mr Keynes, is so much added to the burden of unemployment, and now is the time for everybody, and especially for public authorities to 'spend magnificently'. In so far as trade depression is psychological, this might be sound advice if enthusiastic spending in Great Britain were sufficient to revive industrial confidence throughout the world. If it were not, the consequences (some degree of credit inflation is presumably

---

[1] In the period 1924–9 motor vehicle firms saved 66 per cent of their net earnings and the electrical engineering industry saved 41 per cent.

[2] A. T. K. Grant, *A Study of the Capital Market in Post-War Britain* (1937) pp. 246–7.

[3] *Economist*, 26 Oct 1935, p. 796.

implied) would be a brief and glorious boom for the sheltered industries and a rise in the domestic price level which, through its effect on costs, would give their quietus to the export trades.[1]

The *Economist*'s criticisms show a remarkable inability to distinguish between situations of full employment and general unemployment!

In order to confirm the conclusions drawn from the statistics of consumers' expenditure it is necessary to demonstrate two facts: first, that forces operating in the depression were making for a rise in consumers' disposable income; secondly, that consumers were willing to spend, in spite of the general atmosphere of depression which might have been expected to damage expectations, a high proportion of that increased income. There are several kinds of evidence which can be used to support the former: relative movements in prices and wages, effects of improving terms of trade, transfer payments and other fiscal variations over the cycle, shifts in the distribution of income. The latter proposition is not readily testable. The statistics of the aggregate propensity to consume are consistent with it, but not conclusive since they relate consumption to G.N.P. and not to disposable income. If reasonable hypotheses about consumer behaviour which explain why many consumers were willing to maintain their level of consumption in spite of falls in their income can be put forward, these together with the estimates of increased consumption will have to suffice as an explanation. Such hypotheses can, and have been, tested but the information needed for this period is not available, and the exercise would be a full-scale study in itself.

In depressions one usually finds, on the one hand, a rise in real wages for those left in work because the price of labour is more inflexible than prices in general and, on the other, an increase in unemployment as production falls off. In effect, this means a transfer of income within the lower income groups from the unemployed to the employed. The real value of the earnings of those still in employment rises, while the earnings of those thrown out of work fall to zero, and their subsistence comes from unemployment benefit and other social security payments. The early 1930s were no exception to this generalisation. The estimates of average annual real earnings in Table 4.3 point to a significant rise from 1929 to 1933 (of 12·8 per cent), approximate stability over the next three years followed by a sharp fall in 1937,[2] while unemployment increased from a rate of 10·4 per cent in 1929 to 22·1 per cent in 1932 and the numbers in

---

[1] Ibid., 1 Jan 1931, pp. 107–8.

[2] A. Chapman and R. Knight, *Wages and Salaries in the United Kingdom 1920–38* (1953) p. 30.

employment fell from 16,952,100 in 1929 to 16,103,600 in 1931 but rose by some 70,000 the following year. Money wages did not fall as fast as the cost of living for two main reasons. Firstly, competition in product markets responds to the impact of depression far more than in factor markets because there are strong institutional obstacles,

TABLE 4.3

Estimated Indices of Average Annual Real Earnings, 1929–38
(1930 = 100)

Year	Average annual money earnings	Cost of living	Average annual real earnings
1929	100·2	103·8	96·5
1930	100·0	100·0	100·0
1931	98·6	93·4	105·6
1932	97·0	91·1	106·5
1933	96·4	88·6	108·8
1934	97·4	89·2	109·2
1935	98·8	90·5	109·2
1936	100·7	93·0	108·3
1397	102·6	97·5	105·1
1938	105·7	98·7	107·1

particularly the resistance of trade unions, to price flexibility in the labour market. Collusion between producers to maintain the prices of their goods is much less likely to hold together in times of depression. Even without imperfections in competition, the effect of lags would be such as to make it difficult to reduce wages as quickly as prices fell. Secondly, the cost of living was falling faster than the domestic price level because imported foodstuffs were becoming cheaper relative to other goods; the consequences of improving terms of trade will be given separate treatment below.

The view that trade union resistance was one of the main factors in the differential movements in wages and prices is supported by the fact that *money* wages fell very little in heavily unionised industries. Money wages in manufacturing fell much less than in service industries (where unions were in general weak), and within manufacturing money wages fell less in industries where unions were strong than in other industries. In shipbuilding average annual money earnings fell by only 1·3 per cent between 1929 and 1933, in iron and steel by 2·5 per cent and in coal mining actually rose by 1·7 per cent. The relative stability of money earnings in the depressed staple industries suggests that the strength of unions was more important than the level of activity in the industry. The one depressed manufacturing group where money wages did fall substantially was textiles, but this was to be explained by the predominance of female labour which is generally less able to prevent both wage cuts and unemployment. It is clear that the rise in aggregate real earnings was not due simply to the weighting of prosperous industries with rising money earnings, for the only industries showing a rise in average money earnings between 1929 and 1933 were tobacco and mining, while in printing and publishing money earnings remained stable. That increased real earnings were characteristic of industry in general is shown by the fact that the percentage fall in average money earnings was less than the percentage fall in the cost of living (14·6 per cent, 1929–33) in almost all industries, the exceptions being textile finishing where money earnings dropped 15·9 per cent and fishing with a fall of 17·4 per cent.[1] All this suggests that the growth of real wages was due to the fact that wages were more inflexible than prices, mainly because of the inevitable lags before employers could reduce wages and the successful defence of pre-depression wage rates by trade unions, and not to an upward trend in money wages paid by expanding industries. Another possible explanation, though only a possibility, is that manufacturers benefited so much from falling imported raw material prices, especially in 1930–1 and 1931–2, that this blunted their incentive to try to reduce money wages.

The wage earners and lower-paid salary earners (except for those in Government employment where salaries were cut in August 1931) were benefiting not only at the expense of the unemployed but also at the expense of the middle classes (defined as those having an income of more than £250 per year). The real values of total personal incomes (at 1928 prices) of those with annual incomes below £250 rose from £2,200 million in 1929 to £2,309 million in 1932, while personal incomes above £250 fell from £1,393 million to £1,074 million.[2] Some of the people in this group were affected by national economy measures, others were in jobs where salaries could easily be cut or were dependent on fees which varied directly with the level of activity, but many derived part of their incomes from profits, dividends and interest earned on their capital, all of which fell severely in the depression. On the other hand, their consumption declined by less than 10 per cent suggesting that they had decided to spend more of a lower income. Because income as a whole was not rising, it follows that the growth in real incomes of those in work was merely a transfer of income from the unemployed and from those earning over £250 a year. Can a transfer effect, because it is not an addition to income, stimulate recovery? Certainly, because after the transfer the propensities to consume of the groups concerned will not remain

---

[1] The above analysis is based on Tables 46 and 47, ibid., pp. 104–5.
[2] E. A. Radice, *Savings in Great Britain, 1922–1935* (1939) p. 42.

the same. What happens to the propensity to consume of the gainers is debatable, and is examined later, but there are grounds for holding that it remained at least stable. As for the unemployed, their incomes fell so sharply that they must have dissaved, tending to spend more than the income they received. The upper income groups, as the relative stability in their consumption suggests, tried to maintain their previous consumption levels as their income fell with the result that their propensities to consume rose too.

Another important aspect of increased real incomes was the fact that the terms of trade were moving in Britain's favour throughout the depression phase. The price index of $\frac{\text{exported manufactures}}{\text{imported foodstuffs}}$ rose from 90 in 1929 (1930 = 100) to 114 in 1933 and stayed almost at this peak until 1936, reflecting the very heavy drop in the average price of imported foodstuffs (almost 39 per cent between 1929 and 1933).[1] Improving terms of trade are generally regarded as being the major factor in increased purchasing power for two reasons. Firstly, all classes gained from cheap imported foodstuffs and the gain in real income was significant (certainly for the lower income groups) because imports bulked large in total food supplies. Secondly, the terms of trade aspect is looked upon as an addition to income whereas differential movements in wages and prices and the rise in unemployment in the depression is merely a transfer effect. Neither of these arguments is unassailable, certainly in so far as recovery was concerned. All classes (with the qualification mentioned below) might gain in varying degrees from improving terms of trade, but this was unlikely to assist recovery very much if the increase in real incomes was spent on more imported food for families with low living standards. The many social surveys of the period point to a substantial fraction of the population, including a high proportion of the unemployed, living below the 'poverty line'. For these people any increase in real incomes resulting from favourable terms of trade was almost certain to go on basic necessities such as extra food – with negligible effects on industrial investment. To spread the benefits of rising real incomes thinly over the community as a whole is less effective than concentrating the increase on income receivers who are willing to spend. Moreover, as implied in the analysis of consumers' expenditure earlier, what counts is not the absolute level of purchasing power but where expenditure is concentrated. The ability of increased purchasing power to stimulate recovery will depend on how far it is spent on buying goods which will promote

[1] K. Martin and F. G. Thackeray, 'The Terms of Trade of Selected Countries, 1870–1938', *Oxford University Institute of Statistics Bulletin*, x (1948) 383.

industrial investment and business confidence. If it is dissipated on buying more imported food, its impact on the economy as a whole will be slight.

Similarly, to argue that the improving terms of trade represented a clear addition to income rather than a transfer effect is to exaggerate. Not all the effects on real incomes of improving terms of trade were beneficial. The low incomes of the primary producers meant that they were less able to buy British exports. The primary producers' demand for British exports was probably elastic in respect to both income and price, and one consequence of the movements in the terms of trade was increased unemployment and falling real incomes among workers in British export industries. To a considerable extent, therefore, improving terms of trade meant not so much an addition to income as, once more, a transfer. In both cases (the differential movements in wages and prices and changing terms of trade) a fall in employment and real income via changes in demand was balanced by a rise in real income via changes in price, the only difference being that the terms of trade effect refer to changes in export demand and import prices only, not to aggregate demand and the overall price level (or rather, wages and the prices of commodities included in the cost of living index). Of course, improving terms of trade did not affect each section of the population to the same extent as differential wage–price movements (for instance, the former boosted the real incomes of the unemployed whereas the latter did not), but the two effects operated in more or less the same way.

These criticisms are not intended to denigrate the significance of improving terms of trade but rather to place it in perspective. It was important but no more important than other factors in increased incomes. The tendency to regard the terms of trade improvement as a kind of divine bounty accruing to everyone is certainly misplaced. To argue that movements in the terms of trade were the major element in the expansion of real incomes because they were a net addition to income and because all income groups benefited is to neglect the fact that what is important for recovery is not necessarily greater purchasing power for all income groups including the unemployed but more purchasing power for those sections of the community prepared to spend more on goods which might stimulate investment. The upper strata of wage earners and salary earners, the main beneficiaries of the transfer of income from those out of work to those in employment, probably had a greater propensity to consume *home* goods than the unemployed in that a substantial proportion of the expenditure of the poorest classes went on imported food. This reflected the high proportion of food expenditure in the family budget and the tendency of the poor to buy the cheaper, less favoured imported foodstuffs.

The argument so far is that real disposable income was boosted in the depression by the improvement in the terms of trade (possibly in part a windfall gain) and by rising real incomes for those in work. The latter was achieved by a transfer of income from the unemployed whose earnings fell to zero to the employed whose money earnings either remained almost stable or failed to fall as fast as prices. This resulted in an increase in disposable income simply because the unemployed received unemployment benefit from the Government, virtually all of which (and possibly more) went into consumption. This raises the whole question of variations in Government revenue and expenditure over the cycle as an influence on consumption. The balance of revenue and expenditure on transfer payments (i.e. unemployment benefit, public assistance and other social security payments, where contributions are levied on all participants in the schemes to form a fund out of which such payments are made when the need arises) changes drastically over the cycle. For example, in regard to the Unemployment Insurance scheme total contributions varied directly and total benefits inversely with the level of employment. In the depression when unemployment is heavy, contributions paid by those in work fall off whereas benefits increase sharply so that current expenditure for this purpose is very much in excess of current revenue; in the boom the converse is true. In the early 1930s, therefore, consumption was held up by the fact that total payments for unemployment benefit (even though the level of benefit was reduced by 10 per cent on the May Committee's recommendation in 1931) and by the Public Assistance Boards were greatly increased. Of course, this did not follow from any conscious act of policy but from the automatic functioning of a scheme of this kind unless attempts are made to balance such national insurance funds from year to year. However, one consequence of the 1931 economy campaign was an attempt to make these funds self-balancing.

Tax revenues too, with a *given* structure of tax rates, tend to fall off in slumps and to increase in booms. This is because income and company tax rates are usually graduated, so that the rate applicable rises as incomes and profits rise. In the depression incomes and profits may fall off to such an extent that the taxpayer falls on to a lower tax schedule. Similarly, customs revenues tend to vary directly with economic activity, simply because the demand for imports moves directly with the cycle. In the depression of the early thirties it is difficult to unravel the effect of taxation on the level of disposable income, primarily because tax rates did not remain unchanged.

Under the influence of economy and crisis considerations and of obsession with balanced budget orthodoxy certain taxes were raised, particularly of course import duties; taxes were higher in 1935–6 than they had been in 1929–30. But the share of taxes on incomes and property in total tax revenue fell from 43·9 per cent in 1929 to 40·5 per cent in 1936. The most marked feature of the composition of taxes was the rising share of customs receipts which went up from 17·2 per cent to 26·5 per cent over the same period.[1] This might have been expected to harm consumption since a high proportion of import duties was levied on consumption goods. To assume this would be wrong. In the first place, the introduction of protective tariffs rendered new taxes on domestic consumption unnecessary for customs revenues helped to fill the gap between revenue and expenditure. More important, however, was the fact that most of the increased consumers' demand went on home-produced goods rather than imported goods. One effect of import duties was to divert to domestic industry some of the purchases which had been previously made abroad; electrical appliances were a notable instance of this. It is the consumption of home-produced goods which may stimulate recovery in industrial investment and output; consumption of imported goods only comes into consideration if high import duties combined with a degree of inelasticity in demand for imports lead to purchases of imports absorbing income which might otherwise have been used for buying domestic goods. In the early 1930s this was not the case. Consumption goods where the demand for imports was somewhat inelastic were mainly foodstuffs which were not subject to duty. Where the demand for imported consumer goods was elastic tariffs had a salutary effect on domestic recovery by transferring demand from the foreign to the home producer. Of course, because of the timing of the introduction of the general tariff any effects of this kind were felt in the later stages of the depression and early years of recovery than over the depression as a whole. Nevertheless, it seems reasonable to conclude that changes in taxation did not harm consumption in the depression, and may have benefited it.

Shifts in distribution of income affected consumption not only by raising the level of disposable income but also, and probably more important, by affecting the propensity to spend this income. Of course, intrasectoral shifts (e.g. from the unemployed to the employed) have been discussed above; it is now necessary to look at the overall shift from profit to wage earners. The fall in business savings could have resulted in an increase in consumers' disposable income. Business savings fell off considerably in the depression: it is estimated

[1] League of Nations, *World Economic Survey 1935–6* (1936) p. 223.

that net business savings in manufacturing fell to 30·9 per cent of their 1929 level in 1932 and that 1929 was not overtaken until 1936.[1] One reason why business saving declined is that much of it is done specifically in order to finance new investment by the firm itself, and there is not likely to be much need for this in depression when the inducement to invest is generally low. Yet provided the reduction in such saving did not represent an absolute loss of income, it may well have aided consumption by transferring income to potential consumers. For one thing, business savings were allowed to fall off in order to keep up (relatively) dividends, and those receiving dividends were in view of the evidence on upper- and middle-class consumption using them much more for consumption purposes than they had before. Perhaps even more important, the fall in business savings reflected reduced profits, and an important cause of falling profits in many industries was fierce price competition to gain sales. To the extent that pruning of profit margins was associated with lower prices for the consumer, this had a substantial income effect releasing purchasing power to buy other goods, and therefore raising *real* disposable income as a whole.

Shifts in the distribution of income are much more likely, however, to influence the propensity to consume than the level of disposable income. Any transfer of income from high to low income groups, such as from profit to wage earners, is assumed to mean that income is flowing from people with a low to people with a high propensity to consume (from the hypothesis that the marginal propensity to consume falls as income rises). This assumption is consistent with contemporary evidence which suggests that the average propensity to save of persons with incomes of £250 or more per year varied between 0·30 and 0·36, that is, three to four times the average of income receivers below this figure (their propensity to save varied between 0·075 and 0·10).[2] It is difficult to quantify accurately just how much the distribution of income changed in the depression. Certainly, it moved in the expected direction. Profits earned are estimated to have fallen by 25 per cent between 1929 and 1932 which is far more than any fall in wages over the same period, though profits revived quickly in the recovery, surpassing the 1929 level in 1935.[3] Perhaps a better guide is the estimate for the percentage share of incomes from employment in national income. This rose from 59·5 per cent in 1929 to 64·3 per cent in 1932, though it declined a little

[1] P. E. Hart, *Studies in Profit, Business Saving and Investment in the United Kingdom, 1920–62* (1965) vol. I, p. 118.

[2] Radice, *Savings in Great Britain*, p. 32.

[3] Hart, *Studies in Profit*, p. 21.

in following years.[1] It is impossible to judge how far this change in income distribution affected recovery via changes in consumption. It seems reasonable to argue that it tended to raise the aggregate propensity to consume, but there are, as was stressed above, dangers in using aggregates. Even if a large minority of house buyers consisted of wage earners this may have been less true of purchasers of motor-cars or of some of the newer types of electrical appliances in the conditions of the early 1930s. The fact that consumption of the high income groups fell off so slightly may be more important than any effects of shifts in the distribution of income. Furthermore, even the low income groups saved on a considerable scale; the net growth in small types of savings averaged £66·4 million in the period 1930–5.[2] Radice argued that virtually all the increase in institutional savings between 1929 and 1932 was due to small savers and concluded that 'a considerable part of any increase in the prosperity of the lower income groups is used to increase savings, and that the weight of evidence for the period is that an equalisation of incomes does not tend to decrease individuals' savings, but rather to increase them'.[3] This may be a wrong inference from the evidence; for example, the growth in small institutional savings probably reflected a trend for the working classes to put their savings into institutions instead of hoarding them at home rather than an increase in their propensity to save. Nevertheless, it suggests the need to refer to the effects of changes in the distribution of income with caution.

IV

It is hoped that the case that consumption played an important role at the lower turning-point has been established. The evidence of relatively stable aggregate consumption and of rapidly expanding consumption in certain key sectors where investment in the 1930s was high (housing and consumer durables), of the rising aggregate propensity to consume and of the expanding real incomes for large sections of the community make this conclusion difficult to refute. Yet, to complete the argument it is necessary to explain why people were willing to spend heavily, especially on consumer durables where expenditure is deferrable, in depression. Common-sense reasoning might lead one to think that the working class at least would prefer to save most of the excess above expenditure on necessities for

---

[1] Deane and Cole, *British Economic Growth*, p. 244.

[2] E. Nevin, *The Mechanism of Cheap Money* (1955) p. 250. 'Small' savings are taken to include industrial assurance funds, provident societies, Post Office and Trustees Savings Banks and National Savings Certificates.

[3] Radice, op. cit., pp. 63, 67.

security especially because of the fear of unemployment. In this case common sense would be a poor guide, for the means test which was operated from 1931 meant that an unemployed worker who had a fund of savings was quite likely to receive no benefit or public assist-ance at all. For this reason, if a worker was afraid of being un-employed he might be tempted to spend all he earned rather than to save for bad times.

Apart from this, there are at least three possible reasons why con-sumers were willing to spend a higher proportion of their income in the depression. Firstly, a number of hypotheses about consumer behaviour have been put forward (and tests yielded fairly good results) which suggest that people try to preserve high levels of con-sumption as income falls. There is no direct evidence to substantiate such hypotheses for British experience in the 1930s. Secondly, the development of new products can in certain circumstances stimu-late consumers to spend more. Usually, the result is that consumers reallocate their budgets as between durables and non-durables almost always associated with a sharp fall in savings.[1] The new products which have this effect mostly fall in the consumer durables group, and the reason why they can elicit this response is that the purchase of a consumer durable can be regarded as buying an asset, so that expenditure on consumer durables is a real alternative to saving. There is some evidence that 'new' consumer durables giving rise to these changes were appearing on the British market in the early 1930s. Thirdly, and following from the above factors, there is a particularly strong historical explanation of why many consumers were willing to readjust their expenditure between non-durables and durables and between saving and durables in the early 1930s.

It is obvious that several factors determine the short-run propen-sity to consume. To name a few: consumers' expectations regarding their future incomes and employment prospects, recent price changes, recent changes in the level and distribution of income and the size of liquid assets held. However, generalisation on how these influences work is difficult. More useful as an explanation may be two general hypotheses, the 'relative income' hypothesis associated with J. S. Duesenberry and Franco Modigliani and the 'permanent income' hypothesis elaborated by Milton Friedman.[2] The 'relative income' hypothesis rests on the assumption that where the current level of income stands compared to the highest level of income achieved in

---

[1] J. S. Duesenberry, *Business Cycles and Economic Growth* (1958) p. 175.
[2] For the detailed arguments and the evidence see J. S. Duesenberry, *Income, Saving and the Theory of Consumer Behaviour* (1949) and M. Friedman, *A Theory of the Consumption Function* (1957).

the past is of crucial importance. People, it is argued, tend to adjust their standards of living in an upward direction if the trend of income levels is rising. When incomes fall, however, consumers struggle to maintain the highest level of consumption previously achieved with the result that consumption falls but slowly as income drops. The 'permanent income' hypothesis, on the other hand, argues that a family's consumption is determined not by its *current* income (or even its highest income level in the past) but by its *permanent* or *normal* income. Normal income is a reference mark; it is that level of income which the household expects to receive on average over a number of years, and it is clearly a subjective level. It follows that current changes in income will not alter consumption unless these changes also influence the consumer's belief as to what normal income will be in the medium-term future and not merely in the next time period. Normal income moves much more sluggishly than current income and the hypothesis is that consumption is primarily related to normal income. Generally speaking, therefore, when current income falls consumption will decline only slowly because consumers do not think the decline in income is permanent. Despite their differences, both these theories *might* explain why the propensity to consume disposable income can rise in a depression.

There is rather more concrete evidence that the development of new goods can induce consumers to spend more and cut down on their saving. By 'new goods' one does not necessarily mean brand-new goods appearing on the market for the first time. Initially, knowledge of new products is often so limited and the price so high that demand is very low. After a certain stage, however (which may vary from a year or so to decades after the product's birth), technical progress results in price cuts sufficient to make the product attractive to consumers and information has spread to an extent that consumers convince themselves of the potentiality of the good and its value to them. It is usually around this time that the product reaches a mass market, and is capable of influencing the propensity to consume. The new goods are unlikely to retain this power for long. This is because the demand for consumer durables is affected not only by the level of income but by the amount already owned (the *stock* of goods) and by the proportion of this stock considered obsolescent. Within a relatively short space of time the industry producing the good will attain maturity, when the bulk of its output will be to meet replacement demand. Pending some surge forward in average income levels, sales will cease to expand dramatically. Certainly, by this time the product can have little influence on consumption in a depression. The scrapping rate of the existing stock of the good can easily be slowed down and the purchase of new goods will tend to be deferred until better times.

Several kinds of goods and services, wireless sets, motor-cars and electricity for example, were especially attractive to consumers in the early 1930s. Most of these goods were not new in the strictest sense, but they did become available about this time in sufficient quantity, with quality much improved and the products geared to consumers' tastes, and at prices considerably lower than ever before. The typical radio set of the 1920s was a home-constructed device which required some degree of skill to assemble; manufactured sets were available but prices were very high. The radio assembly industry, however, adopted mass-production methods in the late twenties and early thirties, prices fell and hire-purchase facilities became available.[1] This boosted demand in unprecedented fashion: radio licence holders swelled from three to eight million in the period 1929–36, and increased by 973,000 in 1930–1 and by 877,000 in 1931–2 alone. Motor-cars in the 1920s were large specialist vehicles, costly to buy and costly to run. New production methods and technical refinements in this industry too were adopted towards the end of the 1920s. By 1933 three out of every five motor-cars being produced were 10 h.p. or less as against one in four half a decade earlier. Prices were falling, too: retail prices of motor vehicles fell by over 40 per cent between 1924 and 1932 and by more than 20 per cent between 1929 and 1932. Combined with cheaper running costs this placed motor vehicles within the range of some working- and lower middle-class buyers. Falling relative prices in some branches of the electrical appliance industry also stimulated consumption and here the main factor making price reduction possible was the exploitation of economies of scale due to the fact that domestic products were replacing import demand as well as expanding total demand. In electricity, price reductions led to a substitution of electricity for gas not only in new houses but in many existing houses. The latter did not have much direct effect on consumption, but the conversion of houses to electricity was very often associated with new demands for electrical appliances. Although hire-purchase facilities were provided only on a minute scale compared with postwar developments, there was a *relatively* rapid expansion in such provision in the early 1930s.

The falling off in population growth in the interwar period had important implications for the level and structure of consumption, and this is the basis of the third argument. The number of births had fallen off sharply compared with pre-1914 days. The annual average

[1] For these points see S. G. Sturmey, *Economic Development of Radio* (1958) pp. 169–81.

number of births had dropped from 1,108,100 in the period 1910–12 to 762,000 in 1929, and the annual average number of births for the period 1931–6 was only 694,000 as against 800,000 in the period 1922–30.[1] In the first decade of the twentieth century population grew by 10·3 per cent; in the 1920s the increase was 4·7 per cent and in the period 1930–7 only 3·1 per cent. This retardation in population growth might have been expected to make recovery more difficult to achieve. A rapidly growing population requires sharp increases in the supply of both consumer and capital goods, and hence in the rate of investment. If population grows only very slowly depression will tend to get longer. Moreover, there is little doubt that the relative stagnation of population growth in Europe had been an important cause of the depression, since it meant a slow-growing demand for foodstuffs in a period of rapid technical change in agriculture, and thereby contributed to the excess supply and low prices of primary products on world markets, perhaps the most characteristic feature of the world depression. Moreover, Britain's best customers were the agricultural countries, and this effect of population change had repercussions on the British balance of payments and hence on domestic investment, tending to moderate booms and to intensify slumps.

If this were the complete picture, the falling off in population growth would have depressed consumption. There was, however, a compensating aspect. As less children are born, this frees an increasing proportion of total consumers' expenditure from clothing and food and also frees a certain amount of saving, since saving for one's children's future (for example, for education) was probably one of the strongest incentives to save, for spending on luxury goods or on goods the demand for which is not directly related to family size and needs, especially consumer durables. It is evident that family composition has strong influences on consumption.[2] Investigations have shown that as family composition changes the demand for housing, durables and motor-cars will all be affected, and consumption of housing and cars is a function of both income and family size. Consumption of cars, for example, was found to be inversely correlated with family size. The same correlation was to be noticed with other consumer durables, but the relationship was not universal. The demand for washing machines tended to grow with increasing family size. In housing, the quantity of housing consumed increased with increases in family size, but price per room (an indicator of quality)

[1] *Statistical Abstract of the U.K., 1924–38* (Cmd 6232, 1940) p. 6, and *Report of the Royal Commission on Population* (Cmd 7695, 1949) pp. 45–6.

[2] See for example M. H. David, *Family Composition and Consumption* (1962).

declined. The implication to be drawn from this analysis is that the fall in average family size which accompanied the slowing down of population growth in Britain in the interwar period would tend to raise the absolute demand for many types of consumer durables. Housing was, if these results were applicable to British experience, an exception to this, but reductions in family size might increase the demand for quality housing even if the demand expressed in terms of quantity of house-room fell off. This was consistent with more and more families wanting to buy their own houses, if one assumes owner-occupied houses were superior to those built to let.

This change in the composition of consumption expenditure from non-durables (food and clothing for children) to durables (luxury goods) tended to contribute to instability in consumer demand, since the purchase of consumer durables can easily be postponed and demand is subject to fairly rapid changes in tastes. This change did not necessarily act as a destabiliser, however, for if the decline in population growth was associated with (or even partly caused by) an increased demand for new types of goods, the effect might be to halt the depression and induce recovery. It has already been suggested that new goods influencing the propensity to consume were appearing about this time. Increasing expenditure on consumer durables, because of the links these industries had with key sectors in the economy such as steel and engineering, would tend to promote an increase in investment more rapidly and with more effect than a rise in expenditure on non-durables. In modern times when having children is a matter of individual choice, there is much scope for married couples to revise their scale of consumer preferences at will, rearranging from time to time the priorities given to houses, children, cars, holidays, etc. Tempted by the availability of new types of consumer durables and by the opportunity (because of a large supply, falling building costs and relaxation of borrowing stringency) to buy their own home, many young married couples in the early 1930s preferred to spend their incomes on houses and durables than on having and bringing up babies. This was a relatively painless way of reallocating their incomes between non-durables and durables, and children probably for the first time were regarded as items of consumption absorbing income and for whom other products could be substituted like any other good. Concrete evidence for this argument is almost impossible to obtain, but there is a strong *prima facie* case for it. Of course, the effect of rising incomes in the postwar period has been that consumers may have both children and consumer durables rather than having to choose one or the other. The choice-making decision was probably only crucial for this relatively short historical period of time when average incomes stood at a particular level, when a wide range of new commodities was appearing on the mass market and when people had the physical means to avoid having children without incurring social disapproval. This argument suggests that declining population growth may have been an important factor in recovery via its influence in raising the propensity to consume (reduced saving) and by changing the composition of consumer demand between non-durables and durables in favour of the latter.

V

To sum up the argument: the relative stability of aggregate consumption was a moderating factor in Britain's economic depression in the early 1930s. Consumption was stable for many reasons. Rising real incomes for those in work, gains from the terms of trade, the stabilising effects of Government transfer payments and the effects of taxation raised the share of disposable income in G.N.P. Other factors such as shifts in the distribution of income, the behaviour of consumers in response to falling incomes, and the introduction of new goods influenced the propensity to consume. However, the role of consumption went beyond this, for stable aggregate consumption masked reduced expenditure on some items and increased expenditure on others. Consumers were reallocating their expenditure between non-durables and durables, raising the demand for cars, electrical appliances and houses. The implications of reduced family size were an important relevant factor in this change in the composition of consumer demand. The increased sales of certain groups of consumption goods helped recovery to get under way by inducing new investment in plant and equipment; high capital–output ratios in some of the industries concerned meant that this new investment was of more than marginal significance.

5   The Causes of Business Fluctuations[1*]

D. J. COPPOCK

Introduction

It is now about 100 years since economists began their study of the business cycle and its causes, if Schumpeter was correct in naming Clément Juglar as the first to be concerned with the problem of wavelike movements of prosperity and depression as distinct from the analysis of periodic crises. During this period the fertility of theoretical economics has resulted in a multitude of possible explanations of wavelike movements in the basic economic variables of production and employment. It is probably fair to say that a great deal more effort has gone into the job of constructing theoretical models than has gone into the job of testing the models against the facts. In particular one aspect of the testing process has been, I think, unduly neglected, viz., the comparison of the periodicity of theoretical models in terms of calendar time with the observed periodicity of business fluctuations. The first, and more excusable, reason for the omission is that it is only in comparatively recent years that even tolerably respectable long-run indexes of aggregate production have been constructed so that earlier theorists had of necessity to work with sketchy indicators of real fluctuations. Secondly, even when production series were available they have not been fully exploited since the task of constructing theories is usually much more congenial than that of testing them against the facts, a process which has the additional hazard of producing a heavy rate of stillbirths. In recent times a great deal of attention has been given to dynamic models involving period analysis. These models can define the periodicity of the cycles they produce in terms of numbers of unit periods, but very little effort has gone into the basic problem of measuring the length of the unit period. Yet without such a measure nothing whatsoever can be said concerning the length of the cycles in calendar time.

[1] I am indebted to Mrs H. Collins of the computing section of the Department of Economics, Manchester University, for the preparation of the graphs in this paper.

* This essay was first published in the *Transactions of the Manchester Statistical Society* (1959).

One result of the lack of concern with verification in general and periodicity in particular has been that the general understanding of the pattern of business fluctuations leaves much to be desired. A general idea has developed that there is a 'major' international business cycle with a periodicity of 8–9 years, sometimes known as the Juglar cycle, following Schumpeter. Any theory which seemed vaguely consistent with such timing has been cherished. One of the main conclusions of the present paper is to question this concept of the Juglar as a self-contained major cycle, at least in relation to the experience of the U.K. and the U.S.A.

The study of business fluctuations has, fortunately, not been left to the mercy of the pure theorists and in recent times great progress has been made by writers whose analysis was grounded firmly in empirical study of the pattern of business fluctuations. Such names as N. J. Silberling, A. H. Hansen, W. Isard, A. K. Cairncross, Brinley Thomas, W. A. Lewis, may be mentioned for distinguished synoptic studies, though others have contributed by their detailed analysis of particular periods and aspects. The work of these writers has focused attention on the importance of fluctuations in the residential building industry and leads to the conclusion that this cycle must be given a leading role in the theory of business fluctuations. In many previous discussions this cycle has, if mentioned at all, been introduced only as a humble extra together with such oddities as the shipbuilding, corn-hog and textile cycles.

It would be foolish to claim that the work of the writers mentioned has enabled us to solve the problem of the causes of business fluctuations; there are many formidable problems which have yet to be tackled. But it can be claimed that the result of their work has indicated the general nature of the main forces which have produced the more important fluctuations, and the most fruitful directions for empirical-theoretical inquiry. There is certainly no longer any excuse for casual theorising in an empirical vacuum.

The aim of this paper is to present a general survey of the pattern and probable causes of major business fluctuations in the U.K. and the U.S.A. in the century following 1840. Whilst no originality is claimed for most of the material expounded here, it is necessary to stress that there is, as yet, no general consensus of opinion on this topic beyond that of the crucial role of fluctuations in residential building. Doubtless many of the remarks will be challenged by workers in the field; to this extent, therefore, the account is a personal one.[1]

---

[1] This applies particularly to my conclusion regarding the mythical nature of the Juglar cycle. It is encouraging to find that Mr R. C. O. Matthews seems to have

The Pattern of Fluctuations and Diagnosis

Let us begin by forming some idea of the type of business fluctuations which have occurred in the U.S.A. and the U.K. since 1840. Fig. 5.1 shows the pattern for the U.S.A. from 1860 to 1913 and for the U.K. from 1870 to 1913. For the U.S.A. the graph shows Frickey's annual index of manufacturing production expressed as percentages of the secular trend. For the U.K. Hoffmann's index of industrial production (without building) is graphed in a similar way.[1]

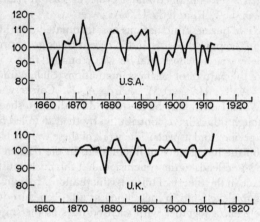

Fig. 5.1. U.S.A. manufacturing production (Frickey):
deviations from trend
U.K. industrial production excluding building (Hoffmann):
deviations from trend

It is obvious even from a casual inspection that the Frickey index does not reveal an 8–9-year major cycle. The pattern is rather a blend of two types of fluctuations: numerous short cycles with an average period of 2–4 years are superimposed on longer cycles whose periodicity is of the order of two decades, with major depressions in the early 1860s, the late 1870s and the early 1890s. From other data

---

reached a similar conclusion, at least for the period 1870–1913. His newly-published book *The Trade Cycle* (Nisbet, Cambridge University Press) arrived too late for this paper to benefit from his excellent survey of the field of business fluctuations.

[1] Data for Fig. 5.1 from E. Frickey, *Production in the U.S.A., 1860–1914* (1947) p. 60, the trend being a straight line to the logarithm of the annual index with an average annual growth rate of 4·95 per cent, and W. Hoffmann, *British Industry, 1700–1950* (1955, trans. W. H. Chaloner and W. O. Henderson) Table 54, by the same method, the average annual growth rate being 1·7 per cent. The Hoffmann index is dated from 1870 because of a noticeable change in the trend value around this year.

we may deduce the existence of a further major trough in the early 1840s.[1] The behaviour of U.S. manufacturing production in the inter-war period shows a similar pattern, with short cycles and a major boom in the 1920s followed by a major slump in the 1930s.

A similar exercise for the U.K. reveals a noticeably different pattern of fluctuations. For the period 1870–1913 both the short cycles and the major swings are absent. Instead we have a fluctuation which is much nearer to the idea of the legendary Juglar with five major peaks and a mean distance between peaks of eight years. Fig. 5.2 shows the pattern of the U.K. cycle from 1830 to 1875 using the same index.[2] The pre-1870 pattern shows a distinct affinity with the

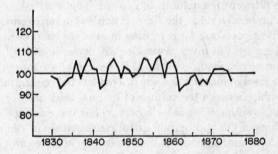

Fig. 5.2. U.K. industrial production excluding building (Hoffmann): deviations from trend

U.S.A. post-1860 pattern with its shorter cycles and suggestion of a major boom and slump in the 1850s and 1860s. Certainly the Juglar peaks and troughs are not clearly defined as they are after 1870. For the inter-war period the U.K. like the U.S.A. experienced the boom[3] from 1921 to 1929 and the slump to 1932, but the U.K. re-

[1] Cf. H. F. Somers, 'The Performance of the American Economy before 1860', in H. F. Williamson (ed.), *The Growth of the American Economy* (1951) p. 330, Fig. 2. Also Brinley Thomas, *Migration and Economic Growth* (1954) p. 315, merchandise imports to U.S.A. at constant prices.

[2] In this case the average annual increase in the index was 3·12 per cent. The graph again shows the index for each year as a percentage of the constant linear trend in the logarithms.

[3] It may seem absurd to talk of boom in the U.K. during the 1920s in view of the persistence of high unemployment. But manufacturing production increased by 57 per cent from 1921 to 1929 compared with 93 per cent in the U.S.A. for the same period. The rate of growth of productivity during the 1920s was about 2 per cent, which is about as high as the best period in the nineteenth century. U.K. production data from K. S. Lomax, 'Production and Productivity Movements in the United Kingdom since 1900', *Journal of the Royal Statistical Society*, series A, CXXII (1959). U.S. production data from *Federal Reserve Bulletin* (Dec 1953).

covery in the 1930s was extremely vigorous compared with that of the U.S.A. Whereas manufacturing production declined in the U.S.A. by 48 per cent the U.K. decline was only 11 per cent. The U.K. peak of 1937 stood 33 per cent higher than the 1929 peak. In the U.S.A. the corresponding increase was only 3 per cent. The pattern of the inter-war period in the U.K., like that in the U.S.A., resembles the pattern of the corresponding 1870–1913 period. It can be argued therefore that the U.K. cyclical pattern after 1870 does support conventional notions of an 8–9-year Juglar cycle but we shall see, presently, that this confirmation is largely spurious.

Having sketched the outline of the cycle in the two countries we can consider possible explanations of the pattern. For the U.S.A. we have two different fluctuations to explain. The short cycles can be disposed of briefly since they are relatively unimportant. There seems to be a good case for regarding most of the short cycles in the U.S.A. since 1919 as inventory cycles, i.e. cycles resulting from the interaction of two features of the U.S. economy, a relationship between the level of incomes and the desired level of consumption and a relationship between the volume of business sales and the desired volume of inventories. It is well known that the existence of such relationships of the appropriate quantitative nature in conjunction with random 'autonomous' variations in expenditure can generate an automatic and recurring fluctuation in production.[1] It is not possible at present to say whether the pre-1913 short cycles in the U.S.A. were caused by this mechanism, though I consider it likely, but an alternative possibility is that the short cycles resulted from temporary interruptions in economic growth caused by the defects of a primitive monetary-banking system without the existence of a Central Bank. It seems unlikely that the short cycles can be explained otherwise than by inventory or monetary factors since their very shortness would seem to rule out the possibility of any cyclical mechanism depending on the period of gestation of fixed capital goods.

For an explanation of the long cycles or secular swings[2] we must look at two important sectors of capital formation, investment in residential building and transportation. The great importance of residential building for the trade cycle has been generally neglected

[1] For a discussion of this subject and references, see my 'Periodicity and Stability of Cycles in the U.S.A.' *Manchester School* (May and Sep 1959). [These articles were superseded by 'The Post-war Short Cycle in the U.S.A.', *Manchester School* (Jan 1965).]

[2] The latter term is due to W. A. Lewis and P. J. O'Leary, 'Secular Swings in Production and Trade, 1870–1913', *Manchester School* (May 1955). Brinley Thomas, *Migration and Economic Growth*, p. 84, refers to them as 'minor secular fluctuations'.

until recently.[1] Investment in houses is important for two reasons. First, because of the great absolute size of such expenditure, and second, because of its nstability. For the period 1889–1908 gross investment in residential construction in the U.S.A. must have comprised about one-quarter of total gross investment. Before 1890 the share must have been higher than this since there is evidence of a downward trend. For the inter-war period the share of residential construction in gross investment was about one-fifth.[2] Apart from its size, the volume of expenditure on housing has also been extremely unstable, being subject to long cycles with an average length between peaks of some 18–20 years. An impression of these cycles can be gained from the following table of indexes of volume for the major turning-points of building cycles since 1860.

TABLE 5.1

Residential Construction, U.S.A.

| | Volume (1920–30 = 100)[3] | | Gross investment[4] ($ m. 1929 prices) | |
	Trough	Peak	Trough	Peak
1864	16		–	
1871		78		–
1880	19		–	
1889		74		2,284
1900	28		1,239	
1909		79		2,705
1918	14		608	
1925		164		5,364
1933	7		571	

The Long index obviously exaggerates the amplitude of the building cycle and this index must become increasingly suspect for the earlier dates, but there are no grounds for disputing the existence of severe fluctuations in the industry. Additional evidence is provided by Census estimates of employment in construction since 1870.[5] From Riggleman's index of building permits per capita in constant

---

[1] As an illustration the editors of *Readings in Business Cycle Theory* (American Economic Association, 1944) did not include one article on the subject in their collection though several worthy of inclusion were listed in their bibliography.

[2] The ratios are based on data in Grebler, Blank and Winnick, *Capital Formation in Residential Real Estate* (1957) pp. 137 and 338, and S. Kuznets, *National Product since 1869* (1946).

[3] C. D. Long, *Building Cycles and the Theory of Investment* (1940) p. 228.

[4] Grebler, *Capital Formation*, p. 338.

[5] *Historical Statistics of U.S.A.* (1949) p. 64.

TABLE 5.2

Construction Workers in U.S.A.

	Number (ooo's)	% increase over decade
1870	700	–
1880	850	21
1890	1,400	65
1900	1,640	17
1910	2,310	41

prices it is clear that the long cycles in residential construction can be traced back to the 1830s with major peaks around 1836 and 1853.[1]

The combination of absolute size and amplitude of swing of expenditure on housing leads to a source of instability of basic effective demand which cannot fail to result in a similar instability in the general level of production. The broad similarity of the major swings in Frickey's index and the building series must derive substantially from the multiplier effects of the long cycle in residential building since Frickey's index does not contain any direct building component.

But residential building is not the only important type of investment which has been subject to long cycles. It has been shown that similar secular swings exist in capital formation in the railroad industry of the U.S.A.,[2] using the annual increase in railway mileage

TABLE 5.3

Gross Capital Formation in U.S. Railroads[3]
($ m. 1929 prices)

	Trough	Peak
1872		604
1876	254	
1882⎫		711
1891⎭		738
1897	207	
1911		1,123

[1] The index is contained in an unpublished thesis. Approximate annual values are given in Thomas, *Migration and Economic Growth*, p. 298. Riggleman's index relates to total building but it is clear from the work of Long, op. cit., that the major source of the fluctuations in total building lies in the residential sector.

[2] N. J. Silberling, *The Dynamics of Business* (1943); Thomas, op. cit.; W. Isard, 'A Neglected Cycle: The Transport–Building Cycle', *Review of Economic Statistics* (1942).

[3] Five-year moving averages.

as an indicator. From 1870 these cycles are confirmed by preliminary estimates of gross investment from the National Bureau of Economic Research. The figures in Table 5·3 for the key turning-points give an impression of the duration and amplitude of the cycles.[1]

The main differences between this series and the building series is the existence of the double peak in the 1880s and the earlier lower turning-point in the 1890s. Both features are present in the Frickey index of production. According to Ulmer railroad gross investment was about 20 per cent of total investment in the 1870s and 16 per cent in the 1880s, falling to about $7\frac{1}{2}$ per cent from 1890 to 1909.[2] Combined investment in housing and railroads must therefore have been of the order of one-half of total investment in the 1870s and nearly one-third from 1900 to 1910. This total together with its time shape and amplitude of swing is almost certainly sufficient to explain the pattern of the major fluctuations in U.S. production from 1870 to 1913 and the argument could probably be extended back as far as the 1850s, since the share of railways in gross investment was then, perhaps, of the order of 12–17 per cent.[3] Silberling has investigated the relationship between his business index and an index of transportation/building and found for the period 1865–1914 a coefficient of multiple correlation of 0·816. For the period 1814–61 the figure was 0·774.[4] The case for interpreting the major swings in production as the results of the transport building cycle seems very strong. The possible causal mechanism is discussed later.

Let us turn now to the cyclical pattern of the U.K. since 1870. The existence here of the 8–9-year Juglar cycle in contrast to the two-decade swings of the U.S.A. and the smaller amplitude of the swings suggests, *prima facie*, that different forces were determining the British cycle. Nevertheless there is evidence of major instability in the British building industry during the period from 1870. The existence of this major swing in building was suggested by Sir

[1] Source: M. J. Ulmer, *Trends and Cycles in Capital Formation by U.S. Railroads 1870–1950* (1954) Table A.1. The figures are five-year moving averages centred on the years given. Annual data available only in graph form.

[2] Ibid., p. 11. Ulmer states that the railway shares are minimum amounts since the national totals include capital expenditures charged to current account whilst the railroad totals exlude such items.

[3] G. R. Taylor, *The Transportation Revolution 1815–1860* (1951) pp. 346–7, quotes an estimate of $600 million for outlay on U.S. railroads from 1851–1858. This compares with a total investment of capital in manufacturing of approximately $1,000 million in 1860 (op. cit., p. 247). If one is prepared to make plausible assumptions about the growth rate of G.N.P. and G.C.F. from 1850 to 1870, it is easy to derive the figures quoted which may well be an understatement. The mileage of track built in the period 1850–9 was approximately half that of the period 1870–9.

[4] *Dynamics of Business*, p. 713.

William Beveridge in his paper to this Society in March 1921, using unemployment statistics to establish the case. Since then the movements have been demonstrated more rigorously in the estimates of the volume of residential building constructed by Professor Cairncross and Mr B. Weber.[1] The U.K. building cycle as revealed by the Weber index shown in Fig. 5.3 has a longer periodicity than the U.S. building cycle. Indeed it may not be valid to use the terms periodicity and cycle for the U.K. since the index from 1856 to 1913

Fig. 5.3. G.B. index of residential construction (Weber),
1900–9 = 100

exhibits only two major peaks, centred on 1876 and 1900, which are separated by an extensive plateau-like depression, lasting almost twenty years. In this case the term secular swing is less question-begging. Since investment in housing in the U.K. must also have shared the U.S. combination of absolute size and amplitude,[2] the question naturally arises why these secular swings in housebuilding

---

[1] A. K. Cairncross, *Home and Foreign Investment, 1870–1913* (1953); B. Weber, 'A New Index of Residential Construction, 1838–1950', *Scottish Journal of Political Economy* (1955). Both indexes strictly relate to Great Britain rather than the U.K. Since the Hoffmann index relates to the U.K. there is an awkward problem of deciding which label to use. I have tended to use the term U.K. as equivalent to G.B. throughout this paper, a procedure which I hope is justified by the relatively small importance of Irish manufacturing industry.

[2] Historical statistics of capital formation in the U.K. are of an exiguous nature. For 1907 Cairncross (*Home and Foreign Investment*, pp. 110, 121), estimates gross expenditure on housing (including repairs) at £53 million, which was 19 per cent of his estimate of gross fixed home investment of £275 million. In 1907, according to Weber's index, housebuilding was about 77 per cent of the 1899 peak level. For 1938 the National Income Blue Book gives gross investment in dwellings at 27 per cent of gross fixed investment. In recent years (1951–8) the share has been 21 per cent. Weber's index shows a 45 per cent decline from 1876 to 1881 and a 105 per cent increase from 1890 to 1898, followed by a 66 per cent decline to 1912.

did not affect the pattern of fluctuation in the U.K. index of production. A minor explanation is the omission of building from the Hoffmann index. With building included the index would reveal a minor secular swing in sympathy.[1] But the U.S. index of production also omits building so that deeper reasons must be sought. The main explanation has been given by Lewis and O'Leary following the work of Brinley Thomas and others. The secular disturbances in effective demand generated by the fluctuations in investment in housing and related domestic investment have been substantially offset by secular disturbances arising from the export trade of the U.K. which have been in opposition to those of the building industry. Thus the major booms and slumps of building and exports have largely cancelled out, leaving as a net effect the 8–9-year fluctuations which have been accepted as the Juglar cycle. The major cycle of the U.K., at least since 1870, is therefore a hybrid cycle whose periodicity and amplitude are not to be explained in terms of fluctuations in any single domestic category of basic effective demand. This is not to deny the existence of minor fluctuations in home investment in phase with export fluctuations and probably derived from them. The point is that it would be misleading to take major and minor peaks of home investment, measure the mean periodicity between peaks and then regard this as an integral cycle to be explained by, say, a multiplier-accelerator interaction model or a Schumpeterian-type innovation model. To emphasise the hybrid nature of the U.K. cycle I therefore propose to call it the pseudo-Juglar.

Having established the proximate causes of the business cycle pattern in the two countries we can seek a closer understanding of the causal mechanism involved. The task seems to fall into three parts, the explanation of the transport building cycles in the U.S.A. from 1840, the explanation of the pseudo-Juglar in the U.K. from 1870 and the explanation of the origins of the pseudo-Juglar or the pre-1870 pattern. The experience of the inter-war period will be considered separately.

The Pure Building Cycle

In view of the key role of the building industry in the diagnosis of the problem it is necessary to begin with a brief account of the structure of the housebuilding industry and its market forces which have made it prone to major instability. Not all writers discussing this problem have given the same story or emphasised the same variables, but the following account can be offered as a rough synthesis.

[1] Cf. Lewis and O'Leary, 'Secular Swings', p. 122.

The main factors which tend to produce instability in the residential building industry may be listed as follows.[1]

(1) The industry produces a very durable commodity. The price of houses/house-room will be determined by the balance of overall demand for housing in relation to the overall stock of houses rather than the current supply which will represent only a small proportion of the overall stock.

(2) The price of houses/house-room tends to have inertia. Ruling prices respond to excess demand or supply in the housing market with a lag. The adjustment of supply to demand tends to take place in the short period via changes in stocks, excess supply leading to unoccupied houses and excess demand leading eventually to doubling up of potentially separate families. By virtue of (1) it may take several years to eliminate an excess demand or supply at ruling prices via adjustments to the current rate of supply.

(3) Further lags in the market adjustment mechanism exist on the supply side. The industry may not respond immediately to the signal of increased rents or prices, either from lack of conviction that the shortage is non-temporary or because of the time needed to recruit a labour force which has been dissipated in a previous slump. The gestation period of houses (say three to six months) adds a further element to the supply lag.

(4) The industry has consisted of a large number of relatively small firms with a strong tradition of speculative building. Therefore it is easy to get erroneous estimates of excess demand/supply which can be aggravated by errors of optimism and pessimism.

(5) The industry has relatively low fixed-capital requirements and relatively high working capital needs. It is therefore dependent on bank credit directly or indirectly via suppliers of materials. It therefore becomes a potent instrument for exploiting the inflationary/deflationary potential of a free banking system which can vary either the cash reserve ratio or its advances/investments ratio in response to changes in the demand for bank advances.

---

[1] Cf. Cairncross, op. cit., pp. 15–18; J. Tinbergen and J. J. Polak, *The Dynamics of Business Cycles* (1950) p. 241; A. H. Hansen, *Fiscal Policy and Business Cycles* (1950) p. 21; N. J. Silberling, *Dynamics of Business*, pp. 175, 190–1, 196; F. Lavington, *The Trade Cycle* (1922). For a general summary of factors determining the demand for housing, see C. E. V. Leser, 'Building Activity and Housing Demand', *Yorkshire Bulletin of Economic and Social Research* (1951) pp. 131–49. Lavington was not ostensibly concerned with the building cycle, but his version of 'Cambridge' cycle theory seems highly relevant for this industry.

From these conditions can be deduced the outline of a pure building cycle. We begin with an excess demand for house-room caused, say, by war or a surge of population growth. The rate of increase of supply may be less than the rate of increase in demand. Rents and prices will rise to give a stimulus to output but the stickiness of rents and the lags in response on the supply side will allow the build-up of excess demand at ruling prices. Given the eventual increase of supply the building boom begins. The increasing weight of expenditure generates a multiplier process and rising incomes raise further the demand for house-room. Eventually errors of optimism lead to an outburst of speculative building. The rate of increase of supply begins to exceed the rate of increase of demand until the excess demand for house-room is converted into an excess supply. Again the lags in the system prevent the adjustment of the current supply until an excess supply has been created. Following recognition of excess supply the building industry contracts, the multiplier process causes an induced decline in demand and errors of pessimism reduce the rate of growth of supply. Eventually the excess supply is converted to an excess demand and the process can repeat itself with a further boom.

The logic of this so-called building cobweb cycle seems reasonable enough but this does not mean it can provide an adequate explanation of the actual building cycles which have occurred in the U.S.A. and the U.K. There is the need to demonstrate an initial excess demand or supply to start the mechanism – not too difficult a task. But there has been a tendency to assume too easily that the building cycle, once started, will have the necessary long periodicity and will be self-sustaining. The pure theory of the building cycle does not exclude the possibility of a highly damped cycle which would disappear but for the existence of periodic exogenous disturbances which could regenerate it. It will be argued presently that the main historical anti-damping factors have been major swings in international migration and the transport booms of the U.S.A. Before considering this evidence, however, it is desirable to glance at the results of an econometric study of the U.S. building cycle from 1914 to 1938. This study by Derksen[1] provides a *prima facie* case for the adequacy of the building cobweb as an explanation of the long periodicity of the building cycle.

In the course of his study Derksen derived an explanation of the level of new building in terms of such variables as the shortage or over-supply of dwellings relative to families (with a two-year lag),

[1] J. B. Derksen, 'Long Cycles in Residential Building, an Explanation', *Econometrica* (1940) pp. 97–116.

average family income, the change in income, the increase in the number of families and the level of building costs, each with an appropriate lag. The general structure of his model is consistent with the theory of the building cobweb. By disregarding all explanatory variables save the first, Derksen then derived an equation for the endogenous building cycle which relates the current level of building to the relative under- or over-supply of houses two years back. The endogenous cycle proved to have a periodicity of twelve years and to be so heavily damped that it would be extinguished after one complete cycle. Derksen commented that this was a surprising result in view of the longer periodicity and persistence of the pre-1913 cycles. He postulated the existence of a longer lag for the pre-war, cycle, which could raise the periodicity to fifteen years, without, however, justifying the assumption.[1] But it is not valid to use a model which assumes income and population growth to be constant as an indicator of the periodicity and amplitude of the real building cycle, since the multiplier effects of building expenditures will induce changes in income levels and in population growth via the effects of varying income on the rate of immigration. The full model would therefore tend to have a greater amplitude and periodicity than the endogenous model, as is indicated by comparison of Derksen's graph showing the actual and theoretical cycle in the 1930s.[2] Thus we must conclude that if the emasculated endogenous cycle can give a periodicity as long as twelve years, this is favourable evidence for the building cobweb as a theory capable of explaining the 18–20 year building cycle. I shall therefore go on to discuss the interaction of immigration and railroad building with the building cobweb in the pre-1913 U.S. transport building cycle.

The Pre-1913 Transport Building Cycle in the U.S.A.

The importance of immigration for the U.S. building cycle has been stressed by Professor Brinley Thomas. He has shown that immigration to the U.S.A. has been subject to secular fluctuations which parallel those in the building industry with an average lead of some two to three years over most of the period. The secular swings in immigration can therefore play two roles which need not be independent; first, as a factor which amplified and maintained the operation of the building cobweb, and second, as an exogenous starting and sustaining mechanism of the building cycle. This assumes that the variations in the rate of net immigration were big enough to have a significant effect on the demand for house-room,

[1] Ibid., p. 116.
[2] Ibid., p. 115, Fig. 3.

which seems to be taken for granted by most writers. The following figures for net immigration certainly suggest a plausible case for the assumption.

TABLE 5.4

Net Immigration to U.S.A. as Percentage of Population Growth[1]

1850–60	22·9
1860–70	17·1
1870–80	10·8
1880–90	20·1
1890–1900	8·4
1900–10	19·9

Yet, surprisingly, the growth of total population was much smoother than the immigration figures would suggest, the average annual intercensal growth rate being about 3·0 per cent from 1840 to 1860, 2·3 per cent from 1860 to 1890 and 2·0 per cent from 1890 to 1910. *Prima facie* the population growth rates are poor material for a building cycle depending on changes in demand via the demographic factor as an amplifying agent. The overall population growth rates are misleading, however, for two reasons. First, a rough coincidence of turning-points of immigration with Census dates tends to minimise the significance of changes in the rate of immigration since the average rate of immigration in the upswing and downswing of the migration cycle need not differ substantially. Secondly, the smoothness of overall population growth conceals irregularity of growth in particular age groups. Since immigrants tended to be concentrated in the middle age groups, periods of high immigration would involve substantial increases in demand for house-room. In fact it can be shown that changes in the 0–10-year age group varied inversely with those of the 11–59-year age group over the Census periods.[2] If the gross rate of immigration per capita is compared between trough and peak years of the immigration cycle, the significance of this factor for the building cycle seems indisputable. The gross rate of immigration rose from about $\frac{1}{2}$ per cent of population to about $1\frac{1}{2}$ per cent from the early 1840s to the 1850s. Even if the rates are discounted by as much as 25 per cent to allow for the unrecorded return flow, the difference represents a considerable variation relative to an average population growth of 3 per cent. The swing from the early 1860s to the early 1870s was about 0·7 per cent

---

[1] From S. Kuznets and E. Rubin, *Immigration and the Foreign Born* (1954, N.B.E.R. Occasional Paper 46) p. 3.

[2] Based on analysis of Table B 81–144, *Historical Statistics of U.S.A.* See Kuznets and Rubin, *Immigration and the Foreign Born*, pp. 6–7, for an explanation. The inverse relationship also holds substantially for the 0–14 and 15–49-year age groups.

gross relative to a population rate of some 2·3 per cent, while from
the late 1870s to the 1880s there was a swing in the gross rate of some
½–1 per cent relative to a population rate of 2·3 per cent. For these
periods net immigration may have been some 15–20 per cent below
the gross rates.[1]

If immigration is to play its part as an amplifying or generating
factor in the building cycle it is necessary to have some explanation
of the secular swings in migration. Some part of the swing in immigration can be regarded as induced by the building cycle itself, but
the apparent tendency for immigration to lead building at the turning-points requires some explanation, particularly if the second role
of immigration is considered important.

In the case of the lower turning-points we can lean heavily on the
exogenous factors connected with immigration and innovation in
railroad construction. Professor Thomas has suggested that the
origin of the secular migration movements may lie in virtual expul-
sions of population from Europe caused by periodic waves of population pressure which in turn may be seen as caused by previous
exogenous waves of excess births.[2] He regards this 'push' element as
particularly important in the period before 1870, since for this period
there is a tendency for turning-points in immigration to precede
turning-points in indicators of economic activity such as railway
miles added and bituminous coal output. After 1870 the sequence is
reversed. He therefore proposes the idea of a structural change in the
U.S. economy in the late 1860s; before then the inflow of immigration was necessary for the development of the U.S. economy, after
that time the economy 'evolved into a more mature phase, and railway building ceased to be the dominant force which it had previously been. Changes in the rate of inflow of population were now
induced by changes in the general level of investment.' But the push
element of population pressure in Europe cannot be excluded as a
causal factor even in the post-1870 period.[3]

This account seems to me to underplay the importance of innovation in railroads as a major causal factor in generating the
sequence of transport/building cycles. It is true that in the first cycle
beginning 1843–4 the influx of immigrants preceded the railroad
boom, but it does not seem plausible to argue that the latter was
dependent on the former. The wave of immigration ending in the
mid-1850s can be regarded as beginning as far back as the early

[1] Based on a rough comparison of the estimates of net immigration by Kuznets
and Rubin with the gross totals, by decades.
[2] *Migration and Economic Growth*, pp. 94–5, 116–18, 155–63.
[3] Ibid., pp. 93–6, also 117–18, 156–8, 162–3.

1820s so that the minor trough in 1843 is not of great causal importance.[1] The railroad boom beginning 1843–4 was the first stage of the massive innovation of this invention and its origins must be sought in entrepreneurial calculation and psychology rather than in population growth, though the latter may have acted as an amplifying factor in the later stages of the boom.[2]

The origins of the second building cycle beginning in 1864 seem fairly clear. The Civil War interrupted both building and railroad construction when these were in any case approaching slump levels. The cycle may therefore be viewed as a typical post-war cycle with no great importance attaching to the lead of immigration in the early 1860s. The second stage of railroad innovation was assisted by the system of Federal land grants to the railroads which played an important part in financing them and also by the first stages of the application of steel to railroad technology.[3]

The influence of rail development in the generation of the third building cycle would seem beyond question in view of the enormous share of the railways in gross capital formation and the lead of rail indicators over immigration and building in the 1870s.[4] The basis of this rail boom probably lies in the second stage of the application of steel, especially to track replacement and laying, and the continued expansion of the rail system, especially in the Western and Prairie States, of which an important part was purely competitive and promotional building.[5]

[1] Professor Thomas uses fiscal year data for immigration. 1843 was a year of changed dating and covers only six months. This tends to exaggerate the 1843 trough on his graphs.

[2] The idea that railroad construction depended on the inflow of migrants as a potential construction force seems distinctly implausible on quantitative grounds. The U.S. Census does not list construction workers separately before 1870, but if construction in 1840 and 1850 represented the same proportion of construction plus manufacturing as in 1870, we may deduce the numbers employed as 1840, 200,000–300,000, and 1850, 315,000–420,000. L. H. Jenks estimated that the maximum number employed in railroad construction at any one time was about 200,000 in the 1880s ('Railroads as an Economic Force in American Development, *Journal of Economic History*, 1944, p. 6). These figures compare with an average annual gross inflow of migrants of about 160,000 for 1840–50. In 1870 (total) construction workers represented 5·4 per cent) of the labour force.

[3] Cf. F. A. Shannon, *America's Economic Growth* (1947) pp. 367–71, 441–2; Williamson, *Growth of the American Economy*, pp. 366–9, 523 (R. C. Overton, 'Westward Expansion since the Homestead Act', and K. T. Healy, 'Development of a National System of Transportation').

[4] Ulmer's graph (*Trends and Cycles in Capital Formation*, p. 19) shows annual railroad G.C.F. as turning in 1875. Apparent consumption of rails turned in 1875 and 1877 (John E. Partington, *Railroad Purchasing and the Business Cycle*, 1929). Immigration shows a clear trough in 1878, residential building in 1880.

[5] Cf. Shannon, op. cit., p. 444; Williamson, op. cit., pp. 523–4, 526–8 (K. T. Healy, 'Development of a National System of Transportation').

Even in the fourth building cycle when investment in the railroad industry had probably begun to be of an induced rather than autonomous nature its expenditures could still have a major influence over the swing of the cycle.[1]

The causes of the upper turning-points in the transport/building cycles can be dealt with more easily. It would be possible to ignore the building cobweb and explain the upper turning-points of building entirely in terms of exogenous declines in immigration, but this does not seem a plausible procedure. Despite Professor Thomas's finding of an average lead of immigration over building of some 2–3 years for the period 1842–1913 (except 1869–79), an examination of the relevant series suggests that in 1853, 1871 and 1890 building began its decline before the rate of immigration. Since this is consistent with the mechanism of the pure building cycle it seems reasonable to regard the endogenous building cycle as the main determinant of the upper turning-points, though the financial crises caused by speculative excesses in railroad building and finance must be allowed an interacting role. The experience of the 1880s when a temporary collapse of rail investment, immigration and manufacturing production did not check the upswing of the building cycle seems to favour the theory that the main shape or inertia of the building cycles was determined by the endogenous structure of the cycle.[2]

It seems possible therefore to explain the main outlines of the major business cycle in the U.S.A. from 1840 to 1913 in terms of a joint transport/building cycle with immigration and railroad innovation plus the Civil War as factors which prevented the potential

[1] Railroads increase in G.C.F. accounted for about 17 per cent of the increase in total G.C.F. (1929 prices) from 1894–1896 to 1906–1907 (data from Ulmer, op. cit., and Grebler, op. cit., p. 428). Using W. H. Shaw's series from *Value of Commodity Output since 1869*, expenditures on locomotives and railroad cars accounted for 28 per cent of the total increase in producer's durables (1913 prices) over the same period. This compares with a 12 per cent share for electrical equipment and is equal to the share of the aggregate of industrial machinery and equipment. Since Shaw's annual series for inter censal years are of doubtful value for the 1890s, the relative increases from 1899–1900 to 1906–7 were tested. The railway share was again 28 per cent compared with 10 per cent for electrical equipment and 30 per cent for industrial machinery and equipment. Electrical equipment is selected as a likely alternative candidate for the role of a major innovation in the period.

[2] The important minor peak in immigration in the early 1880s and the absence of such a peak in the building series may call in question the influence of immigration on residential building. A possible explanation of this discrepancy is the fact that the building series represent urban building whereas over 40 per cent of the new immigrants in this period (1880–3) were from Scandinavia and Germany and may have entered the farm sector rather than the urban sector which was the typical destination of the immigrant to the U.S.A.

damping out of the building cycle by acting as amplifying and re-
generating forces.[1] It would not be greatly damaging to the theory
if the later railroad booms could be shown to depend less on innovational factors and more on a relationship with the rate of change
of economic activity. Writers on the history of railroad building in
the U.S.A. have emphasised the tendencies of building in advance of
demand and the speculative excesses of the railroad booms which
have resulted in periodic overbuilding. These factors help to explain
the discontinuous nature of railroad building and, taken together
with continuous population growth and expansion of traffic, provide
a source of powerful impulses which could maintain an endogenous
building cycle in operation. The precise way in which the railroad
and building cycles interacted to produce similar long cycles and the
details of the mechanism of the upper turning-points provide important problems for the attention of the economic theorist.

The U.K. Pseudo-Juglar, 1870–1913

I turn now to the problem of the U.K. pseudo-Juglar in the period
1870–1913. We saw that the proximate causes of this pattern of
fluctuation lay in the opposing major secular swings of residential
building and exports. It is now necessary to show what sort of
mechanism could produce this opposition of the two major actively
unstable components of effective demand and to examine the link
with the U.S. cycle. The key to this problem lies in two features.
First, the U.K. and U.S. building cycles were in opposite phase at
least from 1876, U.K. building peaks of 1876 and 1898–1903 coinciding with U.S. troughs in 1878–80 and 1900 whilst the shallow
U.K. trough of the 1880s can be matched with the U.S. peak of
1889.[2] Second, the swings in U.K. exports of goods and capital were
in phase with the major swings of the U.S. business cycle. The link
between the two opposing building cycles can be found in the waves
of migration. The possible link between the U.K. export cycle and
the U.S. business cycle is obvious enough since U.S. imports show a
secular fluctuation in phase with the transport/building cycle,[3]
which may be presumed to have influenced the U.K. as the major
exporter of manufactured commodities.

[1] It is perhaps important that the early stages of the railroad booms of the 1840s,
1870s and 1890s coincided with periods of heavy U.S. food exports, some part of
which was caused by European crop failures.

[2] Using dates from Weber, 'New Index of Residential Construction', and Long,
Building Cycles, App. B. 3.

[3] See Lewis and O'Leary, 'Secular Swings', pp. 116–17, and Thomas, *Migration
and Economic Growth*, p. 315.

This suggests a possible mechanism for the pseudo-Juglar.[1] We begin with the generation of a transport/building cycle in the U.S.A. The resulting general boom and prosperity in the U.S.A. induces increased immigration from the U.K. and elsewhere and retards the growth of population in the U.K. Thus the building industry in the U.K. will become depressed relative to trend and home investment dependent on population growth will likewise be affected. Lower home investment releases potential savings for investment overseas. But capital export must be effected via the balance of payments and potential savings will vanish if the U.K. economy becomes seriously depressed. The capital export is effected automatically since the U.S. boom will stimulate U.K. exports directly and indirectly and this will tend to maintain the level of incomes. Thus a surplus on current account will be generated which provides the basis for the capital transfer.[2]

The process described involves two assumptions which may be contested. First, it makes the U.K. building cycle dependent on the U.S. building cycle. Second, it assumes that the secular swing in U.K. exports is directly caused by the foreign trade effects of the U.S. transport/building cycle. It would be possible to reverse the causal sequence whilst retaining the actual process of the pseudo-Juglar, as has been shown by Lewis and O'Leary.[3] Since the U.K. was the main capital exporter and the U.S. a capital importer the timing could be determined by an autonomous U.K. building cycle. Thus the U.S. boom would have to wait for the ending of the British building boom which would then release savings for foreign investment.

It seems easier to justify the idea of a causal sequence originating from the U.S.A. The U.S. building cycle can be traced back to the 1830s as a fairly regular fluctuation whereas the U.K. building cycle, as will be argued later, emerges definitely only after 1870 and lacks a clearly defined cyclical outline. Further the U.S. building cycle is clearly influenced by waves of immigration which are not confined to one source. It is easier to see the emigration waves from the U.K. as part of a general response to the pull of the U.S. boom than as the

[1] For extensive discussions of this problem see Cairncross, *Home and Foreign Investment*, esp. chaps 7 and 8, Thomas, op. cit., esp. chap. 11, and Lewis and O'Leary, op. cit.

[2] The additional imports needed for the additional exports will be offset by lower imports for home investment. In fact as Lewis and O'Leary have shown there was a secular swing in U.K. imports in phase with home investment which assisted the capital transfer (op. cit., pp. 124–5).

[3] Op. cit., pp. 125–6. These authors reject both causal explanations and conclude that the opposition of the two building cycles was accidental.

factor which generated the U.S. boom and so made possible the emigration waves from other European countries.[1] The European emigration waves, in any case, must have been partly exogenous in nature. These factors suggest that the U.S. cycle was causally independent of the U.K. cycle. Nor does the U.S. seem to have been particularly dependent on the import of capital. Lewis and O'Leary have pointed out that this was less than $\frac{1}{2}$ per cent of G.N.P. from 1874 to 1895[2], which would represent about $2\frac{1}{2}$ per cent of gross capital formation. Nor can a stronger case be made out for the period before 1870. It is true that in mid-1853 British and other foreign investors held some 26 per cent of U.S. railway bonds and 38 per cent of State securities, much of which may have represented indirect railway finance.[3] But despite the strategic significance of railroads in the major cycle the origins of the first transport/building cycle can hardly be ascribed to foreign investors. The boom clearly began in 1843–4 during the period of default and repudiation of the State debts, when U.S. securities were being repatriated. After 1848 foreign investment in the U.S.A. revived but can hardly have acted as more than an amplifying factor in the boom. The effects of new gold production were probably more important than capital imports in feeding the boom of the 1850s.[4] A stronger case can be made, perhaps, for the influence of capital imports from Europe in the boom of the 1860s, especially in relation to the financing of the railroad boom.[5] But even in this case it has been stated by Professor L. H. Jenks that 'in only a few cases was it an initiating factor in railroad development'.[6]

What of the export cycle? *Prima facie* it may seem that U.K. exports to the U.S.A. were too small a percentage of total exports to allow them to establish the overall pattern of fluctuation, being about 12 per cent from 1870 to 1890 and about 10 per cent thereafter. But two additional factors have to be considered. First, the effects of U.K. exports to Canada and South America, both of which as heavy exporters to the U.S.A., were linked to the U.S. cycle. The combined exports of the U.K. to North and South America

[1] There is no evidence of a systematic lead in the series for immigration to the U.S. from Britain over immigration from other European countries.

[2] Op. cit., p. 125.

[3] Data from Dorothy Adler, 'British Investment in U.S. Railways', unpublished Ph.D. thesis in University of Cambridge Library.

[4] For discussions which confirm the relative unimportance of capital imports for the U.S.A. during this period see G. R. Taylor, *Transportation Revolution*, pp. 198–206, and D. C. North, 'A Note on Professor Rostow's "Take-off" into Self-sustained Economic Growth', *Manchester School* (1958) pp. 70–2.

[5] See L. H. Jenks, 'Railroads as an Economic Force', pp. 8–9.

[6] Ibid.

amounted to about 25 per cent of total exports between 1870 and 1890 and 22 per cent for the remainder of the period. Second, the enormous amplitude of fluctuation of U.K. exports to the American markets as compared with those to other regions. The combined effect of these two factors can be seen in a rough analysis of changes in the U.K. export volume by regions at some major turning-points in the cyclical pattern of U.K. exports.[1]

TABLE 5.5

Changes in U.K. Exports by Geographical Regions
(£ m, 1913 prices)[2]

Period	Total	Europe	N. & S. America	Asia	Australia	Africa
1872–78	−1·4	−1·7	−30·6	+18·5	+12·9	−0·7
1878–82	+82·5	+13·3	+41·7	+12·8	+9·2	+5·6
1889–93	−39·2	−4·5	−19·6	−4·9	−12·2	+1·8
1901–07	+134·7	+51·4	+54·8	+27·8	+1·9	−1·4

Thus the U.S. factor was the major contributor to the secular swings in U.K. exports being responsible for 50 per cent of the change from 1878 to 1882 and 1889 to 1893 and 40 per cent of the change from 1901 to 1907. In the case of the 1872–8 change the U.S. decline emerges as a leading cause of the spectacular break in trend of U.K. exports after 1870 when the average annual growth rate declined from about 5 per cent from 1830 to 1870 to 2 per cent from 1870 to 1913. Much of the swings in export volume to Asia and Australia must have resulted from variations in capital export determined by the U.S. building cycle if it is correct to regard the U.K. building cycle as the dependent cycle during this period.

The Origins of the U.K. Pseudo-Juglar

We must now inquire why the U.K. pseudo-Juglar becomes evident only after 1870. The explanation for this is, I believe, bound up with the origins of the inverse building cycles. I have suggested that the U.K. building cycle cannot be traced clearly before 1870. This statement contradicts such notable authorities as Brinley Thomas and W. A. Lewis and therefore needs justification. Professor Lewis states

[1] The pattern of U.K. export fluctuations from 1870 to 1913 is shown below in Fig. 5.4.
[2] Source: W. Schlote (trans. W. H. Chaloner and W. O. Henderson), *British Overseas Trade from 1700 to the 1930s*. The figures are derived from approximate volume figures obtained by applying the analysis by value for main regions in Table 19 to the volume of total U.K. exports in Table 7.

that the pattern of inverse building cycles can be traced back to the 1820s but does not give any basis for this assertion.[1] Professor Thomas dates them from 1847 but on the basis of a composite building series involving bricks produced to 1849, railway miles added 1843–68, and Cairncross's building index from 1870.[2] His dating is quite implausible for the period 1847–71; it is just not possible to determine turning-points in residential building from a railway index, and the record of the bricks index is ambiguous. If the thesis of an inverse building cycle between 1847 and 1871 is valid it must be possible to show clearly defined major troughs in U.K. residential building in the region of 1853 and 1871 and a clear major peak around 1862. The Weber index gives no support for the existence of such turning-points from 1856. The index does suggest that residential building rises from a trough around 1860 to a major peak in 1876. If the checks to the major boom which occurred in 1863–5 and 1872–3 are allowed to enter the dating of the building cycle the whole concept of a major secular swing becomes absurd.[3] The course of residential building before 1856 can only be judged on the broad basis of Census data and this suggests building booms in the 1830s and 1850s and a slump in the 1840s.[4] Thus the Census data and the Weber index together suggest that if a U.K. building cycle

[1] Lewis and O'Leary, 'Secular Swings', p. 126.

[2] *Migration and Economic Growth*, pp. 175, 176, 325. The series are used on a per capita basis.

[3] The index becomes less reliable as it is pushed backwards, but consisted of nine towns by 1861 and covered six towns in 1856.

[4] The net increase in total houses in England and Wales was as follows: 1831–41, 515,733; 1841–51, 314,341; 1851–61, 492,666; 1861–71, 596,263. Weber points out ('New Index of Residential Construction', p. 115) that 'some allowance must be made for the greater volume of demolition which accompanied railway construction in the 1840s; and the Census estimates of an increase in the housing stock may be subject to considerable error since, prior to 1851, the interpretation of the term "house" was left to the discretion of the enumerator. Even so it is difficult to see how the volume of housebuilding in the 1840s could have approached the level of the 1830s or the 1850s.' A further point of evidence may be given to support the idea of a trough in housebuilding in the 1840s. Sir William Beveridge ('Some Aspects of Trade Fluctuation', *Transactions of the Manchester Statistical Society*, 1920–1, pp. 45–66) gives the ratio of uninhabited houses per thousand houses for England and Wales from 1841 to 1911. The ratio shows a sharp fall relative to trend from 1881 to 1891 and 1901 to 1911 following the major building peaks of 1876 and 1900. A similar sharp fall occurs from 1841 to 1851. It might be thought that Shannon's series for brick production (*Economica*, 1934, pp. 300–17) could be used to test this question, but the evidence of this series is ambiguous because of demand for bricks for non-housing uses. The average number of bricks produced increased by about 20 per cent from 1831–40 to 1841–9. The annual index follows very closely the shape of the index of railway miles added. Since it is impossible to specify how much of the brick output was consumed by the railways, its performance is not very helpful.

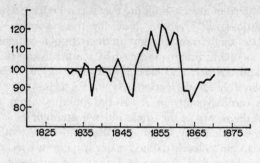

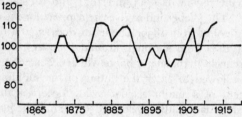

Fig. 5.4. U.K. volume of exports of home products (Schlote):
deviations from trend

existed before 1876 it was roughly in phase with the U.S. building
cycle from 1830 to 1872.

The volume of U.K. exports from 1840 to 1870 followed the
pattern of the U.S. transport/building cycle. Fig. 5.4 shows the
deviations relative to the appropriate trend for the two periods
1830–70 and 1870–1913.[1] Thus, it is not surprising that the pattern
of the cycle as shown by deviations from the trend of the Hoffmann
index (Fig. 5.2) shows signs of a secular swing from 1840 to 1870
instead of the pseudo-Juglar. The severity of this secular swing was
mitigated by a special factor in U.K. home investment, the tendency for housebuilding and railroad building to alternate in the
decades from 1830 to 1860 whereas in the U.S.A. they have swung
together at least since the 1840s.[2] Since investment in the two indus-

[1] The graphs are based on Schlote, *British Overseas Trade*, p. 133, and show the
index for each year as a percentage of the linear trend in the logarithm of the series
for each period. Trend rates are: 1830–70, 4·9 per cent per annum; 1870–1913,
2·0 per cent per annum. Use of A. H. Imlah's series (*Journal of Economic History*,
1950, pp. 177–82) would raise the latter trend to 2·3 per cent per annum but would
not affect the cyclical pattern.

[2] The average annual increase in railway miles added in the U.K. rose from 136
(1832–40) to 520 (1841–50), fell to 381 (1851–60) and rose to 510 (1861–70). Data
from R. C. O. Matthews, *Study in Trade Cycle History* (1959) p. 122; Gayer, Rostow
and Schwartz, *Growth and Fluctuation of the British Economy 1790–1850* (1953)
pp. 254, 318; and W. Page (ed.), *Commerce and Industry* (1919) pp. 170–1.

tries must have dominated British home investment around this time we can say that if aggregate home investment in the U.K. did not swing in phase with U.S. investment it certainly did not swing inversely.

It seems then that emigration from the U.K. (excluding Ireland), though in phase with the U.S. building cycle, did not prove serious enough in magnitude to force an inverse building cycle in the U.K. over this period.[1] The intercensal population increase in Great Britain which had been rising slowly from 1821 to 1841 was checked and remained constant at 2·3 millions from 1841 to 1861. From 1861 to 1871 the increment rose to 2·9 millions despite a parallel increase in the rate of emigration.[2] Hence the parallel expansion of residential building in the two countries in the 1860s. After 1881 the net emigration changes were sufficiently big to cause an absolute decline in the population increment, which declined by 300,000 from 1881 to 1891 following increases in the two previous decades of 600,000–700,000.[3]

The origin of the inverse building cycles seems to have been as follows. Both countries were experiencing a major building boom in the later 1860s. In the U.K. exports and building rose together, not inversely. In 1871–2 there came a sharp reaction in the U.S.A. with rapid declines in rail and housebuilding. U.K. exports also reached a peak in 1871–2 and declined rapidly relative to trend. Emigration from the U.K. to the U.S.A. fell rapidly after 1873 and that to other destinations after 1874. The check to emigration may have given the U.K. building boom a final impetus which carried it to a peak in 1876. Relating the two peaks we do not have inverse phasing: the U.K. peak lagged only by one-quarter to one-third of the normal interval between U.S. peaks. What made the phasing inverse was the extremely rapid reversal of the U.S. building cycle together with a rise in British net emigration to levels previously unattained either absolutely or per capita. The net decennial rate of emigration in England and Wales rose from seven per thousand population from 1871 to 1881 to twenty-three per thousand from 1881 to 1891 and fell to two per thousand from 1891 to 1901 following the collapse of the U.S. transport/building boom in 1890,[4] with a consequent

---

[1] A partial explanation may be found in the offsetting effect of heavy immigration from Ireland to England during the 1840s.

[2] In England and Wales the acceleration dates from the decade 1851–61.

[3] The relevant figures are in millions: 1871–81, 3·6; 1881–91, 3·3; 1891–1901, 4·0; 1901–11, 3·8.

[4] The U.S. was taking about 70 per cent of U.K. emigrants at this period. See Thomas, *Migration and Economic Growth*, pp. 296–8. Examination of the U.S. immigration data does not suggest that the big decline in U.K. emigration was accounted

increase in the rate of population growth and a further building boom in the 1890s.

Thus it seems that Lewis and O'Leary may have been correct in suggesting that the alternation of the U.K. and U.S. building cycles 'was a sheer accident', though the causes of this accident did not lie, as they suggest, in the effects of the Napoleonic Wars,[1] but rather in the different demographic, technical and speculative determinants of the building cycles in the two countries around the 1870s. Once the cycles had attained opposition the natural rhythm of the migration movement[2] would tend to maintain the phasing in the absence of a serious outside disturbance to the system. The First World War provided a possible disturbance of this kind.

The Inter-war Period

Surprisingly the 1870–1913 pattern of fluctuations persisted into the inter-war period though the effects of the First World War should logically have been to break the inverse pattern of the building cycles. The onset of war found the U.K. well into a building slump, with output of houses running, according to the Weber index, at about 30 per cent of the previous peak level. During the war years new construction fell to negligible levels. The U.S.A. had passed the peak of the building boom in 1909 and was in the downswing of the building cycle. The interruption of new building was less serious in this case, though output in 1917 and 1918 was abnormally low, but the ratio of families to houses was increasing from 1915 and continued to increase in the early post-war years whilst building remained at a relatively low level. Thus conditions were ripe in each country for a post-war building boom which might give full play to the building cobweb cycle.[3]

---

for by the Irish element. Immigration from Great Britain declined from 109,000 in 1887 to 23,000 in 1894; the corresponding figures for Ireland were 74,000 and 30,000.

[1] 'Secular Swings', p. 127.

[2] The sudden increase in the relative importance of emigration at this time is rather puzzling in view of the rapid rise in real wages in the U.K. after 1880. For discussion of the problem see Cairncross, *Home and Foreign Investment*, p. 211.

[3] In the U.S. the ratio of non-farm families to houses increased from 94·85 in 1915 to 96·61 in 1919 and 100·65 in 1923 (*Historical Statistics*, p. 173). The acid test of shortage is that during the period of acute deflation from 1920 to 1922 the annual index of consumer prices fell by 11 per cent whilst the rent index rose by 15 per cent (ibid., p. 236). In the U.K. the estimate of the shortage of houses relative to families has been put at 600,000 in 1918 and 800,000 in 1921. Marion Bowley estimated that the average annual increase required for 1921–31 to meet the new demand plus the backlog would be 190,000 or twice the average annual increase from 1901 to 1911 (M. Bowley, *Housing and the State, 1919–1944*, 1945, p. 12).

In the U.S.A. the building boom duly developed and was probably intensified by the massive innovation of the motor-car in the 1920s with its associated development of decentralisation and suburban development.[1] It is possible, therefore, to see the boom of the 1920s as a further example of the effects of the interaction of transport innovation and building, though the relative importance of the motor-car in the boom has not been accepted unanimously.[2]

The boom in residential construction was shorter but more vigorous than the pre-war booms, the number of non-farm houses started rising from 217,000 in 1918–21 to 937,000 in 1925.[3] The potential amplitude of the boom was, however, probably checked by the restrictions imposed on immigration in 1921 and 1924 which reduced the average rate of net annual inflow of immigrants from 584,000 (1908–11), to 376,000 (1920–4) and about 222,000 from 1925 to 1930.[4] By 1924 the ratio of families to available housing was declining and rents were falling relative to other consumer prices. After 1925 rents fell absolutely. The turning-point in output came in 1926; by 1929 aggregate expenditures in 1929 prices had fallen from \$4·8 billion to \$3·7 billion. The following year saw a further fall of \$1·6 billion.[5] Thus the inventory recession of 1929–30 and the effects of the stock market crash and the international disturbances of 1931 came to an economy made vulnerable by a decline in residential building expenditures. The decline in building must have been accentuated by the severe contraction of immigration after 1930. Net immigration fell from 191,000 in 1930 to 35,000 in 1931 and the average for 1932–6 was minus 17,000.[6]

The case for ascribing primacy to the residential building cycle as the main source of the contrast between the prosperity of the 1920s

---

[1] Cf. Silberling, *Dynamics of Business*, p. 235.

[2] Thus R. A. Gordon has commented that at no time during the 1920s were plant and equipment expenditures by the motor-car industry more than 10 per cent of expenditures for the whole of manufacturing industry. ('The Investment Boom of the 1920s' in *Conference on Business Cycles*, N.B.E.R., pp. 189–90). He concedes, however, the need to include a great deal of investment in ancillary industries, roads, bridges, garages and service stations, oil wells, pipelines, oil refining and tyre manufacture, to which might be added glass and rubber. It is also significant that Shaw's estimates of value of passenger cars and accessories, 1920–9, at current producers' prices, amounted to 55 per cent of the value of output of producers' durables.

[3] Grebler, *Capital Formation*, p. 332. The ratio of new dwelling units started to the stock of non-farm dwelling units was 39·5 over the period 1920–9 compared with 34·1 for the period 1900–9 (p. 65).

[4] Kuznets and Rubin, *Immigration and the Foreign-Born*, p. 96.

[5] Compared with a gross capital formation of \$20·1 billion in 1929. Kuznets *National Product since 1869* (1946) pp. 41, 50.

[6] Ibid., p. 96. According to Professor Thomas the maximum permitted under the 1929 Act was about 153,000.

and the depression of the 1930s in the U.S.A. lies in its relative contribution to the decline in capital formation together with the lead of housebuilding at the upper turning-point. The decline in gross expenditures on residential construction from 1929 to 1933 was $3·0 billion (1929 prices) which was 37 per cent of the total decline in expenditures on producers' durables and business construction (including public utilities). But a comparison of the average level of investment in the 1920s and 1930s shows a greater relative importance in the decline in housebuilding. The decline in average non-war gross capital expenditures from 1921–9 to 1930–7 was $7·0 billion (1929 prices). Of this decline residential construction accounted for 39 per cent or practically four-fifths of the average decline in combined business construction and producers' durables.[1] The importance of the decline in housing as an explanation of the depression of the 1930s was pointed out by A. H. Hansen as early as 1941.[2]

In the U.K. the post-war building boom, though based on a more definite backlog of potential demand than that of the U.S.A. did not materialise for several years and did not reach full swing until the 1930s. From 1920 to 1924 the average rate of construction was less than 70,000 per annum or about 37 per cent of estimated needs. Following 1924 the rate of building increased rapidly to 239,000 in 1928, after which there was a check to an annual rate of about 200,000 for the period 1929–33. From 1934 the real boom began with an average rate for 1935–9 of 334,000. The share of private builders in new construction increased from 50 per cent in 1920–4 to 79 per cent for the period 1935–9. The factors determining the time shape of the building boom in the U.K. are undoubtedly complex and can probably be considered as two sets, factors explaining the delay in the initial stages and factors explaining the intensity of the boom in the 1930s.

Under the first heading can be listed the existence of rent control relative to the high level of building costs, a high level of interest rates in the period leading to the return to the International Gold Standard in 1925 at the pre-war parity, restrictive apprenticeship rules by the building trade unions which limited the supply of skilled workers, and administrative failures of the central and local authorities in the subsidised building programme which was the logical result of rent control.[3] Rent control must have been the principal

---

[1] Data from Kuznets, *National Product since 1869*.

[2] *Fiscal Policy and Business Cycles*, p. 25.

[3] See W. A. Lewis, *Economic Survey 1919–1939* (1949) p. 86; M. Bowley, *Housing and the State*, pp. 8–9, 22, 35, 69–73; A. C. Pigou, *Aspects of British Economic History, 1918–1925* (1948 ed.) pp. 91–4; League of Nations, *Economic Fluctuations in the United States and the United Kingdom, 1918–1922*, pp. 66–8.

factor, though it cannot have operated directly, since there was no control of the rents of newly built houses. But the existence of controlled rents at uneconomic levels might be taken as an indication of the probable level to which economic rents must fall following the period of acute shortage and this would discourage new building for letting until the level of costs had fallen appropriately. Under these conditions an adequate level of housebuilding was impossible without some form of government subsidy and the course of production in the 1920s was substantially influenced by the various policies actually pursued, some 65 per cent of all houses produced from 1920 to 1929 being subsidised. Thus the low level of subsidised housebuilding before 1925 reflects the break in Treasury policy between 1921 and 1923, the extent of the Treasury commitment under the 1919 Housing Act having proved somewhat frightening. Unemployment data suggests that supplies of skilled labour were a restraining force only before 1921 and between 1924 and 1927.[1]

The intensity of the boom after 1933 can be attributed to favourable conjunction of several factors. The trend of interest rates was downwards after 1929, the yield on Consols falling slowly to 1932 and then more rapidly to 1935. Mortgage rates followed the trend, with rates moving from 6 per cent in 1930 to $4\frac{1}{2}$ per cent in 1936.[2] Building costs fell by 9 per cent between 1930 and 1934, an acceleration of their previous decline.[3] This mild improvement in the cost factor cannot, however, explain adequately the increase in building after 1933.[4] The main explanations of the boom are to be found in the substantial income effect of falling food prices for the middle and lower middle classes and changes in building society lending techniques which created an effective demand for houses for sale.[5] The introduction of 95 per cent mortgage facilities together with a lengthening of repayment periods were probably more important than the reduction of lending rates.[6] Some 65 per cent of new houses produced between October 1934 and March 1939, with a rateable value of less than £26, were produced for sale.[7] The influence of migration in the phasing of the British building boom is uncertain.

[1] Cf. Bowley, *Housing and the State*, tables on pp. 275 and 281, and *Ministry of Labour Gazette*.

[2] Sir Harold Bellman, 'The Building Trades', in British Association, *Britain in Recovery*, p. 426.

[3] Bowley, op. cit., p. 277.

[4] Cf. A. E. Kahn, *Great Britain in the World Economy* (1946) p. 123.

[5] Cf. F. Benham, *Great Britain under Protection* (1941) pp. 226–7; Bowley, op. cit., p. 175; Bellman, op. cit., pp. 427–9.

[6] See Bellman, op. cit., p. 427, Table X.

[7] Bowley, op. cit., p. 172. Houses of this value represented 88 per cent of total houses produced.

Certainly the outflow of British migrants followed the pre-war pattern, the average for 1924–9 of 150,000 falling to about 30,000 for the period 1931–8.[1] Moreover the depression in the U.S.A. and Dominions induced a considerable rate of immigration to the U.K. during the 1930s so that the net loss to the U.K. by migration from 1921 to 1931 of 667,000 was converted into a net gain of 514,000 for the period 1931–9.[2] The substantial change in the net loss by migration seems to have had very small effects on the actual rate of increase of population, which averaged 215,000 annually from 1931 to 1939 compared with 201,000 for the period 1921–31.[3] Allowing for the age structure it seems probable that the rate of family formation may have been slightly higher in the 1930s. There seems little doubt that the migration factor, if significant, was induced by events in the U.S.A. since the U.S. building slump must have played a leading role in plunging the world economy into depression and in creating the severity of the depression. And, if the real income effect of falling food prices was in fact a major causal factor in the British building boom of the 1930s, it can be argued that the timing of this was determined largely by the effects of the U.S. building slump via the repercussion on world industrial production and the terms of international trade.[4]

Thus the shorter U.S. building boom of the 1920s and the delay in the British building boom served to re-establish the pattern of inverse building cycles in the inter-war period and maintained the pseudo-Juglar in the United Kingdom. The consequences of the delayed building boom for the United Kingdom were not altogether unfavourable. It is true that a 'natural' post-war building boom in the 1920s would have offset substantially, if not completely, the relative stagnation in the export markets caused by the abnormally low level of world trade in manufactures.[5] But the consequences of a combined building and export slump in the 1930s would have been extremely serious. As it was the stable level of housebuilding from 1929 to 1932 mitigated the effects of the export slump and after 1933

---

[1] Data from Thomas, *Migration and Economic Growth*, p. 276, Table 88.

[2] Thomas, op. cit., pp. 70–1, and *Annual Abstract of Statistics*, no. 84, p. 29.

[3] *Annual Abstract*, no. 84, p. 29.

[4] Following the argument developed by W. A. Lewis, 'World Production, Prices and Trade 1870–1960', *Manchester School* (May 1952).

[5] Abnormally low in relation to pre-war trends. The argument again follows from Professor Lewis's analysis (*Manchester School*, May 1952, and *Economic Survey*, *1919–39*). The growth of world exports of manufactures in the 1920s was rapid, but it began from a low level because of the low level of world production in the immediate post-war years. United Kingdom exports shared in the general growth but the rate of expansion in the 1920s fell well short of the average rate for world exports.

exports and building were both expanding. Hence the favourable growth rate of production in the United Kingdom between 1929 and 1937 compared with the poor performance of the U.S.A.

Concluding Remarks

In this account of major business fluctuations in the U.K. and the U.S.A. in the century following 1840 I have tried to show that there is at least a *prima facie* case for believing that the U.S. transport/ building cycle and its international repercussions is capable of explaining both the amplitude and the periodicity of observed major fluctuations. The pattern of fluctuations which resulted seems to suggest that the 8–9-year Juglar cycle is a mythical concept for the U.S.A. and existed in the U.K., after 1870, only as an accidental result of a sequence of turning-points in building and exports which have to be explained, substantially, in terms of the repercussive effects of the U.S. transport/building cycle. Examination of the work of W. A. Lewis and P. J. O'Leary suggests that in Germany also for the period 1870–1913 there is no evidence of a Juglar cycle.[1]

The nature of the approach adopted explains, I hope, why it has been unnecessary to discuss the relative merits of the various traditional theories of business fluctuations, the monetary theory, the over-investment theory, the psychological theory, and so on. To a great extent almost all the theories discussed in the textbooks are relevant and help to explain particular aspects of the basic fluctuations in transport development and housebuilding. Even the acceleration principle finds a part in the building cycle via the importance of the demographic factor – the relationship between the rate of new building and the absolute rate of change of population or family growth. The exclusion of the acceleration principle as a causal factor in relation to general industrial investment in fixed capital is justified by the general failure of attempts to verify this principle empirically.[2] It is true that the acceleration principle can be modified so as to make it a more acceptable theory, both logically and empirically,[3]

---

[1] See their chart of German manufacturing production, 'Secular Swings', p. 131. Clear major troughs occur in 1877, 1892 and 1908–9. The major peaks are less well defined but do not suggest an 8–9 year cycle. The French series, ibid., p. 133 present a more ambiguous picture but do suggest a pattern similar to the U.K. pseudo-Juglar.

[2] See J. Tinbergen, 'Statistical Evidence on the Acceleration Principle', *Economica* (1938), Hollis B. Chenery, 'Overcapacity and the Acceleration Principle', *Econometrica* (1952).

[3] As in Chenery, op. cit., and R. M. Goodwin, 'The Nonlinear Accelerator and the Persistence of Business Cycles', *Econometrica* (1951).

but it has yet to be demonstrated that a modified version of the theory can explain the amplitude and periodicity of the historical cycles of the U.K. and U.S.A.[1] In the absence of such a demonstration we are entitled to favour the transport/building theory which, in any case, can already explain a major part of the observed fluctuations in total investment and, indirectly, fluctuations in exports.

Even if the causal mechanism of the transport/building cycle, as presented in this paper, is rejected, it would seem difficult to deny that the variable course of residential construction in the two countries considered has played a crucial role in historical business fluctuations, and we are entitled to draw the important conclusion that this industry must be watched as a major potential source of future economic instability.

It would obviously be naïve to suppose that history is bound to repeat itself automatically in this field, but the backlogs of demand for housing created in the U.K. and U.S.A. by the Second World War and the existence of post-war housebuilding booms in the two countries point to a clear danger in this respect.

Fortunately, there are several factors which suggest that future building cycles, if they occur, need not be so serious as those of the past century. In the first place, the relative importance of housebuilding in gross investment is certainly declining in the U.S.A. and probably also in the U.K. In the U.S.A. the share of housebuilding for 1948–50 (in current prices) was 16·2 per cent compared with 25 per cent for the mid-1920s, despite the fact that the absolute rates of population growth and family formation were substantially higher in the later period.[2] Thus any given percentage swing in housebuilding will have a smaller destabilising force. But, secondly, it seems doubtful if swings in residential building will have the same amplitude in the future. Immigration restrictions in the U.S.A. will have a powerful damping effect and can be justified on this basis. Also it is difficult to visualise the emergence of any new transport industry – or indeed any industry which is likely to combine a 15–20 per cent share of gross capital formation with as high a degree of instability as that displayed by the U.S. railroads in the 1870s and 1880s. There is also less likelihood that booms and slumps will be exaggerated by financial excesses arising from ill-regulated banking systems and capital markets. Changes in the organisation of the

---

[1] Professor Goodwin does investigate the implied calendar time periodicity of his model and shows that it could produce a major cycle of some 10–11 years. However, his estimation of the relevant parameters is rather casual, and, in particular seems to involve an excessively long average fabrication time for consumer goods.

[2] See Grebler, *Capital Formation*, pp. 429–30; *Survey of Current Business*, U.S. Dept. of Commerce (May 1955) pp. 13, 15.

housebuilding industries, e.g. greater concentration and the switch from rental housing to houses for sale, will presumably have their effects but here I do not feel competent to dogmatise.[1]

If this reasoning is correct there is hope that the problem of business fluctuations need not be so serious in the future as it has been in the past. If fluctuations arising from the root source are likely to be less severe, this, together with the much publicised 'built-in stability' arising from higher proportionate levels of Government expenditures, contra-cyclical social services, and higher marginal rates of taxation, should result in a reduced amplitude of aggregate fluctuations. Moreover, deliberate contra-cyclical policy by Governments should be much easier if the main trouble lies with housing. Economists tend to be sceptical concerning the power of Governments to control the level of private investment, but control of the level of housebuilding should be relatively easy. If fluctuations in private industrial investment expenditures have been substantially induced by the multiplier effects of the major swings in housebuilding and the induced export swings, then there need not be great problems in this direction.

There is time for Governments to work out long-term plans for the stabilisation of housing investment. If this can be done, and it may well involve the acceptance of certain restrictions on individual freedom, we may hope that future business fluctuations will be less severe than those of the past. Minor cycles will remain,[2] and probably little can be, or need be, done to prevent these, though their social effects should be mitigated, but it does not seem unduly optimistic to look forward to an absence of major business fluctuations.

[1] According to Grebler and his colleagues there has been, in the U.S.A., a greater tendency to speculative building since the early 1920s. They seem to visualise an industry more prone to 'pervasive cumulative movements' (op. cit., pp. 42–3). On the other hand Professor C. F. Carter suggests that in the U.K. there has been little speculative building in the post-war period (The Building Industry', in D. L. Burn (ed.), *The Structure of British Industry*, vol. I, p. 60). It is possible, though, that speculative building would have been more serious since the abolition of building licences in 1954 but for the braking effect of the 'credit squeeze'.

[2] e.g. those caused by the pure inventory cycle or *ad hoc* inventory cycles caused by speculative factors. There is also the possibility of temporary declines in the level or growth rate of manufactured exports arising from unbalanced growth of industrial and primary product production, but these are unlikely to be serious in the absence of aggravation caused by severe building slumps.

6 Long Waves in Building in the British Economy of the Nineteenth Century[1*]

E. W. COONEY

I

How good is the evidence for long waves of building activity in Great Britain and the U.S.A. during the nineteenth century? Can such fluctuations be seen clearly in data for the whole period? Or are they evident only in the latter part? And is the picture the same for both countries in this respect? Lastly, how are we to explain the inverse relationship – during at least part of the century – of the waves of activity in building the two countries? The answers to these questions will obviously help to determine our explanation of long waves in building activity. More broadly, they will also influence our ideas about the relationship between the developing economies of the two countries since building accounted for a large part of domestic fixed investment at a time when Britain was exporting increasing amounts of capital and the U.S.A. was a large importer.

In recent years there has been considerable discussion of the long waves in building in the nineteenth century.[2] There can hardly be much doubt that during at least part of that time building activity

---

[1] This article is based on a paper, prepared for a seminar in nineteenth-century British economic history at Oxford in summer 1958. While I am of course responsible for the opinions expressed here the article owes much to stimulating ideas and criticisms from Professor H. J. Habakkuk, Dr R. M. Hartwell and the other members of the seminar. I was helped greatly, too, by reading an unpublished essay by Professor Habakkuk on residential building in the nineteenth century (subsequently published as 'Fluctuations in House-Building in Britain and the United States in the Nineteenth Century', *Journal of Economic History*, XXII (1962) and reprinted in this volume, Essay 7). My thanks are due also to Professor W. Ashworth for helpful criticisms.

[2] A. K. Cairncross, *Home and Foreign Investment, 1870–1913* (Cambridge, 1953) esp. chap. ii *passim* and pp. 187–8, 219–20 (subsequently referred to as Cairncross); Brinley Thomas, *Migration and Economic Growth* (Cambridge, 1954) esp. pp. 102–3 and chap. xi *passim* (subsequently referred to as Thomas); W. Arthur Lewis and P. J. O'Leary, 'Secular Swings in Production and Trade, 1870–1913', *Manchester School of Economic and Social Studies*, XXIII (1955) 113–52.

* This essay was first published in *Economic History Review*, XIII (1960–1).

was marked by fluctuations of about twenty years in length – certainly longer than the general business cycle. They can be seen in statistics for both Britain and the U.S.A.; and at least between 1870 and 1914 there is a substantial inverse relationship of the data for the two countries.[1] For the purpose of the present article I shall therefore take it to be reasonably well established that between 1870 and 1914 there were hyper-cyclical fluctuations in British and United States building activity and that these fluctuations show considerable inverse correlation. (For illustration, see Fig. 6.2, p. 223 below.)

II

The evidence about building activity before 1870 is on the whole a good deal slighter. This is particularly true of Britain between 1849 (when Shannon's index of brick production ends) and 1870 (when Cairncross's estimates of investment in building begin). Even in the case of the U.S.A., where two indices based on building permits issued by cities are available, there is the difficulty that the number of cities providing information is small in the early years.[2]

Despite these difficulties, Brinley Thomas and Lewis and O'Leary, have concluded that a long building cycle, inversely correlated for Britain and the U.S.A., is evident not only after 1870 but also before. Lewis and O'Leary say that 'earlier in the century the alternation was already well established (the U.K. building cycle reached peaks in 1825 and 1847, and the American in 1836 and 1853)'.[3] And they go on to suggest, 'We cannot even rule out the possibility that the alternation of the U.S. and U.K. building cycles was a sheer accident, springing perhaps from the different effects which the Napoleonic Wars may have had upon the progress of residential building in the two countries.'[4] Thomas does not suggest that the cycles can be traced so far back but says they are observable, in inverse relationship, from the late 1840s.[5]

The first main point to be made here is that there does not seem to

---

[1] Thomas, Fig. 37, p. 176 and Tables 108 and 132.

[2] C. D. Long has provided an index which starts in 1856 with data from Philadelphia only, *Building Cycles and the Theory of Investment* (Princeton, 1940). J. R. Riggleman's index, used by Thomas and quoted in the present article, is from 'Building Cycles in the United States, 1830–1935' (unpublished thesis, Johns Hopkins University, Baltimore). An earlier, published version of this index starts in 1875 with figures from New York City, Chicago, Boston and St Louis and builds up to a total of 52 cities by 1900, 'Building Cycles in the United States, 1875–1932', *Journal of the American Statistical Association*, XXVIII (1933).

[3] Lewis and O'Leary, loc. cit., p. 126.

[4] Ibid., p. 127.

[5] Thomas, p. 175.

be enough evidence to establish the existence of a (roughly) twenty-year building cycle in British history before 1870.[1] The second is that the well-demonstrated inverse relation of long cycles in British and American building between 1870 and 1914 arose from differences in the two countries' general economic development and opportunities for growth and was initiated by an unusual combination of circumstances in the 1860s, in which the American Civil War and its after-effects, and the aftermath of the British railway boom of the early sixties, were important elements.

III

In reviewing the data of building before 1870 it will be convenient to look first at the period up to 1850 in order to comment on the generalisations made by Lewis and O'Leary. Here, much the best evidence about building activity in Britain is of course Shannon's index of brick production.[2] This suggests that from 1815[3] there were major peaks and troughs roughly every ten, not every twenty years, until the end of the series in 1849. Admittedly, the definition of major cycles involves a judgement about the amplitude of the movements to be included, but surely it is not satisfactory to overlook the large expansion of brick production in the 1830s with twin peaks in 1836 and 1840. Yet it seems that only by doing so can one accept Lewis's and O'Leary's conclusion that there was a twenty-year cycle from 1815 to 1850 with peaks in 1825 and 1847. Surely the more plausible conclusion is that the characteristic fluctuation in building in Britain in this period was a ten-year cycle conforming pretty closely with the major movements of the general business cycle.[4]

Thomas recognises that an inverse relation of U.S. and British building cycles is not evident between 1830 (when the American data begin) and 1850; but he believes that it 'is clearly marked from 1847

---

[1] A similar opinion has recently been given by R. C. O. Matthews in *The Trade Cycle* (Cambridge, 1959) p. 222.

[2] H. A. Shannon, 'Bricks – A Trade Index, 1785–1849', *Economica*, n.s., 1 (1934) 300–18.

[3] The prolonged expansion of brick production from 1799 until about 1812 can be explained by wartime conditions. Shannon suggests a divergence between the 'market rate' of interest and the 'natural rate' once the Bank Restriction Act of 1797 opened the way for the Bank of England to lend more freely by means of the inconvertible paper currency while it still of course had to observe the 5 per cent limit on interest charges. With rents rising rapidly building must, he concludes, have been abnormally profitable (loc. cit., p. 313).

[4] This is not to deny the possibility that within building activity as a whole there may have been hyper-cyclical movements in activity in particular sections such as housebuilding and railway construction which, however, tended to offset each other. Information is scanty but see B. Weber, 'A New Index of Residential Construction, 1838–1950', *Scottish Journal of Political Economy*, 1 (1954) 114–15.

to 1910'.[1] For the U.S.A. the evidence for long cycles in building is Riggleman's index from the 1830s supported by Long's from the mid-fifties. While recognising the rather narrow basis of these indices in their earlier years they may perhaps be accepted as representing the history of building in much of the U.S.A. In the British case, however, Thomas's use – for want of anything better – of railway building figures (in the form of miles opened per annum related to population) as an index of building activity as a whole seems very questionable. These data suggest a major fluctuation with its trough in 1855 between peaks in 1848 and 1863. They were used by Thomas to bridge the gap between Shannon's brick production index and Cairncross's estimates, i.e. 1849 to 1870.[2] Several comments can be made. Firstly, if evidence of total building can be found it is obviously preferable. Secondly, it seems likely that fluctuations in railway building at this time might differ from those in other forms of building if the demands on resources during the railway booms led to high costs and scarcity of labour and materials. Weber noted that housebuilding in the 1840s was less than in either the 1830s or the 1850s but brick production was higher than in the 1830s.[3] Finally, rail mileage figures may not even be a good indication of building work done on the railways if the network created by the early years of the 1850s was not at first fully equipped with such structures as stations, warehouses, engine sheds and so on.[4] It seems therefore that the railway mileage figures are likely to mislead if they are used to link Shannon's index with Cairncross's. Can better evidence be found for this period?

IV

Although timber, as one of the most important building materials, is sometimes proposed as an index of building activity, and figures of imports are of course available, its disadvantages are evident. The main difficulty is of course that timber has other uses, such as furniture, packing, in mining as pit-props, and on railways as sleepers; and these uses have been of growing importance in the total demand in the last century or so. The growth of coal production, for instance, was accompanied by a large increase in consumption of timber. The position is worse if import figures only are known and if there is no

[1] Thomas, p. 175.

[2] Ibid., Table 132, p. 325.

[3] B. Weber, loc. cit., pp. 114–15. Increase in the stock of houses: 1831–41, 515,733; 1841–51, 313,341; 1851–61, 492,666.

[4] Shannon quotes Lardner's observation that in 1849 on most of the more recently opened railways the stations were incomplete and in some cases depots and other permanent buildings had not been commenced (loc. cit., p. 304).

information about fluctuations in stocks. But the increasing and possibly independently fluctuating consumption of timber outside the building industry is the greatest difficulty.

TABLE 6.1

Imports of Lathwood into the U.K., 1831–70[1]

Year	Fathoms[2]	Year	Fathoms	Loads
1831	11,373	1852	14,110	
1832	10,876	1853	16,671	
1833	10,128	1854	12,588	
1834	9,799	1855	9,611	
1835	12,142	1856	15,579	67,301
1836	12,091	1857	16,922	73,103
1837	12,145	1858	10,911	47,136
1838	13,337	1859	14,842	64,117
1839	12,782	1860[4]	17,269	74,594
1840	12,972	1861	16,664	72,989
1841	12,685	1862	15,655	66,631
1842	9,063	1863	14,767	63,796
1843	10,440	1864	20,118	86,913
1844	11,418	1865	24,303	104,992
1845	14,488	1866	18,771	81,091
1846	12,872	1867	15,960	68,949
1847	10,004	1868	22,493	97,170
1848	9,031	1869	23,944	103,439
1849	8,750	1870	15,398	66,522
1850	12,195			
1851[3]				

A particular kind of timber, lathwood, does not seem to have this defect – at least not in anything like the same degree – and statistics of imports are available for 1831 to 1870.[5] Since lathwood, consisting principally of oak or fir prepared for division into the laths used as a base in roofing and plastering, was part of any buildings constructed along traditional lines (and these accounted for all but a very small

[1] Source: *U.K. Trade and Navigation Accounts.*

[2] One fathom equalled 216 cubic feet.

[3] The figure for 1851 was not published. A nominal 13,000 fathoms was assumed for construction of the moving average in Fig. 6.1.

[4] From 1860 the quantities were given in loads only. For 1856 to 1859 measurement was in both fathoms and loads. For the purpose of this table loads have been converted into fathoms for 1860 to 1870 at the rate of 4.32 loads per fathom.

[5] Definitions of 'lath' and 'lathwood' which are contemporary with the import figures are as follows: 'Lath. A slip of wood used for various purposes in building, namely for hanging tiles and slates, and to form a ground for plastering. . . .' 'Lathwood. Wood prepared for subdivision into laths. . . .' The wood was generally oak or fir. *The Dictionary of Architecture,* ed. W. Papworth (The Architectural Publications Society, 1853–92) vol. v.

proportion in nineteenth-century Britain), its consumption probably varied closely with changes in building activity. That is not to say it is a perfect indication of changes in building activity. Apart from other possible uses, perhaps in packing, for instance, a change of emphasis in building work from, say, houses to factories and warehouses is likely to have meant a change in the consumption of lathwood because of differing proportions of the material used in the various kinds of buildings. There is the further difficulty that the available information consists of import figures only; but it seems likely that any home-produced supplies (which may well have been relatively small in view of Britain's long-standing deficiency in home-grown timber) fluctuated similarly to imports. Finally, the annual figures of lathwood (and other timber) imports show greater short-run fluctuations than are likely to have occurred in building work. No doubt these were the result of speculation.

The usefulness of lathwood imports as an indication of building activity can be tested by comparing them with brick production from 1831 to 1849. As Fig. 6.1 shows, the two series conform pretty closely in their movements. The lathwood imports can therefore be accepted with some confidence when, in filling the gap between 1849 and 1870, they indicate that building in Britain did not undergo a long fluctuation of about twenty years' length with its trough in the 1850s between peaks in the late forties and the early sixties.[1]

v

If the conclusion is correct – that there were no major fluctuations of greater length than the business cycle in British building activity down to the 1860s – what does the evidence suggest about the first major fluctuation? Here, data for London deserve attention. Building in the capital increased very steadily during the 1860s, apparently being little affected by the 1866 crisis. Then abruptly, in 1869, there was a large decline and the industry remained at a depressed level until 1876 when a substantial increase occurred.[2] The lathwood figures unfortunately end in 1870 but so far as they go they broadly agree with the London data (although showing much larger short-run movements) and they end with a sharp decline in 1870.

In the absence of lathwood import figures after 1870 imports of

[1] The relatively large trough in the 1840s, observable in the nine-year moving average shown in Fig. 6.1, is an isolated phenomenon, not an indication of the postulated long waves. It recalls Weber's observation, already noted, that house-building was low in that decade, perhaps because of diversion of resources to railway construction.

[2] E. W. Cooney, 'Capital Exports, and Investment in Building in Britain and the U.S.A. 1856–1914', *Economica*, n.s., xvi (1949) 347–54.

another kind of timber, mahogany, may be worth considering as a possible means of seeing what was happening to building in Britain during the years around 1870. As an index it is undoubtedly inferior to lathwood which was used in all kinds of buildings. Probably the main objections to mahogany are that it was confined to the better-quality houses, offices, shops and public buildings and of course was also used in furniture. Against this, fluctuations in the data conform quite closely with movements in the lathwood series and in brick production (see Fig. 6.1). It is therefore significant that mahogany imports confirm the initial impression, derived from London data,

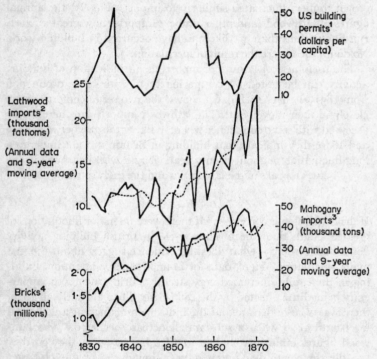

Fig. 6.1. Building activity, timber imports and brick production, 1830–70

[1] J. R. Riggleman's index of annual building permits in the United States, 1831–1913 (dollars of 1913 purchasing power per capita), from Thomas, Table 108, p. 298.

[2] *U.K. Trade and Navigation Accounts.* For quantities, see Table 6.1.

[3] Ibid. For quantities, see Table 6.2.

[4] Shannon, 'Bricks – A Trade Index'.

TABLE 6.2

Imports of Mahogany into the U.K., 1831–80[1]

Year	Gross imports (tons)	Re-exports[2] (tons)	Net imports (tons)	Year	Gross imports (tons)	Re-exports[2] (tons)	Net imports (tons)
1831	11,541			1856	39,751	1,721	38,030
1832	15,864			1857	41,038	2,460	38,578
1833	11,818			1858	33,481	2,128	31,353
1834	16,957			1859	35,701	1,211	34,490
1835	19,087			1860	44,710	2,292	42,418
1836	26,710			1861	53,108	2,617	50,491
1837	28,640			1862	53,798	2,568	51,230
1838	23,336			1863	47,998	3,311	44,687
1839	25,859			1864	41,008	3,201	37,807
1840	23,115			1865	51,376	4,922	46,454
1841	18,439			1866	53,458	2,871	50,587
1842	16,938			1867	52,737	3,560	49,177
1843	20,284			1868	41,925	3,428	38,497
1844	25,622			1869	47,252	3,482	42,870
1845	38,350			1870	32,732	3,345	29,387
1846	40,238			1871	29,335	2,753	26,582
1847	34,009			1872	33,920	3,120	30,800
1848	31,668			1873	53,330	2,536	50,794
1849	29,012			1874	64,674	4,029	60,645
1850	33,650			1875	80,705	3,203	77,502
1851	27,545			1876	52,461	1,635	50,826
1852	41,090			1877	53,600	2,092	51,508
1853	27,495			1878	44,227	3,568	40,659
1854	37,676	722	36,954	1879	45,154	2,256	42,898
1855	37,954	1,403	36,551	1880	41,349	2,470	38,879

of a major slump in building in the early 1870s at a time when the economy generally was in the boom which reached its peak in 1873. Imports of mahogany were abnormally low in 1870–2, having declined erratically since 1866. They increased rapidly from 1873 (see Fig. 6.2). Similarly, in four South Wales towns building activity after running at a high level in the earlier part of the 1860s declined greatly at the end of the decade and was depressed during the early 1870s.[3] Finally, Weber, using local authority records, noted that 'the town indices suggest a depression, varying in severity from place to place, in or before 1873'.[4]

The conclusion put forward therefore is that the onset of the long

[1] Source: *U.K. Trade and Navigation Accounts.*

[2] Not published before 1854.

[3] H. Richards and P. Lewis, 'House Building in the South Wales Coalfield, 1851–1913', *Manchester School of Economic and Social Studies*, xxiv (1956) 289–301.

[4] B. Weber, 'A New Index Residential Construction', p. 127.

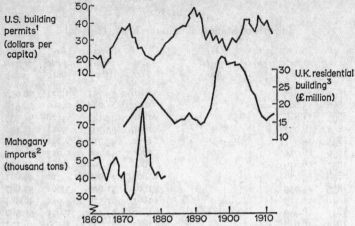

Fig. 6.2. Building activity in U.K. and U.S.A.

waves in building activity in Britain is to be traced to the contra-cyclical movement of building activity during the business expansion of the late sixties and early seventies and during the subsequent business decline of the years from 1873 to 1879. Such a thing does not seem to have happened before.

VI

What are the likely causes of this contra-cyclical movement in building and how is it connected with the occurrence of fluctuations of greater length than the general trade cycle? In considering this it is important to keep in mind that the long waves in building in Britain after 1870 were inversely related to similar fluctuations in American building and that the latter seem to have been occurring since the 1830s.[4] In addition, emigration from Britain and immigration into the U.S.A., and exports of capital from Britain between 1870 and 1914, show the long waves and are correlated with building activity in the U.S.A.[5] While it might be possible to work out an explanation of British building fluctuations between 1870 and 1914 which would be based on causes independent of these circumstances, it is surely more realistic to take them into account.

In the light of the information and conclusions already given, let

---

[1, 2] For sources, see notes to Fig. 6.1.

[3] Value of residential building, 1870–1914, Cairncross, Table 35, p. 157.

[4] On the long waves in American building, see in particular W. Isard, 'A Neglected Cycle: The Transport–Building Cycle', *Review of Economic Statistics*, XXIV (1942) 149–58. Also Thomas, chap. X, *passim*.

[5] Thomas, p. 111, and Cooney, loc. cit. p. 353.

us look at some of the possible causes of the British building fluctuations between 1870 and 1914. One thing seems clearly ruled out: the British fluctuations may have been caused in some way by the American but the opposite is impossible. We have concluded that there was no British long fluctuation before 1870 but we are accepting the evidence which indicates such fluctuations in U.S. building activity before that time. Some possible relationships are:

1. Increases in foreign investment, associated particularly with the twenty-year fluctuations in U.S. development, tended to reduce the supply of capital for building in Britain. In such situations building may not have been able to maintain its financial support because:

(*a*) if new buildings were to be offered at higher rents they would have to compete with the existing stock, much of which was let at rents which could not be quickly increased – either because of long contracts or because, in the case of working-class housing let on a weekly basis, landlords were reluctant to face the complaints and objections of tenants;

(*b*) foreign investment, in the form of easily negotiable Government railway stocks and shares of various denominations, and the like, were in general preferred to the less readily negotiable mortgages for fairly large sums;

(*c*) even if, in the long run, the return on foreign investment was little more than on investment in building by means of loans, at times of expansion its prospects of profits may have seemed much brighter.

2. Building costs may have tended to be higher during periods of heavy foreign investment because at such times industry, especially the export trades, faced strong demands for its products and competed with building for materials such as timber, iron and lead, and for unskilled labour and some kinds of skilled labour (especially carpenters and joiners who could work in shipyards, railway waggon and carriage works and in factories making packing-cases).

3. The increases in emigration from Britain at times of building activity in the U.S.A. reduced the supply of labour to the building industry, both by the departure of urban workers and by reducing the movement of trained builders and unskilled labour from rural areas and small towns to the main towns and cities.

4. The same increases in emigration reduced the demand for houses.

5. Conversely, when foreign investment and emigration were running at low levels, the British urban demand for houses and also for public works and buildings increased relatively fast and more labour and finance were available.

6. In so far as the growth of real income fluctuated in periods longer than, or timed differently from, the general business cycle this would make for hyper-cyclical fluctuations in building activity.

These possible causes are no doubt not exhaustive but they provide a framework within which to discuss the onset and recurrence of the long building waves in Britain.

VII

How did the first long wave in British building activity come about? I have already referred to an unusual feature of the very large trade cycle expansion of 1868–73: not only did building increase after the peak of the boom for some years but there is also evidence that it was depressed during the height of the boom.

Rostow has given a reasonable explanation of the tendency of building activity to run at a relatively high level for some time after a trade cycle peak. 'In general', he says, 'the nature of the trade cycle would suggest the likelihood that decisions to undertake long-term investment be concentrated disproportionately in the latter stages of expansion, rather than spread evenly throughout its course.' And 'the period of gestation of many types of investment was such that projects undertaken in the boom were not completed until some time after the turning-point'.[1] But what one can see in London, in the four South Wales towns, in some of the towns in his index according to Weber, in mahogany imports, and hinted at in the lathwood imports, is an actual decline in building as the boom of the early seventies developed. While it was not unprecedented for the building industry to be busy for some time after the peak of a trade cycle expansion had been reached,[2] there seems no sign of an actual decline in building during earlier booms.

Why did building activity decline instead of sharing in the general expansion in 1868–73? I have set out in general terms some of the possible influences on the demand and supply of building. Is there evidence sufficient to show which of these possible influences was actually at work and which was the most important? While there is a great deal of circumstantial evidence, two things are at present lacking – details of the movements of rents[3] and information about loans to finance building, especially the value of mortgages and the

---

[1] W. W. Rostow, *British Economy of the Nineteenth Century* (Oxford, 1948) p. 55.

[2] In the late thirties and in 1846–7 brick production remained high for some time after the conventional cyclical peaks of 1836 and 1845 (see Rostow, loc. cit., p. 33).

[3] Cairncross, p. 213, gives an estimate of rents for 1870 to 1914. He says (on p. 212) that 'average rents increased between 1870 and 1873 fairly rapidly'. His index shows a rise of 2 per cent.

rate of interest they bore. However, circumstantial evidence certainly suggests a number of factors adverse to a high level of building acti- vity. Emigration, export of capital, and costs of production were all increasing, and the increase in the quantity and value of industrial output requiring finance by means of bank advances and bills may have been making the short-term finance of building work more difficult and more expensive. But all this sort of thing had happened in booms before, yet building seems to have shared in those booms, judging by brick production and lathwood imports. Why should the boom of 1868–73 have been different?

The first things to notice about the expansion of that period are its magnitude and its very marked origin in overseas demand which, as Rostow has said, 'forced the system to full employment and virtually pure inflation . . .'[1] The external causes of this great boom need not be discussed in detail here; it will be enough to mention the more important. Probably the most important single factor was the American Civil War and its economic sequel. As Fels has put it: 'In 1865 the stage was set for one of the bursts of innovating activity such as Schumpeter described'. He goes on to make the following points. Because of depression and conflict, by the end of the Civil War nearly a decade had passed without any considerable railway building. The population was increasing rapidly, large areas west of the Mississippi were ripe for development, and many public authorities were very ready to encourage and assist railway pro- moters. Finally, at a time when immigration was increasing there was a shortage of housing.[2]

Nevins has broadly summarised the extent of the change wrought by the great boom after the Civil War: 'Economically the nation of 1865 – a nation which had hardly advanced to the Missouri, which used iron alone, which had a modest railway system and but one and a half billion dollars invested in manufacturing – was a world away from the nation of 1878 – a nation which had pressed to the Pacific, which was producing huge quantities of steel, and which had in- vested nearly three billions in manufacturing.'[3]

This rapid American expansion was assisted by foreign capital labour and commodities, much of which of course came from Britain. Jenks writes of the revival of British investment in American securi- ties on a large scale at the close of the Civil War as being 'of the

[1] Rostow, loc. cit., p. 81.

[2] R. Fels, 'American Business Cycles, 1865–79', *American Economic Review*, XLI (1951) 327.

[3] Allan Nevins, *The Emergence of Modern America, 1856–1878* (New York, 1927) p. 31. Also A. J. Youngson Brown, *The American Economy, 1860–1940* (1951) p. 47 and pp. 77 ff.

greatest importance in the rise of the American economic system'.[1] And the *Economist*, commenting in 1878 on the boom, took the view that the war 'had so crippled the resources of the Union in capital and people, that it was unable to sustain the vast railway extensions of 1868–73. The railways were made with native and foreign money and native and foreign credit.'[2] Russia, too, had entered into railway extension, 'straining all its resources and credit'.[3] Later in the boom there came the effects of the opening of the Suez Canal, especially in the form of a strong demand for steamships, and the French war indemnity of £220 millions to Germany with the subsequent boom in central Europe. The effect on the British economy can be seen in emigration, in foreign investment and in costs, including those of building.

There was a large increase in emigration from England and Wales and from Scotland in 1869 and further smaller increases every year to 1873 with the exception of 1871. Between 1865 and 1868 annual emigration from England and Wales ran at between 55 and 61 thousand approximately. The figure for 1869 was about 50 per cent higher at 90,000 and the peak was reached in 1873 with about 123,000.[4] While it is reasonable to suppose that such changes in the amount of emigration had some effect on building activity, it may not have been as important as one might think at first sight. It does not seem safe to assume too readily that changes in emigration (or, for that matter, in internal migration) acted fairly quickly by increasing the demand for houses. It is necessary to consider what kind of people the migrants were. The majority were young and unskilled and therefore were also generally unmarried and poor. Such people do not provide a strong direct demand for new houses and their presence or absence in their parents' households or as lodgers in the homes of other people can hardly be seen as a major factor in causing immediate changes in demand for housing. The emigrants in the years around 1870 were predominantly of this kind – young and unskilled.[5] Their going, if it had any immediate influence on building, more probably did so by raising wage costs. But not too much should be made of this because building costs in fact were pretty steady until 1872.[6] Finally, whatever effect emigration did have underwent

[1] L. H. Jenks, *The Migration of British Capital to 1875* (1938) p. 401.
[2] *Review of 1877*, 9 Mar 1878, p. 2.   [3] *Review of 1875*, 11 Mar 1876, pp. 1 ff.
[4] N. H. Carrier and J. R. Jeffrey, *External Migration* (H.M.S.O., 1953) p. 92, Table C (1).
[5] Ibid., chap. 7 *passim*.
[6] K. Maiwald, 'An Index of Building Costs in the United Kingdom, 1845–1938', *Econ. Hist. Rev.*, 2nd ser., VII (1954–5) 192. Table 1 shows (with 1930 = 100): 1867, 50·8; 1868, 50·1; 1869, 50·8; 1870, 51·6; 1871, 52·4; 1872, 57·4; 1873, 63·0.

a 50 per cent increase in 1869 and this is particularly worth noting because in the same year there was also a large increase in foreign investment.

In 1869, according to Imlah's estimates, net income available for lending abroad was £46·1 million compared with £32·9 million in the previous year.[1] The *Economist* at the time noted: 'During 1869, the transactions in American securities in London have been on a more extended scale than in any previous years, and values, with but one miserable exception are materially enhanced.'[2]

Of the several possible causes of the decline in building activity at this time this sharp rise in foreign lending seems most likely to have had the greatest and most immediate effect. I have already given reasons for somewhat discounting the immediate influence of the increase in emigration. By contrast, the increase in foreign investment in 1869 must have been very large in relation to the amounts of money which had been going into new building. Cairncross's estimates show the value of residential building in Great Britain in 1870 as £14·2 millions and loan expenditure of local authorities as £5·47 millions; altogether £19·67 millions. His estimate for all forms of new construction, a category extending beyond building in the conventional sense and comprising housebuilding, shipbuilding, railways, and work for local authorities, is £38·8 millions.[3] This figure is only meant to illustrate the orders of magnitude of the amounts likely to be involved for, while including items which are not the work of the building industry, it does not take account of industrial and commercial premises. The point to be made is that the £13 million increase in foreign investment in 1869 was surely large whether compared with the probable level of investment in building alone or in all forms of new construction. Could such an increase have failed to curtail the flow of funds into building, especially 'non-productive' uses such as housing where the stimulus of export orders could not be directly felt? While recognising the lack of direct proof, it appears highly improbable. And if so, the same can be said of the boom period as a whole, because comparison of Cairncross's and Imlah's estimates of home investment and foreign investment respectively show that the latter increased much more than the former.[4]

To sum up: the conclusion is that a rise in building activity in the late 1860s was sharply checked by the competition of foreign

[1] Albert H. Imlah, 'British Balance of Payments and Export of Capital, 1816–1913', *Econ. Hist. Rev.*, 2nd ser., v (1952) 237.

[2] *Review of 1869*, p. 46.

[3] Cairncross, pp. 143, 157 and 169.

[4] Cairncross, p. 203, Table 46, and Imlah, loc. cit., p. 237.

investment for funds. This does not of course mean that investment in building was completely interchangeable with the several forms of foreign investment, but simply that the capital market was sufficiently homogeneous for a substantial diversion to take place to the disadvantage of building, especially non-industrial building such as housing.

VIII

Let us now consider more broadly what is implied by this discussion and conclusion. We are, in effect, saying what has been said before from various points of view; that is, that the 1870s were a major turning-point in the history of the British economy.[1] From the present point of view the most significant change is the emergence of foreign investment as a much more powerful influence on the economy than hitherto. From that time until 1914 much of home investment, and housebuilding in particular, had to take place predominantly when foreign investment was low. This is what happened – for the first time, it seems – in the 1870s, after 1873, when industrial investment was substantial and there was a housing boom.[2]

Cairncross has discussed in detail the relationship between home and foreign investment, internal migration and emigration, and real wages in the longer period from 1870 to 1914[3] and it is unnecessary to follow him here. One thing however may be noted. The hypercyclical fluctuations which appeared in British building in that period owed their timing and amplitude largely to the impact on British industry, by way of migration and foreign investment, of the succession of long waves which had marked the development of the American economy since the 1830s. But some part at least of the amplitude of the great British building boom centred on 1900 may be reasonably attributed to several factors which were independent of that influence. Briefly, these are the rise in real incomes between 1880 and 1900, the activity of local authorities in the reformed framework of local government, and innovations such as electricity supply and tramways. It would be difficult to argue that these, even taken together, are more likely than the overseas influence to account for the particular timing of the building boom of 1895 to 1905 but they surely added a good deal to its amplitude.

[1] For example, Cairncross, p. 2; W. Arthur Lewis, *Economic Survey, 1919–1939,* p. 74; W. W. Rostow, *British Economy of the Nineteenth Century,* pp. 25–6.

[2] The effect was reinforced by the increase in real wages which rose by about one-sixth between 1870 and 1874 and remained at the higher level until 1880. At the same time rents are estimated to have increased by about 5 per cent during the 1870s. Cairncross, pp. 212–13.

[3] Cairncross, especially chaps. i and viii *passim.*

The story of building and foreign investment might have been different if there had continued to be major innovations at home comparable in their use of capital and promise of profits to the various applications of steam power and iron machinery in early- and mid-Victorian times; but it has been convincingly argued that this was not the case.[1] The last significant railway boom – significant because it can be seen as the main source of business expansion at a time when the cotton industry was in difficulties – reached its peak in 1866 and the financial disasters in which it ended, brought about by contractors' promotion of lines which were never likely to justify themselves, is a well-known story. As the *Economist* remarked: 'The effect of the panic of 1866 had been to shake our credit system more than any panic since 1847. Its effect was worse at first, and it lasted longer, than that of the panic of 1857.'[2] Investment in the economies of countries with greater untapped resources and less developed productive systems henceforth for forty years became the principal regulator of the course of the British economy. The long-term relationship can be summarily indicated by Cairncross's estimate that between 1875 and 1914 British foreign investment increased by about 250 per cent while home investment increased by only about 80 per cent.[3]

[1] For example, Cairncross, especially chap. i *passim*; and D. J. Coppock, 'The Climacteric of the 1890s: A Critical Note', *Manchester School*, XXIV (1956) 22.

[2] *Economist*, 31 Dec 1870, p. 1573.

[3] Cairncross, p. 4.

7 Fluctuations in House-Building in Britain and the United States in the Nineteenth Century[1*]

H. J. HABAKKUK

THE notion that an 'Atlantic Economy' developed in the nineteenth century does not depend simply on the large movements of capital and labour from Britain to the United States. For there were movements of comparable magnitude to other areas. If the economic relations of Britain and North America are to be regarded as distinctive, it is principally because of the reciprocal movement of investment and growth in the two areas.[2] The argument is that the periods of most rapid growth and intensive use of resources in the two economies were inversely related to each other, and that this alternation was established because there existed a common stock of resources, so that when one area drew rapidly on this stock it was at the expense of the other. At one time, investment in buildings and equipment in the United States was particularly rapid, and there was a heavy movement of migrants to America; in Britain the stream of migrants from the countryside was diverted from the industrial districts, and building and home investment were relatively depressed, but the vigorous demand for exports facilitated the flow of funds abroad. In the next period, the position was reversed; development slackened in the United States, and there was a revival of domestic investment in Britain. This, as Phelps-Brown has said, 'is the pattern of the Atlantic Economy, dividing a common fund of incremental energies between its regions in varying proportions from time to time. Whether a house is built in Oldham

---

[1] I have benefited from comments on an earlier draft of this paper by E. W. Cooney, J. R. T. Hughes and S. B. Saul, and from discussion with D. Whitehead.

[2] This relationship has been identified and discussed by E. W. Cooney, 'Capital Exports and Investment in Building in Britain and the U.S.A.', *Economica*, n.s., XVI (Nov 1949) 347–54; by A. K. Cairncross, *Home and Foreign Investment, 1870–1913* (Cambridge University Press, 1953); and by B. Thomas, *Migration and Economic Growth* (Cambridge University Press, 1954), and a number of later studies.

---

* This essay was first published in *Journal of Economic History*, XXII (1962).

depends on and is decided by whether a house goes up in Oklahoma.'[1]

So much importance has been attached to the reciprocal character of long swings in American and British domestic investment, and to the element of stability in the world economy which it afforded, that it may be worth while discussing the problem further. How early can the alternation of British and American investment be discerned? How far was it systematic as opposed to fortuitous? And, in so far as it was systematic, by what means was it established and maintained? The purpose of this essay is to consider these questions in relation to residential building, though some of the discussion will also apply to types of public utility investment closely related to the growth of urban areas. Residential building is the form of investment where the case for alternation has been most clearly presented. It was also of comparable importance in the two economies, though it bulked larger and fluctuated more in America: in the United States, gross residential capital formation as a percentage of gross capital formation ranged from 30·1 per cent in 1891, a high year, to 18·6 per cent in 1903;[2] in England and Wales residential building averaged about 20 per cent of total new construction over the period 1886–96.[3]

It is sometimes argued that both Britain and the United States had long cycles in residential building throughout the nineteenth century and that they were out of phase with each other from the start.[4] So far as the United States is concerned, I do not wish to question the assumption that there were fluctuations in residential building of a twenty-year variety from early in the nineteenth century. The evidence so far available for the period before 1860 and even for the three following decades is thin, but there is a plausible reason for expecting such long swings, since the fluctuations in building were closely associated with the development booms which opened up the country, and these tended to occur every other trade cycle.[5]

[1] In a review of Thomas, *Migration and Economic Growth*, in *Economic Journal*, LXIV 256 (Dec 1954) 820.

[2] L. Grebler, D. M. Blank and L. Winnick, *Capital Formation in Residential Real Estate*, National Bureau of Economic Research, Studies in Capital Formation and Financing, 1 (Princeton: Princeton University Press, 1956) p. 248.

[3] See Cairncross, *Home and Foreign Investment*, pp. 157, 169, 203.

[4] W. A. Lewis and P. I. O'Leary, 'Secular Swings in Production and Trade, 1870–1913', *Manchester School of Economic and Social Studies*, XXIII 2 (May 1955) 113–52, believe that alternation can be discerned from the 1820s. Thomas dates the beginning of the inverse relation in 1847 (*Migration and Economic Growth*, p. 188).

[5] For the American figures see Thomas, *Migration and Economic Growth*, Appendix 4, Tables 108, 109. The data before 1860 are estimates made by Riggleman based on, at most, three cities. These are based for most years on permits for building (not house-building alone), but also take into account Riggleman's judgements based on information about mortgage activity, etc.

Residential building in Britain took place mainly in areas already long settled, and there seems no obvious reason why its fluctuations over the country as a whole should have had a span of as long as twenty years, at least in the early decades of the century. Nor is there any compelling evidence that, up to the sixties at least, there were in fact long swings in total residential building over the country as a whole. The statistical evidence for the first half of the century is limited. The series for individual towns constructed by Weber do not effectively start until the 1850s, and even for this decade their coverage is narrow.[1] For the earlier decades there are only the figures of the stock of houses at each census and certain series relating to building as a whole, for example, the volume of bricks derived from the excise figures and the imports of various kinds of timber. From these it seems reasonably clear that in Britain, house-building up to the 1860s rose over the period as a whole except for a check in the 1840s. The shape of the fluctuations in this growth can only be guessed, but the best guess that can be made is that they coincided generally with those of the trade cycle (cycles with a seven- to ten-year duration), not simply in the sense that house-building rose when trade revived and fell during trade depression, but also in the sense that there was no systematic tendency for house-building to be unusually vigorous or prolonged *every other* trade-cycle boom or unusually and protractedly depressed *every other* depression. From the nature of the evidence we cannot say this is confirmed by the brick index and the

---

[1] For the British evidence see, besides Cairncross and Thomas, A. K. Cairncross and B. Weber, 'Fluctuations in Building in Great Britain, 1785–1849', *Economic History Review*, 2nd ser., IX 2 (Dec 1956) 283–97; B. Weber, 'A New Index of Residential Construction and Long Cycles in House-Building in Great Britain, 1838–1950', *Scottish Journal of Political Economy*, II 2 (June 1955); and J. H. Richards and J. Parry Lewis, 'House Building in the South Wales Coalfield, 1851–1913', *Manchester School of Economic and Social Studies*, XXIV 3 (Sep 1956) 289–300; Herbert W. Robinson, *The Economics of Building* (London: King, 1939) p. 100, gives the census figures of stocks of houses. The small increase in the stock of houses between 1841 and 1851 shown in the census figures is curious, since the railway building of this decade seems, as would be expected, to have stimulated internal migration (Cairncross, *Home and Foreign Investment*, pp. 70, 80). It is possible that the census figures understate the number of houses built, since (a) before 1851 the interpretation of 'house' was left to the individual enumerator, and (b) there was some demolition of old houses as a result of railway building. Shannon's brick index shows an output in 1840–9 greater than in 1830–9 by nearly 25 per cent; but a large part of the output in the 1840s must have been absorbed by non-residential uses, particularly railway construction itself. If the small increase is genuine, the most likely explanation is that a very large amount of building had been done in the 1830s – the proportion of uninhabited houses per thousand in 1841 was higher than in 1811, 1821 and 1831 and than in 1851 and 1861. But the possibility cannot be ruled out that there were difficulties in obtaining finance in the two severe cyclical depressions of 1842 and 1847, and in the intervening railway boom which drew upon the type of savings most likely to be available for building.

census figures on stocks of housing, but it is consistent with them, and there is some confirmatory evidence of a qualitative kind. There are signs of speculative domestic house-building in the boom of 1824–5. A witness before the Select Committee of 1833 on Manufactures, Commerce and Shipping, commenting on severe depression in the building trade in 1826, suggested that all the houses required for 1826 were built in 1825; and other witnesses spoke of speculative building in Sheffield and Liverpool.[1] After a low level of building activity from 1827 to 1834, the rise in incomes between 1834 and 1836 caused an increase in residential building, particularly marked in the textile districts.[2] There seems to have been some revival of building in the uneven trade recovery from 1838 to 1840, but all the evidence suggests that the depression of 1842 brought a drastic fall. The course of residential building during the rest of the decade is not clear, but it is likely that a weak building boom coincided with the trade expansion; and the trade boom of the early 1850s was marked by a high level of building.[3]

In particular regions, fluctuations may well have had a different pattern. Matthews has suggested that in the period 1833–42 the long swings in British building activity were mainly regional, as opposed to the large national swings characteristic of the last quarter of the century.[4] Possibly there were long regional swings which bore no systematic relation to the trade cycle; in London the fall in building after the boom of 1825 was more severe and prolonged than for the country as a whole, and – presumably in part as a consequence – there was a rise in new houses from 1835 to 1842 sustained throughout the trade-cycle depression.[5] But the building market in London was in several respects exceptional, and any long regional swings else-

---

[1] S. C. on Manufactures, Commerce and Shipping (1833), Qu. 1719, 4787, 2887, 2888. The year 1816 was also one of distress in building (Qu. 1777).

[2] R. C. O. Matthews, *A Study in Trade-Cycle History: Economic Fluctuations in Great Britain, 1833–1842* (Cambridge: Cambridge University Press, 1954) pp. 116–17. The 1836 Act for the Regulation of Benefit Building Societies, passed because of the rapid increase in their number since the passing of the Friendly Society Act of 1834, suggests vigorous house-building.

[3] J. R. T. Hughes, *Fluctuations in Trade, Industry and Finance: A Study of British Economic Development, 1850–1860* (Oxford: Clarendon Press, 1960) pp. 225–7. It would be worth investigating the local press for evidence of building activity. See the *Hampshire Independent* for 6 September, 1856. 'The progress made by Southampton during the past few years is strikingly apparent on all sides . . . whether we look at the new streets . . . or the erection of public buildings in every part of the town. We are astonished when passing through the new parts of the town to find the houses occupied before they are completed . . . proving incontestably the great demand for houses.'

[4] Matthews, *A Study in Trade-Cycle History*, p. 117.

[5] Cairncross and Weber, 'Fluctuations in Buildings', pp. 292–3.

where are most likely to have occurred because so much building was done in one trade cycle that it was not absorbed until the next cycle but one; the swings took the form of a building boom every other trade revival. If these regional swings were not synchronised – and in the still disunited economy of the first half of the century there was no obvious mechanism to ensure that all regions had their building booms in the same cycle – their effect would be to produce in the national aggregate fluctuations which coincided with the trade cycle.

Reasons can be suggested for a coincidence of building fluctuations with the trade cycle in the first half of the century. So far as the expansion phase of the cycle is concerned, it had unfavourable as well as favourable influences on building. On the one hand, the influx of migrants from the countryside into the industrial areas and the rise of industrial incomes increased the demand for houses. On the other hand, the increase in industrial activity competed for labour and building materials and drove up costs. Builders and potential house-purchasers had to face greater industrial competition for funds as industrialists, in order to finance expansion, drew in their loans and/or borrowed from local men who would otherwise have financed the construction or purchase of houses. Moreover, builders to some extent depended for finance on credits from those who supplied them with materials, and such credits were possibly less readily available in the later stages of a trade expansion; finance for building may have become more difficult before (or even without) a decline in the funds available for mortgages. Since finance is a larger part of total costs in the provision of houses than in the production of most other kinds of goods, building was particularly sensitive to such changes. The point is not merely that the decision to build houses, like the decision to undertake other forms of long-term investment, tended to be made only when recovery was well advanced, but that in its progress the recovery engendered forces unfavourable to residential building as well as forces that were favourable. In the first half of the century, however, favourable influences predominated over the country as a whole.[1] Migration from the countryside took place mainly during the trade-cycle booms. On the supply side, even at the height of a boom, unskilled building labour was abundant. The total supply of money and money substitutes during the boom was highly elastic, and since,

---

[1] Though the small increase in the stock of houses between 1841 and 1851 may be due to the fact that railway building competed with building for finance and labour more directly than did the dominant forms of investment in other cycles.

down to about 1850, the return on Consols tended to *fall* in periods of rising activity, we may reasonably deduce that there was a substantial increase in the funds available for mortgages.[1] Though finance may have limited building in particular areas, there is no evidence that house-building over the country as a whole was damped down by shortage of funds *before* the downturn of the trade cycle from the end of the Napoleonic wars to the 1850s. The net effect of a trade revival was to stimulate house-building.

During the trade-cycle depressions of the first part of the century, on the other hand, there were depressing influences on house-building from both the demand and supply side. The contraction of incomes was generally abrupt and severe. Moreover, because people were poorer than later in the century, they either doubled up in existing accommodation during depressions or went back to the villages, which was easier for a recently recruited labour force than for second- and third-generation urban workers. Migration to the towns died away.[2] Even where effective demand might have warranted a higher level of building in depression, it was difficult after the collapse of a trade-cycle boom to raise finance. The downturn in the early decades of the century was normally accompanied by a commercial and financial panic, as a result of which there was a rapid contraction of funds for all types of investment – house-building and industrial investment as well. Because the English banking system in the earlier nineteenth century was unstable and the range of assets available was narrow, the desire for liquidity was very strong, and it absorbed even the funds available for new mortgages and led to reluctance to renew them. (It also led to the sale of Consols, which is why, from the 1780s to the 1850s, the yield on Consols fell during booms and rose during depressions.) The trade-cycle crisis broke the speculative building boom and made many builders bankrupt; when the immediate effects of the crisis had worn off and finance again became available for building, the industry was in the doldrums. How far building booms ceased because of the fall in demand during depression and how far they were cut short by financial crises in circumstances in which demand would have warranted a continuation it is impossible to say. The only point I wish to make here is that

---

[1] Possibly, also, to a greater extent than later in the century, house-building was financed by industrialists out of profits.

[2] *Hansard*, 3rd ser., LXLV, 118, 1248. Tooke attributed the depressed state of agricultural workers in 1844 'to the accumulating results of the interruption of the customary migration from the agricultural to the manufacturing districts, during the long and severe depression of the latter'. (Thomas Tooke and William Newmarch, *A History of Prices*, 6 vols in 4 (reproduced from the original and published New York: Adelphi, 1928) vol. IV, pp. 56–7.)

the nature of the trade-cycle downturn in this period tailored fluctuations in building to fit the trade cycle.

So long as this was the case, there was no regular alternation between British and American building fluctuations.[1] British building tended to move with the trade cycle, and American building with the development booms. These development booms tended to occur roughly every other trade cycle, and since there was a rough synchronisation of the trade cycle in the two countries the peaks in building tended to coincide as often as not. There are some signs of alternation in the 1860s – the British had a marked building boom in the early 1860s, while, because of the Civil War, the American building boom was deferred to the second half of the decade. But the signs are not very marked. Building fluctuations in the two countries did not become clearly out of phase until the 1870s. In both America and Britian, building rose in the trade revival of the late 1860s and was high during 1869–72; but American building declined abruptly after 1872, while building in Britain, though it fell slightly in 1873, rose again to new heights between 1874 and 1876. This is the first unambiguous instance of a building boom in Britain coinciding with a trough in American building. Thereafter the building cycles continued to alternate in the way Cairncross and Thomas have described, with British building low in the eighties, rising in the 1890s to a peak in 1903 and low again between 1907 and the outbreak of war, and American building moving in the reverse direction.[2]

Even of these periods of alternation it should be observed that the available indices, which are primarily of building in urban areas, probably exaggerate the extent to which building fluctuations in the two countries diverged. In Britain, except in certain of the coalfields, most of the urban growth in the second half of the nineteenth century took place in or around centres which were already urban in 1851. In the United States, on the other hand, more of the urban growth took the form of the appearance of new large towns: an index based on the figures for the administrative areas of towns is in general likely to be a more accurate measure of American than of British

---

[1] There seems to be no evidence for the view of Lewis and O'Leary ('Secular Swings in Production', p. 176) that alternation was evident from the 1820s. Thomas's view that the alternation started as early as 1847, and that English building was low in the 1850s when American building was high, is based on the assumption that railway miles added in England are an index of building. His conclusions, so far as residential building in the 1850s is concerned, are difficult to reconcile with the census figures for housing in 1851 and 1861.

[2] There was also some alternation in the 1920s and 1930s, with English building relatively low in the first decade and high in the second; but this period falls outside the scope of this essay.

building. Furthermore, when there was a significant change in the proportions of suburban building in the two countries, the existing indices would mislead. In the 1900s a large amount of building in England was suburban. Weber's index of thirty-four major English towns therefore understates total English house-building in this decade, as indeed is evident from the figures of intercensus increase. Between 1901 and 1911 the number of houses in England and Wales as a whole rose by 12·5 per cent and in 'urban districts', that is, the smaller urban areas, by as much as 19·2 per cent. These figures, while they do not necessarily indicate a cyclical pattern different from that in Weber's figures, do suggest a higher level of building.

Thus alternation is confined to the forty or so years before 1914. It will be observed, also, that the beginning of this alternation came about because of a change in the character of British building fluctuations, by which they ceased to follow the path of the trade cycle and became longer and more widely spaced in time. The building boom which started in the later 1860s is the first clear case in which the national peak in English house-building occurred a considerable time after the peak of the trade cycle. That this building boom was unprecedented is suggested by the fact that the proportion of uninhabited to inhabited houses in 1881 was much the highest in the century – eighty per thousand.

At first sight it seems obvious enough that British building fluctuations were accommodating themselves to the American. But the British cycle in the later nineteenth century was the product of its own previous history as well as of contemporary events in the United States, and there are reasons why it should have changed its character quite apart from any events in the United States. More specifically, there are reasons of domestic origin why the relation between British building fluctuations and the trade cycle should have changed and, in particular, why a long wave of building activity should have appeared.

There were first of all changes which, in the later nineteenth century, weakened the influences which stimulated building during a trade expansion. The association between internal migration and trade expansion became less close. Not only was urbanisation more rapid in the first half of the century, but it was in this period that the contribution of migration to urbanisation was relatively greatest; and in this sense building was more subject to the influence of migration. There were changes in the social composition of the migrants in the later decades of the century: to judge from the rapid growth of middle-class towns in the twenty years before 1900, there was an increase in the proportion of middle-class migrants, and their movement was less directly dependent on trade fluctuations.[1]

While the favourable influences exerted during the boom on the demand side were becoming less powerful, the unfavourable influences exerted on the availability of finance and on costs became more powerful. There are signs that finance had become a restraint on residential building in the 1850s and 1860s. In the boom of the 1850s, housebuilding was curtailed before the crisis of the trade cycle, and it was suggested that this was the result of difficulty in negotiating mortgages. 'Persons can now realise from 5 to 6 per cent very readily upon loans, or merely by deposits at joint-stock banks, and, therefore, are not to be satisfied with 4 or 5 from builders encumbered with the business of mortgages and other securities.'[2] In 1865 and 1866 building was again cut off by shortage of funds well before the boom broke. Finance became more difficult during the boom as a result of the development of a more stable and unified banking system – particularly the growth of joint-stock banks with more considered policies about reserves – and the increasing assumption by the Bank of England of central banking functions. Possibly, too, the increasing perfection of the capital market worked to the disadvantage of house-building in the boom. There were more places in the first half of the century than in the second where builders and house-purchasers found it easy to obtain funds during a boom simply because local money men could find little else to do with their money. It also became more difficult for builders to obtain labour during the boom; there were complaints of general labour shortage in the 1850s, and the contemporary already quoted attributed the decline in building in January 1857 to higher wages as well as higher interest rates. Probably there was some general tendency for housing to be squeezed at the height of the boom, as the reserve army of labour was depleted and as supplies of credit became less responsive in the upswing of the cycle. Resources were less easily able to accommodate an increase in all types of investment during a boom, and pressure was greater in the 1850s and 1860s than in the twenties and thirties.

Changes in the methods of financing house-building made it more vulnerable to high interest rates and shortage of funds at the

---

[1] Discussion on R. Price Williams. 'On the Increase of Population in England and Wales', *Journal of the Royal Statistical Society*, XLIII (3) (Sep 1880) 500–1; T. A. Welton, *England's Recent Progress* (London: Chapman & Hall, 1911) pp. 564–9.

[2] A letter in *The Builder* of Jan 1857, quoted by Tooke and Newmarch, *History of Prices*, vol. VI, pp. 175–6.

height of the boom. A witness before a Commons Committee said in 1857:

> Forty years ago what houses were built upon speculation were built out of the savings and the profits of builders upon their ordinary jobbing business, and it answered very well at that day. But at present the general practice is to build upon a large scale . . . and raising money upon mortgage as the buildings proceed. Almost the whole of Belgravia and Tyburnia, and the countless thousands of villas round London, are built upon that principle. A man makes an arrangement with some solicitor, who has clients ready to advance money, and he says. 'As you go on we will advance a certain portion on Mortgage.' That is the way that the builder generally finances.[1]

If this witness was right, speculative housing at the end of the Napoleonic wars was financed by the savings and profits of the jobbing business more than by mortgage. This dependence on the builders' savings and profits was probably a temporary phenomenon – it does not seem to have been characteristic of building in the eighteenth century – due not only to the strong demand in the jobbing business in the years after 1815 but to the exceptional difficulty of raising money upon mortgage in the later stages of the Napoleonic wars and the time needed afterwards to re-establish fully the links between the building industry and the mortgage market. But, whatever the cause, it seems likely that by the 1850s a larger proportion of building was done by builders building ahead of demand for a market financed by mortgages, as opposed to men building with their own capital. Since the mortgage rate was, from the nature of the instrument, more stable than the industrial or commercial rate and the rate on, for example, commercial bills, the relative attraction, to the investor, of loans to builders tended to diminish in the trade-cycle boom and to increase during the slump. Housing suffered in the competition for funds not merely because the stickiness of rents made it difficult to pass on any increase in costs, but also because mortgage rates were sticky – solicitors had only heard of one rate. Moreover, the development of joint-stock banking, while it may have made it easier for builders to obtain advances, also made the bank deposit an alternative asset to the mortgage. These changes made the building industry more sensitive to given fluctuations in the supply of finance, and, if this had been the only determinant, building fluctuations would have been anticyclical.

[1] S. C. on the Bank Acts, 1857, Qu. 5414.

These developments meant that in the 1850s and 1860s not all the houses were built during the boom that were warranted by the level of demand during the boom or even by the lower level of demand for housing after the downturn of the cycle. Independent of events abroad, there was some frustrated demand which tended to sustain this form of investment into the trade-cycle depression. Though the high building of the mid-seventies is the first clear instance of a boom in building of longer duration than the trade cycle, the revival of building after 1866 was sufficiently prompt to suggest that it was stimulated by a backlog of demand from the previous period of industrial activity.

For building to be sustained after the downturn of the trade-cycle boom, effective demand for houses had to be sustained and funds had to be available. The growing stability of the banking system after mid-century and the increase in the range of assets available, while they reduced the power of building to compete for funds during a boom, greatly improved its position during a depression. The downturn ceased to be accompanied by a general commercial and financial convulsion. The year 1866 was the last of the genuine panics. Moreover, since persons and institutions held a greater diversity of assets, the pressure for liquidity in the later nineteenth century was no longer exerted on bonds and mortgages, but on short-term securities. Indeed, in depression there was a shift to funds *into* such assets as Consols and mortgages, and this is why the yield on Consols in the second half of the century, in contrast to the first, moved in sympathy with industrial activity and fell during depressions.[1]

Thus the increase in the stability of English financial institutions tended to detach building from the trade cycle. In the earlier decades of the century, because of imperfections in the capital market, house-building during a trade-cycle boom had a full head in some areas and was constrained in others; but once the boom had broken, conditions became unfavourable to building in all areas, partly because of a general unwillingness to lend and partly because the contraction of incomes reduced demand for housing. The increased availability of finance for building in depression in the second half of the century allowed building to go ahead in those areas where, even in depression, demand conditions were favourable.

Absence of a commercial panic affected not only the availability of finance for building, but also effective demand for houses. The

---

[1] This is the main explanation of the change in the behaviour of Consols over the trade cycle noted by Sir William Beveridge, 'The Trade Cycle in Britain Before 1850', *Oxford Economic Papers*, no. 3 (Feb 1940) p. 91.

point is not merely that stringencies of the boom meant there was an unsatisfied demand for houses at the level of income prevailing during the cyclical boom, but that the level of income was better sustained during the depression. The possibility should also be considered that the change in the character of British building fluctuations, whereby they ceased to coincide with the trade cycle, was partly due to an increase in the relative importance of the type of area in which, even in the earlier nineteenth century, the net effect of trade revival was to inhibit rather than stimulate residential building.

These changes in the character of the trade cycle in Britain would lead one to expect a change in the response of building to the trade cycle. But why, it may be asked, should they produce *long swings* in building? Building fluctuations may be related to the trade cycle in a number of different ways and still remain of the same length as the trade cycle. They may be positively and synchronously tied to the cycle; but they may also be inversely related; or industrial demand for resources may regularly depress building in the second half of trade-cycle expansions and slack industrial demand stimulate it in the second half of recessions. Or, again, the favourable and unfavourable effects on building of the various phases of the cycle may offset each other, and the balance of trade-cycle influences might shift over time between these possibilities without affecting the length of building fluctuations.

The changes I have examined in fact produced long waves because the shift in the balance of favourable and unfavourable forces was gradual, so that, at some point of time, the building boom came to overlap the trade cycle, rising during trade expansion but continuing to rise after the cyclical downturn. Once this had happened there was an increase in the number of regional long cycles, since, after such a long wave, building would skip the immediately following trade revival. Once the pattern of building fluctuations had been modified in this way there was no reason why it should revert to its previous shape.

To the extent that these regional waves were not synchronised, they would tend to produce greater steadiness in the national aggregate, the building boom in some regions overlapping one trade cycle and those in other regions overlapping the trade cycle immediately following. But so long as the two classes of region were not equally important as centres of building, there would be a tendency for long swings to appear in the national aggregate. As the British economy became more closely integrated geographically in the course of the nineteenth century, it is probable that there was an increasing degree of synchronisation between regional building fluctuations. But quite apart from this, an increase in the number of regional long swings would tend to lengthen, as well as moderate, the swings for the country as a whole.

I wish to suggest that the appearance of the first long wave in the 1870s is primarily to be explained by influences of this kind. The depressing influences on building during the trade revival of 1869–72, while sufficient to leave a backlog of demand for housing, did not prevent an increase in building, and the favourable influences after the cyclical downturn of 1873 boosted building to a peak in 1876. So much building had been done between 1869 and 1876 that in most areas there was little scope for a revival of building in the trade revival of 1879–82; there had been built not only the houses needed at the level of incomes prevailing in the 1870s but a large part of those that were needed at the income level of the early eighties.

There is another general development which one might expect to have produced a longer rhythm in British building fluctuations – the increasing importance of suburban building, particularly for middle-class people. At first, builders filled in the settled areas of a town and then made piecemeal additions on the outskirts; in this way, a town might grow very large without the provision of new transport facilities, for increasing dispersion of industry within an urban area could allow inhabitants to live near enough their work to walk to it. There came a point beyond which further expansion of the town involved the provision of trams or trains, and additional public utilities. Whether at this point transport and housing moved simultaneously into the suburbs under a common stimulus or whether one or the other was the initiating influence depended not only on the accidents of local history but on the form of transport. The increased use of horse-trams at the end of the seventies and the early eighties seems to have been a *consequence* of the housing boom of the mid-seventies; these lines enabled people to live further out – people could now walk to the terminus – but the lines were very short and did not generally reach the suburbs and did not stimulate much building on the outskirts in the eighties. On the other hand, the boom in electric trams at the end of the 1890s, though we cannot say how far it influenced the volume as opposed to the location of building, was primarily an independent stimulus and not a response to new house-building. In the case of suburban railway lines, there are instances where lines were built ahead of the house-building which was to justify them. But whether transport and other facilities or the houses came first, building was likely to have a longer rhythm than that of an earlier period whenever urban expansion involved investment in developing a new area. Once the minimum of transport facilities and public utilities had been provided, the area provided opportunities for a large amount of building; builders could expect not only profits on the sale of houses, but also gains from rising land values; and they could expect such gains more confidently than builders in existing urban areas where the price of land was more likely to discount the future. Builders thus had an inducement to buy land during trade depression, when it was cheap, and hold it ready to develop at the first sight of an increase in demand for houses. The prospects of capital gain might ensure that such development, once started, proceeded even after house prices had ceased to rise. Where new houses were being built in the suburbs and people were migrating from the central areas of towns, the number of empty houses in the centre might increase for several years without affecting the profitability of suburban building in the way in which a comparable amount of building nearer the central area would have done. (In these circumstances a high proportion of empty houses might not be a sign of over-building but merely of the location of new building.) After such building activity, a renewed influx of migrants from the country into the towns would find a concentration of empty houses in the central urban area which would need to be taken up before there was a demand for new housing, and this again would tend to lengthen the intervals between building booms.

It might be objected at this stage that to confine attention to residential building is to beg the question. For long swings have been found in other items of British domestic investment in the later nineteenth century – in the expenditure of local authorities, in railways, and – though on more fragile evidence – in industrial investment. Are the long swings in these items also to be explained by reference to domestic influences? Is it not more probable that they were the result of systematic interaction with American long swings? And, in this case, is it not likely that it was the long swings in these other items of domestic investment which caused the long swings in residential building?

It is indeed likely that, in a developed country like Britain, fluctuations in residential building would be a passive response to movements in other items of investment to a greater degree than in a country still in process of settlement. But the movements to which they responded were, I wish to suggest, those of the trade cycle; and the appearance of long swings outside residential building is itself the result of changes in the character of the cycle.

Because British trade cycles ceased to come to an end with a commercial convulsion or financial panic, the forces sustaining investment and income after the downturn were much more effective than they were earlier in the century. Lumpy projects begun in the boom needed to be completed and provided with ancillary equipment; projects completed in the boom were filled in. Some fresh investment was undertaken as the result of opportunities created by boom investment, for example, the external economies resulting from railway building and the extension of knowledge and know-how resulting from a mining boom or the introduction of new types of blast furnace. Projects deferred because of high costs were taken up when costs fell, and perhaps financed from the high profits of the preceding boom. For example, English railway investment was high in the mid-seventies partly because of the abnormally high profits of the preceding boom, and because track, once started, had to be finished and furnished with new rolling stock.

Influences of this kind are, of course, present in any cyclical depression, but in England they operated more immediately in the late than in the early nineteenth century. And in the late nineteenth century they operated more strongly in Britain than in America or in other overseas regions whose banking systems were more vulnerable and whose booms had a stronger 'mania' element. There has recently been some suggestion that in England after the 1860s the trade cycle was not an independent phenomenon but simply the result of lack of synchronisation between the long swings in foreign and domestic investment.[1] The view taken here is the reverse of this: it was the long swings which were the epiphenomena and the trade cycles the reality, in the sense that when the character of the individual cycles has been explained there is no residue which needs to be attributed to the behaviour of a long cycle. The appearance of alternation in British and American long swings is the result of the fact that British trade cycles no longer came to a violent end but the American ones often did.

This section has been an attempt to attribute the appearance of long waves in British building in the later nineteenth century to domestic influences; though there are obvious dangers in attempting to isolate the domestic elements in an economy so dependent upon foreign trade, some such changes as we have described might be reasonably expected even in a closed economy. Nor can the possibility be ruled out that the inverse relationship which these long waves proved to bear to the long waves in American building was fortuitous, for the inverse relationship is not all that exact; it is only a

[1] R. C. O. Matthews, *The Trade Cycle* (Cambridge University Press, 1959) pp. 215–23.

few fluctuations that are in question, and the logical possible number of relationships between them is small.[1]

Systematic alternation existed in so far as the two areas drew on a common stock of resources. Where building is concerned the resources of most interest are migrants and funds, though if we were considering investment as a whole, certain types of skill and capital equipment would have to be considered.

The suggestion most commonly made is that the alternation was established and maintained by fluctuations in the number of migrants. The simplest case would be one in which the building cycle in both countries was determined by migration, that is, where migrants depressed the demand for British houses when they left Britain and raised the demand for American houses when they entered the United States.

So far as the United States was concerned it seems clear that fluctuations in residential building were sensitive to fluctuations in the volume of immigration from all sources. An increase in immigration did not *initiate* a revival of building; the revival was started by changes in migration within the United States which preceded changes in immigration, that is, the economic events which attracted immigrants would in any case have caused some boom in building. But the immigrants strengthened and prolonged the boom. Since the periods of heavy emigration from Britain tended to coincide with the periods of heavy immigration from all sources into the United States, we should expect the periods when American building was active to have coincided with heavy emigration from Britain. This by itself, however, would not have been sufficient to produce an alternation of building cycles.

For the connection between emigration and building fluctuations in Britain is much less obvious. It is clear that fluctuations in the number of emigrants were too small to have had a direct influence on fluctuations of activity in the British building industry; for the rate of increase in *total population* (or, what is more relevant, the total number of households) was very little lower in the periods of heavy emigration, and the absolute increase was as large as in periods of low emigration.

The argument in the case of Britain, however, does not rest on fluctuations in total emigration, but on the relation of these to the rate of urbanisation in Britain. The argument has rested on changes not in total population but in urban population, and the supposition has been that British towns grew most rapidly in the periods of low

[1] Any alternation in the 1860s was due to the American Civil War, which was fortuitous in this context.

emigration. As Cairncross puts it 'urban expansion and colonisation tended to alternate with each other in successive decades'; or as Thomas says, 'when a relatively large number of people are leaving the country, internal mobility is low'.[1] There are really three distinct issues involved:

(a) How far, in fact, did internal migration alternate with emigration?

(b) In so far as it did, how far were the alternations causally connected? How far, for example, were the variations in the volume of internal migration in Britain determined by fluctuations in external migration as compared to changes in the disparity between English agricultural and urban incomes, changes in the costs of internal migration and in the geographical distribution of industry?

(c) How great an influence did changes in internal migration in Britain have upon the British building cycle?

In dealing with the first point we are handicapped by paucity of data, for though there are annual figures relating to emigration, for internal migration there are only the decennial census figures which sum up the net result of the preceding decade. The movements inside each decade can only be guessed. There were clearly years in the nineteenth century when internal migration and emigration moved together; the boom of 1869–73 saw both urbanisation and expansion of the area of overseas settlement. But there were also occasions where there was alternation. The position in the 1870s is ambiguous; it is not clear whether the rise in English residential building activity in 1874–7 indicates an increase in migration to the towns in these years, or accommodation for people who had migrated in the previous trade-cycle boom. There must have been some increase in migration to the towns in the later 1880s but it was slight compared with the increase in emigration; 1894 to 1901 was a period of relatively low emigration, and probably of considerable internal migration. The years after 1900 saw considerable emigration and relatively small net urbanisation. From 1880 on, therefore, there is a plausible case for supposing that English urbanisation alternated with American 'colonisation'.

At first sight the notion that, when migration to the towns was low and emigration high, the high emigration *caused* the low migration, seems obvious common sense; if people had not gone abroad a sufficient number would have gone to the towns to make a significant difference to the level of residential building in England. But the

[1] Cairncross, *Home and Foreign Investment*, pp. 68, 74; Thomas, *Migration and Economic Growth*, p. 173.

assumptions underlying this view need checking. The main assumption is that English towns competed with the United States in a common reservoir of potential migrants from the English countryside, the size of which was determined by fairly long-term factors. When one competitor made more rapid claims on this reservoir, the flow to the other fell off; the level of income and opportunity prevailing at any time in English towns and in the United States made more difference to the division of the stream of migrants between them than to the size of the stream.[1]

But it is possible to conceive other situations. The total stream of migrants may have been very sensitive to short-term changes in economic opportunity, so that, when both British towns and America drew simultaneously, one did not obtain migrants at the expense of the other but both obtained them at the expense of a more rapid flight from the English countryside. A high level of migration to one area might indeed, by force of example and by loosening social bonds, induce some people to migrate to the other. Of course when one competitor was prosperous and the other depressed, the prosperous one would get the migrants, but one could not say that the one area was depriving the other of migrants, for if both had been depressed neither of them would have had many; and if both had been active both would have had all the migrants they wanted. As a third possibility one can suppose that English towns and the United States each drew on its own particular pool of migrants, in which case, even if neither pool were elastic, the demands of one area would not compete with those of the other.

These are theoretical possibilities, but they correspond to three recognisable types of motive and situation. There was the man who was determined to leave the English countryside in any case sooner or later, whose decision when to leave was determined by random factors like the harvest or his age, but whose choice of destination was very sensitive to the relative attractiveness of the English towns and the United States at the moment when he decided to leave. At the other extreme was the man who was decided on one particular destination, the timing of whose move depended on the varying conditions in that destination. There must, for example, have been many men for whom the choice was to emigrate or to stay in the countryside – men who waited for good conditions before emigrating but who would not be attracted to the English towns by any conjunction of circumstances. There may also have been people, especially among the older people, whose preference was very strongly for the

[1] B. Thomas, 'Wales and the Atlantic Economy', *Scottish Journal of Political Economy*, VI 3 (Nov 1959) 169–71.

English town and who never seriously considered emigrating. In between these groups are people with a range of different preferences about the timing of their migration and their destination, whose decisions on both points were subject to short-term variations in economic conditions.

It cannot therefore be assumed without further argument that if emigration had been lower in any period internal migration would have been very much higher. It may be, for example, that in the mid-seventies migrants moved to English towns because activity in them remained high, not because emigration had become less attractive. It is even more likely that the more rapid urbanisation of the later nineties would have taken place even in the face of larger emigration; the towns grew because they were seats of innovation, not because migrants were diverted from America; and if the demand of the primary producing areas for migrants had been higher they would probably have got them from other countries or by a higher level of migration from the English countryside rather than at the expense of English urbanisation. Even for the period after 1900, when it seems most obvious from the census figures that emigration was at the expense of the growth of towns, there are some qualifications to be made. In the first place, the loss to the urban areas as defined for census purposes represents in part simply the growth of suburbs and not a loss to towns in the wider economic sense. In the second place, the centres of industrial expansion in these years – the coalfields of South Wales and Yorkshire, the Lancashire cotton towns, and centres of new industry like Coventry – attracted a considerable number of migrants: they were evidently able to compete with the attractions of emigration. Nevertheless it is reasonable to suppose that, but for attractions abroad, those urban areas where demand for labour was not expanding, and areas like London from which labour was migrating, would have had a higher level of building. Probably also in the 1880s, people would have left agriculture in any case, but in the absence of good opportunities abroad they would have gone to English towns.

There is, therefore, some sense in saying that in the 1880s and in the 1900s a large number of people emigrated who would otherwise have gone to (or stayed in) the English towns. This was probably a new feature. In the first half of the century emigration was much more a *pis aller*; migrants went to English towns in booms and emigration tended to be highest in depression; of the early period it would be truer to say that when migration and emigration alternated, emigration was determined by internal migration.

But even where the fluctuations in internal migration after, say, the 1870s were dominated by those in emigration, it by no means follows, even in this period, that the English building cycle was dominated by internal migration. There are two objections which must be met before this view can be accepted. In the first place, though there was a fall of about 10 per cent in the absolute numbers of the population of the rural areas as a whole from 1861 to 1901, it was only in the 1880s that the fall was significant, and between 1901 and 1911 there was an increase.[1] In these circumstances, why should *migration* – as opposed to the increase of total population, which has already been ruled out as an inadequate explanation – have had any effect on the total demand for housing? Would not the migrants to the towns have had to find accommodation even if they had stayed in the countryside? In the second place, many of the migrants were young and unskilled, who must have found difficulty in obtaining work and have earned low wages at first; many were single and would naturally fit into existing households, often enough with urban relations. This is to say the newcomers may have represented only a very small effective demand for new houses.

To the first objection there are reasonable answers. Though in the *aggregate* the absolute fall in rural population may not have been significant for our purposes, there were several areas where there *was* such a significant fall. On the most rigorous assumptions, therefore, some of the movement to the towns represented a net addition to the need for houses; if the migrants had stayed in the country, the existing house-room there would have been ample for them. Even when there was no absolute fall in the rural population, the additional population was more likely to stimulate a demand for new houses if it moved to the towns than if it stayed in the countryside. For country accommodation was probably more stretchable. It is true that conditions in Liverpool or Manchester suggest that accommodation was very stretchable in some towns. But migrants came from each of a very large number of villages and went to a small number of towns, that is, the sources of migrants were diffused but their destinations were concentrated. So it was easier to accommodate a man in his village than when he moved to the town. The migrant to the town, furthermore, was more likely to have to *pay* for additional accommodation among strangers; had he stayed in his village he would probably have been fitted in, at little or no cost to him, with his family or with relatives. Then again movement to the town must have meant for the migrants as a whole an increase in money in-comes, and therefore an increase in money demand for houses. More-

[1] A. L. Bowley, 'Rural Population in England and Wales', *Journal of the Royal Statistical Society*, LXXVII (6) (May 1914) 605–6.

over, it is not only the effective demand of the newcomers to the urban areas which must be considered: the demand of the people pushed out of the older parts of the towns by these newcomers was probably substantial. Immigrants from the country concentrated in the areas where housing was poorest, areas on the verge of becoming slums, and their influx led to the exodus of some of the existing occupants and to the extension of suburbs; migration of the countryside caused a building boom in Didsbury rather than in central Manchester, just as migration from the Mississippi causes a housing boom in Westchester not in Harlem. For all these reasons a shift of people from country to town probably meant an increase in the demand for houses and not merely a change in the place where houses were demanded. Finally, there is no doubt that a given increase in demand for house-room was more likely to be met by additional building when it was exerted in the town than when it was exerted in the village, because the building industry was organised to meet urban rather than rural demand. For one thing, urban demand was more concentrated. For another, in the countryside, a substantial part of the housing was provided by the landowners at low rent and in part payment of wages, and the supply of houses was not determined by market considerations, so that even a rural wage earner who could have afforded a better house would, in many villages, not have found one available.[1]

There is also an answer to the second objection. The argument is not that an influx of migrants into English towns in the seventies by itself stimulated a housing boom, or even that the slower pace of urban immigration in the 1880s by itself prevented one. The argument is that in the mid-seventies, when finance was easy and construction costs low, and when there was a backlog to be made up, building was able to continue at a high level because demand was reinforced by a stream of immigrants; migration into the towns explains not why the building boom started but why it continued so long. Contrariwise, in the mid-eighties, when there were signs of a revival of building, the argument is that it did not proceed further because demand was no longer braced by newcomers. There is, therefore, no reason in principle why migration should not have made the English building cycle alternate with the American, but the discussion suggests that the variations would need to have been very substantial to have had this effect.

[1] 'The general complaint all over the country with regard to rural matters and the agricultural industry is the want of accommodation; old dwellings are condemned on account of their condition, and it does not pay to build new ones.' (Cd. 2751 of 1905, Qu. 21698.)

Overseas regions competed with the British building industry for funds as well as for migrants. I argued, in an earlier section, that house-building had to compete for finance with certain other types of domestic investment. The point which may be urged about foreign investment in the later nineteenth century is that it was a more serious and direct competitor for the funds available for English house-building. There had developed during the eighteenth century, principally because of the growth of the national debt, a substantial class of passive investors. The numbers and resources of this class were enormously extended during the wars against France between 1792 and 1815, and interest payments on the debt further increased their accumulations. Tooke, writing of the early 1850s, refers to 'the increased wealth of the country, and the peculiar social arrangements which confine a considerable part of the accumulations to investment in the public funds'.[1] These savings were not readily diverted into the London money market; for most of the century English industry did not make large claims upon them, partly because its own savings were sufficient for the increase in capacity which it wished to undertake, partly because it could not easily offer securities which were attractive to the passive investor. The coming of limited liability did not fundamentally alter this position. The passive investor favoured Government securities or investments of a public utility type – transport improvements, urban developments, housing – investments financed largely by bonds or mortgages. Foreign investment was financed in ways which were attractive to this type of investor. A large part of it consisted of Government borrowing; much of the private borrowing was of a public utility type, and the need to obtain funds often compelled foreigners to finance projects which were not of this type by the issue of bonds bearing a fixed interest.

There was, therefore, a substantial amount of saving done by passive investors who switched, not between British industry and British public utilities, but between British public utilities and foreign investment. Substantial shifts in the disposition of new funds could take place with small or even negligible changes in return; a mere increase in the relevant type of securities might be sufficient.

Until the 1850s and 1860s the claims of foreign investment on these *rentier* savings were circumscribed, partly because few foreign countries were developing so rapidly that they needed to borrow heavily, and partly because a high degree of risk still attached to their securities. There was, moreover, a strong domestic demand for such savings. Up to 1815 the increase in Government debt absorbed

[1] Tooke and Newmarch, *History of Prices*, vol. v, p. 315.

much of them. In several of the trade revivals, the dominant form of investment was of a public utility type – canals and turnpikes in the 1790s and railways in the 1830s and 1840s; even in the revival of the fifties railways raised large amounts of capital, and there was in addition Government borrowing during the Crimean War. It is true that even before the 1850s there was competition between British and foreign investment; foreign investment tended to fluctuate with the trade cycle and influenced the size of the pool of *rentier* savings available for domestic investment; it is significant that the first large foreign investment boom of the nineteenth century occurred during the trade revival of the mid-1820s, when the pace at home was made by metals and textiles and not by public utilities. But by and large the main competition which English housing had to meet in the first half of the century came from other domestic claimants rather than from abroad.

In the decades after the 1850s, foreign demand for the savings of English *rentiers* grew and the risks probably diminished. So far as domestic investment was concerned, the main demand for such savings now came from housing and closely allied urban developments, and some of the money which in the 1840s would have gone into English railways, in the 1870s went into mortgages. But domestic mortgages, though more attractive than other available domestic alternatives, were in several respects unsatisfactory: they were unhomogeneous and the market in them was very imperfect; it was difficult to adjust the terms on which they were contracted in such a way as adequately to discount this disadvantage whenever supplies of foreign bonds, especially Government bonds, became available. In the competition for the savings of the passive investor, domestic housing was much less powerful vis-à-vis foreign investment than domestic railways had been in the 1830s and 1840s. This indeed is one of the reasons for the magnitude of British foreign investment between 1870 and 1914 – with one exception the booms in England were dominated by developments in industry, in which the English passive investor did not participate. Except when the Government was borrowing during the Boer War, there were few domestic claimants for *rentier* savings sufficiently attractive to stand up to the competition of foreign borrowers, since the market in foreign securities was well organised.

Since most of the English trade-cycle booms coincided with high activity in the primary producing areas, foreign competition with housing mortgages was exerted in the boom. While English trade expansions no longer ended with a financial crisis, those in primary producing areas usually did, so that during a depression, *rentier* savings were very sharply deflected back to such secure domestic assets as mortgages. Thus the character and timing of foreign investment reinforced both the pressure on building finance during the trade-cycle boom and the availability of funds for building during the following depression.

Exactly how sensitive the flow of funds was must await investigation. It depended partly on the particular foreign security: on the face of it one would expect English mortgages and the securities of Argentinian railways to have appealed to different classes of investors. It must also have depended on the scale of operations of the builders and of the solicitors, who negotiated many of the mortgages, which varied from area to area. In some areas, for example in South Wales, most house-owners owned only a few houses, bought from the profits of a small business – a public house, etc. – or with a mortgage financed from such sources. One would not expect such people readily to divert their savings into foreign bonds during a boom. On the other hand, in the 1880s, as J. D. Bailey has shown, Scottish funds were switched directly out of Scottish into Australian mortgages.[1] This evidence relates particularly to a switch between Australia and Scotland, and may be exceptional since Australians borrowed much more on mortgage than other primary producing areas, and Scottish investors were more dependent on solicitors than the English. But English investors also invested heavily in the debentures of Anglo-Australian land mortgage companies and placed large sums on deposit with Australian financial institutions. At the end of the 1880s there was no difficulty in inducing Englishmen to lend on Australian debentures at $3\frac{1}{2}$ or 4 per cent. It is a fair presumption that there were many passive investors who readily switched their savings between home and foreign assets of comparable types.

There is some general probability about the notion that foreign demand for funds was at the expense of building finance. Very large sums were invested abroad in periods of heavy foreign investment. Some of these funds must have come from saving out of increased incomes, but it seems likely from the national income figures that a large part must have come from a switch from some item of domestic investment. The increase in foreign investment and the fall in building and public utility-type investment are of the same general order of magnitude, and this in itself suggests that the switch was at the expense of building. Finally, the existence of a large pool of savings, the size of which was not sensitive to changes in income, which could

[1] J. D. Bailey, 'Australian Borrowing in Scotland in the Nineteenth Century', *Economic History Review*, 2nd ser., XII 2 (Dec 1959) 268–79.

be drawn into the finance of building, was a necessary condition of the persistence of a housing boom over a cyclical depression.

Thus, besides the domestic factors discussed in an earlier section, there were foreign influences tending to inhibit building during the expansion phase of the trade cycle and encourage it during the depression phase. They may be summarised as follows:

(a) In the early nineteenth century people went to the towns when business was booming there, and stayed in the country-side or emigrated in slumps: that is, internal migration was dominated by the fluctuations in United Kingdom prosperity. But in the later part of the nineteenth century, internal migra-tion was influenced by emigration, that is, by fluctuations in the prosperity of the regions of recent settlement. Costs of emigration had fallen, particularly in relation to the incomes of the potential migrants, and this tended to decrease the proportion of migration to the towns which took place during the trade-cycle expansion.

(b) The primary producing regions accentuated the shortage of funds available to the British building industry during the trade-cycle boom, by borrowing sums which in relation to contemporary British domestic investment were much larger than in the first half of the century, and by borrowing on securities more directly comparable and competitive with housing finance than were the securities of British industry.

The problem posed by the hypothesis of the Atlantic economy is the balance between domestic – and in this context fortuitous – in-fluences on the one hand, and foreign and systematic influences on the other. The first long wave of British building in the 1870s is best interpreted as the result of domestic influences. Cooney has argued that the heavy foreign investment during the trade-cycle boom of 1869–73 diverted funds from building and in this way thrust the period of heavy building forward into the mid-seventies.[1] His argu-ment seems to exaggerate the decline of building during this boom; with the principal exceptions of London and South Wales, housing activity rose fairly continuously from 1866 to 1876 with only a slight check in 1873. While it may be true that there would have been more building between 1869 and 1873 had it not been for the foreign demand for funds, I am inclined to think that the continued rise in building up to 1876 is principally to be explained by the fact that the

---

[1] E. W. Cooney, 'Long Waves in Building in the British Economy of the Nine-teenth Century', *Economic History Review*, 2nd ser., XIII 2 (Dec 1960) 264–6, re-printed in the present volume, Essay 6.

trade-cycle boom did not come to an end in England with a financial panic, and that industrial activity remained at a high level even after 1873. These facts were not, of course, independent of events abroad, but they were not related in the direct way implied in the argument about systematic alternation.

But if British building had continued to repeat its pattern of the 1870s, it would have risen in the revival and continued on into the depression of every other trade cycle, and there would have been a partial overlapping instead of an inverse relationship. This is not what happened; the British building boom missed not one but two trade cycles. There was, it is true, an increase in building in the trade revival of the later eighties but there was no boom. There was indeed no general building boom between 1876, which saw the end of one, and 1896, which saw the beginning of another – a longer swing in fact than twenty years.

It is conceivable that a British building boom failed to develop in the late eighties because of the character of the industrial investment most prominent in the trade revival of those years. This was a revival after a very severe depression, concentrated mainly in exports and in the shipbuilding industry. There was a good deal of slack in the areas where the industries mainly concerned were situated, and a substantial increase in output and employment could take place with a relatively modest increase in internal migration.

But the main explanation is likely to have been the effect of the overseas development booms of these years. The 1880s are in many ways an exceptional decade. Foreign investment and emigration were sustained at a high level for a longer period than at any other time in the century. The cause of this is reasonably clear. Up to the 1870s by far the greater demand from regions of recent settlement for British migrants and funds had come from the United States. In the later 1870s and 1880s a sizeable demand arose from Australasia. The development booms did not coincide in all parts of Australasia, nor did Australasia coincide with the United States. There was also a large demand from South America. Whereas the overseas demand for finance and for migrants had previously tended to a considerable degree to be concentrated in the trade-cycle boom, it was now sustained for a decade and was, in addition, unusually heavy during the boom. It was so strong that, while not preventing the cyclical revival of the later 1880s in Britain, it drew off the migrants and/or funds which would have sustained a simultaneous boom in British building. This is the only occasion on which foreign influences clearly deflected British building fluctuations from the course they would otherwise have taken.

As between migrants and funds, it is unlikely that this deflection was produced by the outward flow of the latter.[1] For this was a decade of low interest rates – Consols were converted from 3 per cent to $2\frac{3}{4}$ per cent in 1888 – and funds were pushed abroad rather than pulled. The experience of the building societies does not suggest shortage of funds: at times during the eighties the directors of the Abbey Road Society were compelled to suspend the issue of shares because of the superabundance of money seeking investment.[2] In this decade the case for the importance of foreign influences must rest on emigration. Even in this decade the magnitude of emigration was in considerable measure the result of domestic influences. It is not merely that overseas areas were pulling migrants; English agriculture was pushing and English industry was not pulling hard enough. A large-scale migration from the English countryside was by then inevitable – by the later 1880s it was difficult to interpret the agricultural depression as the result of temporary circumstances. It is probable, too, that the depth of cyclical depression in 1879 and 1885 and the weakness of the intervening revival had made many industrial workers decide to emigrate, and that they acted on their decision as soon as the improvement of conditions provided them with the means to do so. But if certain regions of recent settlement had not been booming in this decade, more agricultural labourers would have gone to the English towns, and more urban workers would have stayed in them. This is the clearest case of emigration at the expense of urbanisation.

Once the fluctuations had been deflected from their former pat-

---

[1] Detailed comparison with German building fluctuations might shed light on the relative importance of migrants and funds. German foreign investment and exports went principally to Europe, and German emigrants went principally to America, and went during American booms; if the German building cycle had been determined by migration it ought, Lewis and O'Leary have argued, to have synchronised with the British. Instead, they believe it virtually coincided with the U.S. building cycle, with peaks in 1873 and 1890 ('Secular Swings in Production', p. 130), and with periods of heavy German capital exports (p. 142). But this does not shed much light on the problem because (*a*) German emigration was very much smaller in relation to total German population and did not necessarily bear the same relation to migration within Germany; (*b*) the evidence is, in fact, too slight to assert that the German building cycle coincided with the British.

[2] Sir Harold Bellman, *Bricks and Mortals* (London: Hutchinson & Co., 1949) pp. 66–7. The accounts of building societies are difficult to interpret because (*a*) each society was subject to individual influences; (*b*) the movement as a whole was affected by the failure of the Liberator Society (1892) and the Birkbeck (1911). Such as it is, the experience of the Abbey Road and the Co-operative Permanent suggests that the fluctuations in demand were much more important than those in funds. Certainly in periods of trade depression, for example 1885–6 and 1893–5, advances fell while receipts often rose. (A. Mansbridge, *Brick upon Brick* (London: Dent & Sons, 1934) pp. 62–8.)

tern, there was no reason why they should revert, even in the absence of further disturbance from abroad; indeed, on the view I have taken, there was every reason why the former pattern should *not* re-establish itself. One would expect the deficient building of the later 1880s to have produced a strong echo effect; so that even if there had been no subsequent fluctuations in foreign competition for funds and migrants after the eighties, building would probably have been high in the 1890s. If, as a result of events abroad in the second half of the eighties, the house-building of these years was unduly low, even for the level of demand in that decade, there would have been a backlog to be made up in the 1890s over and above houses for the migrants who in that decade turned away from the United States to English towns.

It is true that the extreme discredit which overtook foreign investment after the Australian and South American financial crises in the early nineties enhanced the attractions of domestic building mortgages to the passive investor; abundance of funds actively seeking such outlets allowed the building boom of the nineties to develop on a larger scale than might otherwise have been the case. But in the housing boom of the 1890s the contemporary influences which were most important were domestic. In this decade there was a change from industrial booms based on established industries to those based on new industries. Many of these developed in areas where there was no substantial surplus of labour at the beginning of the revival and where growth therefore stimulated considerable internal migration. As Charles Booth said in evidence before the London Transport Commission:

> The new industries that are started are not started in towns; they are started outside. I think anyone who travels through England cannot but notice the large new works that have been built in recent years and are being built near important stations, or still more near important junctions ... the development of trade at present is largely taking that shape. It is not so much that they are going out of the towns, but they are not coming into the towns. But it must tend to move the population to a great extent; in fact, you see the houses of the working people being erected near these great new factories.[1]

Thus the character of the industries most prominent in the cycle was favourable to house-building.

It was in the nineties, moreover, that electricity was applied to

[1] R.C. on London Transport (Cd. 2751 of 1906, Qu. 19104, evidence given in March 1904).

transport in England with a resultant stimulus to suburban building. This illustrates better than anything else the random element in the relations of British and American building cycles. In the United States, electricity began to be applied to traction in the 1880s, and this had been one of the causes of the high level of American house-building in the eighties. If Britain had made similar advances in electricity in the 1880s, she would have had a more substantial building boom in that decade. Thus the alternation of American and British housing activity in the eighties and nineties partly reflects the different rate at which electricity was applied to traction in the two countries. This was, in the present context, almost certainly fortuitous. It is, of course, true that if emigration from the United Kingdom in the 1880s had been smaller, urban authorities would have had more incentive to undertake improvements in local transport facilities. But the English lag in using electricity for this purpose was part of the lag in her use of electricity for all purposes, and this has nothing to do with the volume of migration to the United States and the heavy foreign investment during the 1880s. It was primarily the result of the relative efficiency of the English gas industry, and the unfortunate history of the electrical companies founded in the trade revival of the early eighties.

After 1903 there was a decline in building over the country as a whole, but as S. B. Saul has shown, this fall in the national total covers considerable diversity of regional experience.[1] Building was well sustained not only in the main centres of the export boom of this decade – in the coalfields of South Wales and Yorkshire, in the Lancashire cotton towns and in Liverpool – but in the East Midlands, which had been one of the main seats of engineering in the boom of the later nineties and where industry continued to expand. It is possible that where building was low it was because emigration depressed the demand for housing, and foreign investment depleted the funds. The main influence on internal migration, however, was not the level of emigration, but changes in the distribution of British industry, and where building declined after 1903 there is no evidence that it was because funds were diverted abroad. Except where demand was sustained by the continued growth of new industries or by the boom in exports, a decline in building was to be expected after 1903 simply because the previous housing boom had been so vigorous. There is no need to invoke foreign influences, and if they are invoked it can be argued that the demand of the primary producing regions for English goods in these years did more to stimulate

---

[1] S. B. Saul, 'House Building in England 1890–1914', *Economic History Review*, xv (Aug 1962).

building in England than their demand for migrants and funds did to depress it. It was only in the years immediately before 1914 that there were complaints that foreign investment was inhibiting British building, and the outbreak of war came too soon to enable us to judge how effective this competition for funds would ultimately have been in preventing the building revival which, from previous history, one would have expected in the second decade of the twentieth century.[1]

As an instance of the importance of not merely domestic but local influences on fluctuations, I take the case of London – exceptional in many ways, no doubt, but important since it has considerable influence on the behaviour of the national aggregate. In London there was a decline in building after 1903, which at first sight it might seem natural to attribute to foreign influences. But the fall can be accounted for by local circumstances. In the first place, London industries were principally consumer industries, and these were not expanding rapidly in the decade or so before 1914 because real wages were stationary.[2] There is a link here with events abroad – the favourable terms of trade for primary products which partly accounted for the stagnation of real wages. But the link was indirect. The attractions of London as an industrial centre – mainly a large supply of cheap and diversified labour – were increasingly offset by the rising price of sites within the central area.[3] While one effect of this was to induce factories to move from central London to outlying areas, possibly increasing the demand for houses there, it must have deterred new manufacturers coming to London and impaired the competitive power of London manufacturers against those of less densely populated areas.

Building in London had been unusually active in the 1870s, stimulated by the development of the horse tramway – the peak of building was not reached in London till 1881. There was in these years a large amount of building in Camberwell, Walworth, Forest Hill, Stamford Hill and Tottenham, much of it associated with improved transport facilities.[4] The Great Eastern Railway, whose London stations were in the crowded parts of the East End, ran

---

[1] For evidence of a shift from housing to foreign investment in the 1910s see *Report of the Land Enquiry Committee*, II (London, 1914). It was, of course, not only foreign investment which competed with housing but, for example, small joint-stock companies in textiles. (Ibid., pp. 89–91.)

[2] Between 1901 and 1911 there was a net emigration from the Greater London area of 228,733. J. C. Spensley, 'Urban Housing Problems', *Journal of the Royal Statistical Society*, LXXXI (2) (Mar 1918) 173.

[3] R.C. on London Traffic, Cd. 2597 of 1905, Qu. 21651 ff., 21678.

[4] R.C. on Housing of the Working Classes, P.P. 1881, VI, Qu. 3987.

cheap workmen's trains, under statutory obligation from the mid-1870s.[1] There was a large amount of speculative building of working-class houses. The building boom of the 1870s was therefore more prolonged in London than almost anywhere else. Some of the activity in the London building boom of the later 1890s was in areas where there had already been very considerable building as recently as 1881, Tottenham, for example, and it might for this reason be expected to peter out earlier.[2]

Then again, a large part of the building in this boom of the later 1890s was in places where transport facilities were already available. 'The enormous migration of people into Tottenham, Edmonton, West Ham and Walthamstow and such districts', said one witness before the Commission on London Transport of 1905, 'is simply caused by the facilities that have been given by the railway companies.'[3] It was the provision of cheap workmen's trains running out considerable distances that was said to be the most important cause of the exceptionally rapid growth of population in the districts of London adjacent to the suburbs.[4] It was cheap trains which had caused the increase in population, not vice versa. This was a type of business which the railway representatives before the Commission made it clear they disliked. Its concentration at peak hours would in itself – quite apart from the limit on fares – have made it uneconomic, and cheap workmen's fares, by changing the social composition of the suburbs to which they were available, tended to reduce the more profitable types of traffic. There were also special difficulties in London in building new suburban lines – mainly the high cost of land and the difficulty of acquiring it – and there were particular difficulties in the provision of tramways.

Thus the fluctuations in London building are partly to be explained by independently determined changes in the provision of cheap travelling facilities. The explanation of the relatively low level of London building after 1903 is not simply that demand for housing was growing less rapidly in London than elsewhere. There is a large amount of evidence given before the Royal Commission on Means of Locomotion and Transport in London which suggests that there was

[1] Ibid., P.P. 1881, VII, Qu. 1444.

[2] There was probably also a long-standing tendency for London building to be out of phase with that of industrial areas. Thus the 1830s seem to have seen less building in London than in the rest of the country – between 1831 and 1841 the number of inhabited houses per hundred of population rose over the country as a whole, but fell in Middlesex. (Matthews, *A Study in Trade-Cycle History*, p. 118.) This disparity of experience may have had some echo effect in later decades. It also suggests the possibility that migration into London tended to vary inversely with the prosperity of the industrial districts.

[3] Cd. 2597 of 1905, Qu. 2751, 3799.   [4] Ibid., Qu. 5058.

still in 1904 a large unsatisfied demand for housing in London. The cost of land and the high rates made it virtually impossible to build profitably in any central district.[1] Commercial builders would not build around London until means of access at cheap rates were assured. Building therefore depended on the creation of cheap suburban transport, and this was slow for reasons which have little to do with events abroad, for example, the fact that the suburban fares were too low, and the limited capacity of the London stations.

That very local factors had an important effect on fluctuations is not of course a demonstration that the systematic influence was not the crucial variable. But the study of a particular area does reinforce one's scepticism.

The argument of this essay is not that emigration and foreign investment had no effect on British building fluctuations, but only that except in the later eighties they were of minor importance compared with domestic factors. These foreign influences were of such a nature that they *could* have dominated British building, but it is only in the later eighties that it may reasonably be supposed that foreign influences did in fact deflect it from the path dictated by its previous history and by contemporary developments of a primarily domestic origin. The argument has been confined to the influence on British fluctuations of the overseas demand for British funds and migrants, because this seems the direction in which effects hypothesised by the theory of the Atlantic economy are most likely to have worked. But it would of course be equally a verification of the theory if an exceptionally strong British demand for funds and migrants called a temporary halt to growth in the overseas regions; it has indeed been argued that the British boom of the later 1890s inhibited the flow of capital and labour to Canada and held up a revival which was warranted by purely Canadian conditions.[2] This part of the argument must be left to transatlantic historians, but since the overseas economies were growing more rapidly than the British and their cyclical booms were more vigorous, I should expect to find the autonomous element in their fluctuations even more evident than in the British.

---

[1] R.C. on London Traffic, Cd. 2751 of 1906, Qu. 5799, 5908. This is also related to the social structure of London. A very large proportion of London's industrial labour was employed in domestic industry – in the small workshop. There was, therefore, more residence near place of work than in factory towns. Morever, though there was a class of prosperous artisans, the mass of London's domestic workers enjoyed lower earnings than factory workers. They could less easily afford the economic cost of travel from the suburbs.

[2] K. A. H. Buckley, *Capital Formation in Canada, 1896–1930* (Toronto: University of Toronto Press, 1955).

8 The Long Swing: Comparisons and Interactions Between British and American Balance of Payments, 1820–1913[*1]

JEFFREY G. WILLIAMSON

IN the past decade there has been an extremely active interest in the evidence and importance of the twenty-year building cycle, or Kuznets cycle as Lewis suggests we call it, in both American nineteenth-century development and British development after 1870.[2] The evidence of building cycles in the United States is perhaps more extensive and seems clearly, in the research accumulated by Kuznets, Burns and Abramovitz, to indicate a long swing in the general process of growth, not just long swings isolated to the building trades.[3] Whereas American long swings pervade all domestic series of output, income and investment, British experience seems somewhat different. After 1870 long swings in British capital exports alternated with long swings in domestic investment in a fashion which eliminated excess

[1] See Jeffrey G. Williamson, *American Growth and the Balance of Payments* (Chapel Hill: University of North Carolina Press, 1964).

[2] See for instance R. C. O. Matthews, *The Business Cycle* (Chicago: University of Chicago Press, 1959) esp. chap. 12; Moses Abramovitz, 'Resource and Output Trends in the United States since 1870', *American Economic Review*, XLVI 2 (May 1956) 5–24; Brinley Thomas, *Migration and Economic Growth* (Cambridge: Cambridge University Press, 1954); and most recently, E. W. Cooney, 'Long Waves in Building in the British Economy of the Nineteenth Century', *Economic History Review* 2nd ser., XIII (Dec 1960) 257–69 (reprinted above, Essay 6).

[3] Simon Kuznets, *Long Term Changes in National Income of the United States since 1869*, Income and Wealth, Series II, published for the International Association for Research in Income and Wealth (Cambridge: Bowes & Bowes, 1952); Moses Abramovitz's work is most recently summarised in *The Nature and Significance of Kuznets Cycles*, mimeographed for the Stanford Research Center in Economic Growth (Dec 1960), and which appeared in *Economic Development and Cultural Change*, IX 3 (Apr 1961) 225–48; Arthur Burns, *Production Trends in the United States since 1870* (New York: National Bureau of Economic Research, 1934).

---

* This essay was first published in *Journal of Economic History*, XXII (1962).

fluctuations in income and output, which would have been due mainly to fluctuations in aggregate demand.[1]

Most of these investigations into long swings in the process of development concern domestic movements; their evidence in American development extends back into the nineteenth century at least as far as the 1820s, while significant evidence of these swings in British history seems to be available only after 1870. Apart from one recent exception,[2] no important attempts have been made to extend the Kuznets cycle analysis to encompass the international flow of goods, capital and specie, although there has been an investigation of swings in labour migration, most notably by Thomas. Surely one important reason for the lack of attention to this aspect of the long swing has been due to the unavailability of net capital flow estimates. This statistical gap has been filled quite recently with research done by Douglass C. North, Matthew Simon and Albert H. Imlah.[3]

The purpose of this paper is not primarily to examine long swings in the United States balance of payments. Although I will review the evidence of long swings in the flow of international capital, goods and specie in American nineteenth-century history, my major goal here will be an examination of two aspects of their evidence in British balance of payments. First, did the domestic long swing mechanism produce similar movements in British capital exports, merchandise imports and merchandise exports with the same violence that was exhibited in American movements? The first purpose of this paper, then, is a comparison of the effects of a domestic long swing upon the international transactions of a relatively developed, high-income, chronic capital exporter with the balance of payments movements of

[1] This relationship has perhaps been most energetically pursued by A. K. Cairncross, *Home and Foreign Investment, 1870–1913* (Cambridge: Cambridge University Press, 1953); Thomas, *Migration and Economic Growth*; and W. A. Lewis and P. J. O'Leary, 'Secular Swings in Production and Trade, 1870–1913', *Manchester School of Economic and Social Studies*, XIII (May 1955) 113–52.

[2] Douglass C. North, *The Economic Growth of the United States, 1790–1860* (Englewood Cliffs, N.J.: Prentice-Hall, 1961). This excellent little book appeared after this manuscript was completed.

[3] Douglass C. North, 'The United States Balance of Payments, 1790–1860', *Trends in the American Economy in the Nineteenth Century*, Studies in Income and Wealth, vol. 24, of the National Bureau of Economic Research (Princeton: Princeton University Press, 1960) pp. 573–627; Matthew Simon, 'The United States Balance of Payments, 1861–1900', *Trends*, pp. 629–715; Albert H. Imlah, *Economic Elements in the Pax Britannica* (Cambridge, Mass.: Harvard University Press, 1958).

In the research contained in this paper I have used North's and Simon's estimates to cover nineteenth-century United States and Imlah's estimates for British balance of payments 1820–1913. The estimates for net capital movements over United States borders from 1901 to 1913 are taken from Raymond W. Goldsmith, *A Study of Saving in the United States*, 3 vols (Princeton: Princeton University Press, 1955) vol. 1, pp. 1078–93, Tables K-1 through K-7.

a relatively underdeveloped, capital-scarce, net capital importer undergoing these same internal swings in the process of growth. Very little research has been devoted to British experience with long swings in the balance of payments prior to 1870, and the analysis of the nineteenth century in the literature as a whole has not been very systematic. Second, and perhaps even more interesting, what is the mechanism of interaction between these two members of the nineteenth-century Atlantic economy? Is there a *systematic* relationship between British and American development in the nature of an inverse Kuznets cycle, and is it possible that this interrelated mechanism had its source in one of the two countries? And finally, if a *systematic* inverse relation between the rate of domestic growth of Great Britain and America did indeed exist, did it arise predominantly from independent internal conditions or by the direct effects of fluctuating international demands for, and supplies of, goods, securities and specie or by the indirect effects of labour migration? These are some of the major questions towards which this paper will be directed.

American demands for goods from, and in part supplies of goods to, the international market do indeed reveal long swings as early as 1820, and are clearly evident without the sometimes questionable methods of moving averages, trend removal and calculated rates of change. The movements are easily identifiable in the unadulterated annual estimates. Over the nineteenth century as a whole imports of goods into the United States are positively related to composite dating of Kuznets cycles in domestic activity, and after 1860 deflated imports reveal an extremely high positive correlation with income, output and investment series; that is, from 1830 to 1870, deflated imports are positively related to the Riggleman building index with $r = \cdot 95$; from 1860 to 1900, deflated imports are positively related to the Frickey index of manufacturing production and railroad mileage added where $r = \cdot 822$ and $r = \cdot 938$ respectively; and from 1890 to 1914, deflated imports are positively related to the Riggleman building index, $r = \cdot 871$, and railroad mileage added, $r = \cdot 903$.[1] Without exception the fluctuations in American imports over the Kuznets cycle in domestic growth had more violent amplitude than export movements. Imports dominated the trade balance from 1820 to 1913, with exports only randomly affecting the timing and amplitude of the trade balance. During periods of extremely rapid growth, on

[1] In these tests, both series were smoothed by a five-year moving average after their trends had been removed by

$$\log y = \alpha_0 - \alpha_1 t - \alpha_2 t^2.$$

the upswing of a Kuznets cycle, the trade balance became progressively worse, reflecting increasing excess demands for goods in the domestic system. These periods of worsening in the trade balance alternated with periods of improvement, when domestic growth was sluggish or more seriously involved with protracted periods of deficiencies in aggregate demand.

This description of a Kuznets cycle in merchandise imports, which also reflects itself in the balance of trade, slights the importance of the export market in *conditioning* the pace of American development prior to the Civil War. Although they were less severe in amplitude, before 1860 exports also exhibited long secular swings positively related to the pace of domestic growth. Indeed, in its undeveloped state our development was very much a function of conditions in the export market: a market dominated by cotton and, to a lesser extent, grain. Some have supported the view that the long swing in American development (during a period of export monopoly) was *initiated* by a persistent and endogenous lag of raw material and foodstuff production behind supply price.[1] In other research which is not reviewed here, I found no evidence which would throw doubt on this thesis. On the contrary, any new evidence which I compiled strongly supports the view that long swings in the American economy prior to the 1850s could be explained by fluctuations in export supply as described above.[2] Nevertheless, at the end of the American Civil War, after a period of secular transition, export movements no longer displayed similar long swings, and over the nineteenth century as a whole they did not interfere with the singular importance of imports in dictating the state of the trade balance.

Concomitant with alternation in the pace of real growth over the long swing and alternating excess demands for goods reflected in the trade balance, there must have been variations in (*ex-ante*) excess demands for money as well. During periods of rapid growth in income and output, tendencies towards heavy excess demands for increments in real money balances are the rule, while during periods of sluggish growth and prolonged depressions the tendency may be even towards an excess supply. Under a nineteenth-century gold

---

[1] Douglass C. North has presented this argument most cogently, an argument to which I also subscribe, in 'Location Theory and Regional Economic Growth', *Journal of Political Economy*, LXIII 3 (June 1955) 243–58; 'Agriculture and Regional Economic Growth', *American Farm Economic Association Proceedings*, XLI 5 (Dec 1959) 943–51; 'International Capital Flows and the Development of the American West', *Journal of Economic History*, XVI 4 (Dec 1956) 493–505; *The Economic Growth of the United States, 1790–1860*.

[2] See also my note, 'International Trade and United States Economic Development: 1827–1843', *Journal of Economic History*, XXI 3 (Sep 1961) 372–83.

standard system, how was it possible to eliminate price deflation and/or serious deficiencies in aggregate demand which could have interfered with maximum growth performance over the long swing? In the face of an increasingly unfavourable trade balance during periods of rapid growth and concomitant import demand, how was it possible to eliminate gold outflow and cause an inflow of specie as well, when under 'normal' conditions an internal supply of gold was insufficient to satisfy excess demands for money? There is evidence that prior to the western gold discoveries, 1820–50, and after the Resumption, 1879–1914, there was a long swing in the rate of inflow of gold positively related to income growth and postulated excess demands for real money balances; there is also evidence that during the period 1879–1904, at least, the external flow of gold was primary in determining the rate of growth of the money supply.

Extensive periods of rapid development were accompanied by rising net capital imports during upswings in Kuznets cycles – so much so that fluctuations in the trade balance were overshadowed by this flow of American securities abroad. Long swings in the rate of net capital import are perhaps the most obvious evidence of long swings in balance of payments. The kinds of securities which foreigners, mainly British, were induced to purchase when every acceleration in the pace of development created an increasingly unfavourable trade balance were particularly of one type. From 1820 to 1913, about three-fifths to four-fifths of all American securities accepted abroad were either state and municipal bonds (used to finance a developing transportation network) or railroad stocks and bonds. Trade deficits generated during periods of rapid growth were

TABLE 8.1

U.S. Balance of Payments Dating for Long Swings, 1817–1915
(Smoothed Data)*

	Imports (current value)	Imports (deflated)	Net capital inflow (current value)		Trade balance (current value)		Exports (current value)	Exports (deflated)
Peak	1817	–	1817	Trough	1817	Peak	1818	1832
Trough	1822	1822	1825	Peak	1825	Trough	1822	1835
Peak	1837	1837	1837	Trough	1837	Peak	1838	1847
Trough	1842	1842	1842	Peak	1842	Trough	1844	1848
Peak	1858	1859	1852	Trough	1855	Peak	1858	1860
Trough	1863	1863	1858	Peak	1860	Trough	1863	1863
Peak	1873	1874	1871	Trough	1871	Peak		
Trough	1877	1877	1879	Peak	1879	Trough		
Peak	1891	1895	1888	Trough	1888	Peak		
Trough	1896	1896	1900	Peak	1900	Trough		
Peak	1915	1915	1911	Trough	1908	Peak		

* Although these dates are for the series after smoothing by a five-year moving average, there is no significant difference between those and the dates for peak and trough derived from the annual data.

financed, then, by systematic recurrences in transportation development positively related to (causing?) rates of income and output
growth.

We have in American experience Kuznets cycles in our balance of
payments. The flow of goods, capital and specie (and, of course,
labour migration) exhibit definite long swings over the course of
American development. Their dating in terms of peaks and troughs
is given in Table 8.1, and the movements in net capital imports can
be seen in Fig. 8.5.

There are two excellent justifications for a simultaneous examination of British balance of payments with an investigation of
domestic long swings and their effects upon American trade. First,
since there is preliminary evidence of a long swing in many British
domestic series *after* 1870, and especially in home investment,[1] it
seemed fruitful to study British experience to throw further light
upon the question of Kuznets cycles and their effect upon the international flow of goods, capital and species.

Realistically, we should be prepared for different secular movements in the balance of payments of an important capital exporter
compared with those of a chronic capital importer, even when faced
with the evidence of internal long swings in both the lending and
receiving nations. But as in the relation between American internal
development and her capital imports, British capital exports should
exhibit an inverse relation with the pace of internal development or
with domestic outlets for domestic savings; that is, when the pace of
British internal development was low, English investors should have
shifted increasingly to more lucrative investments abroad, just as
when American business slowed there was a net reduction in capital
imports or even a serious net export of capital. So much for similarities. Dissimilarities may arise for at least two major reasons. First,
because of its resource endowment and small size, foreign trade
played and does play a much greater role in the British system than
in the American. Thus, although British and American experience
may *both* reflect an inverse relation between domestic and foreign
investment over the Kuznets cycle, net foreign investment assumed
a much more important role as a determinant in British than in
American aggregate demand. Cairncross estimated that between
1875 and 1914 a little more than 40 per cent of British capital investment was in net capital exports, while in 1913 the share was as large

[1] As indicated earlier in this paper, Cairncross, Matthews, Lewis and O'Leary,
and Thomas have shown the most interest in the evidence of long swings or Kuznets cycles in British home investment, as well as the apparent inversion between
British home and foreign investment.

as 50 per cent.[1] This averages about *three or four times* the American estimates; in the post-1860 period, the highest share of net capital imports in total capital accumulation was 27 per cent, while the average share from 1870 to 1900, *during periods of positive inflow alone*, lies between only 10 and 15 per cent.[2]

For these very reasons, and apart from relative internal conditions, we would anticipate much less violent fluctuations in aggregate output over the long swing in home investment, due to the offsetting effects of net capital exports on aggregate demand. British import demand should, therefore, reveal mild fluctuations since imports are generally written as some function of national output. In this respect, however, Cairncross, Lewis and O'Leary, and Matthews put the argument in much stronger terms than either Thomas or I would. Those authors imply that evidence of a long swing in British national output, and in all expenditures related to it, would be lacking. It seems more cautious, but more nearly correct, to suggest that a dampening of the domestic long swing likely occurred, and that severe depressions and excessive booms in aggregate demand at the troughs and peaks of long swings in the rate of development were more likely to be avoided. Although severe fluctuations in aggregate demand may have been cushioned over the long swing, this does not imply a constant growth path of capacity output, or that fluctuations in domestic investment were completely offset.

A second suspected difference between British and American balance of payments movements over the Kuznets cycle would lie in export movements. As a capital exporter, and especially under the assumption of mild import fluctuations, the rate of expansion of the export industry ought to be very closely related to the outflow of foreign capital – the real transfer should be facilitated mainly by export increments. Whereas American experience revealed import movements dominating the trade balance to facilitate the real trans-

---

[1] Cairncross, *Home and Foreign Investment*, pp. 2, 4.

[2] Of course changes in net foreign investment would be more pertinent than absolute levels in determining the relative importance of capital movements as a stabilising component of aggregate demand. However, American fluctuations in the import of capital were not so very much more violent than British variations in the export of capital. For that matter, it is also true that net capital flows are not precisely measures of net foreign investment.

Cairncross's estimates are consistent with some recent estimates of the importance of external trade (exports plus imports of goods) as a share in total income. Deutsch and Eckstein estimate that from 1860 to 1920 British external trade was from 50 to 60 per cent of national income. The same share in the United States was 15–20 per cent from 1819 to 1839 and 10–15 per cent from 1859 to 1909. K. W. Deutsch and A. Eckstein, 'National Industrialisation and the Declining Share of the International Economic Sector, 1890–1959', *World Politics*, XIII (Jan 1961) 267–99.

fer, we should expect that British trade-balance fluctuations were dominated by exports. And finally, since export movements should be inversely related to long swings in British home investment, the trade balance should have reached peak deficits at high levels of British home investment and at low levels of net capital exports – movements, though caused in a different manner, precisely like those found in United States experience.

Besides using this excursion into British balance of payments movements in a comparative manner, there is also a second and perhaps more pertinent justification for the research. I have attempted with some success to include conditions in Great Britain as an explanatory factor for American net capital imports,[1] but did American Kuznets cycles also have *direct* effects upon British economic conditions via movements in the balance of payments?[2] That is, did fluctuations in United States import demand have profound, and direct, effects upon total British exports, or was the American market too small, or did other developing nations take up the slack, or both? The problem can be reworded more elegantly to ask whether or not the United States simultaneously created its own increasing supply of foreign capital on the upswing of a Kuznets cycle by dominating fluctuations in the rate of expansion of British export markets, and thereby creating a concomitant trade balance surplus in Great Britain; if not, then the interrelationship becomes much more subtle.

The second possible direct influence is via prices of traded goods. We may find that any evidence of a mild long swing in British import demands is eliminated by raw material and foodstuff price movements. If grain and cotton prices dominated British import price movements, American export prices in cotton and, to a lesser extent, grain may have had a profound influence upon British imports *in current prices* at least prior to 1860–70. Prior to the 1860s, American export prices were positively related to domestic activity, while over the nineteenth century as a whole British and American internal development moved inversely. It is likely that British import demand moved inversely with American export prices, and thus it seems reasonable to expect that American export prices had a smoothing influence on British imports in current prices.[3]

---

[1] See below, p. 276, n. 1.

[2] By *indirect*, I have in mind the effects of the migration of labour upon income and prices in both nations.

[3] United States imports and import prices exhibit a reasonably significant positive correlation over the long swing. This *may* be explained in the same manner since in this case American import demand and British export prices move in sympathy. Given our assumptions above, it is more likely that British imports and import prices move inversely.

Earlier research has made it clear that supply conditions of investment funds in Great Britain played an important role in determining the amplitude of American net capital imports.[1] The final direct effect of United States balance of payments upon British balance of payments might include the importance of American security markets in influencing British capital exports. It was not necessary that America's share of British capital export be large, only that its fluctuations in demand for British capital were excessive enough to dictate long swings in British capital exports.

It should be frankly admitted at the outset that this paper actually raises more questions than it answers, especially with regard to the framework of the Atlantic economy envisioned by Thomas or the broader interactions in nineteenth-century development of capital-scarce, agricultural, raw material-producing nations and capital-rich, manufactures-producing nations. The major question of the evidence of long swings in Australian, Argentine, Canadian, etc. development and international interactions over the course of nineteenth-century expansion must be deferred until a later time.

Our expectations concerning import movements are supported by the data.[2] Even after removing the trend, British imports in current

---

[1] Although not in its timing, the amplitude of long swings in American net capital imports is in part explained by inverse conditions in Great Britain ('push'). In regression analyses to test the explanatory power of British and American stock prices in explaining United States net capital imports, when we include only American ('pull') conditions, $\bar{R}^2 = \cdot624$ (1873–1914), but when we include conditions in both countries,

$$\dot{K}^t = 112\cdot42 + 420\cdot71 \ P^{t-3} - 552\cdot39 \ P^{t-2}, \ \bar{R}^2 = \cdot83.$$
$$(64\cdot41) \ \text{U.S.} \quad (72\cdot52) \ \text{G.B.}$$

The same results occur in the period 1844–60; if we use only American stock prices, $\bar{R}^2 = \cdot769$; if we include conditions in both countries, $\bar{R}^2 = \cdot910$. These tests were done where $\dot{K}$, net capital movements, and both P's, general stock prices in Great Britain and railroad stock prices in American, are trendless and smoothed.

[2] All British balance of payments estimates are taken from Imlah, *Economic Elements*. Imlah utilises the same techniques employed by North and Simon in estimating nineteenth-century net capital flows. However, it should be noted that Imlah's transportation account, which is an important part of his balance of payments, has been the subject of criticism. See particularly the article by Douglass C. North and Alan Heston, 'The Estimation of Shipping Earnings in Historical Studies of the Balance of Payments', *Canadian Journal of Economics and Political Science*, xxvi 2 (May 1960) 265–76.

The sources of the British data which are used in the charts are primarily from Imlah, *Economic Elements*, pp. 94–8; I have removed trends or calculated rates of change (those series which result from such adjustment are available upon request). The index of home investment and imported foodstuffs on Fig. 8.1 is from Thomas, *Migration and Economic Growth*, pp. 297 and 328 respectively. In Fig. 8.2, exports of finished iron and steel goods are also from Thomas, op. cit., p. 293.

prices reveal no evidence whatever of long swings. What trend removal *does* exhibit are longer movements associated with 'Kondratieff' swings in import prices. In the trendless series, British imports in current prices fall steadily for about twenty years from the mid-twenties to the mid-forties, rise consistently over a longer period of thirty years until the mid-1870s, fall to a secular trough in the mid-1890s and then expand until the First World War. Not surprisingly, this configuration is very much like the general movement of import prices (see Figs. 8.1 and 8.2). Even if we examine growth rates in imports in current prices, there is absolutely no evidence of Kuznets

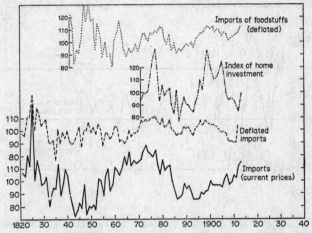

Fig. 8.1. British imports deflated and in current prices,
and home investment: original data as percentage of trend, 1820–1915.
Source: see above, p. 276, n. 2.

cycles which might be identified with hypothesised British income–output movements.

At first sight, the lack of evidence of long swings in imports in current prices, even after trend removal, would seem to support the implied position of many current students of British economic history that the interaction of home and foreign investment eliminated Kuznets cycles in aggregate income and output. After further study, however, this conclusion does not seem justified.

When we deflate import values by import prices, deflated imports do indeed reveal long swings after 1860, while the movements prior to 1860 are questionable (Fig. 8.1). It is not a violent fluctuation even in the trendless index, but this is precisely what we hypothesised, given the inverse relationship between home and foreign investment and the resulting relative stability in aggregate demand over the long swing. So mild are the fluctuations in income, that movements in real import demand over the long swing are completely smothered by raw material and agricultural foodstuff price movements.[1]

Are British deflated import movements positively correlated with income? Assuming a positive correlation between income growth (or some relevant component of income which exhibits long swings, such as consumption) and the rate of domestic investment, we can make some meaningful tests.[2] Cairncross's series of British home

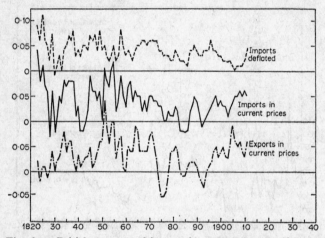

Fig. 8.2. British exports and imports in percentage rates of change, 1820–1915 (smoothed by 5-year moving average)
Source: see above, p. 276, n. 2.

investment from 1871 to 1913 is available, and has been used. Both the home investment and deflated imports series were used after removing their trends and smoothing. A simple univariate regression exhibits a positive correlation between the two series, where the

[1] One cannot explain the evidence of long swings in deflated British imports by terms of trade movements. Imlah's net barter terms of trade *do* reveal long swings positively correlated with domestic investment and with deflated imports. However, these long swings in the net barter terms of trade occur with even more violent amplitude prior to the 1850s, while deflated imports reveal long swings only *after* the 1850s.

[2] After this paper was submitted, Feinstein's estimates of British domestic investment and net national income appeared in the *Economic Journal*. Regretfully, his estimates did not appear soon enough for me to make use of them in this study. C. H. Feinstein, 'Income and Investment in the United Kingdom, 1856–1914', *Economic Journal*, LXXI 282 (June 1961) 367–85.

explanatory power of domestic investment (I^{uk}) over deflated imports (M_D) is surprisingly high:

$$[1871\text{--}1913]\ M_D = 73\cdot47 + \cdot2597\ I^{uk} \qquad R^2 = \cdot837$$
$$(\cdot0190) \qquad\qquad R = \cdot915,$$

and as we might have expected, the coefficient of I^{uk} is low, $\cdot26$, reflecting the relative mildness of income movements compared with domestic investment.

The tentative conclusion is that not only were there long swings in deflated imports but that they were positively related to 'income' movements, although mild enough to be eliminated by active, and inversely correlated, import price movements. When deflated imports were at high levels in the late 1840s and early 1850s import prices reached a secular trough; when deflated imports troughed in the mid-1860s, prices achieved fantastic heights; and finally, when deflated imports peaked in the mid-late 1890s, prices again fell to a secular trough. Although general world price movements were little different from British import price movements, the violence in amplitude of those prices must surely be partially explained by supply conditions in the American cotton and grain markets prior to 1870–80. Thus, it is the variation from the general world price trend in agricultural and raw material prices which removes the evidence of long swings in British import demand. For approximately two decades, the 1860s and 1870s, American wheat exports played an extremely important role in dictating the state of the grain market, while prior to 1860 the cotton market was almost entirely dominated by American exports. Both these commodities make up by far the largest share of British imports.

One more observation might be made before discussing the more violent swings in export movements. Deflated imports reveal Kuznets cycles after the late 1850s and until 1913, but the evidence of long swings *before* the American Civil War is thin indeed. This lack of long swings in British history prior to the 1850s is also true of net capital exports, which had configurations closer to seven- to ten-year cycles than to twenty-year cycles, and of merchandise exports, which did not reveal long swings until the late 1840s and early 1850s. Was the same thing true of British income movements?

Since net capital exports were certainly no more severe in their amplitude and were less important as a share in total investment prior to the 1860s,[1] any explanation for observed stability in income–output movements should be attributable to the pattern of British home investment itself. In this respect, Thomas disagrees with Lewis

[1] Matthews, *The Business Cycle*, p. 222.

and O'Leary, since he believes that there is no evidence of British building cycles from 1830 to 1850.[1] Cooney, in a recent article, puts the argument in even stronger terms: 'The first main point to be made here is that there does not seem to be enough evidence to establish the existence of a (roughly) twenty-year building cycle in British history before 1870.'[2] Cairncross and Weber also support the view that, prior to 1850 at least, there is evidence of inherent seven- to ten-year cycles but none of building cycles.[3] Based mainly on Shannon's brick index,[4] Cairncross and Weber date major peaks in 1819, 1825, 1836, and 1847, and major troughs in 1821, 1832 and 1842.

Over the Kuznets cycle the movements in British exports were much more apparent than in imports. Generally, the rate of expansion in British exports was inversely related to deflated imports (and thus, presumably, to income), and exhibited more violent amplitude; this is true in both rates of change (Fig. 8.2) and in the trendless series (Fig. 8.3).

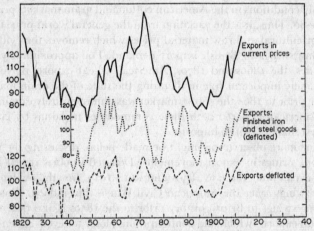

Fig. 8.3. British exports deflated and in current prices, as percentage deviations about trend, 1820–1915
Source: see above, p. 276, n. 2.

[1] Thomas, *Migration and Economic Growth*, p. 175.
[2] Cooney, 'Long Waves in Building in the British Economy of the Nineteenth Century', and above, Essay 6.
[3] A. K. Cairncross and B. Weber, 'Fluctuations in Building in Great Britain, 1785–1849', *Economic History Review*, 2nd ser., IX 2 (Dec 1956) 283–97.
[4] H. A. Shannon, 'Bricks – a Trade Index', *Economica* n.s., no. 1 (1934) 300–18.

Deflated exports, as percentage deviations about a trend, exhibit almost four long swings. The first rose from low levels in the 1840s to increasingly higher rates of export in the late 1850s and terminated with a trough in the early mid-1860s. The next long swing rose to a peak in the early 1870s and fell to a trough late in the 1870s. The third rose to a double peak in the early and late 1880s with an intermediate trough, and then fell to a trough at the turn of the century. Exports, then, expanded continually up to 1913 and the war. These long swings are less evident in the trendless current price series, but they are quite clear in rates of change.

The dating for deflated exports and imports with their trends removed is given in Table 8.2. After 1870, the inverse correlation between export and import movements is quite striking, with imports generally leading by from one to three years. Prior to 1870 the inverse relationship almost disappears, while before 1860, of course, there is not enough evidence of a long swing in imports to date them. The inverse relationship between imports and exports seems to have become more consistent and precise as the century progressed. Can we go one step further and suggest that the same would also hold true of net capital exports and the rate of home investment?

Deflated British exports moved inversely with deflated British imports, at least over most of the latter half of the nineteenth century, but they also moved *directly* with United States import fluctuations. This was true for the period after the later 1840s and until 1913, but there was no long swing in deflated British exports from 1820 to 1850. (There *was* a long swing in the rates of growth of exports in current prices over the nineteenth century as a whole, including 1820–50. This is discussed below.) Table 8.2 compares the dating of deflated British exports and deflated American imports. Although there is obvious similarity in movement and timing throughout – but not in amplitude – the lead–lag relationship is much better in the latter half of the nineteenth century. Indeed, the timing of the British and American series is so close after 1860, especially for a comparison of annual data, as to suggest that American import demand may have played an important role in determining the rate of expansion of total British exports.

Fortunately we can apply a better test than this to determine the importance of the American market in conditioning the state of the British export industry. Increments in total British exports to foreign countries and British exports to the United States can be compared – the data are available in the British *Parliamentary Papers*. Were Kuznets cycles in the rate of expansion of British exports in current prices caused by violent fluctuations in American demand? The

TABLE 8.2

Long Swings in Exports and Imports (Deflated Series),
U.S. and U.K., 1821–1913

	(1) U.S. deflated imports (*trendless and annual*)	(2) British deflated exports (*trendless and annual*)		(3) British deflated imports (*trendless and annual*)
Trough	1821			
Peak	1836			
Trough	1843	1848		
Peak	1854	1860		
Trough	1862	1864		
Peak	1872	1871	Trough	1864
Trough	1878	1878	Peak	1877
Peak	1883	1882	Trough	—
Trough	[1885]	[1885]	Peak	—
Peak	[1888]	[1889]	Trough	1886
Trough	1898	1901	Peak	1898
Peak	1913T*	1913T*	Trough	1910

* T means last year in series.

average share of total British exports going to America is significant: the highest occurred between the decades of the 1880s and 1890s, when approximately 20 per cent of British exports to foreign nations went to the United States. The marginal share, the ratio of first differences, was much higher, reaching its peak in the 1890s when 45 per cent of changes in British exports was attributable to changes in exports to the United States. The decade averages are given in Table 8.3.

Even more impressive is the striking similarity between the movements of first differences in total British exports and exports to America shown in Fig. 8.4. From 1850 to 1900 these series move together both in the smoothed and annual data. In the decade and a half after 1900 the series exhibit much less similarity, when American markets apparently ceased to play as vital a role for British export industry over the long swing. It should be clear, however, that fluctuations in American demand must have been a major cause for long swings in the rate of expansion of the British export industry from 1850 to 1900.

In the 1830s and 1840s, although there is no evidence of a long swing in deflated British exports, the data on current exports in rates of change do reveal a long swing positively related to movements in American imports. In rates of change, British exports fell to a trough in 1824, reached a peak in 1834 and fell to a trough in 1839. United States imports, in rates of change, rose from a trough in the 1820s to a peak in 1833 and fell to a trough in 1842. Averaged over the period 1833–42 as a whole, the value of British exports to the United States constituted only 15 per cent of the total value of British exports. The *proportional* fluctuations, as in the period 1860–1900, were much greater. The average ratio of changes in exports to the United States to changes in total British exports was as high as 58 per cent. There is only one year between 1833 and 1842 when the series move in opposite directions.

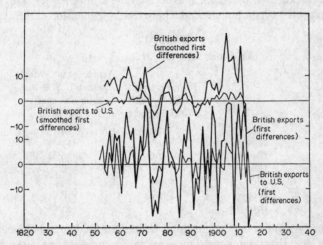

Fig. 8.4. British exports to America and total British exports, first differences, 1850–1915 (£m.)
Source: derived from British *Parliamentary Papers*

Matthews concludes from this evidence that 'the state of the American market was therefore the most important single factor in bringing prosperity or depression to British export industries'.[1] There are two problems, however, about such a strong conclusion concerning the effect of American import demand on English industry during the 1830s and 1840s. First, American imports in current prices *and* deflated exhibited long swings. Why were British exports affected only in current prices? This was not true of later years. Second, the fluctuation in British exports in current prices was extremely mild even in rates of change, and certainly nothing like those which appeared after the 1860s. It is thus difficult to believe that American import demands seriously imposed long swing

[1] R. C. O. Matthews, *A Study in Trade Cycle History*, pp. 43–4.

fluctuations on the British export industry at this stage of the nine-teenth century, and certainly there is no evidence that the British economy as a whole was enmeshed in the long swing mechanism. It seems more likely that the direct effects of the American long swing on British development began during the period 1848–64 when evidence of Kuznets cycles in British exports became clear (although the British domestic economy at this stage was not yet undergoing long swings).

There is another interesting aspect of this comparison. Prior to and after 1870, when both series expanded rapidly, increases in British exports exceeded increases in exports to the United States. This is to be expected over a long period where secular expansion of the export

TABLE 8.3

British Exports to U.S.A., 1850–1913

	British exports to U.S. ÷ total British exports	Net change in British exports to U.S. ÷ net changes in total British exports
1850–9	·19	·14
1860–9	·13	·17
1870–9	·14	·39
1880–9	·18	·38
1890–9	·19	·45
1900–9	·16	·18
1910–13	·16	·20

industry was not dependent upon United States demand alone. It is also true that changing American factor proportions must have caused a proportional shift out of British exports over time. But things are quite different at troughs of long swings. Prior to 1870 and in periods of depression in the American market, total British exports decreased at a lesser rate than did American imports from Great Britain, while after 1870 changes in total British exports moved more violently during *both* booms and prolonged depressions over the Kuznets cycle. This suggests that prior to 1870 only the United States was undergoing long swings in demand for British products, while after 1870 other developing nations with demands for British manufactures must also have been undergoing long swings similar in timing to American movements. This conclusion seems consistent with earlier movements as well, since Matthews's figures show consistently lower negative first differences in total British exports than in British exports to the United States during American depressions from 1833 to 1842. I will return to this point below in the discussion of British capital exports.

In summary, it appears that long swings in United States development had an immediate effect upon British conditions through British export movements and, to a much lesser extent, via British import prices.

The similarities begin with balance of trade movements. Just as with American trade balance movements, the British trade balance deficit grew progressively worse during periods of domestic boom, becoming less unfavourable during periods of domestic depression and massive capital export. After 1860, American trade balance fluctuations inversely related to domestic long swings were almost entirely due to violent income, and thus import, movements. British trade balance fluctuations were certainly less violent, but their significant amplitude was due entirely to fluctuations in the rate of export expansion, since imports in current prices reveal no long swing. Thus, improvement in the British trade balance during depressions in domestic investment is not normally to be explained by a reduction in import values (although real import demand decreased) but rather by an expansion of export values.

Long swings in the British balance of trade really did not begin until 1860. However, choosing a somewhat arbitrary date of 1847, the trade balance exhibited a mild secular improvement from the large deficit of 1847 up to 1859, became sharply unfavourable from 1859 to the early mid-1860s, but remained constant and finally

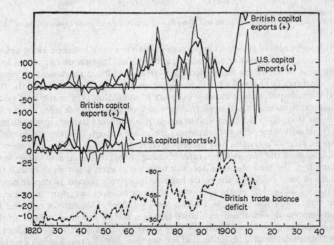

Fig. 8.5. British trade balance and net capital exports (in £500,000), and American net capital imports ($m.), 1820–1915
Source: see above, p. 276, n. 2.

improved gradually up to 1872. From 1872 to the late 1870s, the trade balance was progressively unfavourable until 1886; from 1886 until 1902, it again deteriorated cumulatively, at which point it again improved until about 1911 (see Fig. 8.5). Severe movements resembling long swings did not begin in the trade balance, then, until the late 1850s, which were also the initiating years of the more violent long swings in exports.[1] The dating of deflated exports, the trade balance, deflated imports and domestic investment is given in Table 8.4. I should point out that imports in current prices do not exhibit long swings, but deflated values are included only as an approximation of hypothesised 'income' movements.

In the British balance of payments, just as in American experience,

TABLE 8.4

Long Swings in Trade Components and Home Investment, U.K., 1847–1913

	Inverted British trade balance deficit (annual data)	Net export of British capital (annual data)	Deflated exports (trendless)		Home investment (trendless)	Deflated imports (trendless)
Trough	1847(?)		1848			
Peak	1859	1859	1860			
Trough	1868	1862	1864			
Peak	1872	1872	1871	Trough	1871	1864
Trough	1877	1877	1878	Peak	1877	1877
Peak	—	—	1882	Trough	—	—
Trough	—	—	[1885]	Peak	—	—
Peak	1886	1890	[1889]	Trough	1887	1886
Trough	1902	1898	1901	Peak	1899	1898
Peak	1911	1913T*	1913T*	Trough	1912	1910

* T means last year in series.

Source: The home investment series was taken from Thomas, *Migration and Economic Growth*, Table 100, p. 290.

[1] Although rates of growth of imports in current prices do not reveal long swings over the nineteenth century as a whole, and deflated imports do not reveal long swings prior to the 1850s, the period 1828–41 *does* exhibit a movement in import values (in rates of change) similar to export movements. Indeed, this is the *only* period when import values indicate evidence of something akin to the long swing mechanism. Apparently, although real income movements do not seem to reveal a long swing from 1820 to 1840 and thus similarly for deflated imports, price fluctuations (primarily American cotton prices) are severe enough to cause a movement in import values similar to, and exceeding in rate of change, export movements. Thus, in spite of the long swing in rates of change of exports in current values from 1824 to 1839, the trade balance does not reflect it in such a way as to extend the evidence of long swings in the trade balance (positively related to export movements) back before the 1850s. Compared to other nineteenth-century movements this is a very unusual period in English history indeed. One cannot help but be further impressed with the dissimilarity between British movements prior to the 1850s and afterwards. Apparently the long swing, which was already so evident in United States development, either had not yet foisted itself upon English development, or whatever endogenous conditions were necessary to generate the long swing were not yet in evidence. Surely the popularised mechanism of the interaction of the Atlantic economy was not the same prior to the 1850s as after those years.

the most obvious evidence of Kuznets cycles is in the flow of capital. The timing of net capital exports was similar to export and trade balance movements, but the amplitude of capital flows was more violent – though not as violent as American net capital imports. After 1870, net capital exports and home investment did indeed complement each other in a consistent fashion. Nevertheless, there is no evidence of long swings in the rate of capital export prior to the late 1850s and early 1860s; after that time the amplitudes of these long swings in capital flows unquestionably became more severe. Prior to the late 1850s, net capital exports from Great Britain played a much smaller role in British development and as a share in total investment. It is also true that prior to the late 1850s any fluctuations in net capital exports seem to have been primarily of the seven- to ten-year variety, peaking in 1835, 1844, 1850 and 1859, troughing in 1840, 1847 and 1853. At least from 1830 to 1845, net capital exports moved consistently with building indices;[1] nor is this positive relation inconsistent with experience after 1870, when domestic and foreign investment moved inversely over the long swing, for in that period as well domestic and foreign investment moved positively over *short* cycles.[2]

From a peak outflow of capital in 1859, net capital exports fell to a trough in 1862. The first complete swing rose from there to an extremely high level of capital outflow in 1872 and then fell to a severe trough in 1877. This long swing rose rather gradually to the end of the 1860s before the massive outflow, peaking in 1872. The second secular swing rose from a trough in 1877 to a peak in 1890, then fell into the prolonged depression of the 1890s – 1898 being the poorest year. From the decade of the 1890s, capital exports continued to increase until 1913, quite sharply from 1905 to the war (see Fig. 8.5).

The net export of British capital, therefore, is positively correlated with the export of goods, and negatively correlated with the trade balance deficit, home investment and deflated imports. On average, net capital exports lead deflated exports by about two years (the lead would possibly be longer if export movements were expressed in annual data). And we find home investment (inverted) leading net capital exports by one or two years. Consequently, foreign and domestic investment do not quite mesh over the long swing: it may be quite true that this lag of British savers moving out of domestic and into foreign investment explains the apparent evidence of a Juglar cycle.

[1] Cairncross and Weber, 'Fluctuations in Building in Great Britain', p. 285.
[2] Cairncross, *Home and Foreign Investment*.

Although the evidence seems to support the hypothesis that American import demands played an extremely important role in determining the level and movements of British exports, at least after 1850, it is more difficult to make the same statement for capital flows. Surely the timing and general pattern of British exports and American imports of capital were extremely similar. Nevertheless, it is difficult to say much more than this for the nineteenth century as a whole. Prior to the late 1850s, there was no long swing in the rate of British capital exports and yet there was in American capital imports. After the 1850s, it is clear that American capital imports moved as if they dominated British capital exports due to the similarity of timing and pattern over the long swing, but could this be due to long swings in other countries as well? One bit of evidence which positively points to the importance of American demands for capital has its source in Madden's research.[1] His estimates show that from 60 to 65 per cent of the fluctuations in British capital exports from 1860 to 1880 were due to fluctuations in American demands for capital over the long swing. If this were true of all the long swings in the nineteenth century we could conservatively conclude that American demands did indeed directly determine the extent and timing of British capital export fluctuations over the long swing.

If we discard the temptation to apply Madden's research to all the long swings in capital flows after the 1850s, then it would seem that it takes a combination of *three* things to cause a long swing in net capital movements in the case of a capital exporter. Long swings in the demand for capital in the United States were not enough to cause similar British movements (that is, pre-1850s) either because the United States was too small as a source of demand or, *and more likely*, one of the other two necessary ingredients was missing. If income growth was approximately constant in the rest of the world outside of the United States, it should have been relatively simple for British investors to shift between American securities and those of other countries according to the vitality of American development and the return on capital, as was apparently the case before the 1850s. Thus, a long swing in American development and demands for foreign capital need not be reflected in total British capital exports as well: nor, for that matter did long swings in British exports of goods (1848–64) have an *immediate* effect upon the pattern of growth of the British economy.

---

[1] John J. Madden, 'British Investment in the United States, 1860–1880', Conference on Research in Income and Wealth, unpublished manuscript (Sep 1956) Table 10, p. 46. I would like to thank Professor Madden for allowing me to refer to his work.

One of the missing ingredients may be the lack of similar and inverse movements in the pace of development of the lending country. If Great Britain were undergoing a long swing as well, surely one would also expect to find a long swing in the rate of British capital export. The problem then is why there is so little evidence of long swings in British internal development prior to the 1850s. Can we then suggest that American long swings in some indirect way triggered movements in Great Britain?[1] This supposition seems more likely than to attribute the creation of a domestic long swing mechanism in Great Britain to something purely endogenous to the British system. For why do British and American movements exhibit this curious and suspicious inverse relation, and why did British long swings come relatively late in the century after the United States had been undergoing them for some time?

The second ingredient, which seems to be in evidence only after 1870 and which may help explain the appearance of Kuznets cycles in British capital exports after 1860, is the possible new occurrence of long swings in the pace of growth in other newly developing, raw material- and foodstuff-producing nations. Not only did Canada, Australia and Argentina, for example, exhibit what look like long swings in their consumption of foreign capital after 1870, but their movements were inversely related to British internal development as well. If, however, Madden's estimates quoted above are applicable to a large part of the period 1860–1913, then the importance of variation in demand for British capital in other countries, similar in timing to United States demands, seems very much reduced. For that matter, fluctuations in net capital imports into Canada, Australia and Argentina may have been the effect, not the cause, of fluctuations in British capital exports.

This paper is not intended to examine exhaustively the possible direct interactions between British and American balance of payments, nor is it intended to determine and test the causes of British balance of payments fluctuations over the long swing. What I have attempted here is to leave open the door so ably set ajar by Brinley Thomas in his examination of the interactions in the development of the Atlantic economy. The general impression in this preliminary analysis is that the systematic relationship between British and American development, in the nature of a Kuznets cycle, had its source not in Great Britain but in the United States. If that statement is supported by future research, it is only a small step to imagine how the powerful inverse relation in Anglo-American

[1] For an assertion of this intuitive feeling see Cooney, 'Long Waves in Building in the British Economy of the Nineteenth Century', and above, Essay 6.

development spilled over into other newly developing nations with factor endowments similar to those of the United States.

It seems clear that a large part of the Anglo-American interaction can be explained by the direct effects upon British export industry of fluctuating United States demands for imports. Nevertheless, this conclusion is not meant to depreciate the importance of labour migration as an explanation for the inverse pattern of growth between these two countries. Long swings in American demands for imports can be traced back at least as far as 1820, but migration of labour from Europe to America did not really attain impressive heights until the 1840s and 1850s; long swings in British development do not seem to be in evidence before that time, but very soon afterwards. However, we now have a second alternative hypothesis: from 1848 to 1864 British exports (current *and* deflated) showed definite long swings, but net capital exports and home investment did not. Could these fluctuations in British exports reflect an initiation of the transfer of American long swings into British development via demands for British exports? It seems more likely, however, that the interaction was a result of both the demand for goods and for migrants: variations in American import demands strengthened the inverse movement, which became clear after the first really important flow of factors, notably labour, across the Atlantic.

Select Bibliography

THERE is a considerable volume of literature on business cycles, though much of the empirical work relates to American experience. The following bibliography is selective and includes those studies which are most relevant to British conditions. It is divided into three sections: (1) works primarily theoretical in content; (2) studies relating to the standard business cycle; and (3) literature on long swings in economic activity.

1. *Theoretical Studies*

IRMA and FRANK ADELMAN, 'The Dynamic Properties of the Klein–Goldberger Model', *Econometrica*, XXVII (1959).

IRMA ADELMAN, 'Business Cycles: Endogenous or Stochastic?', *Economic Journal*, LXX (1960).

E. AMES, 'A Theoretical and Statistical Dilemma: The Contributions of Burns, Mitchell, and Frickey to Business-Cycle Theory', *Econometrica*, XVI (1948).

S. BOBER, *The Economics of Cycles and Growth* (1968).

H. B. CHENERY, 'Overcapacity and the Acceleration Principle', *Econometrica*, XX (1952).

J. S. DUESENBERRY, *Business Cycles and Economic Growth* (1958).

J. A. ESTEY, *Business Cycles*, 3rd ed. (1956).

W. FELLNER, *Trends and Cycles in Economic Activity* (1956).

R. FRISCH, 'Propagation Problems and Impulse Problems in Dynamic Economics', in *Economic Essays in Honour of Gustav Cassel* (1933).

R. M. GOODWIN, 'Innovations and the Irregularity of Economic Cycles', *Review of Economic Statistics*, XXVIII (1946).

——, 'The Non-linear Accelerator and the Persistence of Business Cycles', *Econometrica*, XIX (1951).

——, 'The Problem of Trend and Cycle', *Yorkshire Bulletin of Economic and Social Research*, V (1953).

——, 'A Model of Cyclical Growth', in E. Lundberg (ed.), *The Business Cycle in the Post-war World* (1955).

R. A. GORDON, 'Investment Behaviour and Business Cycles', *Review of Economics and Statistics*, XXXVII (1955).

——, *Business Fluctuations*, 2nd ed. (1961).

J. D. GOULD, 'Agricultural Fluctuations and the English Economy in the Eighteenth Century', *Journal of Economic History*, XXII (1962).

G. HABERLER, *Prosperity and Depression* (1958).

A. H. HANSEN, *Business Cycles and National Income* (1951).

J. HICKS, *A Contribution to the Theory of the Trade Cycle* (1950).

B. HIGGINS, 'Interactions of Cycles and Trends', *Economic Journal*, LXV (1955).

N. KALDOR, 'A Model of the Trade Cycle', *Economic Journal*, L (1940).

——, 'The Relation of Economic Growth and Cyclical Fluctuations', *Economic Journal*, LXIV (1954).

M. KALECKI, *Theory of Economic Dynamics* (1954).

R. C. O. MATTHEWS, *The Trade Cycle* (1959).

P. SAMUELSON, 'Interactions Between the Multiplier Analysis and the Principle of Acceleration', *Review of Economic Statistics*, XXI (1939).

J. TINBERGEN and J. POLAK, *The Dynamics of Business Cycles* (1950).

R. N. WAUD, 'An Expectations Model of Cyclical Growth: Hicks on the Trade Cycle Revisited', *Oxford Economic Papers*, XIX (1967).

T. WILSON, 'Cyclical and Autonomous Inducements to Invest', *Oxford Economic Papers*, V (1953).

2. *The Business Cycle*

D. H. ALDCROFT, *The Inter-War Economy: Britain, 1919–1939* (1970) chap. 2.

—— and H. W. RICHARDSON, *The British Economy, 1870–1939* (1969) section A II.

T. S. ASHTON, *Economic Fluctuations in England, 1700–1800* (1959).

W. H. BEVERIDGE, 'Unemployment in the Trade Cycle', *Economic Journal*, XLIX (1939).

——, 'The Trade Cycle in Britain Before 1850', *Oxford Economic Papers*, III (1940).

——, 'The Trade Cycle in Britain Before 1850: A Postscript', *Oxford Economic Papers*, IV (1940).

A. F. BURNS, *The Business Cycle in a Changing World* (1969).

D. C. CORNER, 'Exports and the British Trade Cycle: 1929', *Manchester School*, XXIV (1956).

A. G. FORD, 'Notes on the Role of Exports in British Economic Fluctuations, 1870–1914', *Economic History Review*, XVI (1963–4).

——, 'Bank Rate, the British Balance of Payments and the Burdens of Adjustment, 1870–1914', *Oxford Economic Papers*, XVI (1964).

——, 'Overseas Lending and Internal Fluctuations, 1870–1914', *Yorkshire Bulletin of Economic and Social Research*, XVII (1965).

A. D. GAYER, W. W. ROSTOW and ANNA J. SCHWARTZ, *The Growth and Fluctuation of the British Economy*, 2 vols. (1953).

E. J. HOBSBAWM, 'Economic Fluctuations and Some Social Movements since 1800', *Economic History Review*, V (1952).

J. R. T. HUGHES, 'The Commercial Crisis of 1857', *Oxford Economic Papers*, VIII (1956).

——, *Fluctuations in Trade, Industry and Finance: A Study of British Economic Development, 1850–1860* (1960).

J. R. T. Hughes, 'Wicksell on the Facts: Prices and Interest Rates, 1844 to 1914', in J. N. Wolfe (ed.), *Value, Capital and Growth: Papers in Honour of Sir John Hicks* (1968).

R. C. O. Matthews, *A Study in Trade Cycle History: Economic Fluctuations in Great Britain, 1833–1842* (1954).

——, 'Postwar Business Cycles in the United Kingdom', in M. Bronfenbrenner (ed.), *Is the Business Cycle Obsolete?* (1969).

F. V. Meyer and W. A. Lewis, 'The Effects of an Overseas Slump on the British Economy', *Manchester School*, XVII (1949).

I. Mintz, *Trade Balances during Business Cycles: U.S. and Britain since 1880* (1959).

W. C. Mitchell, *Business Cycles and their Causes* (1950).

O. Morgenstern, *International Financial Transactions and Business Cycles* (1959).

F. W. Paish, 'Business Cycles in Britain', *Lloyds Bank Review*, no. 98 (Oct 1970).

J. S. Pesmazoglu, 'Some International Aspects of British Cyclical Fluctuations, 1870–1914', *Review of Economic Studies*, XVI (1949–50).

——, 'A Note on the Cyclical Fluctuations of British Home Investment, 1870–1913', *Oxford Economic Papers*, III (1951).

E. H. Phelps Brown and G. L. S. Shackle, 'British Economic Fluctuations, 1924–38', *Oxford Economic Papers*, II (1939).

W. W. Rostow, *British Economy of the Nineteenth Century* (1948).

J. A. Schumpeter, *Business Cycles*, 2 vols. (1939).

J. Tinbergen, *Business Cycles in the United Kingdom, 1870–1914* (1951).

C. N. Ward-Perkins, 'The Commercial Crisis of 1847', *Oxford Economic Papers*, II (1950).

3. Long Cycles

M. Abramovitz, 'The Nature and Significance of Kuznets Cycles', *Economic Development and Cultural Change*, IX (1961).

——, 'The Passing of the Kuznets Cycle', *Economica*, XXXV (1968).

Irma Adelman, 'Long Cycles: Fact or Artifact?', *American Economic Review*, LV (1965).

A. K. Cairncross, *Home and Foreign Investment, 1870–1914* (1954).

—— and B. Weber, 'Fluctuations in Building in Great Britain, 1785–1849', *Economic History Review*, IX (1956).

E. W. Cooney, 'Capital Exports and Investment in Building in Britain and the U.S.A.', *Economica*, XVI (1949).

John H. Dunning, *Studies in International Investment* (1970).

R. A. Easterlin, 'Economic-Demographic Interactions and Long Swings in Economic Growth', *American Economic Review*, LVI (1966).

A. R. Hall, 'Long Waves in Building in the British Economy of the Nineteenth Century: A Comment', *Economic History Review*, XIV (1961).

W. G. Hoffmann, *British Industry, 1700–1950* (1955).

W. Isard, 'A Neglected Cycle: The Transport–Building Cycle', *Review of Economic Statistics*, XXIV (1942).

W. Isard, 'Transport Development and Building Cycles', *Quarterly Journal of Economics*, LVII (1942).

A. C. Kelley, 'International Migration and Economic Growth: Australia 1865–1935', *Journal of Economic History*, XXV (1965).

——, 'Demographic Change and Economic Growth: Australia 1861–1911', *Explorations in Entrepreneural History*, V (1968).

——, 'Demographic Cycles and Economic Growth: The Long Swing Reconsidered,' *Journal of Economic History*, XXIX (1969).

S. Kuznets, 'Long Swings in the Growth of Population and Related Economic Variables', *Proceedings of the American Philosophical Society*, CII (1958).

——, *Capital in the American Economy: Its Formation and Financing* (1961).

J. P. Lewis, 'Growth and Inverse Cycles: A Two-Country Model', *Economic Journal*, LXXIV (1964).

——, *Building Cycles and Britain's Growth* (1965).

W. A. Lewis and P. J. O'Leary, 'Secular Swings in Production and Trade, 1870–1913', *Manchester School*, XXIII (1955).

A. Lösch, 'Population Cycles as a Cause of Business Cycles', *Quarterly Journal of Economics*, LI (1937).

G. M. Meier, 'Long Period Determinants of Britain's Terms of Trade, 1880–1913', *Review of Economic Studies*, XX (1952–3).

M. Melnyk, *Long Fluctuations in Real Series of American Economy* (1970) Printed Series No. 9, Bureau of Economic and Business Research, Kent State University, Ohio.

S. B. Saul, 'Housebuilding in England, 1890–1914', *Economic History Review*, XV (1962).

M. Simon, 'The Pattern of New British Portfolio Foreign Investment, 1865–1914', in John H. Adler (ed.), *Capital Movements and Economic Development* (1967).

B. Thomas, *Migration and Economic Growth* (1954).

——, 'The Rhythm of Growth in the Atlantic Economy', in Hugo Hegeland (ed.), *Money, Growth and Methodology and Other Essays in Honour of Johan Åkerman* (1961).

——, 'The Historical Record of International Capital Movements to 1913', in John H. Adler (ed.), *Capital Movements and Economic Development* (1967).

J. G. Williamson, *American Growth and the Balance of Payments, 1820–1913* (1964).

Index of Names

Abramovitz, M., 60n., 268, 293
Adelman, F. L., 23n., 291
Adelman, I., 1, 5, 23n., 60, 207, 291, 293
Adler, D., 207n.
Aldcroft, D. H., 10n., 37n., 50n., 54n., 58n., 62, 292
Ames, E., 5, 291
Andrews, P. W. S., 44n.
Ashton, T. S., 2n., 3n., 36, 37, 38, 40, 292

Bailey, J. D., 259
Bain, A. D., 44n., 49n.
Bellman, H., 171n., 215n., 262n.
Benham, F., 215n.
Beveridge, W. H., 11n., 26, 43n., 52, 75, 76, 91n., 196, 246n., 292
Blank, D. M., 237n.
Blaug, M., 41n.
Bloomfield, A. I., 50n., 144n.
Bober, S., 4n., 34n., 291
Booth, C., 263
Bowley, A. L., 77n.
Bowley, M., 212n., 215n.
Buckley, K. A. H., 267n.
Burns, A. F., 9, 18, 57, 75n., 86n., 88n., 100, 268, 292

Cagan, P., 47, 51n.
Cairncross, A. K., 61, 68, 69, 189, 196, 198n., 212, 228n., 230n., 234, 235n., 236n., 237n., 238n., 239n., 242, 252, 269n., 273, 274, 278, 280, 287n., 293
Carrier, N. H., 232n.
Carter, C. F., 219n.
Chapman, A., 173n.
Chenery, H. B., 217n., 291
Cole, W. A., 38n., 168n., 181n.
Cooney, E. W., 236n., 260, 268n., 280, 289n., 293
Coppock, D. J., 235n.
Corner, D. C., 292

Cramp, A. D., 46n., 47n.
Creamer, D., 166n.

David, M. H., 185n.
Deane, P., 7n., 8, 13n., 38n., 168n., 181n.
Derksen, J. B., 199, 200
Deutsch, K. W., 274n.
Duesenberry, J. S., 182, 291
Dunning, J. H., 68n., 70n., 293

Easterlin, R. A., 66, 293
Eckstein, A., 274n.
Ellison, T., 100n.
Estey, J. A., 5n., 291
Evans, M. K., 19n., 51n.

Feinstein, C. H., 8, 61n., 278n.
Fellner, W., 58n., 291
Fels, R., 231n.
Flamant, M., 16n.
Forchheimer, K., 14, 15
Ford, A. G., 26n., 50n., 292
Frickey, E., 190, 194, 195
Friedman, M., 44, 45, 182
Frisch, R., 23, 56, 291

Gayer, A. D., 11, 42n., 55n., 58n., 85n., 97, 292
Goldsmith, R. W., 269
Goodwin, R. M., 1n., 6n., 22, 35, 217n., 218, 291
Gordon, R. A., 4, 18n., 27n., 213n., 291
Gould, J. D., 39, 292
Grant, A. T. K., 172n.
Grebler, L., 193n., 213, 218n., 219n., 237n.
Guttenberg, J. M., 51

Haberler, G., 39n., 292
Hall, A. R., 293
Hamilton, H., 93n.

Hansen, A. H., 4n., 15, 189, 198n., 292
Hart, P. E., 180n.
Hawke, G. R., 37n.
Hawtrey, R. G., 43, 49
Healy, K. T., 203n.
Henderson, H., 44n.
Henderson, W. O., 16n.
Heston, A., 276n.
Hickman, B., 24
Hicks, J. R., 22, 49, 94, 160, 292
Higgins, B., 6n., 292
Higonnet, R., 145n.
Hilton, J., 77n.
Hobsbawm, E. J., 292
Hoffmann, W. G., 7n., 11, 60, 64n., 75, 190, 293
Hoskins, W. G., 3n.
Hughes, J. R. T., 43n., 53n., 55n., 292, 293
Hyman, S. H., 20n.

Imlah, A. H., 7n., 127, 128, 233n., 269, 276n., 278n.
Isard, W., 60n., 189, 194n., 228, 293, 294

Jeffrey, J. R., 232n.
Jenks, L. H., 207n., 232n.
Jevons, W. S., 38
Johnson, H. G., 44n.
Jones, E. L., 41n., 42
Juglar, C., 188

Kahn, A. E., 215n.
Kaldor, N., 22, 44, 47, 292
Kalecki, M., 23n., 292
Kelley, A. C., 60n., 71n.
Keynes, J. M., 44, 92, 158, 172, 173
Knight, R., 173n.
Kondratieff, N. D., 4n.
Kuznets, S., 35n., 59, 193n., 201, 202n., 213n., 268, 294

Leser, L. E. V., 198n.
Lewis, J. P., 60, 61, 62n., 71, 73, 227n., 238n., 294
Lewis, W. A., 189n., 192n., 205n., 208, 209n., 212, 217, 221n., 222, 234n., 237n., 242n., 262n., 269n., 273, 274, 293, 294
Lomax, K. S., 7n.
Long, C. D., 193n., 205n., 221n.
Lösch, A., 294

Madden, J. J., 288, 289

Maiwald, K., 232n.
Mansbridge, A., 262n.
Martin, K., 176n.
Mathias, P., 1n.
Matthews, R. C. O., 2n., 3n., 8, 9n., 11n., 42, 56, 61n., 64n., 189n., 222n., 239, 250n., 266n., 268n., 273, 274, 279n., 283, 284, 292, 293
Mayer, T., 52n.
Meade, J. E., 44n.
Meier, G. M., 70n., 294
Melnyk, M., 59n., 294
Meyer, F. V., 293
Mintz, I., 25n., 293
Mintz, L. W., 49n.
Mitchell, B. R., 13n.
Mitchell, W. C., 4, 14, 15, 18, 21, 75n., 86n., 88n., 100, 293
Modigliani, F., 182
Moore, H. L., 38
Morgan, E. V., 53n., 54n., 55n., 110, 111
Morgenstern, O., 16, 52, 148n., 293

Nevin, E., 181n.
Nevins, A., 231
North, D. C., 207n., 269, 271n., 276n.

O'Leary, P. J., 192n., 205n., 209n., 212, 217n., 221n., 222, 237n., 242n., 262n., 269n., 273, 274, 294
Overton, R. C., 203n.

Paish, F. W., 3n., 26n., 293
Papworth, W., 224n.
Pesmazoglu, J. S., 26, 142n., 155n., 156n., 293
Phelps Brown, E. H., 26n., 293
Pigou, A. C., 39, 95n.
Polak, J. J., 22n., 198n., 292

Radice, E. A., 175n., 180n., 181n.
Richards, H., 227n.
Richards, J. H., 238n.
Richardson, H. W., 37n., 54n., 58n., 62
Riggleman, J. R., 193, 226n.
Robertson, D. H., 39, 54n., 59n., 158
Robinson, H. W., 238n.
Rostow, W. W., 9n., 11n., 12, 25, 40, 42n., 55n., 58n., 97, 230n., 231n., 234n., 292, 293
Rowe, D. A., 169n., 170n.
Rubin, E., 201n., 202n., 213n.

Samuelson, P., 6n., 292
Saul, S. B., 71, 264, 294
Sayers, R. S., 1n., 50n., 51, 52n., 54n., 144
Scammell, W. M., 50n.
Schlote, W., 99n., 117, 208n.
Schumpeter, J. A., 4n., 5, 6, 33, 34, 35, 36, 37, 86, 108, 109, 188, 293
Schwartz, A. J., 11n., 25, 42n., 45, 55n., 58n., 97, 292
Shackle, G. L. S., 26n., 293
Shannon, F. A., 203n.
Shannon, H. A., 222n., 223n., 280
Shaw, W. H., 204n.
Silberling, N. J., 53n., 56n., 189, 194n., 198n., 213n.
Simon, M., 17n., 63n., 151n., 269, 294
Singer-Kérel, J., 16n.
Spensley, J. C., 265n.
Staller, G. J., 11n.
Stone, J. R., 169n., 170n.
Sturmey, S. G., 184n.

Taylor, G. R., 195n., 207n.
Thackeray, F. G., 176n.
Thomas, B., 61, 68, 70, 189, 192n., 194n., 200, 202, 203, 204, 208, 209, 210, 211n., 213, 221, 223, 228n., 236n., 237n., 238n., 242, 253n.,

268n., 269n., 273, 276n., 279, 280n., 289, 294
Thorp, W. L., 14
Timoshenko, V. P., 38
Tinbergen, J., 22n., 25, 27n., 142n., 145n., 198n., 217n., 292
Tooke, T., 74, 107, 108n., 120, 241n., 257

Ulmer, M. J., 195, 203n.

Viner, J., 86n.

Walters, A. A., 45, 46
Ward-Perkins, C. N., 42n., 53n., 293
Waters, J. A., 46n.
Waud, R. N., 23n., 292
Weber, B., 196, 205n., 209, 222n., 223n., 227n., 238n., 239n., 243, 280, 287, 293
Welton, T. A., 244n.
Williams, D., 50n.
Williams, R. P., 244n.
Williamson, J. G., 268n., 294
Wilson, T., 24, 292
Winnick, L., 237n.
Wood, G. H., 100

Youngson, A. J., 231n.

Subject Index

Abbey Road Society, 262
Acceleration principle, 20, 217–18
Argentina, 149, 289
Atlantic economy thesis, 60–72, 147, 205, 236–7; *see also* Emigration; Housebuilding; Overseas investment; United States
Australia, 146, 147, 149, 259, 263, 289

Balance of payments, 20, 127–8, 137, 138, 139, 140, 142, 162, 185; fluctuations in, 95, 137 ff.
Balance of trade, fluctuations in, 285
Bank Rate, cyclical behaviour of, 95, 137 ff.
Brazil, 147, 149
Brick production, 79, 92–3, 101–2, 107, 111, 222
Building societies, 170, 171
Business cycles, 4, 74, 79, 99, 190, 197, 205, 217; amplitude of, 2–3, 14, 85–90, 162; control of, 218–19; dominance over short cycle, 83–5; duration of, 75–8, 80, 98, 161–3; economic models of, 24–5; endogenous theories of, 21–4, 33; exogenous theories of, 21–4, 33; features of, 17–21; and investment, 92–4, 101–6, 111 ff.; relationship with housebuilding, 206, 241–7, 249–50, 260–1; relationship with innovations, 32, 33–7; relationship with overseas investment, 258–9; *see also* Exports; Money stock; United States

Camberwell, 265
Canada, 149, 267, 289
Canals, 258
Capital–output ratio, 167, 187; in building, 171
Chicago School, 46
Chile, 149
Coal industry: exports of, 153; influence on housebuilding, 72; lack of long cycle in, 64
Consumer-goods industries, 171
Consumers' expenditure in depression, 181–7
Consumption: between the wars, 165–87; fluctuations in, 20
Corn Laws, 43
Cost of living index, 174
Cotton industry, 110; influence on housebuilding, 72
Coventry, 254

Demographic change: effect on consumers' expenditure, 184–7; and long cycle, 59, 60, 61, 62–3, 65, 71–2; *see also* Emigration; Housebuilding; United States
Didsbury, 256
Drink, expenditure on, 169–70
Durable goods, expenditure on, 169–70

Earnings between the wars, 173–6
Echo effect, 66, 263
Edmonton, 266
Egypt, 146
Electricity, 36, 70; influence on housebuilding, 264
Emigration, 63, 65, 69–72, 200–2, 206–7, 211–12, 213, 229, 232–3, 251–6, 260, 261–4, 267; *see also* Atlantic economy thesis; Housebuilding; United States
Enclosure, 101
Exports, 3, 21, 36, 133; amplitude of, 27–9; demand for, 177; fluctuations in, 121–6, 143, 146–54, 207–8, 274–5, 279, 280–5, 290; and instability, 115–16, 121–6, 133–7, 139, 143, 146–54, 162, 205, 207–8; role of in business cycle, 25–32, 78, 111, 115–16, 126–30, 134–7, 139, 162, 205; role of in short cycle, 81–4, 99; *see also* Inventory fluctuations

Family size, influence of on house-
building, 65–6
First World War, 165
Fluctuations: *see* Business cycles; Har-
vest fluctuations; Long cycle; Short
cycle
Food, expenditure on, 169–70
Forest Hill, 265
France, 14, 15, 16, 232, 257

General Strike, 58, 161
Germany, 14, 15, 16, 232
Glasgow, building and emigration, 68
Gold, loss of, 124, 125
Government expenditure, 110–15, 178–
9

Harvest fluctuations, 32, 38–43, 59,
90–1, 94, 102, 105, 126, 129, 130
Holland, 146
Housebuilding, 19, 27, 36, 105;
between the wars, 62, 164; causes of
instability in, 64–6, 197–200, 214–17,
227–8, 229–35, 240–2, 247–9; emigration and, 65, 211–12, 229, 232–3,
251–6, 260, 261–4, 267; expenditure
on, 170–2; finance of, 257–9, 260;
fluctuations in, 60, 61–2, 71–3, 109–
10, 195–7, 206–7, 214, 218, 220–3,
225, 250 ff.; inverse nature of fluctuations in, 205, 208–12, 216, 220–3, 228,
242–3, 250–3, 260; migration and
instability in, 252–6, 260; relationship with business cycle, 241–7,
249–50; transport and instability in,
62, 66–7, 265–7; *see also* Atlantic
economy thesis; Overseas investment; United States

Imports, 21; fluctuations in, 115–21,
122–3, 124–5, 128, 275–9, 281–6
Income: distribution of, 179–81, 187;
increases in, 176–8
India, 146, 147, 149
Industrial production, cyclical beha-
viour of, 11–13, 21
Industry between the wars, 164–5
Inventory fluctuations, 21, 81–3, 126,
127, 130
Investment, fluctuations in, 155, 167–8,
171–2, 286; *see also* Housebuilding;
Inventory fluctuations; Overseas
investment
Iron production, lack of long cycle in,
164

Juglar cycle, 3, 8, 13, 34, 36, 59, 189;
see also Business cycles

Kitchin cycle, 4; *see also* Short cycle
Klein–Goldberger model, 23, 57
Kondratieff cycle, 34, 36, 59
Kuznets cycle; *see* Long cycle

Lathwood, imports of, 223–5
Liverpool, 239, 255, 264
London, 254, 260; housebuilding in,
72, 225, 239–40, 265–7
Long cycle, 4, 27, 158, 268–70;
demographic factor in, 59, 60, 61,
62–3, 65, 71–2; *see also* Atlantic
economy thesis; Balance of payments;
Emigration; Housebuilding; Overseas investment; United States

Mahogany wood, imports of, 226–7
Manchester, 72, 255, 256
Major cycle: *see* Business cycles
May Committee, 178
Means test, 182
Minor cycle: *see* Short cycle
Monetary policy, 48–56, 163–4, 171;
counter-cyclical effects of, 48–9, 52–3;
historical development of, 49–51,
53–6
Monetary system, its influence on
instability, 94–6, 103
Money income as indicator of insta-
bility, 131 ff.
Money stock and fluctuations, 32, 44–8,
94–6, 103, 143–6, 157–8
Motor vehicles: demand for, 187;
expenditure on, 169–70; sales of, 184

National debt, 257
National income, 27–8, 135–7, 138,
145, 147, 149, 155, 168–9
Neilson's hot-blast iron production, 93
New Zealand, 146, 147

Overseas investment, 27, 155; and
exports, 148–54, 158; fluctuations in,
63, 273, 276, 279, 286–9; and
housebuilding instability, 229, 233–5,
257–9, 261, 265, 267; and interest
rates, 140–3; *see also* Atlantic
economy thesis; Emigration; United
States

Patents, 36–7
Poverty line, 176

Prices as index of instability, 91–2
Profits, fluctuations in, 157, 171–2, 180

Quantity theory, 91

Radios, sales of, 184
Railways, 101, 105, 114, 223, 258
Random factors, 4, 32, 56–9
Rate of interest and instability, 48–56; *see also* Bank Rate; Monetary policy
Rent control and housebuilding, 214–15
Russia, 232

Savings, fall in: of businesses, 179–80; of institutions, 181
Scotland: flow of overseas capital from, 259; iron industry in, 93
Sheffield, speculative housebuilding in, 239
Shipbuilding, 93, 105, 157
Short cycle, 99, 100, 103, 191; amplitude of, 82–3; definition of, 79; disappearance of, 80, 83–5, 86–7; duration of, 77, 80, 98; investment and, 101–2, 109; *see also* Exports; Imports; Inventory fluctuations
Silberling index, 97
South Africa, 149
South America, 141, 146, 147, 263
South Wales, 72, 254, 260, 264
Speculative activity, role of in fluctuations, 106–10, 119–20
Suez Canal, 232
Sunspot theory, 38–9

Tariffs, 165, 178–9
Taxation, 169, 178–9
Terms of trade and instability, 69–70, 176–8
Timber, imports of, 101
Tobacco, expenditure on, 169–70

Tottenham, 265, 266
Trade cycle: *see* Business cycles
Transfer payments, 169, 178, 187
Transport, fluctuations in, 27, 62, 66–7, 200–5, 206, 217, 218, 265–7
Turkey, 146
Turnpikes, 258

Unemployment, 167, 173, 175; as indicator of instability, 85, 88–9, 103, 104–5, 132
United States, 14, 15, 16, 17, 58, 122, 124, 130, 162, 165, 166; balance of payments, fluctuations in, 255, 272–3; building, cyclical behaviour of, 192–4, 206, 211, 213–14, 216, 218, 223, 237, 251, 264; capital imports, fluctuations in, 272, 286–9; Civil War in, 79, 203, 204, 231–2; exports, fluctuations in, 271; immigration and building, 206–7, 211–12, 213, 251, and instability, 200–2; imports, fluctuations in, 207–8, 270–1, 281–5, 290; long cycle in, 59, 61; money supply, instability in, 271–2; short cycle in, 190–2; transport–building cycle in, 66–7, 200–5, 206, 217, 218; *see also* Atlantic economy thesis; Housebuilding; Overseas investment

Wages, 166
Walthamstow, 266
Walworth, 265
War, French Revolutionary, 110–15; *see also* United States
Westchester, 256
West Ham, 266
Wheat, imports of, 118–19
Woollen industry, 59

Yorkshire, 254, 261